Urban Sociology

Urban Sociology

Edited by

ERNEST W. BURGESS

and

DONALD J. BOGUE

THE UNIVERSITY OF CHICAGO PRESS

CHICAGO & LONDON

This book is an abridged edition of
Contributions to Urban Sociology
which is available in a clothbound edition from
THE UNIVERSITY OF CHICAGO PRESS

International Standard Book Number: 0-226-08056-0

THE UNIVERSITY OF CHICAGO PRESS, CHICAGO 60637
The University of Chicago Press, Ltd., London

Preface

This volume is the first in a series of monographs to emerge from a comprehensive program of research on the topic, "Problems of Living in the Metropolis," being conducted under a grant from the Ford Foundation to the Social Science Division of the University of Chicago.

Within the past ten years there has been a tremendous increase in urban research. Literally millions of dollars are now being poured into many large-scale and smaller urban studies projects. The new funds are being made available for a wide range of studies on all major aspects of city life—population trends, residential and social mobility, housing, family organization and disorganization, juvenile delinquency, family life education, family planning, and social institutions and their problems.

The funds for urban research are being granted not only by foundations but also by the federal government through the media of the National Science Foundation, the Institute of Public Health, the Social Security Administration, and other bureaus and departments. Moreover, industrial concerns, which have recognized the inadequacies of market research which limits itself to inventorying current consumer preferences, are seeking to comprehend the changing nature of society and to anticipate the content and pattern of the future material demands which may be expected of the public of twenty-five or more years from now.

As social research, both basic and practical, becomes a way of life of American institutions there is a growing appreciation that the context for the future is the urban and metropolitan community.

This interest in the significance of social change and its meaning for human welfare and progress has burgeoned so rapidly that there is real danger that studies will be poorly planned and that the findings will be either superficial or meaningless because of inadequate attention to the conceptual design and the methods of operation. While joining in the enthusiastic chorus welcoming technological advance that facilitates research, the editors fear that urban sociology may fritter away much of its current financial popularity by excessively large expenditures of research funds in massive but haphazardly designed projects processed through super-computers. In this day and age it seems that computers can do anything and everything from predicting the election results much earlier and more accurately than trained political analysts to translating books from one language to another. But they cannot arrive at empirical formulations without guidance. The basic variables and forces—especially those involved in the all-important topic of change—must be conceived in the human mind and programmed into machine language before they can be measured and correlated. The social scientist with access to this modern miracle is under real pressure to place undue reliance upon this super-computer as a substitute for inductive originality. The temptation is very appealing to substitute hundreds or even thousands of correlations for conclusive evaluations based upon a prior conceptual scheme that will reduce masses of isolated interrelationships into a coherent system. Progress will come from a mix-

v

ture of fact-digestion and insightful abstraction; to the extent that there is a tendency to substitute correlations for ideas, there is the disturbing prospect that we are faced with another wave of naïve raw empiricism such as that which followed the advent of the IBM counting sorter. Only this time the insufficiency of fundamental thoughts and concepts may be more attractively camouflaged with higher mathematics.

One way to avoid such an unfortunate result in the field of urban sociology is to engage in a careful review of what we already do and do not know from the research cumulation to date, especially from one coherent program of urban research. Such is the purpose of this volume of reports on the projects undertaken by a group of graduate students in the Department of Sociology at the University of Chicago during the past forty years. Most of these studies have been inaccessible to students of urban life either because they were not published or because they were published in books now out of print. In the judgment of the editors their value is immensely increased by presenting in one place the highlights of many related research projects. It is hoped that the reader will find that the selections fall naturally into an organized framework, wherein each chapter gets added significance from its relation to the other contributions.

If our work has been done properly, this volume should become far more valuable than the worth of its individual components, although each affords a highly provocative vantage point from which to view the urban scene. It is intended to become a guide book on urban research, with a look backward to perceive the directions taken by research in the past and a probing search forward to indicate what further research should now be undertaken. Because the number of collaborators was so very large, we have been forced to suppress our own ideas of future directions in order to provide space for each expert to speak for himself.

This volume is one of genuine collaboration between the editors and the authors of the individual research articles. Each contributor was asked to write a chapter derived from his doctoral dissertation and to supplement his original work with research carried out later and his current ideas of further research deemed to be desirable and feasible. Thus, this volume embodies the latest thinking of the authors on directions to be followed in current research. All too often, the prime recommendation (and correctly) is for replication in places other than Chicago and for more recent dates.

Almost all of our collaborators turned in oversized manuscripts; after all, to compress an entire dissertation into a few pages, and then to evaluate it and make insightful recommendations, is almost an impossible assignment. Considerations of space forced the editors to cut and trim drastically. Most authors saw their papers after the first round of such trimming but not after the second. Because of human inability to keep all promises made in this overworked professional world, the publication of the book was delayed for two years by late delivery of the last few manuscripts. We decided to risk offending the prompt and faithful by being dictatorial in the final editing rather than by further inexcusable delay.

In a few cases where the authors could not accept our invitation to write the chapters assigned to them, the editors have taken the liberty of making an abstract of the original dissertation. This means that the chapter does not have the benefit of the author's present thinking on the subject and his suggestions for further research. The editors therefore must take the responsibility for the text of these chapters. They have attempted to make a faithful report of the author's ideas at the time he wrote. But, of course, some of the authors may not wish to be bound today by every word written as a graduate student several years ago.

It is our hope that this volume can be used as a text in urban sociology, although teachers must be energetic enough to supply information on topics not covered here or not fully brought up to date with a review of recent research. Under whatever contexts it is used, we sincerely hope that it will stimulate even more profound research in the field of urban sociology.

We want to acknowledge the generosity and patience of the contributors during the four years required to complete the task. All have shown good humor at our editorial pruning. We want to express our gratitude to Annice Cottrell and Basia Miller for their assistance in typing and retyping the various drafts and in assisting with the editorial work.

ERNEST W. BURGESS
DONALD J. BOGUE

Contents

Research in Urban Society: A Long View

ERNEST W. BURGESS AND DONALD J. BOGUE

INTRODUCTION: THE GOALS OF THIS VOLUME

Few fields of social life are now being subjected to more intensive study than the urban community. Urban sociology is a basic course in many undergraduate and certainly in most graduate schools of sociology. Several universities and colleges have ambitious urban research programs under way. In addition, urban research is now being done by a host of agencies and persons that are comparative newcomers to the scene of the analysis of urban life. Among them are:

City planning commissions
Administrative offices of religious bodies
Urban renewal agencies
Real estate agencies and investment firms
Public and private housing agencies
Market analysts
Transportation analysts
Economists of industrial and commercial location
Public administration analysts
Medical and public health researchers
Researchers in school and educational systems
Research units of departments of welfare

In short, in the 1960's urban research is "big business." It is grinding out reports, textbooks, and monographs at a pace so rapid that reading them could itself be more than a full-time job. Prospects for a greatly expanded sphere of knowledge in the area of urban communities have never been brighter. Unfortunately, in the context of uninhibited individual research there is much opportunity for mere fact-reporting, repetition without replication, and failure of the whole program to "add up" very fast because of failures to per-

ceive basic issues and work along similar lines in many different organizations.

The present volume is dedicated to the proposal that in the midst of all this activity there may be a place for a calm "long view" that scrutinizes current events in this field while looking backward and peering into the future. The backward look should review some of the significant events that led up to the present hyperactivity; the forward look should undertake to foresee emerging lines of study that will be of unusual significance for theory-building and practical action. Implicit in such an undertaking is the intent to stimulate a critical evaluation of current thinking, teaching, and research in urban sociology. This is the first of the two major goals of this volume.

The other of the two major goals of the book is to present, as succinctly as possible, a substantial amount of research information that hitherto has been in the realm of "fugitive literature." Significant urban research, some of it performed many years ago, has never been adequately reported in a way that would bring it conveniently to the attention of those varied professionals interested in urban life. An equally large amount is now equally inaccessible to younger scholars because it is published in books now out of print. This volume seeks to rescue some of this work from too early oblivion. It also seeks to attract renewed interest in certain classic and well-known studies, using the authors themselves to summarize and refurbish their original insights.

We have chosen to take our "long view" in terms of a particular line of development—the program of urban research at

1

the University of Chicago. Inasmuch as
the University of Chicago was one of the
foci of the early urbanism studies, a critical evaluation by the reader of the sequence of development at this one institution (written against a background of
developments elsewhere) should help
furnish the historical perspective needed
to view present research efforts throughout the country more objectively. The full
history, in terms of research thinking, of
this program has never been recorded.
Even more important, some of the important research findings of this program
have never been fully brought to the attention of the public. The files of the University of Chicago Department of Sociology and the Chicago Community
Inventory contain a considerable body of
useful and insightful research which is
unknown to many persons working on
similar topics today. This volume has undertaken to distil many theses and research reports in order to extract ideas
and factual findings that are pertinent today. Thus, the "research contributions"
reviewed here are primarily those made
by students while in residence at the
University of Chicago.

The purpose behind this review has
been to chart the future. The sociology
department at Chicago has recently
launched into a renewed cycle of activity
in urban research. Much thought has
gone into the questions, "What are the
most profound lines of basic research in
the field of urban sociology?" "What was
good about past programs that should be
preserved and developed further, and
what was unfruitful and should be
avoided in the future?" "What are the
unique opportunities that merit exploiting because others are passing them by?"
"What lines of research should now be
left to public and non-academic agencies,
and what lines of research are most
appropriate for university sponsorship?"
The volume was developed by the following process. First, the entire list of
Ph.D. thesis topics was reviewed, and

those dealing with topics of urban sociology were identified. The Ph.D. theses
were reviewed, and certain ones that
represented unique contributions at the
time they were written were singled out
for special review in this book. The author was contacted and requested to perform two tasks: (*a*) to summarize his
original work within the confines of a
single chapter-length statement in a book
and (*b*) to indulge in "mature second
thoughts" based upon his experience
since leaving the University of Chicago.
This latter part was to include not only
self-criticism but also positive suggestions for further research in this area.
Needless to say, a few major items which
we sought could not be included because
of other work pressures upon the original
authors or because the author was de-
ceased. Several such works have been
summarized by the editors.

The contributions are grouped into
four sections. Each section opens with a
statement by the editors and is followed
by the edited papers submitted by the invited participants. The intended purposes
of each section are to view critically what
is being done in that particular field,
while reporting a body of research findings which may be largely unfamiliar to
the reader or to review familiar research
with the intent to explore its implications
for the future.

Despite the fact that in our formal outline we have confined ourselves to Chi-
cago-generated materials, the reader will
quickly discover that we (and our contributors) freely discuss the total context within which the research has taken
place.

A SHORT HISTORY OF URBAN RESEARCH
AT THE UNIVERSITY OF CHICAGO
BEFORE 1946°

The sociological studies of Chicago
began with an article which Dr. Park

° This section is a revision of a talk given by
Ernest W. Burgess before a seminar dealing
with "New Directions for Urban Research."

wrote, "The City: Suggestions for the Investigation of Human Behavior in the Urban Environment," published in the *American Journal of Sociology*, 1916. I returned to Chicago to join the staff in 1916, after having graduated from the Chicago Department of Sociology in 1913. It was my good fortune to be placed in the same office with Dr. Park (the east tower of Harper Library); and we began a collaboration that continued as long as he was at the University of Chicago. Our office arrangement was most fortunate for me, because Dr. Park had a most creative mind. He lived and slept research. I never knew when I would get home for dinner, because we would spend whole afternoons discussing both theoretical and practical aspects of sociology and social research.

Dr. Park had been a newspaperman before he turned to sociology. He had been fascinated by the city. The problems which the city presented interested him greatly. He was interested in the newspaper, its power of exposing conditions and arousing public sentiment, and in taking the lead in crusades against slums, exploitation of immigrants, or corruption in municipal affairs. The exposés by Lincoln Steffens, and the whole tradition in journalism which he stimulated, was the point of departure in this thinking. But Dr. Park found that, while newspaper publicity aroused a great deal of interest and stirred the emotions of the public, it did not lead to constructive action. He decided that something more than news was needed, that you had to get beneath the surface of things. So he returned to the university. He went to Harvard University, where he studied in the departments of psychology and philosophy. Then he went to Germany, where he studied at Berlin and Heidelberg, and wrote his doctor's thesis in German on "The Crowd and the Public."

When he returned to this country, he was offered the opportunity to teach at a major northern university, but instead he went to Tuskegee Institute in Alabama, where he worked with Booker T. Washington. He chose this course because he felt that the Negro problem was a significant one, and that Booker T. Washington was dealing with it not sentimentally but realistically. Some years later, Professor W. I. Thomas, visiting Tuskegee, was impressed by Dr. Park. He invited him to the University of Chicago for a summer term in the year 1913. Professor Park stayed on to make his career here.

When I joined Dr. Park at the University of Chicago in 1916, I had not the background of experience he possessed. After graduating in sociology under Professors Small, Thomas, Henderson, and Vincent (the "Big Four" of sociology in those days), I had gone to Toledo University for one year, then to the University of Kansas for two years, and finally to Ohio State University for one year. At the University of Kansas I had come in contact with the social survey movement under Shelby Harrison: I had made the recreation study for the Topeka Survey, had co-operated with the Health Department of the university in making a study of Belleville, Kansas, and then made a social survey of Lawrence. By the time we joined forces and began urban studies in Chicago, I had also become very interested in the urban community and its problems and in studying those problems by research.

At Chicago Dr. Park and I taught the first course, Principles of Sociology. Dr. Small was chairman; like each of the "Big Four" he was a great individualist and a forceful character. We had to teach six sections of this course a year because students came from all parts of the university to hear Dr. Park. It was during this time we wrote our *Introduction to the Science of Sociology*. After a few years Dr. Park and I began a course in Field Studies together. Meanwhile, I had students in my course on Social Pathology making maps of all types of social problems for which we could get data. From this began to emerge the realization that there was a definite pattern and structure to the city, and that many types of social problems were correlated with each other. Then, with Professor Millis of the Department of Economics, I had the students in the Principles of Sociology course study 40 blocks in a Chicago Survey of Health Insurance. The students interviewed all the families in those blocks, to get all the facts about their health, whether they had health insurance, and many facts about their living conditions and social life that we included for scientific inquiry.

Meanwhile, Professor Thomas had started his study of the Polish peasant. He made yearly trips to Europe, studying peasants from country to country, using anthropological methods to study the peasant community. When he left the university, he had begun a study of the Polish community in Chicago. Under his influence I had made an investigation of the Russian peasant and had become interested in ethnic groups.

It is important to make clear that the Department of Sociology studies were not the first field studies in Chicago. If you go back as far as 1895 in the Hull-House Papers, you will find urban studies. It would be correct to say that systematic urban studies in Chicago began with these Hull-House studies. Edith Abbott and Sophonisba Breckenridge, in what was then the Chicago School of Civics and Philanthropy (later the School of Social Service Administration of this university), had carried on a series of studies of the immigrant and of the operation of Hull-House. They began these studies as early as 1908. And of course there were other isolated studies of Chicago during the early decades of the twentieth century. Similar work had been going on in New York City and in other cities where there had been social surveys or investigations of slums.

Although he was not there first, the sociologist made a big difference in urban research. It was sociology that emphasized science and the importance of understanding social problems in terms of the processes and forces that produce them.

Perhaps it would be useful in understanding the development of urban research if I would try to communicate to you the situation that existed in those days. Chicago had been flooded with wave after wave of immigrants from Europe. The number of new arrivals had been especially heavy from 1890 to 1910. World War I had caused this flow to cease, but immediately after the war there was great speculation that it would be renewed—with perhaps even greater activity. By the time our studies began, the various ethnic neighborhoods were well established, with each ethnic group having its own churches, schools, newspapers, restaurants, stores, social clubs, politicians, and welfare stations. By this time, too, public sentiment had crystallized into rather firm prejudice and discrimination against the new arrivals from Eastern and Southern Europe. Anti-Jewish, anti-Polish, anti-Italian, and anti-Czech feelings were especially strong in particular neighborhoods. In those days, even Germans, Irish, and Swedes were regarded by the old-line English families as being socially inferior. Landlords were taking advantage of the crowded housing situation and the ignorance of the newcomers to offer substandard living units at exorbitant rents. The public prejudice and desire for segregation of the foreign stock made it possible to maintain a housing shortage for these groups despite rapid building in other parts of the city. Fertility was high, families were large, and the overcrowding was very great. Health, educational, and other municipal services were definitely inferior in the ethnic neighborhoods to those in the upper-class and middle-class areas.

The children of immigrants, standing between two cultures, were loyal neither to their parents nor to America, although they identified themselves with the New World. They had formed street corner groups that were acting in open defiance of both the desires of their parents and the social rules of the community at large. The city administration was commonly regarded as being corrupt, and politicians were manipulating the ethnic neighborhoods for their own advantage. Many families were desperately poor; widows struggling to bring up a brood of children were very common in those days, since mortality rates were high and death of the breadwinner during the prime of life was not uncommon. There was much need for charitable social service in the ethnic neighborhoods.

The social scientists at the University of Chicago did not share, for the most part, the prejudices against these people that were commonly expressed. Quite often they defended the foreign groups publicly and spoke out for tolerance, sympathy, and understanding. Much of the earliest "social research" was little more than the discovery and reporting to the public that the feelings and sentiments of those living in the ethnic slums were, in reality, quite different from those imputed to them by the public. By the early 1920's this "social work" orientation had given way, in the Department of Sociology to an ambition to understand and interpret the social and economic forces at work in the slums and their effect in influencing the social and personal organization of those who lived there. Although the objective was scientific, behind it lay a faith or hope that this scientific analysis would help dispel prejudice and injustice and ultimately would lead to an improvement in the lot of slum dwellers.

It was not only the sociologist and social worker who had reacted to this situation. Studies were carried on in other departments of the social sciences. For example, Professor Merriam of the Political Science Department had been alderman of the Fifth Ward (University of Chicago), and had fought the "gray wolves" in the City Council. He had run for mayor and after his defeat had somewhat retired from active participation in politics but was very much interested in studying the political system and especially the political process that was not observable to the press. Under his guidance were made some of the earliest scientific studies of metropolitan government. Meanwhile, the School of Social Service Administration had continued a wide range of studies of social agencies and social problems. The Department of Economics, though perhaps not quite as active as these other groups, was also carrying on studies of the urban economy in the 1920's. The geographers had studied Chicago's physiographic situation thoroughly and were gradually developing within their own discipline the concept of the metropolitan region, which later was to be stated explicitly and fully by the sociologist R. D. McKenzie.

With this brief description of what had gone on before 1916, or what was going on in other departments, I will now concentrate on describing the program of urban research that came to be called "The City as a Sociological Laboratory." This program, as I knew it, may be subdivided into three phases.

Phase 1: The Period without Funds: Discovering the Physical Pattern of the City

The first period of our study we might call "the period without funds." Certainly, during our first years there was very little financing for urban research. This covers the period from 1916 to 1923. The work of this period was conducted very largely by the students in our classes. In every course I gave I am sure there were one or two students who made maps. I think the maps of juvenile delinquency were the first ones undertaken. They were followed by maps showing the distribution of motion picture houses. Then came maps showing the distribution of the patrons of the public dance halls. The students made maps of any data we could find in the city that could be plotted.

This phase might also be called, "Discovering the Physical Pattern of the City." We were very impressed with the great differences between the various neighborhoods in the city, and one of our earliest goals was to try to find a pattern to this patchwork of differences, and to "make sense of it." Mapping was the method which seemed most appropriate for such a problem.

At this time we made contacts with agencies throughout the city in search of the data they could furnish. We secured the co-operation of the Juvenile Court, the Health Department, the many social settlements, the Council of Social Agencies that was getting under way, the Association of Commerce, and the Urban League. One of our students collaborated with Graham Romeyn Taylor in publishing the book on the race riots in Chicago. He was Charles S. Johnson, who was later to become president of Fisk University, a leading sociologist, and a leading public figure in this country.

The courses that Dr. Park and I gave at this period may be of interest to you. He gave courses on the Social Survey, the Newspaper, the Negro in America, in addition to his famous course on the Crowd and the Public. Besides the Introduction to Sociology course I gave courses in Social Pathology, Crime and Its Social Treatment, the Theory of Personal Disorganization, and the Family. In the winter of 1918, Dr. Park offered his first field study course. The following autumn I joined him in giving the field study course, and we gave it every quarter as long as he was at the university. After he left, Dr. Wirth and I continued to give this course, as long as we were both at the university.

I should mention one study that was made and published in this period without funds, *The Hobo*, by Nels Anderson. Actually, there was a small fund for this study: $300, that Dr. Ben Reitman, the king of the hobos, solicited from Dr. Evans, who wrote the health column in the Chicago *Tribune*. This small amount of money enabled Nels Anderson to exist in the hobo district, and write this book, which the University of Chicago Press accepted for publication as the first volume in the Sociological Series.

Phase 2: Birth of an Organized Research Program

The period with funds came suddenly upon us. Beardsley Ruml, who had been an instructor in psychology at the University of Chicago, became director of the Laura Spelman Rockefeller Foundation. He induced the trustees of this foundation to devote funds to social science research. In 1923 the National Social Science Research Council was established under a grant and with the prospect of funds for research from the same foundation. Dr. Ruml and his board of directors also decided to support social science research at a number of universities. The first university to apply and to have its proposal approved for sponsorship was the University of Chicago. The funds did not descend upon us out of the clouds. We had to make application. We had to show some basis for receiving funds. Fortunately, the studies we had under way made quite an impressive exhibit. Thrasher was already beginning to study the gang, and other studies were in progress. The School of Social Service Administration had a number of projects also under way. So they gave us a grant, as I recall, of $25,000 for the first year. That wouldn't seem very large to social scientists of the present. But when you had had only $300 for one study, it seemed like a great amount, and we were promised much larger funds in the future. I think the next year they gave us $50,000 and $25,000 additional, contingent upon raising $25,000 in the community. This program continued for about ten years and I think every year the civic and social welfare agencies of the community joined with us in raising $25,000 so we could get the extra $25,000 from the foundation.

It was understood that in Chicago, because of the beginning we made in the study of the city, the research would be concentrated and limited to the studies of the community. The first Local Community Research Committee was set up with Dean Leon C. Marshall, who was then the head of the Department of Economics (chairman of the committee), Professor Merriam from political science, Dr. Edith Abbott from social service administration, and Professor Jurnigon from history. I was the representative from sociology.

What were the points of view and the methods of research with which we began our studies? We assumed that the city had a characteristic organization and way of life that differentiated it from rural communities. Like rural communities, however, it was composed of natural areas, each having a particular function in the whole economy and life of the city, each area having its distinctive institutions, groups, and personalities. Often there were wide differences between communities which were very sharply demarcated.

We early decided that the natural areas could be significantly studied in two aspects:

First, their *spatial pattern:* the topography of the local community; the physical arrangements not only of the landscape but of the structures which man had constructed, that sheltered the inhabitants and provided places of work and of play.

Second, their *cultural life:* their modes of living, customs, and standards.

Now the first of these aspects, the spatial aspect, gave rise to ecological studies; all that could be mapped; the distribution, physical structures, institutions, groups, and individuals over an area. It was interesting what discoveries came from mapping data. For example, this

first map showed that juvenile delinquents were concentrated in certain areas of the city and that they tended to thin out in other areas. That was quite surprising, strange to say, to the personnel of the juvenile court, because they knew they had cases in all parts of the city. This finding was not accepted by visitors from other cities. They said, "That may be what happens in Chicago; but in our city, juvenile delinquents are evenly scattered all over the area."

But some years later, Clifford R. Shaw studied the spatial distribution of juvenile delinquency in other cities, and found the same phenomena. Delinquents were concentrated in what we call the areas of deterioration and transition; they thinned out and almost disappeared in the better residential neighborhoods. There were, of course, juvenile delinquents in almost every area, but their distribution followed the zonal pattern.

These studies of juvenile delinquency distribution convinced us of the need for basic social data. We realized that population data were essential for social studies of the city. We co-operated with the health department, the Association of Commerce, and with many other agencies including the welfare agencies of the city. We obtained data from the United States Census—unpublished and especially tabulated data, by census tracts. The census tracts for Chicago originally had been laid out in 1910. Little use had been made of them. We secured the tract data for 1920 and 1930. When the census was taken in Chicago in 1930, Dr. Philip M. Hauser was a student. He was in charge of enumeration in one of the districts in the city and began his career that later led him to be the acting director of the 1950 census.

Phase 3: The Economic Depression and War Years

In 1934 we took a population census of Chicago. This was the period of the depression, and of WPA projects. The idea came to me of having a city census. The data could be contrasted with those of 1930 and, later, with those of 1940. I got in touch with the Department of Health and the mayor of the city. I wrote the ordinance under which the census could be conducted. We had the promise of the WPA that they would furnish the enumerators. I attended the meeting of the council because I was afraid if any questions were to be asked of the mayor by the aldermen, he would not be able to answer them. This fear showed my naïveté, because Mayor Kelly made a short speech in which he spoke of all the persons out of work. He said this census would give 1,000 unemployed men jobs. And I heard the aldermen say, "pass, pass." No formal vote was taken. I went over to a reporter and asked what had happened. He said, "Don't you know? They voted unanimously to have this census taken." Two of our graduate students, Charles Newcomb and Richard Lang, directed this census of Chicago. I think it was as good as any other census taken, but the U.S. Bureau of the Census, when it made the 1940 census, did not rely upon the distribution of population which we found in 1934, but went back to their own census of 1930. As a result, they got into real difficulties. Certain areas which we showed having decreased population, had less population than they anticipated, and other areas had gained in population. But I suppose it is only natural that the federal agency would consider that only under its auspices could an adequate census be taken.

An early project was the preparation of a basic map for social data. This map has on it what we regard as basic data; railroads, streetcar lines, business property, residential property, unoccupied property indicated, property occupied by industry, by parks, and by boulevards.

We made a study in order to find the boundaries of the different natural areas of the city. That was the study in which the city was divided into its constituent

local communities. The city council passed a resolution that in the future the census division would tabulate population not by wards but by these local communities. This system was accepted by the health department for recording their data and by the Council of Social Agencies for indicating distribution of agencies in the city. The *Local Community Fact Book of Chicago,* of which the first edition, by Wirth and Furez, appeared for 1930, has been reissued after the 1940, 1950, and 1960 censuses. It has been very valuable not only to students engaged in studies but also to the social agencies of the city. It shows population data by local communities.

At that time it was possible to get many research projects accepted by WPA. At one time we had so many research projects in the department, it was said that every graduate student had a project. That wasn't literally true, but there was enough truth in it to warrant the statement. We were able to make certain studies that would otherwise have been impossible, unless we had had grants far beyond the foundation's interest in local community studies. The Ford Foundation at that time had not yet been established.

The book by Faris and Dunham on *Mental Disorders in Urban Areas* would not have been possible without the data that was accumulated in this way. Dr. Hauser wrote his thesis on differential fertility, mortality, and net reproduction in Chicago. He had a force of students employed under WPA at the health department working machines every night, the only time they were available. That would hardly have been possible without great funds. A map showing the distribution of over a hundred thousand relief cases during the depression was made possible in this way.

Statistical data and map-plotting tell us much, but they don't tell us all. They tell us many very interesting things which require further investigation. For example, Shaw, in his studies of all the different social and health conditions related to the distribution of juvenile delinquency, found the highest correlate with juvenile delinquency was tuberculosis. Now, of course, we know that tuberculosis doesn't cause juvenile delinquency; nor does juvenile delinquency cause tuberculosis. But it meant that the same community conditions that give rise to tuberculosis, give rise to juvenile delinquency—non-white population, immigrant population, bad housing. All the factors of community deterioration that lead to one lead also to the other.

These statistical data raise questions. Many of these questions, of course, can be further studied by statistical investigation; others, to be understood, require us to get below the surface of observable behavior. Cooley thought that these could be studied by what he called sympathetic introspection. He advocated this method as the ideal one for sociologists to use; but it is quite apparent that sympathetic introspection has many fallacies. If you and I try to imagine how a hobo feels—we have not been a homeless man, we have not ridden the rails—our mental picture is quite likely to be very different from what goes on in the mind of a hobo. So the superior method, as sociologists have discovered, is that of communication, of securing personal documents, and the life history. Psychologists and psychiatrists have introduced other methods, other tests, to get beneath the conscious responses of the person to our underlying motivations.

But by the use of a personal document we are able to get at the subjective aspects of life in the city.

Blumenthal, in his book *Small Town Stuff* (a study of a small mining community), exploded the common sense notion that in a small town everybody is constantly rating and re-rating everyone. But when he had interviews with persons, he didn't say, "I want your life history, I want a personal document." He said, "I want you to tell me the history of the community." The history of the community is something that everyone, at least the old-timers, is interested in narrating; and before they knew it, they were telling their life story. Blumenthal found out that what he got from the life story of the individual's self-conception was quite different from his rating in the community.

Of course, this rating in the community is also important, because it enters into the status of a person, into his conception of himself, but is only part of the story. Self-conception is not readily revealed, except perhaps by egocentric persons who tell everything to anyone who will listen, or by the use of the technique of getting personal documents and life histories.

I recall Nels Anderson telling me he was greatly bored by his landlady, in the roominghouse district where he was studying the homeless man, telling him her life history. I told him, "Why, this is valuable, you must get it down on paper." I still have this document; it is most revealing. Who becomes a roominghouse keeper? What are the problems of a roominghouse keeper? Who is the star boarder? How do you keep a roominghouse orderly against all the tendencies toward disorder in a roominghouse district? Out of this one document you get more insight into how life moves in the roominghouse area, and especially from the standpoint of the roominghouse keeper, than you do from a mountain of statistics that might be gathered. So what we get from the life history, of course, also enables us to pose more questions to the statistician, to get to the other answers.

It is very interesting how studies begun in the department tended to get incorporated into other agencies in the community. While working on the study of juvenile delinquency, Mr. Shaw did get some funds during the period without funds from the Chicago Woman's Club, which was interested in the problems of juvenile delinquency. He also lived at a settlement house that was interested in what a sociologist would say about the problems of the gang.

In 1929 Mr. Shaw was appointed head of the Department of Sociological Research at the Institute of Juvenile Research and after that carried on this series of studies and of publications, both ecological and cultural. This is a very good illustration of combining statistical methods, of finding out everything in the community that can be correlated with juvenile delinquency, of establishing the delinquency areas of the city, and of securing intensive life histories. *The Jack-Roller* shows how a person becomes a delinquent—an actual history of a delinquent career. Later Mr. Shaw was engaged in another, even more difficult, task of trying to find out the process by which a delinquent is rehabilitated. It seems to be easier to become a delinquent than to cease to be a delinquent; easier to explain why a boy becomes a delinquent than what factors really are involved in his rehabilitation.

The Church Federation of Chicago and the Chicago Theological Seminary employed Dr. Samuel C. Kincheloe to direct research on churches, especially problem churches and dying churches. On the basis of his studies, he presented to the church alternatives to action. One rather interesting effect was this: that the presentation of these facts to the church members hastened the death of many of these dying churches. Otherwise they would have continued the futile struggle to survive years longer.

The Chicago Council of Social Agencies, as I indicated before, adopted the community areas as did also the Recreation Commission and the health department. At Northwestern University Ernest R. Mowrer continued his studies of the family and in his book, *Disorganization—Personal and Social*, presents an exhaustive amount of data on family disorgani-

zation classified by the local community areas of the city.

My reason for reviewing the past has been primarily to raise the question of the conceptual system for current urban studies and what seem to be the most appropriate opportunities at present for further studies of the city. It is my firm conviction after a quarter-century of urban research, that *the conceptual system for urban studies should take in the whole field of sociological theory.* Social organization with its class structure; social change as the result of technological discoveries and inventions; collective behavior; social control, ecological studies, and population studies, all give us clues. But whatever is done in one of these fields should not fail to acknowledge principles established by research in other areas of urban life. Personal and social disorganization are of peculiar interest in the study of the city because of the fact of change, because of the change of tempo of city life. But social disorganization needs to be studied not so much from the standpoint of social pathology (although that also requires certain attention) but as an aspect of an interaction and adjustment process that eventually leads into social reorganization. Many trends in social disorganization lead to personal disorganization, community breakdown; but others are attempts at community reorganization. Some of the reorganizational efforts are successful and these of course need to be most carefully observed and studied as they occur. Merely charting past trends, and extrapolating them into the future can never suffice for an entity so dynamic and adaptable as the urban community!

Personal disorganization may be the result of community disorganization; but personal and community disorganization are not necessarily involved together. We have some very vigorous, well-organized personalities developing in situations of community disorganization; it may be a failure of a person to relate to community organization, or it may be a precondition leading to personal reorganization.

Mobility is the key process in understanding the rapidly growing city; mobility of persons, families, and institutions. Here we mean not only residential mobility, and not only the fluidity of the population change; we mean also social mobility. Very often spatial mobility is an index of social mobility, as a person changes residences, moves away from the family and upward or downward in the class scale. Then, too, the group loses or gains status as old residents and institutions move from the community and are succeeded by newcomers. As yet we have only scratched the surface of the mobility research field.

In the growth of the city we have differentiated the series of concentric zones which is one way of indicating as the city expands outward from its center, how each successive zone tends to encroach upon the further outlying zones. We are now witnessing a new zonal phenomenon, as urban renewal begins at the core and gradually encroaches on slums as they develop in an ever widening arc. While I do not have time enough to speak in any detail of the appropriate ecological conceptual system as related to urban research, I don't want to underestimate its importance; because the ecological aspect permeates and conditions all others, and the findings of the sociological studies will be strongly influenced by the degree to which the ecological conceptual system and the actual areas of the city are recognized in the assembling data for the questions that are being raised.

There are at the present time certain very interesting opportunities in the field of mobility for sociological research. The Negro in the city, the recent Southern white and the more recent Puerto Rican are significant from the standpoint of mobility, but for different reasons. The Ne-

gro, like the Southern white, is American in culture and aspirations, but finds discrimination, particularly in employment, and is underprivileged in many community and social services. I would like to see a study of the services available to the Negro as compared to the white in areas of similar economic level.

The Southern white, at least so one of our recent studies indicates, considers himself a sojourner in the northern city; so did all our immigrants from Europe; but our earlier immigrants were thousands of miles away with ocean lanes between them and their home country. The Southern mountaineers are a very short distance by automobile, and so the Southern white can readily go back and forth. Thinking of himself as a sojourner, he tends not to participate in community institutions. We need to know how and under what circumstances the home ties are broken so that he eventually comes to look upon the Northern metropolis as home.

The Mexican tends to remain loyal to Mexico and loath to change his nationality; this introduces another facet into the problem.

The Puerto Rican, at least at first, was largely a non-family man and brought with him the problems that come in a predominantly male group and those arising from the lack of domestic ties. Now the Puerto Rican community is getting a more even sex balance. We know very little, sociologically speaking, about Spanish speaking communities in urban areas.

Another situation that seems to me to present a real opportunity is this comparatively new phenomenon, urban redevelopment: demolishing the obsolescent structures and rebuilding a community. We have several such demonstrations of this in Chicago at the present time. The most important problem in redevelopment and the provision of model housing is likely to be completely overlooked in urban research. It is how to maintain the gains of renewal in view of the adverse trends in city growth. Comparative studies of different redevelopment projects, in regard to their social organization, their management, ways of maintaining neighborhood organization and preventing community disorganization and physical deterioration would, I think, be significant not only from the standpoint of social organization but from the lessons that could be gathered in directing these projects in the future.

I think it would be quite significant to look over again the program Dr. Park outlined in the article I referred to, "The City: Suggestions for the Investigation of Human Behavior in the Urban Environment." Although it is nearly half a century old, you will see there much that has been achieved. You will also see much that has not been studied; and I think certain of the very important aspects of urban life are still relatively neglected, or at least underinvestigated from the sociological standpoint.

Restudies are an important opportunity for future research. They are significant because great changes have taken place. Dr. Bogue has updated Nels Anderson's study of hobohemia. You may recall that Anderson did his research in the pre-depression period. Then came the great depression; Sutherland and Locke made their study of 20,000 homeless men. The present period is one in which there are social security and old-age assistance, and one in which you might say the economic basis for hobohemia has been removed.

A restudy of the Gold Coast and the slum would be most interesting; great changes have taken place in that area since Zorbaugh made his famous study. A new study of the gang is indicated. A new study of the ghetto cannot be made; there is no longer any ghetto. But the absorption of the Jewish population, in the city and in the suburbs, is a sociological event that should be studied. The tendencies for particular religious groups and the remnants of ethnic groups still to concentrate in certain areas, despite the fact that the reasons for their original concentration have disappeared, would be of great research interest.

And so we could go through the whole series of the studies that were conducted in the Sociological Series. The new studies of the city are about to emerge. There will be no danger of copying the methods of research of the older studies, because research methods have had a great advance in the last thirty years, and these new methods need to be utilized to their full.

We have new conceptions of what is significant, and there are new conditions, all of which must be taken into account in designing the new series of studies. The objectives of the earlier studies still hold good: the attempt to describe and analyze the natural areas which together make up the city in order to understand human behavior, institutions, and social types. The prospect of launching a new series of urban studies is exciting to all of us. The city of Chicago is a great laboratory. At this university there is perhaps the greatest collection of basic social data of any city in the world. There are now research groups here constantly collecting data on the city, which have come into existence as the importance of urban study became apparent and which represent, of course, a marvelous facility, not only because of the data that have been collected, but also the way in which they can command the further collection of data. There are great stores of data on health, housing, and civic, social, and planning agencies of the city that still have not been fully investigated or interpreted.

Studies of the problems of city life are now possible on a scale thought impossible in my day of urban study. Studying the great social problems of the city can and will be of great theoretical significance in advancing our knowledge of human behavior in the urban environment. They will also be of practical importance in providing a sound basis for the application to the problems of urban living the problems confronted by the institutions, by the welfare and civic agencies, and by the inhabitants of the city.

POSTWAR PERIOD: THE CHICAGO
COMMUNITY INVENTORY

In 1946, Professors Louis Wirth and Ernest W. Burgess sought and obtained funds to establish a permanent research organization devoted to research, informational, and advisory activity with respect to urban life. Under a grant from the Wieboldt Foundation of Chicago, the Chicago Community Inventory was established with Louis Wirth as its director. In 1951, Philip M. Hauser assumed the directorship, which he still holds. The Chicago Community Inventory (CCI) is the heir of the older urban studies program, and its archives contain basic research papers and materials dating back to the early 1920's.

The research activities of this center have focused primarily on demographic and ecological aspects of the urban and metropolitan community; some most outstanding contributions have emerged from this specialization. Working as a team, Otis and Beverly Duncan, Evelyn M. Kitagawa, Philip Hauser, and Donald Bogue have carried out research studies on a wide variety of ecological aspects of metropolitan structure and demographic processes and situations. Most of their research has been conducted with student research assistants, so that their operation has provided a valuable training facility to supplement the formal instruction in the Department of Sociology.

Far from being an ivory tower retreat from which to take a detached and academic view of the city, the CCI has been active as an information resource to municipal, business, and welfare organiza-
tions in the Chicago Metropolitan Area. It has published the *Local Community Fact Book of Chicago* after the 1950 and the 1960 censuses. These made available for each of the 75 community areas of Chicago a wide variety of statistics. In addition, much valuable information concerning census tracts was reported in the form of percentages and rates which could be easily interpreted. The CCI maintains current unofficial estimates of the population of Chicago and its environs, and a long-range population projection. It has prepared numerous analytical and interpretive reports that are of use to urban planners, urban renewal programs, and business firms. It has been a leading force in maintaining the system of census tracts, in extending the tracts to cover the entire metropolitan area, and in obtaining special tabulations of census tract data. It has pointed the way both methodologically and by example, for more intensive and extensive use of these valuable resources in urban research. The work of the Duncans has been especially noteworthy in transforming human ecology from a science of mapping to one of highly refined discipline of statistical and mathematical inference with a coherent and distinctive viewpoint and theoretical underpinning. The techniques of demographic analysis appropriate for dealing with small local populations have been developed and put to work in exploring fertility, migration, and mortality events in the urban setting. Studies of the urban labor force, labor mobility, racial segregation, and the changing location and pattern of ethnic neighborhoods have become models which are being emulated at other research centers. Recently, the ecological and demographic work of the center has culminated in a series of researches aimed at comparing metropolitan areas with each other.

To a limited extent, the Chicago Community Inventory has made studies of ecological and demographic events in cities outside the United States. Further work in this area is contemplated.

A major gap in urban research had persisted for some decades at the university in the urban studies program. This was lack of a facility for carrying out systematic research on more distinctively sociological and social psychological aspects of urban life, for which data are not provided by official censuses. A move to correct this deficiency was made in 1961. At that time the Family Study Center (established in 1951 by E. W. Burgess with Nelson Foote as its first director) was reconstituted as the Community and Family Study Center, with a mandate from the Division of Social Science to develop a diversified program of research in urban sociology exclusive of the demographic and ecological aspects being exploited so thoroughly by the Chicago Community Inventory.

The Community and Family Study Center is directed by Donald J. Bogue, with Ernest W. Burgess as director emeritus. In addition to a continuing program of family research, this center has launched into an ambitious program of sociological analysis of urban and metropolitan life. The present volume is the first report of this program. A second report, *Skid Row in American Cities,* has also been published. Currently, a series of monographs is in preparation exploiting the results of a sample survey, "Problems of Living in the Metropolis." Still another research program centers around an experimental effort to induce low-education urban families to try to resolve some of their problems, or gain further insight concerning them. This project is called "Self-Help with Family Problems." Among the series of experiments being conducted is a project to see whether low-education families can be stimulated to adopt birth control by an especially designed program of mass communication.

It is intended that the Community and Family Study Center, with its sister center, the Chicago Community Inventory, will together carry out a sustained program of research and training which will cover all aspects of urban sociology.

PART 1

Urban Ecology and Demography

The starting point for urban analysis traditionally has been with demographic and ecological study. Knowledge about the population—its size, composition, and growth trends—is the foundation upon which other research may be based. Knowledge of the "economic base" of the community, and of how the various occupational and industrial units are organized with respect to the major community institutions—both in their livelihood activity and in the spatial location of their residences—follows quickly after the population analysis. For this reason, urban demography and urban ecology are usually linked or combined in a single research effort; instead of being treated as separate fields they tend to be looked upon as a single field with twin focus.

Once the demographic and ecological facts are known, and the forces which account for existing patterns and present trends are spelled out, they provide a context within which the social and cultural life, the intergroup alliances, bonds and tensions, and the patterns of attitudes and values can be assessed and understood. For this reason, the traditional sequence has been followed in arranging the materials of this book; the present section is devoted to contributions in the field of urban ecology and demography.

Because demography and ecological considerations are a fundamental starting point, and also because reliable data could be made available readily from censuses and other official sources, this branch of research got off to an early and very strong start. Robert E. Park was especially intrigued by the spatial patterning both of institutions and of people within the city, and by the tendency for "natural areas" to develop, based upon differences of income, occupation, ethnic background, religion, race, or other traits. He never tired of pointing out to his students how this process of differentiation conditioned almost every aspect of urban social life, and that spatial segregation and aggregation were physical manifestations of social and psychological processes at work in the city, as well as of the economic and ecological processes. This tendency toward spatial patterning attracted the attention of some very talented students early in the urban studies program, and they selected it as a topic for dissertation research. Zorbaugh's *The Gold Coast and the Slum,* and McKenzie's study of neighborhoods in Columbus, Ohio, were early instances of research in this area. As has already been described in the Introduction, the mapping of a wide variety of phenomena and efforts to develop explanations for the observed patterns comprised a substantial part of the urban research at the University of Chicago during the 1920's.

The zonal hypothesis of concentric circular zones of typical combinations of land use was derived as an abstraction from the findings of several different ecological and demographic studies. The hypotheses of sector specialization (Hoyt) and of multinucleation (Harris), which followed it, were derived in similar fashion—from research.

The items of research summarized in this section are only a selection of the total work that has been performed. Each one, however, was a pioneer undertaking at the time it was begun. The authors not only report their research, but review the results in the light of national and international developments to make recommendations for future research on urban ecology and demography.

1. *Variables in Urban Morphology**

BEVERLY DUNCAN

Students of urban structure have lived for some time with the uncomfortable realization that their theories—or rather, their abstract, schematic descriptions—of urban growth and form are not very susceptible to empirical testing. Given a map of land uses and residential characteristics, any investigator can discern evidence of concentric patterning, of multiple nucleation, and of sector differentiation.[1] Evidence favoring one of these does not rule out the plausibility of the others, however; and no way has been found to assess the relative contributions of the three types of tendency to the total configuration of the city. Such an impasse is perhaps typical of the stage of investigation in which natural-history observation has been followed by the formulation of ideal types. Some methodologists believe that it can be escaped only by resorting to more sophisticated measurement devices and formal multiple-variable analysis. These techniques will be productive, however, only if investigations are guided by realistic hypotheses about the determinants of community structure.

The economic efficiency associated with elaborate functional specialization of the urban work force requires a more or less pronounced separation of places of work from places of residence and a marked functional differentiation of areas wherein work is carried on.[2] The intra-community pattern of industrial location presumably evolved as part of the total process of city growth, but also in response to such specific locational determinants as space requirements, linkage to transportation and communication facilities, and site characteristics of available land. The pattern of socioeconomic residential differentiation likewise reflects the city's history of growth—on this point the concentric-zone and sector hypotheses are agreed—and in particular the several contingencies as to layout of mass-transit routes, residential amenities, and timing of settlement. Moreover, the patterns of industrial location and socioeconomic residential differentiation developed together, each changing under the influence of the other.

Salient in any accounting of the configuration of the city are factors which might be subsumed under the headings: G, Growth; A, accessibility; S, site; and P, persistence. The GASP scheme is offered not as a "theory" of urban structure but as a device for calling attention to some basic structural determinants.

A city grows over a period of time. Parts of the city are recently occupied;

* The analyses reported here were carried out in 1960–62 with the aid of a grant from the National Science Foundation. This paper was brought to completion as part of the program in Comparative Urban Research carried on at the Population Research and Training Center, University of Chicago under a grant from the Ford Foundation.

[1] The best synthetic discussion of these generalizations is still that of Chauncy D. Harris and Edward L. Ullman, "The Nature of Cities," first published in 1945 and reprinted (among other places) in *Cities and Society*, edited by Paul K. Hatt and Albert J. Reiss, Jr. (Glencoe, Ill.: Free Press, 1957).

[2] Beverly Duncan, "Intra-Urban Population Movement," in Hatt and Reiss, *op. cit.*; Leo F. Schnore, "Three Sources of Data on Commuting: Problems and Possibilities," *Journal of the American Statistical Association*, LV (March, 1960), 8–22.

17

others were built up decades ago; and some may have passed through one or more cycles of urban renewal or a succession of land uses. Areas, either industrial or residential, built up at a particular time will differ in character from older as well as more recently developed areas, for the relevant conditions of growth are modified through time. Hoover and Vernon, for example, point to the increasing land-per-worker ratio at industrial sites associated with new industrial processes and the decreasing importance of rail sidings in plant location paralleling the shift from "river to rail to rubber" in the assembly of materials and distribution of goods.[3] Rodwin considers the effect of rising real income, along with improvements in local transport technology, on the spatial configuration of "workingmen's homes."[4] Duncan, Sabagh, and Van Arsdol have demonstrated temporal changes in the density of residential settlement,[5] and Sabagh and Van Arsdol have shown the relevance of recency of occupancy in an accounting of intracity differentials in fertility.[6]

Accessibility to the city center, wherein the exchange of information and goods is co-ordinated, has long been regarded a key factor shaping the location of workplaces and residences. In studies of the location of industrial activity, Duncan and Davis found several highly centralized industries in the commercial com-

plex and only two centralized manufacturing industries—textiles and apparel, and printing and publishing.[7] The character of the centralized manufacturing industries is instructive. Both have unusually low ratios of area per establishment and area per worker as compared with other types of manufacturing;[8] and the garment and printing industries are "communication-oriented" to a much greater degree than are most manufacturing industries.[9] Economists such as Muth and Alonso, abstracting from all other factors shaping urban structure, have built impressive models deriving residential differentiation from accessibility to the city center.[10] There also is increasing evidence that accessibility to non-central industrial or commercial concentrations, as well as to the city center, influences residential differentiation and *vice versa*.[11]

Studies of the urban community carried out at the University of Chicago during the 1920's placed heavy emphasis

[3] Edgar M. Hoover and Raymond Vernon, *Anatomy of a Metropolis* (Cambridge, Mass.: Harvard University Press, 1959), pp. 31, 37.

[4] Lloyd Rodwin, *Housing and Economic Progress* (Cambridge, Mass.: Harvard University Press and Technology Press, 1961), pp. 94 ff.

[5] Beverly Duncan, Georges Sabagh, and Maurice D. Van Arsdol, Jr.,"Patterns of City Growth," *American Journal of Sociology*, LXVII (January, 1962), 418–29.

[6] Georges Sabagh and Maurice D. Van Arsdol, Jr., "Suburban Transition and Fertility Changes: An Illustrative Analysis," Paper No. 113, International Population Conference, 1961, organized by the International Union for the Scientific Study of Population.

[7] Otis Dudley Duncan and Beverly Davis, *Inter-Industry Variations in Work-Residence Relationships of the Chicago Labor Force* (Chicago: Chicago Community Inventory, University of Chicago, 1952), p. 20.

[8] Otis Dudley Duncan and Beverly Davis, *Ecological Aspects of the Labor Force in the Chicago Metropolitan Area* (Chicago: Chicago Community Inventory, University of Chicago, 1953), pp. 50–55.

[9] Hoover and Vernon, *op. cit.*, pp. 63–67.

[10] Richard F. Muth, "The Spatial Structure of the Housing Market," *Papers and Proceedings of the Regional Science Association*, VII (1961); William Alonso, "A Theory of the Urban Land Market," *Papers and Proceedings of the Regional Science Association*, VI (1960), 149–57.

[11] One example, results of which are summarized subsequently, was first reported in Beverly Duncan and Otis Dudley Duncan, "The Measurement of Intra-City Locational and Residential Patterns," *Journal of Regional Science*, II (Fall, 1960), 37–54. See also Willard B. Hansen, "An Approach to the Analysis of Metropolitan Residential Extension," *Journal of Regional Science*, III (Summer, 1961), 37–55.

on both growth and accessibility.[12] Because the physical expansion of the city typically proceeds outward from the city center and areas occupied at different times differ in character, a "zonal" hypothesis of urban areal differentiation was set forth by Burgess.[13] On this assumption of the form of urban expansion, accessibility to the city center is greatest in the inner and oldest "zones" of the city and less in the outer, recently developed "zones." Perhaps for this reason, the roles of growth and accessibility in shaping the city were not explicitly distinguished; and, given the more restricted range of techniques then available for measuring areal patterns, both factors were indexed by distance from the city core.

It is true, to be sure, that the relationship between mile distance from the city center and various indicators of the socioeconomic level of the resident population or the prevalence of non-residential units, such as plants, stores, or amusement centers, is imperfect. The looseness of relationship, however, does not rule out growth and accessibility as potent explanatory factors. Until their influence on urban structure has been evaluated with the most sophisticated measurement techniques available, the formulations of the "Chicago school" cannot be rejected. We have investigated the areal association of mile distance from the heart of the central business

[12] See, for example, Ernest W. Burgess, "The Growth of the City: An Introduction to a Research Project," and R. D. McKenzie, "The Ecological Approach to the Study of the Human Community," in *The City*, edited by Robert E. Park, Ernest W. Burgess, and Roderick D. McKenzie (Chicago: University of Chicago Press, 1925); Robert E. Park, "The Urban Community as a Spatial Pattern and a Moral Order," and Harvey W. Zorbaugh, "The Natural Areas of the City," in *The Urban Community*, edited by Ernest W. Burgess (Chicago: University of Chicago Press, 1926).

[13] Ernest W. Burgess, "The Growth of the City: An Introduction to a Research Project," in Park, Burgess, and McKenzie, *op. cit.*

district with age of the housing inventory, accessibility to manufacturing workplaces, and accessibility to commercial workplaces, respectively, in metropolitan Chicago c. 1950.[14] Correlations among the measures are shown below:

Item	Age of Housing (Per Cent pre-1920)	Workplace Accessibility	
		Manufacturing	Commercial
Distance from center.	−.54	−.79	−.73
Age of housing......	....	.65	.59
Mfg. accessibility....	....	....	.86

Although the inter-correlations among the measures are sizable, they provide a strong empirical basis for distinguishing age of housing, i.e., growth, from accessibility, quite aside from theoretical justifications.

Rather less attention has been directed to site and persistence, the remaining elements of the GASP scheme. Items falling under these rubrics may be "facts" and as such, uninteresting to theoretically oriented students of urban structure. Those who ignore the facts, however, are likely to experience difficulty in accounting for the configuration of the city.

Places within a city differ in terms of topography, substratum, elevation, proximity to bodies of water, orientation to prevailing winds, and other physical qualities. Qualitative differences also obtain with respect to such man-made features as rapid transit lines, interurban rail lines, expressways, and parks. For that matter, areas will differ with respect to nearly any quality. It is beyond question that site qualities of an area influ-

[14] Correlations are based on a sample of 211 quasi-tracts in the Chicago Metropolitan District as defined in 1940. Accessibility to workplaces is measured by workplace potential. The sampling procedure and the calculation of workplace potential are described in Duncan and Duncan, *op. cit.*, pp. 41–44.

ence the types of uses which develop. The location of a complex of trans-shipment facilities, such as the harbor area, or a string formation of industrial or commercial activity can scarcely be explained without reference to site qualities. Areal variation in residential densities may reflect differences in topography or substratum: Can high-rise structures be built? The importance of elevation and orientation to prevailing winds in the socioeconomic differentiation of Durban has been documented by Kuper, Watts, and Davies.[15]

Finally, sheer persistence is a powerful factor. The activity whose present location makes "no sense" often can be explained by reference to the past. An excellent example is the Chicago meatpacking industry, located within a few miles of the city center and now surrounded by residential neighborhoods. In 1864, when Chicago's population was just over 100,000, a peripheral area with only a few scattered farms was selected as the site of the stockyards. Nine railroads engaged in transporting cattle extended spur lines to the site, and four major stockyards companies constructed stock pens and an exchange and bank building.[16] The capitalization of structures and facilities bound the industry to the site for nearly a century although innovations in processing and shipping had modified locational requirements in the industry and the prevailing winds carried noxious odors to many residential areas of the city. There also is evidence of strong stability over time in the relative positions of residential neighborhoods with respect to housing and population characteristics. Given the rather long life-expectancy of residential struc-

tures, stability over a decade or quarter-century in housing characteristics might be attributed to the fact that the same dwellings are the base of initial and terminal measurements. The high rates of population mobility within urban areas, however, render this argument untenable for population characteristics; initial residents account for only a fraction of the terminal residents. Probably less than a fifth of the dwellings in a "middle-aged" United States city are now occupied by their original tenants.[17] The ranking of residential neighborhoods by socioeconomic level at the end of a decade has been shown to be much the same as their initial ranking, even in areas where a substantial shift in racial composition occurred within the ten-year period.[18] Some preliminary results suggest that socioeconomic differentials among neighborhoods persist over much longer time periods. To illustrate, we can cite the coefficient of correlation of .81 between the proportion of employed males in professional occupations in 1950 and the proportion of gainfully occupied males in professional service in 1920, based on 124 areas, a 25 per cent sample of 1920 Chicago census tracts.

These observations about basic determinants of industrial location and socioeconomic differentiation of residential neighborhoods provide a framework for assessing the results of a recent investi-

---

[15] Leo Kuper, Hilstan Watts, and Ronald Davies, *Durban: A Study in Racial Ecology* (London: Jonathan Cape, Ltd., 1958), pp. 107–42.

[16] *Local Community Fact Book for Chicago: 1950*, edited by Philip M. Hauser and Evelyn M. Kitagawa (Chicago: Chicago Community Inventory, University of Chicago, 1953), p. 250.

[17] The maximum proportion of dwellings in the city of Chicago in 1940 which could have been occupied by their original tenants is 19 per cent. The estimate is derived from tabulations of dwellings by year of original construction and households by duration of occupancy published for community areas in *Residential Chicago*, Vol. I of the Chicago Land Use Survey (Chicago: Chicago Plan Commission, City of Chicago, 1942).

[18] Otis Dudley Duncan and Beverly Duncan, *The Negro Population of Chicago* (Chicago: University of Chicago Press, 1957); Alma F. Taeuber, "A Comparative Urban Analysis of Negro Residential Succession" (Unpublished Ph.D. dissertation, Department of Sociology, University of Chicago, March, 1962).

gation of patterns of residential differentiation according to the industrial affiliations of the work force. The results first were reported in Duncan and Duncan, "The Measurement of Intra-City Locational and Residential Patterns."[19]

RESIDENTIAL DIFFERENTIATION BY INDUSTRY

The research reported by Duncan and Duncan rests on two bodies of small-area data for the Chicago Metropolitan District *c.* 1950. One pertains to the areal distribution of workplaces, i.e., number of jobs, by industry; the other concerns the distribution of the resident labor force by industry. Two features of these data call for special comment. First, statistics are available for the entire CMD (Chicago Metropolitan District), an area approximating the city of Chicago, its suburbs and urban fringe in 1950. Within the CMD there is commutation into the city from white-collar dormitory suburbs, as well as flows of manufacturing workers from the city into satellite industrial areas. The CMD as a whole, however, constitutes a more or less closed labor market, a prerequisite for the subsequent analysis. Second, the areal detail with which employment in manufacturing establishments is reported and the relatively complete coverage of workplaces are somewhat unique. Census-tract data of rather good quality are available for the two-fifths of the labor force in the fourteen manufacturing industries separately identified in the 1950 Census of Population. Less detailed and comprehensive statistics for the three-tenths of the labor force in the commercial complex are available for some 100 subareas of the CMD. Workplace information is not available for the remaining three-tenths of the labor force whose workplaces are assumed to be distributed more or less evenly over the CMD.

The analysis relies heavily on a sum-

mary measure of the areal distribution of workplaces termed "workplace potential." The workplace potential at a particular site in the CMD is the sum over all workplaces in the CMD of the reciprocals of the mile distance separating each workplace from the site. On the assumption that accessibility declines as distance increases, workplace potential is interpreted as a measure of the accessibility of the site to workplaces in the CMD.

Isolines of workplace potential for two industries in the CMD—non-electrical and electrical machinery—can be seen in Figures 1 and 2.[20] Each industry employs about 4.5 per cent of the CMD work force. The configuration of contours is less "peaked" for the non-electrical machinery industry than for the electrical machinery industry. This reflects the fact that workplaces in the non-electrical machinery industry are distributed more evenly over the CMD. The density of non-electrical machinery workplaces is comparatively high throughout the central industrial area west of the city center, and a few sizable outlying establishments ring the city. By contrast, a fifth of the employment in the electrical machinery industry is concentrated at a single site some seven miles southwest of the city center; and an equal number of electrical machinery workplaces are found within three miles northeast of this site.

Another variable playing an important role in the analysis is termed the "expected" proportion of the resident work force in an industry on the basis of occupational composition. A variation on the "method of expected cases" was se-

[19] In *Journal of Regional Science,* II (Fall, 1960), 37–54.

[20] Maps showing isolines of workplace potential for two other industries, fabricated and primary metal, appear in "The Measurement of Intra-City Locational and Residential Patterns." Isolines are identified in terms of "workplaces per mile," the sum of the reciprocals of the mile distance separating each workplace (job) from the site. The potential depends on the site's position with respect to the total configuration of jobs.

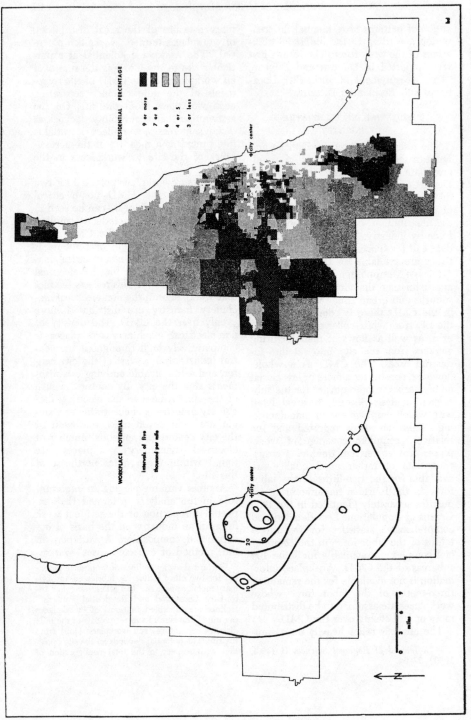

FIG. 1.—Workplace potential and residential distribution for the machinery, except electrical, industry group in the Chicago Metropolitan District, c. 1950

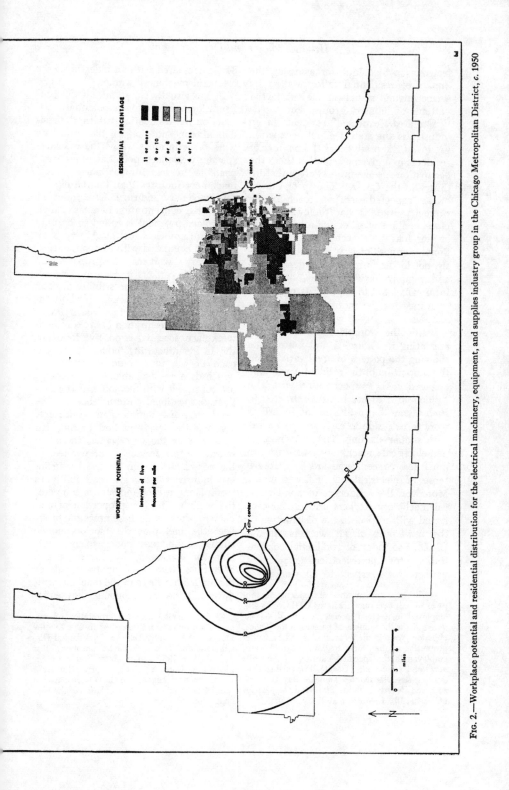

FIG. 2.—Workplace potential and residential distribution for the electrical machinery, equipment, and supplies industry group in the Chicago Metropolitan District, c. 1950

lected as a technique for assessing the impact of residential differentiation by socioeconomic status on the residential patterns of industry groups. For a particular area, "expected" residents in an industry is the sum over all occupation groups of the products of the number of residents in a given occupation times the occupation-specific proportion in that industry in the CMD.[21] The special merit of the "expected cases" approach for the present purpose is that it allows the "socioeconomic status" of the area (insofar as this may be reflected in its occupational composition) to enter the analysis, not in the form of some generalized and vaguely justified "index," but in a form calculated to capture its particular relevance for the industry group under analysis.

Beside the workplace potential maps appearing in Figures 1 and 2 are maps showing the pattern of areal variation in the proportion of the resident work force engaged in the respective industry. The residential map has been constructed in such a way that a fifth of the industry's work force reside in each group of areas with similar shading. The residences of non-electrical machinery workers are much less concentrated areally than are those of electrical machinery workers. Moreover, the residences of non-electrical machinery workers are less concentrated with respect to the distribution of the residences of all workers in the CMD. The index of residential concentration for non-electrical machinery workers with respect to all workers is

34, as compared with an index of 46 for electrical machinery workers.[22]

If one visually superimposes the configuration of workplace-potential contours on the residential pattern, the residential concentration of the industry's work force in areas where the industry-specific workplace potential is high appears to be less for the non-electrical machinery industry than for the electrical machinery industry. The index of residential concentration in areas of high workplace potential is found to be only 8 for the non-electrical machinery work force, as compared with 31 for electrical machinery workers. Disproportionate numbers of workers in each industry reside in areas where accessibility to their workplaces is high, however, for both indexes are positive. In fact, the index of residential concentration in areas of high workplace potential is positive for 13 of the 14 manufacturing industries and for each of the four trade industries for which data are available. These findings are consistent with the notion that an industry's locational pattern influences the residential distribution of its work force.

Along the lakefront and in the area just west of the city center, there are relatively few residences of workers in the non-electrical and electrical machinery industries although accessibility to workplaces in each industry is comparatively high. The low proportion of machinery workers in these areas might reflect the fact that the "socioeconomic status" of the areas renders them unsuitable for occupancy by craftsmen and operatives, who make up two-thirds of the male labor force in the machinery industry. If the socioeconomic differentia-

[21] The expected number of residents in the jth areal unit (census tract in the CMD) who are employed in a given industry equals $\Sigma_i X_{ij} Y_i$, where X_{ij} is the number of persons in the ith occupation group in the jth areal unit and Y_i is the proportion of the ith occupation group who are employed in the specified industry in the universe of j areal units (CMD). For further discussion, see Otis Dudley Duncan, Ray P. Cuzzort, and Beverly Duncan, *Statistical Geography* (Glencoe, Ill.: Free Press, 1961), pp. 120 ff.

[22] The calculation and interpretation of concentration indexes are described in Otis Dudley Duncan and Beverly Duncan, "Residential Distribution and Occupational Stratification," first published in 1955 and reprinted (among other places) in Hatt and Reiss, *op. cit.* The 1,178 census tracts making up the CMD were classified into 12 to 15 intervals for calculation of the concentration indexes.

tion of residential areas does influence the residential distribution of an industry's work force, the industry's residential distribution should differ less from its "expected" distribution than from the residential distribution of all workers. For the non-electrical machinery industry, the index of residential concentration with respect to "expected" residences of the industry group is only 27, as compared with the index of 34 reported earlier. The index of residential concentration falls from 46 to 38 for electrical machinery workers, when the base of comparison is shifted from all residences to "expected" residences of the industry group.

These results imply that the residential pattern of an industry group is shaped by the locational pattern of the industry, the occupational composition of its work force, and the residential patterns of the several occupation groups. Any model which seeks to account for the residential distributions of industry groups solely on the basis of the location of industrial activity or solely on the basis of the differentiation of the city by socioeconomic level should be demonstrably deficient. A model which incorporates both factors and permits an assessment of their independent as well as joint effects is described below.

The residential pattern of an industry group within the metropolitan district, or more specifically areal variation in the proportion of the resident labor force employed in a particular industry, is the phenomenon to be accounted for. Two probable determinants of residential patterns have been identified: interarea differences in accessibility to the industry's workplaces; and interarea differences in socioeconomic status (occupational composition). Accessibility is measured by the industry's relative workplace potential in the area, i.e., the percentage of the area's total workplace potential accounted for by the industry-specific workplace potential. The frequent coincidence of areas of high workplace potential for two or more industries suggests that relative workplace potentials should be more efficient predictors of residential structure than workplace potentials *per se*. Such a hypothesis would follow if one conceived of total workplace potential as indicative of the total demand for residence in a particular area, on the assumption that demand varies directly with accessibility to workplaces. The industrial composition of the area's resident work force, then, would mirror the industrial composition of its total workplace potential, assuming the effective demand for residence is constant over industries. The socioeconomic status of the area is measured by the "expected" proportion of residents in the industry. This means, of course, that an area has no single index of socioeconomic status, i.e., occupational composition, but rather a distinct index for each industry examined. The percentage of the resident labor force in the industry, the "expected" percentage of the resident labor force in the industry, and the relative workplace potential for the industry were computed for each of 14 manufacturing industries for a sample of 211 residential neighborhoods in the CMD. The 14 manufacturing industries are taken to represent 14 "tests" (albeit not wholly independent ones) of the model's goodness of fit.

A quick overview of the results, summarized in Table 1, would stress the facts that accessibility to workplaces and socioeconomic status together account for more than a fourth of the areal variation in the residential proportion and that each, "holding constant" the other, has a significant effect on the residential distribution in 11 of the 14 "tests." The 14 industries are arrayed in order of decreasing employment size in Table 1, and it can be seen that the "tests" in which the model performs least efficiently are those based on the industries of smallest employment size. The measurement problem may be particularly difficult for these industries, or a distinctive residential pattern may emerge only as an industry attains substantial size.

For each manufacturing industry, there is a direct association, significant in the statistical sense, between the residential

workplaces, for in ten of the 14 "tests" the association between actual and "expected" residential proportions in the industry is weaker than that between the residential proportion and relative potential.

As measured by the respective regres-

TABLE 1

SUMMARY OF REGRESSIONS OF RESIDENTIAL DISTRIBUTIONS ON WORKPLACE POTENTIALS AND
"EXPECTED" RESIDENTIAL DISTRIBUTIONS, FOR MANUFACTURING INDUSTRIES, BASED ON
SAMPLE OF 211 QUASI-TRACTS IN THE CHICAGO METROPOLITAN DISTRICT, *c.* 1950

MANUFACTURING INDUSTRY	CORRELATION AND REGRESSION COEFFICIENTS[1]								
	r_{Y1} (1)	b_{Y1} (2)	r_{Y2} (3)	b_{Y2} (4)	r_{12} (5)	$R_{Y.12}$ (6)	$R^2_{Y.12}$ (7)	$b_{Y1.2}$ (8)	$b_{Y2.1}$ (9)
Primary metal industries.........	.86	2.41	.45	2.99	.25	.90	.80	2.23	1.68
Electrical machinery, equipment, and supplies.................	.65	1.22	.50	2.13	.07[2]	.80	.63	1.16	1.95
Food and kindred products.......	.69	0.74	.41	1.99	.20	.74	.55	0.68	1.38
Machinery, excluding electrical....	.29	0.80	.54	2.10	.13[2]	.58	.34	0.61	1.99
Fabricated metal industries.......	.27	0.64	.56	1.83	.18	.59	.35	0.41	1.72
Printing, publishing, and allied industries......................	.39	0.55	.36	1.13	−.36	.66	.44	0.85	1.82
Other durable goods.............	.47	0.75	.52	1.49	.12[2]	.66	.44	0.65	1.34
Other non-durable goods.........	.78	2.59	.30	2.12	.23	.79	.62	2.49	0.91
Apparel and other fabricated textile products..................	.60	1.01	.42	1.23	.36	.64	.40	0.87	0.70
Chemicals and allied products.....	.64	1.94	.13[2]	1.84[2]	−.03[2]	.65	.43	1.95	2.17
Furniture, and lumber and wood products.....................	.39	1.25	.37	2.07	.37	.46	.21	0.94	1.44
Motor vehicles and motor vehicle equipment	.20	0.23	.32	1.21	.25	.34	.12	0.15[3]	1.09
Transportation equipment, excluding motor vehicle..............	.51	1.31	.10[2]	1.44[2]	.07[2]	.51	.26	1.30	0.85[2]
Textile mill products.............	.37	0.35	.20	0.89	.13[2]	.40	.16	0.32	0.68[3]

[1] Identification of symbols:
  Y, per cent of resident employed persons in the specified industry, by quasi-tract;
  r_{Y1}, r_{Y2}, and r_{12}, zero-order correlations;
  b_{Y1} and b_{Y2}, zero-order regression coefficients;
  $R_{Y.12}$, multiple correlation coefficient, Y on X_1 and X_2;
  $b_{Y1.2}$ and $b_{Y2.1}$, partial regression coefficients.
[2] Coefficients not significant at .05 level.
[3] Coefficients significant at .05 level; all other coefficients differ significantly from zero at the .01 level.

proportion and relative workplace potential on an area-by-area basis (Col. 1, Table 1). The percentage of the resident work force in the industry also varies directly with the area's "expected" percentage in the industry; the relationship is significant, in the statistical sense, for 12 of the 14 industries (Col. 3, Table 1). Socioeconomic level is, on the average, a less efficient predictor of an industry's residential pattern than is accessibility to

sion coefficients (Col. 2 and Col. 4, Table 1), however, the average influence of areal differentials in socioeconomic level on the residential pattern is often more than that of interarea differences in accessibility. Possibly a more accurate statement would be that the influence of socioeconomic level on the residential distribution is consistently substantial, while the influence of accessibility may be substantial or negligible.

Areas in which accessibility to an industry's workplace is high need not have occupational compositions which are conducive to residence by members of the industry. In the case of the printing industry, there is, in fact, an inverse relationship between relative potential and the "expected" residential proportion in the industry (Col. 5, Table 1). For six industries, relative potential varies over areas more or less independently of the "expected" proportion. Areal differentials in relative potential reinforce socioeconomic level in shaping the residential pattern for only half the manufacturing industries; and even in these cases, the association is rather loose.

As a consequence of this loose association between the determinants of industrial residential distributions, accessibility to workplaces and socioeconomic level together more fully account for the residential pattern of an industry than does either alone. Over a third of the variance in the residential proportion for the industry group is accounted for by the combination of relative industry-specific potential and "expected" residential proportion in the industry for each of the ten largest manufacturing industries in the CMD (Col. 7, Table 1). The two factors combined account for an eighth to a fourth of the variance in the residential percentages for the four smaller industries. The effect on the residential distribution of each factor, independent of the other, is significant for all but the three smallest industries (Col. 8 and Col. 9, Table 1). Owing to the generally low correlation between the two predictor variables, the interindustry differences with respect to the partial regression coefficients are much like those with respect to the zero-order regressions. Hence the observation stands that occupational composition has a more consistently substantial effect on residential distribution, but that relative workplace potential has the stronger effect for a few industries.

WORKINGMEN'S NEIGHBORHOODS

Despite the restrictions on generalization imposed by having only one city as a case study, the results reported above indicate that any adequate theory of urban residential structure must reckon with both the locational pattern of industrial activity and the socioeconomic differentiation of residential areas which comes about through general city growth. To deduce the location of the "zone of workingmen's homes," Burgess, in his schematic presentation of urban residential structure, relied primarily on the latter factor, the sequence of settlement in the course of urban expansion. He was not unaware of the influence of industrial location, however, for he described the zone of workingmen's homes as "inhabited by the workers in industries who have escaped from the area of deterioration but who desire to live within easy access of their work."[23] "Workingmen's suburbs," or industrial satellites, also have been identified; and the location of outlying industrial concentrations is presumed to be a key factor in their occurrence.[24] Attempts to include both in a single hypothesis have been few, however.

The relative number of manufacturing workers living in a neighborhood can be shown to vary with both the area's position in the sequence of urban expansion and its accessibility to manufacturing workplaces. Moreover, the relevance of a site factor, lakefront location, in shaping the pattern of workingmen's neighborhoods becomes evident. The regression of the percentage of the resident labor force employed in manufacturing on distance from city center, age of

[23] Ernest W. Burgess, "The Growth of the City: An Introduction to a Research Project," in Park, Burgess, and McKenzie, *op. cit.*, p. 50.

[24] See, for example, Leo F. Schnore, "The Growth of Metropolitan Suburbs" and "Satellites and Suburbs," first published in 1957, and reprinted in *The Suburban Community*, edited by William M. Dobriner (New York: G. P. Putnam's Sons, 1958).

housing, relative accessibility to manufacturing workplaces, and lakefront location for the Chicago CMD *c.* 1950 is summarized in Table 2. A low zero-order association between the residential percentage in manufacturing and distance from the city center might be interpreted by some investigators as adequate simultaneously, however, each factor is found to have a statistically significant, independent effect on the residential proportion in manufacturing. The four factors, in combination, account for 36 per cent of the variance in the relative number of manufacturing workers.

TABLE 2

SUMMARY OF REGRESSIONS OF RESIDENTIAL DISTRIBUTIONS OF MANUFACTURING WORKERS AND WHITE-COLLAR MALES ON DISTANCE FROM CENTER, AGE OF HOUSING, MANUFACTURING POTENTIAL, AND LAKEFRONT LOCATION, BASED ON SAMPLE OF 211 QUASI-TRACTS IN THE CHICAGO METROPOLITAN DISTRICT, *c.* 1950

DEPENDENT VARIABLE AND STATISTIC	INDEPENDENT VARIABLE			
	Mile Distance from Center	Age of Housing (Per Cent pre-1920)	Relative Manufacturing Potential	Lakefront Location
Per cent of employed in manufacturing, by quasi-tract:				
Zero-order coefficient				
Correlation	.07[1]	.18	.42	− .32
Regression	.13[1]	.06	1.04	−11.34
Partial regression coefficient				
Standard measure	.43	.28	.49	− .21
Raw-score form	.78	.10	1.22	− 7.63
Per cent of employed males in professional, managerial, and sales occupations, square root transform, by quasi-tract:				
Zero-order coefficient				
Correlation	.19	− .54	− .30	.31
Regression	.05	− .03	− .11	1.60
Partial regression coefficient				
Standard measure	− .19	− .62	− .15[2]	.30
Raw-score form	− .05	− .03	− .01[2]	1.58

[1] Coefficients not significant at .05 level.
[2] Coefficients significant at .05 level; all other coefficients differ significantly from zero at the .01 level.

quate grounds for rejecting the Burgess hypothesis. The relationship between the residential proportion and distance is found to be weak, even when allowance is made for the curvilinearity implied by the hypothesis. The coefficient of multiple correlation between the percentage of manufacturing workers and (*a*) mile distance from the city center and (*b*) the square of mile distance is only .15 (not significant at the .05 level). When distance, age, workplace accessibility, and lakefront location are considered

Workingmen's neighborhoods might be identified on an occupational rather than an industrial criterion. The residential distributions of males in professional, managerial, and sales occupations resemble one another and are quite distinct from the residential patterns of males in clerical and blue-collar occupations.[25] Within the CMD in 1950, the

[25] Otis Dudley Duncan and Beverly Duncan, "Residential Distribution and Occupational Stratification," first published in 1955 and reprinted (among other places) in Hatt and Reiss, *op. cit.*

inter-correlations among the professional, managerial, and sales proportions are
.8 or more; each of the three proportions
has an inverse association, significant in
the statistical sense, with each blue-collar major occupation group and varies
more or less independently of the clerical proportion. Workingmen's neighborhoods, then, might be defined as those
in which the residential proportion in
professional, managerial, and sales oc-

and each factor, holding constant each
other factor statistically, is the same
whether the areas of workingmen's
homes are defined in industrial or occupational terms. A relatively high accessibility to manufacturing workplaces is
conducive to residence by workingmen.
Older housing is directly associated with
the residential proportion of workingmen. A lakefront location deters residence by workingmen. The final net

TABLE 3

MEANS OF RESIDENTIAL PERCENTAGES OF MANUFACTURING WORKERS AND WHITE-COLLAR MALES,
OBSERVED AND CALCULATED FROM MULTIPLE-REGRESSION EQUATION, BY DISTANCE ZONE FROM
CENTER, BASED ON SAMPLE OF 211 QUASI-TRACTS IN THE CHICAGO METROPOLITAN DISTRICT,
c. 1950

MILE DISTANCE FROM CITY CENTER	MANUFACTURING WORKERS		WHITE-COLLAR MALES (SQ. RT.)		INDEPENDENT VARIABLE[1]				NUMBER OF AREAS
	Observed	Calcu-lated	Observed	Calcu-lated	X_1	X_2	X_3	X_4	
All zones..	39	39	4.9	4.9	8.6	59	42	.11	211
Less than 3..	41	34	3.6	4.2	2.1	91	40	.14	21
3 to 6.......	42	42	4.1	4.2	4.5	84	45	.10	62
6 to 9.......	36	39	5.4	5.1	7.3	55	43	.14	56
9 to 12......	36	35	5.8	5.9	10.2	26	41	.15	34
12 to 15.....	39	38	5.6	5.3	13.2	39	40	.09	11
15 to 18.....	36	37	6.2	5.4	16.2	34	38	.17	6
18 or more...	46	43	4.6	4.8	23.9	34	37	.05	21

[1] Identification of symbols:
X_1, Distance from center of city, in miles;
X_2, per cent of 1950 housing inventory built in 1919 or earlier;
X_3, relative workplace potential of all manufacturing industries;
X_4, proportion of quasi-tracts located within one mile of Lake Michigan.

cupations is low. The four factors—distance, age, accessibility to manufacturing workplaces, and lakefront location
—account for 44 per cent of the variance
in the residential proportion of males in
professional, managerial, and sales occupations (square root transform thereof). Again the zero-order association
between the residential proportion and
mile distance from the city center is
rather loose. Within the multiple-factor
framework, however, each factor has an
independent effect on the residential
proportion.

The direction of the net relationship
between "workingmen's neighborhoods"

relationship is perhaps more surprising:
the proportion of workingmen increases
with distance from the city center. This
relationship can scarcely be explained in
terms of workplace location, for relative
accessibility to manufacturing workplaces has been controlled statistically.
Two alternative explanations can be
suggested, speculatively to be sure. First,
accessibility to the specialized retail outlets, centers for cultural events, firms
offering special services, and the like
which are concentrated in the core of
the city may be a less important de-
terminant of residential location for
workingmen than for white-collar males.

Second, given a decline in land values with increasing distance from the city center, residential areas with more or less equivalent housing and amenities may command substantially higher rentals if they are centrally located.

Given these net relationships, the sequence of urban expansion and the location of manufacturing activity in Chicago would have resulted in zonation of workingmen's neighborhoods. The lakefront location factor, incidentally, would lead to a sector pattern of differentiation superimposed on the zonation. In Table 3, the zonal pattern of variation in the residential proportion of workingmen expected on the basis of the multiple-regression equation is compared with the observed zonal pattern. On either the industrial or occupational criterion, the proportion of workingmen is expected to be high in the area surrounding the city core and on the periphery of the urban area. The proportion is expected to be lowest in the middle distance band, nine to twelve miles from the center. The actual zonal distribution evidences this double "peaking," the first peak suggesting a "zone of workingmen's homes" and the second a "ring of industrial satellites." The major discrepancy between the expected and actual pattern of zonation occurs in the innermost zone of the city, where the proportion of workingmen is substantially higher than expected.

The first peak in the zonal pattern or the inner zone of workingmen's homes might be anticipated on the basis of the Burgess hypothesis of city growth and differentiation, but this growth model does not suggest the presence of workingmen's suburbs on the periphery of the urban area. The zonal model, abstracting from reality, assumes expansion emanating from a single core over an undeveloped area. Actually a city in the course of its growth encroaches upon and engulfs outlying, once independent settlements with their own complements of industrial activity. The proportion of pre–World War I housing in the CMD, for example, falls from a peak near the city center rather regularly for some twelve miles and then rises as some settlements predating the city core are reached. The remoteness of these settlements from the central commercial complex results in a high relative accessibility to manufacturing workplaces located in the immediate area. The failure of the growth model to anticipate workingmen's surburbs should not be regarded as a weakness of the hypothesis as such; rather it stems from the particular abstraction which underlies the model. Traces of early settlement patterns persist in the area over which the city spreads.

Perhaps by re-examining earlier findings with more powerful analytical techniques guided by a GASP framework, some gaps in our understanding of urban morphology can be closed.

2. Trends in Differential Fertility and Mortality in a Metropolis—Chicago*

EVELYN M. KITAGAWA AND PHILIP M. HAUSER

INTRODUCTION

The studies of differential fertility and mortality in Chicago, conducted now over four decades, had their origin in two interests in sociology at the University of Chicago in the late 1920's. One was the interest in human ecology sparked by the insights of Robert E. Park and the theoretical bent and empirical researches of Ernest W. Burgess. The second was the interest in quantitative method and research spearheaded by William F. Ogburn who was, also, among the first sociologists to offer a course in population and to conduct demographic research.

The series of researches summarized and updated in this report was initiated in the doctoral dissertation of Hauser, in which the merger of human ecological and demographic interests is evident.[1] It is of more than historical interest that the Chicago studies of differential fertility and mortality had their origin in a merger of interests in human ecology and demography, for without the developments in human ecological research and the growing fund and utilization of census tract data stimulated by such research, the individual studies drawn upon here could not have been conducted; nor could the trends in differential fertility and mortality within an urban area be measured. Birth and death certificates, their primary purpose being non-statistical, contain only limited information about the characteristics of individuals and do not permit analysis of differentials by meaningful socioeconomic categories. But the allocation of birth and death certificates to census tracts makes possible the aggregation of fertility and mortality data for various combinations of census tracts classified by summary characteristics of their populations, including socioeconomic characteristics. Thus, the combination of birth and death data by census tracts provide the numerators, and the combination of population data by census tracts the denominators, of the various birth and death rates.

Five studies of fertility or mortality in Chicago have provided the foundation for this summary report.[2] In the effort to

* The present paper integrates a continuing line of investigation, the history of which is described in the text. This task was supported in part (collection of 1950 data and analysis of 1920 to 1950 time series of socioeconomic differentials) by a PHS research grant (No. RG–7134) from the National Institutes of Health, Public Health Service.

[1] Philip M. Hauser, "Differential Fertility, Mortality, and Net Reproduction in Chicago, 1930" (unpublished Ph.D. dissertation, Department of Sociology, University of Chicago, 1938).

[2] Hauser, op. cit.; Melvin L. Dollar, Vital Statistics for Cook County and Chicago (Chicago: Works Projects Administration Publications in Research and Records, 1942); Albert J. Mayer, "Differentials in Length of Life in Chicago: 1880–1940" (unpublished Ph.D. dissertation, Department of Sociology, University of Chicago, 1950); Evelyn M. Kitagawa, "Differential Fertility in Chicago: 1920–40" (unpublished Ph.D. dissertation, Department of Sociology, University of Chicago, 1951). The fifth study provided the basic data for 1950 and was supported by a grant (to Hauser and Kitagawa) from the National Institutes of Health, Public Health Service.

analyze changes in patterns of differential fertility and mortality over time, however, most of the measures for 1920–40 were recomputed to effect greater comparability.

The study of fertility and mortality transcends matters of immediate demographic concern. For both fertility behavior and the incidence of mortality, although they possess important biological components, are also functions of the social milieu in which they occur. This basic premise, which in a large measure accounts for the interest of the sociologist in demography and the capture by him in academic United States of most of the teaching and research in demography, is well supported by research findings—those dealt with here and in other studies. To set forth patterns of differential fertility or mortality is to reveal much about social stratification and subcultures in a society; and to point to basic differences in personal attitudes, values, and behavior, as well as the net effect of all the forces operating within a society on the life chances of the individual. Differential fertility may be viewed as an important measure of the extent to which a society is homogeneous or heterogeneous, integrated or pluralistic, static or experiencing rapid social change. Differential mortality may be interpreted as the supreme measurement of the net effect of differential opportunities, for it provides an index of the ability of the person or a group to retain life itself.

DIFFERENTIAL FERTILITY

Until 1950, most of the available statistics indicated an inverse relation between fertility rates and size of city, and an inverse relation between fertility and socioeconomic status although there were some exceptions in respect to the marital fertility of particular population groups. However, the increases in birth rates since 1940 have been much greater in the upper-status groups than in the lower-

status groups, with the result that socioeconomic differentials in 1950 were considerably narrower than in 1940.[3] Preliminary statistics currently available for 1960 indicate that differential increases in fertility during the decade 1950–60 may have eradicated or even reversed some of the long-term patterns of differential fertility in the nation, as increases in fertility apparently continued to be greater in the former low-fertility groups.

The most "advanced" patterns of social and economic differentials in fertility have been sought in the metropolis where, presumably, births are subject to a higher degree of control.

The phenomenon of differential fertility according to occupational or socioeconomic status has sometimes been described as a transitional phase of declining fertility. The theory is that the declines begin in the so-called "upper" occupational classes in urban areas. Later, the declines affect the so-called "middle" classes and finally the so-called "lower" occupational classes. In the meantime the declines spread outward to the rural areas and presumably the process runs the same type of course there.[4]

From this perspective, a time series of statistics on differential fertility in a metropolis should shed light on emerging patterns of differential fertility. The unique body of data available for Chicago for the period 1920–60 is analyzed here with this objective.

The time series of statistics on differential fertility in Chicago also permits the comparison of fertility trends in a major metropolis with trends in the nation as a whole. The section that follows analyzes the available statistics from this perspective.

The Metropolis and the Nation

In Table 1 Chicago and U.S. fertility rates are presented from the earliest date

[3] Wilson H. Grabill, Clyde V. Kiser, and Pascal K. Whelpton, *The Fertility of American Women* (New York: John Wiley & Sons, 1958), chapters v, vi, vii.

[4] *Ibid.*, p. 180.

for which reliable statistics are available for both areas, namely, 1920. In conformity with the expected pattern, Chicago fertility was significantly lower than that for the total United States from 1920 through 1950, although the "relative differential" shows a steady decrease throughout the period (Table 2). For example, Chicago native white women had a total fertility rate that was 44 per cent lower than the nation's in 1920, but in 1950 the Chicago rate for white women was only 17 per cent below that of the nation.[5] By 1960, Chicago's total fertility rate for white women was only 5 per cent lower than the nation's, and if we base our comparison on the Chicago Metropolitan Area instead of the city—perhaps a fairer comparison because the central city is selective of single women —we find that the white total fertility rate of the Chicago Standard Metropolitan Statistical Area (SMSA) was slightly higher than that of the nation.[6]

When births are expressed as ratios to ever-married women, as in the marital fertility rates shown in Table 1, the size of the differential between Chicago and the nation is considerably narrower than the difference in total fertility, at least for white births from 1930 to 1950 (Table 2).[7] For example, in 1930 the city's native white marital fertility was 26 per

[5] In this analysis of fertility trends, "native white" fertility in 1920 and 1930 is compared with "all white" fertility in 1940 and later years, primarily because the trend in "all white" fertility prior to 1940 was due in large part to the declining proportion of foreign white women, who had much higher birth rates than native white women prior to 1940. By 1940, however, differences between native white and foreign white fertility were negligible. For example, the total fertility rate of native white and foreign white women in Chicago in 1940 was 155 and 154, respectively, and in the U.S. both groups had a total fertility rate of 223.

[6] Unfortunately the necessary birth statistics are not available to compute fertility rates for the Chicago SMSA prior to 1950, and the requisite data on married women by age are not available to compute marital fertility rates for 1950.

cent below that of the nation, as compared with a total fertility rate 34 per cent lower; and in 1950 Chicago's white marital fertility rate was only 6 per cent lower than the nation's although its white total fertility rate was 17 per cent lower. By 1960, however, the marital fertility differential had clearly reversed its direction, both for the city and the metropolitan area. That is, the city's white marital fertility rate was 5 per cent higher than the nation's in 1960, and the SMSA's rate was 6 per cent higher.

The relatively higher rates for the metropolis where fertility is measured in relation to married women are explained by the selective composition of the metropolis. A significant proportion of the growth of large cities has been the result of net in-migration, and white female migrants in particular are disproportionately weighted with young single women. Consequently, measures of white fertility not controlled for marital status tend to depress the fertility rate of the metropolis relative to that of the nation.

As might be expected, there are wide variations in fertility among cities of similar size, and not all individual cities fall into place in conformity with the average relation.[8] As a result, trends in the comparative fertility of a particular metropolis and the nation may or may not be indicative of trends for other metropolises. Nevertheless, it is highly significant that the very substantial differences in white marital fertility between Chicago and the nation steadily decreased after 1920 and were reversed by 1960.

[7] The extent to which differentials in fertility may depend on the particular measure of fertility used is demonstrated in Tables 1 and 2. In general, the crude birth rates of the white population in Chicago and the nation differ less than do their total fertility rates, and their marital fertility rates differ least of all. The crude birth rate indicates the proportionate increase in total population due to births; the total fertility rate is controlled for age and sex composition; and the age-standardized marital rate is controlled for age, sex, and marital composition.

[8] Grabill, Kiser, Whelpton, *op. cit.*, p. 85.

TABLE 1

CRUDE AND STANDARDIZED FERTILITY RATES, BY COLOR, FOR THE UNITED STATES AND THE CITY OF CHICAGO, 1920–60

YEAR AND COLOR	CRUDE BIRTH RATE (BIRTHS PER 1,000 PERSONS)		TOTAL FERTILITY RATE[1] (PER 100 WOMEN)		MARITAL FERTILITY RATE[2] (PER 1,000 EVER-MARRIED WOMEN)	
	U.S.	Chicago	U.S.	Chicago	U.S.	Chicago
1960	23.7	24.9	365	372	149	161
White	22.7	21.3	353	337	143	150
Non-white	32.1	36.8	453	476	192	187
1950	24.1	21.6	309	261	130	119
White	23.0	20.0	298	247	126	118
Non-white	33.3	31.2	393	331	158	120
1940	19.4	14.8	230	158	114	90
White	18.6	14.5	223	155	112	91
Non-white	26.7	18.1	287	198	124	83
(Native white)			(223)	(154)	(105)	
1930	21.3	16.9		180		94
Native white	21.4	16.2	250	166	125	92
Non-white	27.5	19.3[3]	296	184[3]	113	64[3]
1920	27.7	21.8		232		
Native white	24.2	16.3	315	177		
Non-white	35.0	19.8		188		

[1] The total fertility rate is defined as the sum, over single years of age, of the annual birth rates per 100 women 15–44 years old. It was computed by adding age-specific birth rates for 5-year age groups and multiplying the result by five.

[2] All births (legitimate and illegitimate) per 1,000 ever-married women 15–44 years old, standardized for age using the age composition of white ever-married women in Chicago in 1950 as the standard.

[3] Rate refers to Negro population.

SOURCE: Birth statistics from Grabill, Kiser, and Whelpton, *The Fertility of American Women*, pp. 26 and 31; *Vital Statistics of U.S., 1960*, Vol. I, Sec. 2, Tables 2–12, pp. 2–20; *Vital Statistics—Special Reports*, Vol. XLIV, No. 8, Table 6 and Vol. XXXIII, No. 8, Table 3. Population statistics from decennial census publications except for ever-married women in U.S. in 1960, compiled from *Current Population Reports—Population Characteristics*, Series P-20, No. 105, Tables 1 and 3.

TABLE 2

PER CENT DIFFERENCE BETWEEN CHICAGO AND UNITED STATES FERTILITY RATES, BY COLOR, 1920–60 (CHICAGO RATE MINUS U.S. RATE, EXPRESSED AS PER CENT OF U.S. RATE)

YEAR AND COLOR	CHICAGO CITY AND U.S.			CHICAGO SMSA AND U.S.		
	Crude Birth Rate	Total Fertility Rate	Marital Fertility Rate	Crude Birth Rate	Total Fertility Rate	Marital Fertility Rate
1960	+ 5	+ 2	+ 8	+ 3	+ 2	+6
White	− 6	− 5	+ 5	− 1	+ 1	+6
Non-white	+15	+ 5	− 3	+13	+ 5	−3
1950	−10	−16	− 9	−10	−13	
White	−13	−17	− 6	−10	−13	
Non-white	− 6	−16	−24	− 7	−16	
1940	−24	−31	−21			
White	−22	−30	−19			
Non-white	−32	−31	−33			
1930	−21					
Native white	−24	−34	−26			
Non-white[1]	−30	−38	−43			
1920	−21					
Native white	−33	−44				
Non-white	−44					

[1] Based on Negro rate for Chicago and non-white rate for U.S.

SOURCE: Tables 1 and 10.

Trends in Chicago-U.S. fertility differentials for non-whites are similar to those for whites, although the interplay of compositional factors is somewhat different. The general pattern of decreasing differences between the city and the nation holds for non-whites. In the case of the non-whites, however, marital fertility differences were greater than total fertility differences. For example, in 1950 the non-white marital fertility rate for changes over time in their respective fertility rates. Table 3 shows the per cent change by decades in the fertility rates of the city and the nation since 1920. The fact that the city's total fertility rate decreased less than the nation's from 1920 to 1940 and increased much more than the nation's from 1940 to 1960, accounts for the virtual elimination by 1960 of what was a sizable deficiency in the city's rate in 1920.

TABLE 3

PER CENT CHANGE IN FERTILITY RATES, BY DECADE, UNITED STATES AND CHICAGO, 1920–60

DECADE AND COLOR	CRUDE BIRTH RATE		TOTAL FERTILITY RATE		MARITAL FERTILITY RATE	
	U.S.	Chicago	U.S.	Chicago	U.S.	Chicago
1950–60...........	− 2	+15	+18	+43	+15	+35
White...........	− 1	+ 7	+18	+36	+13	+27
Non-white......	− 4	+18	+15	+44	+22	+56
1940–50...........	+24	+46	+34	+65	+14	+32
White...........	+24	+38	+34	+59	+13	+30
Non-white......	+25	+72	+37	+67	+27	+45
1930–40...........	....	....	....	−12	....	....
Native white.....	....	....	−11[1]	− 7[1]	− 7	....
Non-white......	− 3	− 6	− 3	+ 8	+10	+30
1920–30...........	−23	−22	....	−22	....	....
Native white.....	−12	− 1	−21	− 6	....	....
Non-white......	−22	− 3	....	− 2	....	....

[1] Based on 1930 and 1940 rates for native whites. In 1940 total fertility rates for native whites and all whites were virtually identical, both in Chicago and the U.S. (see Table 1).

SOURCE: Table 1.

the city was 24 per cent lower than the nation's, while the total fertility rate was only 16 per cent lower. The greater deficiency in the city's non-white marital fertility is attributable to selective inmigration of young married non-white women to the metropolis (discussed further below) which tends to deflate the city's non-white fertility relative to that of the nation when marital status is controlled. In 1960, the marital fertility of non-whites in Chicago was still slightly below that of the nation, although its total fertility rate was 5 per cent higher.

These trends in the size of fertility differences between Chicago and the nation are the result, of course, of differential

The importance of compositional factors is again evident in Table 3, since the three measures of fertility give very different impressions of fertility trends. For example, between 1940 and 1950 the crude birth rates increased much less than the total fertility rates, and between 1950 and 1960 the nation's crude birth rate actually decreased by 2 per cent despite an 18 per cent increase in its total fertility rate. However, because age at marriage decreased after 1940, the per cent increases in marital fertility rates after 1940 were considerably smaller than the increases in total fertility rates, especially during the decade 1940–50, when most of the decline in median age at marriage occurred.

Color differentials.–The sharp increases in Negro fertility and the resultant reversal in the relationship between non-white and white marital fertility constitute the outstanding facts about color differentials in fertility between 1930 and 1960. The "per cent differences" shown in Table 4 support the conclusion that Negro marital fertility was *lower* than white marital fertility until the 1930's for the nation as a whole, and until the 1940's in Chicago.[9] Despite the inclusion of illegitimate births in the numerator of the marital fertility rates used here–which con-

tility in Chicago was 2 per cent higher than white, and by 1960 it was 25 per cent higher. It is difficult to estimate accurately the effect of illegitimate births on the "marital rates" shown in Table 1. However, the statistics on illegitimacy discussed later in this section indicate that the higher non-white marital fertility rate in Chicago in 1950 was entirely due to illegitimacy, and this may also be true for 1960.

The change between 1940 and 1960 from lower marital fertility for non-whites than whites to a pattern of higher

TABLE 4

PER CENT DIFFERENCE BETWEEN NON-WHITE AND WHITE FERTILITY RATES, FOR
THE UNITED STATES AND CHICAGO, 1920–60 (NON-WHITE RATE MINUS
WHITE RATE, EXPRESSED AS PER CENT OF WHITE RATE)

YEAR	CRUDE BIRTH RATE		TOTAL FERTILITY RATE		MARITAL FERTILITY RATE	
	U.S.	Chicago	U.S.	Chicago	U.S.	Chicago
1960.......	+41	+73	+28	+41	+34	+25
1950.......	+45	+56	+32	+34	+25	+ 2
1940.......	+44	+25	+29	+28	+11	− 9
1930[1]......	+29	+19[2]	+18	+11[2]	−10	−31[2]
1920[1]......	+45	+21	....	+ 6	....	....

[1] Figures for 1920 and 1930 are based on difference between non-white and native white rates except as noted.
[2] Refers to difference between Negro and native white population.
SOURCE: Table 1.

siderably overstates the marital fertility of the Negro relative to the white population–the rate for non-whites in Chicago was 31 per cent lower than the rate for whites in 1930, and 9 per cent lower in 1940. By 1950, non-white marital fer-

[9] Measures of non-white fertility and mortality are taken as representative of Negro fertility and mortality, since Negroes in the United States during the period studied comprised more than 95 per cent of the non-white population, except for 1960 when the addition of Hawaii and Alaska reduced the proportion to 92 per cent. In Chicago between 1920 and 1960, Negroes comprised more than 97 per cent of the non-white population except for 1930, when as a result of the inclusion of "Mexicans" in the non-white group the per cent was somewhat lower. It is for this reason that in 1930, the Chicago rates were computed for Negroes instead of non-whites.

marital fertility for non-whites was the result of larger increases in Negro marital fertility during the period (Table 3). In fact, Negro marital fertility even increased between 1930 and 1940, the decade of the economic depression when white fertility was declining.

Because of compositional differences between the white and non-white populations, the size and pattern of color differentials varies tremendously with the fertility measure used. For example, even when the Negroes had lower marital fertility rates, their crude birth rates and total fertility rates were considerably higher than the white rates (see the rates for 1930 and 1940 in Table 4). Moreover, in 1960, when non-whites in Chicago had a marital fertility rate 25 per cent higher than whites, their total fertility rate was 41 per cent higher and their crude birth rate 73 per cent higher. That is, the size of Chicago's color differential obtained from crude birth rates was almost three times as large as the differential based on marital fertility rates. Thus, compositional factors were responsible for almost two-thirds of the difference between the crude birth rates of whites and non-whites in Chicago in 1960.

The "relative" fertility of the non-whites in relation to whites has been much higher in the nation as a whole than in Chicago. In 1950, for instance, the non-white marital fertility rate was 25 per cent higher than the white rate in the nation as a whole, whereas in Chicago it was only 2 per cent higher. Similarly, in 1930 the non-white marital rate for the nation was only 10 per cent lower than the white rate, whereas in Chicago it was 31 per cent lower. This "relatively higher" fertility for non-whites in the nation as a whole results, at least in part, from the larger proportion of non-whites living on farms. In 1950, 21.2 per cent of the nation's non-whites were "rural farm" dwellers, as compared with only 14.6 per cent of the white population.

While the total United States approximates a "closed" population in the sense that there has been relatively little in- and out-migration since 1920, the situation in the large metropolis has been quite different. Migration has played an important role in the growth of large cities and their suburbs and in recent years, especially, has effected great changes in the composition of the central cities of many large metropolitan areas despite insignificant changes in the size of the total population living in these central cities. Proportionate changes in the white and non-white population of the City of Chicago (the central city of

the Chicago Metropolitan Area) are summarized in Table 5. The trends in white–non-white differentials in fertility summarized in Table 4 no doubt have been influenced by the very large in-migration of Negroes to Chicago—which more than septupled the non-white population between 1920 and 1960—and the net loss of one-eighth of its white population during one decade, 1950 to 1960. Estimated rates of net migration to Chicago between 1940 and 1960 are summarized in Table 6 for the most impor-

TABLE 5

POPULATION OF CITY OF CHICAGO, BY COLOR, 1920–60

	Total	White	Non-white
Population:			
1920.........	2,701,705	2,589,169	112,536
1960.........	3,550,404	2,712,748	837,656
Per cent change:			
1920–30......	+25.0	+21.2	+112.7
1930–40......	+ 0.6	− 0.7	+ 18.0
1940–50......	+ 6.6	− 0.1	+ 80.5
1950–60......	− 1.9	−12.8	+ 64.4
1920–60......	+31.4	+ 4.8	+644.3
Per cent distri-bution:			
1920.........	100	95.8	4.2
1960	100	76.4	23.6

tant childbearing age groups. Differences in the marital composition of whites and non-whites also have an effect on their fertility differentials. Table 7 summarizes several aspects of marital composition and provides indirect evidence of the selective marital composition of migrants to Chicago.

These data on net migration and marital composition explain why the patterns of marital fertility differ so markedly from the patterns of total fertility and crude birth rates in Chicago. Non-white migrants were concentrated in the childbearing ages—more than doubling the non-white population 20–34 years old during the decade 1940–50, for example —and apparently were selective of young

TABLE 6

NET MIGRATION RATES, BY COLOR (AND BY SEX FOR 1950–60), CHICAGO, 1940–50 AND 1950–60
(NET MIGRANTS PER 1,000 POPULATION AT THE BEGINNING OF THE DECADE)

| | 1940–50 | | 1950–60 | | | |
	All White	All Non-white	White Males	White Females	Non-white Males	Non-white Females
All ages......	−90	+ 635	−225	−209	+301	+316
15–19.......	−49	+ 532	−276	−189	+377	+526
20–24.......	+62	+1218	− 20	+ 38	+580	+726
25–29.......	+64	+1370	+ 25	− 75	+689	+676
30–34.......	−78	+1026	−169	−266	+546	+419

SOURCE: Donald J. Bogue, *An Estimate of Metropolitan Chicago's Future Population: 1955 to 1965*, Table 6; Bogue and Dandekar, *Population Trends and Prospects for Chicago-Northwestern Indiana Consolidated Metropolitan Area: 1950 to 1990*, Table 13, p. 23.

TABLE 7

PER CENT OF WOMEN 15–44 EVER MARRIED, AND PER CENT WITH SPOUSE PRESENT, BY COLOR, CITY OF CHICAGO AND UNITED STATES, 1930–60

| YEAR | CITY OF CHICAGO | | UNITED STATES | |
	White	Non-white	White	Non-white
	Per Cent of Women 15–44 Ever Married[1]			
1960.......	70.8	77.3	75.7	72.4
1950.......	71.9	80.8	74.9	74.7
1940.......	61.6	74.1	64.5	69.0
1930.......	57.0[2]	79.9[3]	62.5[2]	70.9
	Per Cent Widowed or Divorced (of Ever-Married)[4]			
1960.......	......	......	4.5	10.1
1950.......	6.5	12.1	5.1	9.5
1940.......	6.8	15.9	5.6	12.1
	Per Cent with Husband Present (of Ever-Married)			
1960.......	......	......	91.4	71.3
1950.......	90.4	66.9	91.5	73.5
1940.......	89.4	60.7	90.7	74.7

[1] Per cent of all women 15–44 who were reported as "ever married" in decennial census.
[2] Refers to native white women.
[3] Refers to Negro women.
[4] Per cent of ever-married women 15–44 who were reported as widowed or divorced in decennial census.

married women, as evidenced by the higher proportions married among non-white women in Chicago than in the nation. White women in Chicago, on the other hand, were selective of young single women. As a result, the proportion of ever-married among women of child-bearing age was considerably higher for non-whites than for whites in Chicago, which accounts, of course, for the smaller non-white–white differences in marital fertility rates than total fertility rates. However, broken families were much more common among non-whites, especially in Chicago, as evidenced by their higher proportions widowed or divorced and their much lower proportions with husband present in the same household (Table 7). The census classification of marital status and living arrangements, combined with the large proportion of non-white illegitimate births and the possibility that census enumerations legalize a considerable number of non-white "marriages," makes it difficult to reach definitive conclusions about white and non-white marital fertility, and the influence of marital status on color differentials in fertility in the metropolis.

It is clear from Table 4, however, that the size of the non-white–white differential has increased in recent decades. All three measures of fertility confirm this conclusion. In Chicago, for example, the non-white total fertility rate was only 6 per cent higher than the white rate in 1920, but by 1960 it was 41 per cent higher. And, since 1940 marital fertility rates have increased more for non-whites than for whites (Table 3). Decreases in fetal mortality, venereal disease control programs, and other health improve-

non-white birth rates were higher at every age, although the size of the difference remained much greater below age 25. In 1950, the only year for which birth rates are shown for five-year age intervals in Table 8,[10] the non-white rate for ages 15–19 was 105 per cent higher than the corresponding white rate, but for

TABLE 8

TOTAL BIRTHS PER 1,000 WOMEN EVER MARRIED, BY AGE AND COLOR,
CITY OF CHICAGO AND UNITED STATES, 1930–60

| | CHICAGO | | UNITED STATES | | PER CENT DIFFERENCE | | | |
| | | | | | Non-white/white | | Chicago/U.S. | |
YEAR AND AGE	White	Non-white	White	Non-white	Chicago	U.S.	White	Non-white
1960:								
15–24 years........	385	563	389	564	+ 46	+45	− 1	0
25–34 years........	180	197	163	200	+ 9	+23	+10	− 2
35–44 years........	38	47	38	55	+ 24	+45	0	−15
1950:								
15–24 years........	283	381	308	453	+ 35	+47	− 8	−16
25–34 years........	147	125	152	164	− 15	+ 8	− 3	−24
35–44 years........	31	25	38	49	− 19	+29	−19	−49
1940:								
15–24 years........	236	332	284	363	+ 41	+28	−17	− 9
25–34 years........	110	65	129	121	− 41	− 6	−15	−46
35–44 years........	22	15	35	45	− 32	+29	−37	−67
1930:								
15–24 years........	236[1]	208[2]	295[1]	281	− 12	− 5	−20	−26
25–34 years........	107[1]	59[2]	139[1]	115	− 45	−17	−23	−49
35–44 years........	29[1]	18[2]	52[1]	52	− 38	0	−44	−65
1950:								
15–19 years........	415	852	425	797	+105	+88	− 2	+ 7
20–24 years........	267	296	282	352	+ 11	+25	− 5	−16
25–29 years........	188	159	190	201	− 16	+ 6	− 1	−21
30–34 years........	110	89	113	124	− 19	+10	− 3	−28
35–39 years........	49	37	56	69	− 25	+23	−13	−46
40–44 years........	12	10	17	25	− 17	+47	−30	−60

[1] Refers to native white women.   [2] Refers to Negro women.   SOURCE: Same as Table 1.

ments are no doubt responsible for at least part of the increase in Negro fertility. Data are not available, however, to evaluate the relative importance of these factors.

Age-specific birth rates (per 1,000 ever-married women).—In Chicago, higher non-white fertility has been concentrated at ages 15–19, and prior to 1960 births to married women over 25 years old were consistently lower for non-whites than whites (Table 8). By 1960,

each age group above age 25 the non-white rate was considerably lower than the white rate. Therefore, the slightly higher age-standardized marital fertility rate for non-whites in 1950 (2 per cent higher, in Table 4), was due entirely to the excessively high fertility of non-whites 15–19 years old.

[10] Ten-year age groups of ever-married women were used throughout the time series because 1960 data for Chicago were available only in these age intervals.

For the nation as a whole, non-white fertility has been much higher than white fertility both at the beginning and end of the childbearing age span. In 1950, for example, the non-white rate was 88 per cent higher at ages 15–19, only 6 per cent higher at ages 25–29, and 47 per cent higher at ages 40–44.

Most of the higher non-white than white fertility at ages 15–19 is attributable to illegitimacy and the fact that we have related *all* births (legitimate and illegitimate) to "ever-married women" in cago, 45 per cent of all births to non-white women 15–19 years old were illegitimate, as compared with less than 25 per cent for other ages (Table 9). In contrast, only 11 per cent of the births to white women 15–19 years old were illegitimate, and the proportion for older ages never exceeded 3 per cent. If 1960 marital fertility rates for Chicago are computed by the conventional procedure of relating legitimate births to ever-married women, the non-white rate is 6 per cent lower than the white rate. Hence

TABLE 9

LIVE BIRTHS BY AGE AND COLOR OF MOTHER, BY LEGITIMACY, CITY OF CHICAGO, 1960

AGE AND COLOR	TOTAL			WHITE			NON-WHITE		
	Total Births	Illegitimate Births	Per Cent Illegitimate	Total Births	Illegitimate Births	Per Cent Illegitimate	Total Births	Illegitimate Births	Per Cent Illegitimate
Total.....	88,537	10,182	12	57,673	1,726	3	30,864	8,456	27
15–19.....	11,488	3,172	28	5,746	614	11	5,742	2,558	45
20–24.....	30,807	3,072	10	20,636	616	3	10,171	2,456	24
25–29.....	22,718	1,952	9	15,091	234	2	7,627	1,718	23
30–34.....	14,202	1,232	9	9,573	142	1	4,629	1,090	24
35–39.....	7,472	614	8	5,262	92	2	2,210	522	24
40–44.....	1,850	140	8	1,365	28	2	485	112	23

SOURCE: Illegitimate births from *Vital Statistics of U.S.*, *1960*, Vol. I, Table 2–22. Total births from tabulation provided by Illinois Department of Public Health.

computing the marital fertility rates shown in Tables 1 and 8.[11] In 1960, 27 per cent of the non-white births in Chicago were illegitimate, as compared with 3 per cent of the white births; and in 1950, the corresponding figures were 22 and 2 per cent, respectively. However, the proportion of illegitimate births is much greater at the younger than at the older ages. For example, in 1960 in Chi-

11 The conventional practice of defining nuptial fertility as the ratio of "legitimate births" to "currently married women" was not followed for two reasons: (1) undoubtedly, census enumerations "legalize" many living arrangements in the census returns, especially in the Negro community where "cohabitation without legal marriage" is more common; (2) birth data for Chicago were not tabulated by age, color, and legitimacy.

the 25 per cent higher marital rate for non-whites shown in Table 1 for Chicago in 1960 may be entirely due to illegitimacy. As was mentioned earlier, however, the conventional procedure was not used to measure marital fertility both because the requisite data were not available for the time series and because of the likelihood that an unknown proportion of unwed mothers are classified as married in the census enumerations. Moreover, in view of the cultural differences which account for non-white–white differences in marriage and illegitimacy, the practice we have followed undoubtedly provides a better comparison of non-white–white fertility differentials than the conventional practice would afford.

The Central City and the Ring

The tendency for young married couples to move to the suburbs of the large metropolis to raise their children is well known. One might expect, therefore, to find total fertility rates lower in the central city than in the "ring" of the metropolitan area. Marital fertility in the central city also may be expected to be lower than in the ring if we assume that married couples currently having children are more likely to move to the ring.

Both of these expectations are confirmed for the white population in Table 10. In 1950, the white total fertility rate was 16 per cent higher in the ring than in the central city of the Chicago SMSA, and in 1960 it was 11 per cent higher. The white marital fertility rate, however, was only 2 per cent higher in the ring in 1960, indicating that most but not quite all of the difference in total fertility was due to the presence of relatively more married women in the ring. In fact, the proportion of all white women 15–44 who had ever been married was only 71 per cent for the City of Chicago, as compared with 78 per cent for the ring of the SMSA.

For the non-white population only the second expectation—higher marital fertility in the ring—is confirmed. Residential segregation and other factors curtail the movement of Negroes to suburban housing. In 1960 only 8 per cent of the Chicago SMSA's non-white women 15–44 years old resided in the ring, as compared with more than half of the white women 15–44; and, contrary to the white pattern, the proportion of non-white women who had ever been married was slightly larger in the city than in the ring. Consequently, non-whites in the ring of the SMSA had a total fertility rate 2 per cent below the central city's in 1960, despite a marital fertility rate that was 3 per cent higher.

It is also significant that despite the ring's higher marital fertility among both whites and non-whites, the marital rate for the total population was 4 per cent *lower* in the ring than in the central city in 1960 (Table 10). Again, compositional factors are the explanation, since non-whites comprise 28 per cent of all ever-married women 15–44 in the central city but only 3 per cent of all ever-married women 15–44 in the ring. As a result, the high non-white rate is more heavily

TABLE 10

CRUDE AND STANDARDIZED FERTILITY RATES BY COLOR, FOR CENTRAL CITY AND RING OF CHICAGO STANDARD METROPOLITAN STATISTICAL AREA, 1950–60

AREA AND COLOR	CRUDE BIRTH RATE		TOTAL FERTILITY RATE		MARITAL FERTILITY RATE
	1950	1960	1950	1960	1960
Total:					
Chicago SMSA[1]..	21.8	24.5	268	374	158
City of Chicago	21.6	24.9	261	372	161
Ring.........	22.2	24.0	288	376	155
White:					
Chicago SMSA[1]..	20.7	22.4	259	355	152
City of Chicago	20.0	21.3	247	337	150
Ring.........	22.0	23.7	287	373	153
Non-white:					
Chicago SMSA[1]..	30.9	36.5	332	475	187
City of Chicago	31.2	36.8	331	476	187
Ring.........	28.5	33.3	346	466	192
	Per Cent Difference (Non-white and White)[2]				
Chicago SMSA..	+49	+63	+28	+34	+23
City of Chicago	+56	+73	+34	+41	+25
Ring.........	+30	+41	+21	+25	+25
	Per Cent Difference (Ring and City)[3]				
Chicago SMSA..	+ 3	− 4	+10	+ 1	− 4
White........	+10	+11	+16	+11	+ 2
Non-white....	− 9	−10	+ 5	− 2	+ 3

[1] The Chicago SMSA includes Cook, DuPage, Kane, Lake, McHenry, and Will counties in Illinois.

[2] Non-white rate minus white rate, expressed as per cent of white rate.

[3] Ring's rate minus city's rate, expressed as per cent of city's rate.

weighted in the total city's rate than in the rate for the total ring.

Non-white fertility is consistently higher than white fertility, both in the central city and in the ring of the Chicago SMSA.

Socioeconomic Differentials

Statistics on socioeconomic differentials in fertility in Chicago from 1920 to 1940 were analyzed in an article published in 1953.[12] Since then, similar data have been compiled for 1950.[13] In all, the following time series of fertility rates by socioeconomic status are available for the City of Chicago: (1) total fertility rates, by color, for five socioeconomic groups for selected years between 1920 and 1950, and also by nativity of the white population for the period 1920 to 1940; (2) marital fertility rates for the white population in five socioeconomic groups, for 1930 and 1950. The data permitted the computation of rates for eight time intervals during the 30-year period: 1919–21 (average), 1930, 1931, 1932, 1933, 1934–36 (average), 1940, and 1950. Average annual rates for 1919–21 and for 1934–36 will be referred to as for 1920 and 1935, respectively.

The five socioeconomic groups used in the analysis were obtained by assigning residents of each of the 935 census tracts in Chicago to a socioeconomic group on the basis of median rent (1920 to 1940) or median family income (1950) of the tract. The underlying rationale was to al-

locate the population of Chicago to the five socioeconomic groups in approximately the same proportionate distribution on each date. In 1930, census tracts were classified as being in one of five socioeconomic groups according to 1930 median rent as follows: I, under $30; II, $30–$44; III, $45–$59; IV, $60–$74; V, $75 or more. Tracts were left in these 1930 rent groups for the preparation of the rates for 1930 to 1935 inclusive, and for the 1920 rates.[14] In 1940, tracts were classified in five socioeconomic groups according to 1940 median rent as follows: I, under $20; II, $20–$29; III, $30–$39; IV, $40–$49; V, $50 or more. In 1950, tracts were classified in five socioeconomic groups according to median family income. However, the heavy immigration of low-income Negroes to Chicago during the decade 1940–50 resulted in a disproportionate weighting of Negroes in the low-income groups and made it impossible to use the same income intervals to define socioeconomic groups of whites and non-whites without grossly violating the condition that their proportionate distribution by socioeconomic groups should be approximately the same on successive dates.[15] For this reason, different income intervals were used to define white and non-white socioeconomic groups in 1950, as specified below:

[12] Evelyn M. Kitagawa, "Differential Fertility in Chicago, 1920–1940," *American Journal of Sociology*, LVIII (March, 1953), 481–92.

[13] Specific sources of basic data for 1920–40 are cited in Kitagawa, *op. cit.*, pp. 483–84. Birth statistics for 1950 were obtained from the Chicago Board of Health, who provided a duplicate deck of their birth cards for 1950 occurrences to Chicago residents, and the Illinois Department of Public Health, who provided a set of birth cards for births occurring outside Chicago to Chicago residents. Population statistics for 1950 were tabulated from census tract summary cards purchased from the U.S. Bureau of the Census.

[14] See Kitagawa, *op. cit.*, p. 484, n. 16. Median rent in both 1930 and 1940 included the equivalent monthly rental value of owner-occupied dwelling units.

[15] For example, if both the white and non-white population in tracts with less than $3,250 median family income were assigned to socioeconomic Group I in 1950, this group would include 18 per cent of the total population of Chicago and would therefore be in line with the proportion of the total population in Group I in earlier years. However, Group I would then include 88 per cent of the non-white population in 1950 and only 6 per cent of the white population, making it impossible to compare 1950 socioeconomic differentials in each color group with their socioeconomic differentials for previous years.

WHITE POPULATION		NON-WHITE POPULATION	
Group	Median Income of Tract	Group	Median Income of Tract
I....	Less than $3600	I....	Less than $2400
II...	$3600–3999	II....	$2400–2999
III...	$4000–4499	III–V.	$3000 or more
IV...	$4500–5099		
V....	$5100 or more		

As a result, the socioeconomic groups of whites and non-whites in 1950 are not comparable, and therefore do not provide a basis for measuring white–non-white differences in fertility at comparable socioeconomic levels in 1950. This limitation does not apply to the rates for 1920 to 1940, however, since white and non-white socioeconomic groups are defined on the same basis in these years.

Total fertility rates.—Changes in total fertility rates in Chicago between 1920 and 1950 are summarized by color, nativity, and socioeconomic status in Table 11. The following conclusions appear warranted from an examination of these data:

1. Total fertility generally declined from 1920 to 1933 and then increased to 1950.[16]

[16] See Kitagawa, *op. cit.*, Table 1, for evidence that 1933 was the "low point" in the fertility decline.

TABLE 11

TOTAL FERTILITY RATES BY COLOR, NATIVITY, AND SOCIOECONOMIC STATUS, CHICAGO, 1920–50

COLOR AND SOCIO-ECONOMIC STATUS	TOTAL FERTILITY RATE					INDEX OF RATE				
	1920[1]	1930	1933	1940	1950[2]	1920	1930	1933	1940	1950
Total..............	232	180	144	158	....	....	....	....	....	....
I (low)..........	376	256	199	186	....	301	229	226	154	....
II...	232	199	163	166	....	186	178	185	137	....
III..............	196	166	131	152	....	157	148	149	126	....
IV...............	155	151	121	145	....	124	135	137	120	....
V (high).........	125	112	88	121	....	100	100	100	100	....
All white........	235	180	142	155	246					
I (low)..........	391	252	194	180	260	310	225	220	148	114
II...............	239	201	160	162	248	190	179	182	133	109
III..............	197	170	133	152	246	156	152	151	125	108
IV...............	155	152	120	145	234	123	136	136	119	103
V(high).........	126	112	88	122	228	100	100	100	100	100
Native white.......	177	166	132	154						
I (low)..........	263	232	183	181	....	210	200	208	146	....
II...............	193	187	151	161	....	154	161	172	130	....
III..............	167	158	124	150	....	134	136	141	121	....
IV...............	141	146	114	144	....	113	126	164	116	....
V (high).........	125	116	88	124	....	100	100	100	100	....
Foreign white......	358	222	....	162						
I (low)..........	525	300	....	196	....	380	316	....	178	....
II...............	333	245	....	169	....	241	258	....	154	....
III..............	272	202	....	158	....	197	213	....	144	....
IV...............	222	184	....	150	....	161	194	....	136	....
V (high).........	138	95	....	110	....	100	100	....	100	....
Non-white[3]........	188	184	161	198	326					
I (low)..........	211	241	204	252	368	122	170	162	159	123
II...............	181	198	176	205	314	105	139	140	130	105
III–V (high).....	173	142	126	158	300	100	100	100	100	100

[1] Based on 1919–21 births.

[2] Rates for white and non-white population in each socioeconomic level *cannot be compared* because income intervals used to assign white population to socioeconomic levels differed from those used to assign non-white population to socioeconomic levels. For the same reason, rates could not be computed for the total population by socioeconomic status. Instead, 1950 rates were defined to measure the extent of socioeconomic differentials within the white population and within the non-white population.

[3] Rates for 1930 and 1933 refer to Negro population (because persons of Mexican ancestry were classified as non-white in these censuses). Negroes comprised 97.3 per cent of the non-white population in 1920, 98.4 per cent in 1940, and 96.6 per cent in 1950.

2. Ratios of 1940 to 1920 total fertility rates illustrate the dominant role of the very sharp decline in foreign white fertility in the decreases in the all-white rate during the twenty-year period.[17] While the total fertility rate for all native whites decreased by only 13 per cent from 1920 to 1940, the rate for all foreign whites decreased by 55 per cent. Thus, the 34 per cent decrease in the rate for all whites reflects, for the most part, sharp decreases in foreign white fertility and

30-year period. The indexes shown in Table 11 document the extent of the inverse relationship and the convergence. For example, the total fertility rate for the lowest socioeconomic group of the white population was 210 per cent higher than the rate for the highest group in 1920, but only 14 per cent higher in 1950.

This convergence of socioeconomic differentials was the result of different patterns of change in total fertility rates among the five status groups during the

TABLE 12

PER CENT CHANGE BETWEEN TOTAL FERTILITY RATES FOR SELECTED PAIRS OF YEARS,
BY NATIVITY, COLOR, AND SOCIOECONOMIC STATUS, CHICAGO, 1920–50

COLOR AND SOCIO-ECONOMIC STATUS	1920–30	1930–33	1933–40	1940–50	1920–50
All white..........	−23	−21	+ 9	+59	+ 5
I (low)..........	−36	−23	− 7	+44	−34
II...............	−16	−20	+ 1	+53	+ 4
III..............	−14	−22	+14	+62	+25
IV...............	− 2	−21	+21	+61	+51
V (high).........	−11	−21	+39	+87	+81
Native white........	− 6	−20	+17	....	....
I (low)..........	−12	−21	− 1	....	....
II...............	− 3	−19	+ 7	....	....
III..............	− 5	−22	+21	....	....
IV...............	+ 4	−22	+26	....	....
V (high).........	− 7	−24	+41	....	....
Non-white..........	− 2	−12	+23	+65	+73
I (low)..........	+14	−15	+24	+46	+74
II...............	+ 9	−11	+16	+53	+73
III–V (high)......	−18	−11	+25	+90	+73

SOURCE: Table 11.

also the declining proportion of foreign whites during the twenty-year period.

By 1940, the very large differences between native white and foreign white fertility had virtually disappeared. In 1920, the total fertility rate for foreign white women was twice as high as the native white rate, but in 1940, it was only 5 per cent higher (Table 11).

3. Among the white population of Chicago there was a consistent inverse relationship between total fertility rates and socioeconomic status at each date, but also a marked convergence of socioeconomic differentials in fertility during the

[17] See Kitagawa, *op. cit.*, Table 2, p. 487.

30-year period. Between 1920 and 1930 the decreases in white fertility were inversely related to socioeconomic status (Table 12). During the depression years, 1930–33, the relative decrease in white fertility was roughly the same for each socioeconomic group (between 21 and 23 per cent). After 1933, total fertility rates increased at all socioeconomic levels and the amounts of increase were directly related to socioeconomic status. Thus, the convergence of socioeconomic differentials was the result of larger decreases in the fertility of the low-status groups from 1920 to 1933 and smaller increases in their fertility after 1933.

In 1920, socioeconomic differentials in fertility were much greater among foreign white women than among native white women. By 1933, the pattern of socioeconomic differentials for native whites and foreign whites were much more similar, and by 1940 they were almost identical (see the indexes in Table 11).

4. Socioeconomic differentials in Negro fertility followed a very different pattern than white between 1920 and 1950. The relatively small differences in 1920, when the total fertility rate for the low-status group (I) was only 22 per cent above the rate for the high-status group (III–V combined) changed to wide differences by 1930, when the rate for Group I was 70 per cent above the rate for Groups III–V (see the indexes in Table 11). This expansion in socioeconomic differentials was the result both of an increase in the rate for the low-status group and a decrease in the rate for the high-status group.

Between 1930 and 1933, Negro fertility decreased slightly more in the lowest socioeconomic group than in the two higher groups, 15 per cent as compared with 11 per cent (Table 12). But, in contrast to the rates for white women, the 1933–40 increases in Negro fertility showed no consistent relationship to socioeconomic status. However, in each group the 1933–40 increase more than offset the 1930–33 decrease. In general, the index numbers in Table 11 show a slight convergence of socioeconomic differentials in Negro fertility during the decade 1930–40, primarily as a result of the larger decrease in the fertility of the lowest group during the first three years of the depression.

Between 1940 and 1950, increases in Negro fertility were directly related to socioeconomic status. The net result was a considerable narrowing of socioeconomic differentials so that in 1950, the total fertility rate for the low-status group was only 23 per cent above the

rate for the high-status group, as compared with a difference of 59 per cent in 1940. Socioeconomic differentials were larger in 1950 among Negroes than among whites, despite the less detailed classification of status groups among Negroes.

Possibly the small socioeconomic differentials in fertility among Negroes in 1920 reflected a relatively new, more or less homogeneous, migrant group from the South. During the decade 1920–30 the Negro population more than doubled (Table 5), and the differentiation by socioeconomic status between 1920 and 1930 may reflect the emergence of a Negro middle class and, therefore, the development of more divergent socioeconomic levels in the Negro community. The beginnings of convergence between 1930 and 1940 may reflect accommodation to the urban way of life, especially since there was a relatively small influx of Negroes to Chicago during this period. This hypothesis is supported by Drake and Cayton's observation that between 1920 and 1930 a professional and business class arose upon the broad base of Negro wage-earners, and additional migrants from the rural South poured into the city.[18]

The marked convergence of socioeconomic differentials in Negro fertility between 1940 and 1950, despite the very high rates of in-migration during the decade (Table 6), needs further study. The generally accepted thesis that the fertility of upper-status white groups is rising faster than that of the lower-status white groups because of the increasing practice of birth control in the lower groups at a time when the upper groups are purposely increasing their already "controlled" fertility, is not readily applicable to the Negro population at its present stage of urban in-migration and adaptation to urban living. The interac-

[18] St. Clair Drake and Horace Cayton, *Black Metropolis* (New York: Harcourt, Brace & Co., 1945), p. 78.

tion of the very high rates of Negro in-migration to Chicago—much of it from the rural South—and the impact of city living on Negro fertility, as well as the extent to which birth control is practiced by various segments of the Negro community, are for the most part unknown factors at the present time.

TABLE 13

PER CENT DISTRIBUTION OF POPULATION BY COLOR AND SOCIOECONOMIC STATUS, CHICAGO, 1920–50

Color and Socio-economic Status	1920	1930	1940	1950[1]
Total.........	100	100	100	......
I (low).......	26	18	18	......
II...........	27	24	25	......
III..........	26	25	27	......
IV...........	16	24	21	......
V (high)......	5	29	9	......
White.........	100	100	100	100
I (low).......	25	17	17	17
II...........	27	23	23	21
III..........	26	25	28	33
IV...........	17	25	22	17
V (high)......	5	10	10	12
Non-white[2]....	100	100	100	100
I (low).......	32	22	22	30
II...........	45	38	45	47
III–V (high)..	23	40	33	23
Total.........	100	100	100	100
White........	96	92	92	86
Non-white[2]...	4	7	8	14

[1] The income intervals used to define the white socioeconomic groups were different from those for the non-white socioeconomic groups.

[2] 1930 data refer to Negroes.

5. In 1920, non-white fertility was lower than white fertility at each socioeconomic level. For example, the non-white rate for the lowest-status group (I) was 20 per cent below the native white rate and 60 per cent below the foreign white rate for the same group (Table 11). In 1930, non-white rates at each socioeconomic level were slightly higher than corresponding rates for native

whites, but still considerably lower than foreign white rates. By 1940, however, non-white rates for each socioeconomic group were substantially higher than either the native or foreign white rates. (This comparison cannot be made for 1950, since the socioeconomic groups were not defined on the same basis for the white and non-white population in 1950.)

The average socioeconomic status of the Negro population in Chicago is considerably lower than that of the white population. The proportionate distributions by socioeconomic status shown in Table 13 indicate, for example, that in 1940 only 33 per cent of the non-white population was in Groups III–V, as compared with 60 per cent of the white population. In 1950, the average socioeconomic level of whites and non-whites differed so greatly that 88 per cent of the non-whites lived in census tracts with a median family income of less than $3250, as compared with only 6 per cent of the white population. In order to compare the over-all level of white and non-white fertility *holding constant their differences in socioeconomic status,* total fertility rates standardized for socioeconomic status were computed for each census year from 1920 to 1950. The results are summarized below.

PER CENT DIFFERENCE BETWEEN NON-WHITE AND WHITE TOTAL FERTILITY RATES: CHICAGO, 1920–60

	1920	1930	1940	1950	1960
Total fertility rate: Unstandardized	−20	+2	+28	+34	+41
Standardized for socioeconomic status[1]........	−30	−6	+19	+5	.....

[1] Computed by indirect method, using five socioeconomic groups for 1920 to 1940 and 15 income categories in 1950, and using the total population on each census date as the standard

The standardized total fertility rates indicate that in 1950 almost all of the difference between white and non-white total fertility could be accounted for by differences in socioeconomic status. That is, the non-white total fertility rate was only 5 per cent higher than the white rate when socioeconomic status was held constant, although the unstandardized non-white rate was 34 per cent higher. The requisite data are not yet available to compute such standardized rates for 1960.

Marital fertility.—In 1930 marital fertility rates (per 1,000 ever-married women, standardized for age)[19] followed a

19 The age composition of "ever-married white women" in Chicago in 1950 was used as the standard; five age groups were used for the computation: 15–19, 20–24, 25–29, 30–34, and 35–44. Since the age composition of ever-married women in each socioeconomic group was not available from census data, it was estimated by the following procedure:

The number of ever-married women 15 and older in each socioeconomic group, and the total number of ever-married women in each 5-year age group in the city, were available from census tabulations. Thus, the marginal totals of the cross-classification of ever-married women by age and socioeconomic status were known. Also known were the total numbers of women cross-classified by age and socioeconomic status.

A first approximation to the cross-classified distribution of ever-married women by age and socioeconomic status was obtained by computing "proportions ever-married" from the classification of native white women by age, marital status, and rental value of home in U.S. cities of 250,000 or more population in 1940 (obtained from Bureau of the Census, *Differential Fertility, 1940 and 1910, Women by Number of Children Ever Born*, pp. 178–79). The ten "rental categories" by which these data were classified were summarized into five socioeconomic groups yielding as nearly as possible the same proportion of women in each socioeconomic group as in the 1930 native white population of Chicago, and age-specific proportions of ever-married women were determined for these five groups. Within each age group, the resulting "proportions ever-married" for the five rental groups were adjusted by the same number of percentage points in such a manner as to produce the known total number of ever-married women in that age group when the proportions were applied to the known total number of women classified by age and socioeconomic status. The estimated number of ever-married women by age and socioeconomic group obtained by applying these "adjusted proportions ever-married" to the known "total numbers of

J-shaped pattern among white women in Chicago, with the lowest rate in the middle socioeconomic group. Among native white women, for example, marital fertility in Group I (the lowest-status group) was 38 per cent higher than in Group III, while the rate for Group V (the highest-status group) was 15 per cent higher than the Group III rate (Table 14). The same general pattern obtained for all white women, although the variation by socioeconomic level was slightly less. By 1950, there was a consistent direct relationship between socioeconomic status and marital fertility among white women in Chicago. That is, the marital fertility rate for the lowest socioeconomic group was 20 per cent below the rate for the highest group, and there was a steady increase in fertility with rising socioeconomic status.

Thus, in spite of the consistent inverse relationship between total fertility and socioeconomic status discussed in the preceding section, when differences in marital composition are taken into account we find a positive relationship between fertility and socioeconomic status. Whereas the positive relationship was limited to the three upper-status groups

women by age and socioeconomic group" were used as first approximations to the desired cross-classification.

The final cross-classification was obtained from this first approximation by adjusting the latter to the two sets of known marginal totals, utilizing the method outlined in W. E. Deming and F. F. Stephan, "On a Least Squares Adjustment of a Sampled Frequency Table When the Expected Marginal Totals Are Known," *The Annals of Mathematical Statistics*, Vol. XI (1940).

Insofar as the writers could determine from alternative techniques tested, the net result of the method utilized tends to err in the direction of underestimating the *differences in proportions married by socioeconomic status* and hence also to underestimate the degree of positive relationship between marital fertility and socioeconomic status. (Specifically the method probably overestimates the number of ever-married women in the high status groups, and therefore underestimates the marital fertility rates of these groups.)

in 1930 (who comprised 60 per cent of the white population), by 1950 the direct relationship held for the entire range of the socioeconomic classification.

The change from a partial to a complete positive association between marital fertility and socioeconomic status during the 20-year period resulted from quite different changes in fertility rates in the various socioeconomic groups. The rate for the lowest-status group decreased slightly during the period, while the other groups showed significant increases in marital fertility, with the largest increase in the highest-status group. Per cent changes in marital and total fertility rates for the 20-year period were as given in the last table on this page.

There were much larger increases in total fertility than in marital fertility because age at marriage was declining during the period. The proportions below indicate the effect of younger marriages on the proportion of women ever married at each age.

PER CENT EVER MARRIED, BY AGE

	15-19	20-24	25-29	30-34	35-44
1930—Native white	6.7	45.5	71.8	80.7	84.3
1930—All white....	6.9	46.2	73.6	83.7	88.4
1950—All white....	9.7	57.4	80.4	86.2	87.9

The fact that socioeconomic status is directly related to marital fertility and inversely related to total fertility is explained by the tendency of women in the high-status groups to marry later than women in lower-status groups. Consequently, the relatively low "total fertility" of the upper-status groups is attributable to their smaller proportions of married women in each age group up to age 35, and not to lower fertility of their married women in each age group. The estimated proportions ever married, by age and socioeconomic status, are summarized below for all white women in Chicago in 1950.

ESTIMATED PER CENT EVER MARRIED, 1950[1]

Socioeconomic Status	15-19	20-24	25-29	30-34	35-44
1 (low).......	15	70	84	87	86
II..........	10	62	83	88	89
III.........	9	57	81	87	88
IV.........	7	48	78	85	88
V (high).....	6	37	69	82	87

[1] The method of estimation probably overstates the proportion married in the high-status groups at the older ages (see note 19).

DIFFERENTIAL MORTALITY

Trends in mortality in the United States have been in one direction—downward—and are less complex to interpret in the sense that motivational factors do not play the important role they do in fertility. Mortality is much less subject to individual control, although of course individuals do vary in the extent to which they choose or can afford to obtain medical services, in how faithfully they follow medical advice, and in their attitudes and exposure to "dangerous" activities.

The Metropolis and the Nation

For at least the last 40 years, mortality rates have been slightly higher in the city of Chicago than in the nation as a whole. In 1920, for example, white males in Chicago had an average life expectancy of 54.4 years, or 2 years less than the life expectancy of all white males in

PER CENT CHANGE 1930-50

	Total	I	II	III	IV	V
Marital fertility rate......	+23	−4	+15	+33	+29	+ 39
Total fertility rate........	+37	+3	+23	+45	+54	+104

TABLE 14

MARITAL FERTILITY RATES BY SOCIOECONOMIC STATUS, WHITE POPULATION, CITY OF CHICAGO, 1930 AND 1950

Socio-economic Status	1930 Native White	1930 All White	1950 All White	Index of Rate[1] Native White 1930	Index of Rate[1] All White 1930	Index of Rate[1] All White 1950
Total............	92	96	118	....	....	....
I (low).........	117	114	110	138	128	100
II..............	95	98	113	112	110	103
III.............	85	89	118	100	100	107
IV.............	91	95	123	107	107	112
V (high)........	98	99	138	115	111	125

[1] The socioeconomic group with the lowest marital fertility rate is used as the base of the index in each case.

TABLE 15

LIFE TABLE VALUES, BY SEX AND COLOR, CITY OF CHICAGO AND UNITED STATES, 1920–60

Year	White Males Chicago	White Males U.S.	Non-White Males Chicago	Non-White Males U.S.	White Females Chicago	White Females U.S.	Non-White Females Chicago	Non-White Females U.S.
				Expectation of Life at Birth ($\overset{\circ}{e}_0$)				
1960[1].....	65.2	67.3	60.9	60.9	72.0	73.9	66.5	66.2
1950.....	65.2	66.3	58.3	58.9	71.0	72.0	63.9	62.7
1940.....	62.6	62.8	51.0	52.3	67.1	67.3	56.7	55.5
1930.....	57.7	59.1	42.7[2]	47.6[2]	61.8	62.7	47.1[2]	49.5[2]
1920.....	54.4	56.3	41.2	47.1[2]	57.4	58.5	43.0	46.9[2]
				Increase in $\overset{\circ}{e}_0$, 1920–60				
1920–60..	10.8	11.0	19.7	13.8	14.6	15.4	23.5	19.3
1920–40..	8.2	6.5	9.8	5.2	9.7	8.8	13.7	8.6
1940–60..	2.6	4.5	9.9	8.6	4.9	6.6	9.8	10.7
				Infant Mortality Rate (q_0)				
1960[1].....	26.8	26.3	42.6	48.4	19.7	20.0	36.3	40.1
1920.....	96.3	80.3	121.9	105.0	77.5	63.9	105.4	87.5

[1] United States figures refer to 1959.
[2] Refers to Negro population.
SOURCE: U.S. Life Tables from *Vital Statistics of U.S., 1959*, Table 5–C.

the nation.[20] Between 1920 and 1940, more than 8 years were added to the average length of life of Chicago's white males, and the mortality difference between the city and the nation had virtually disappeared (Tables 15 and 16).

TABLE 16

DIFFERENCES IN EXPECTATION OF LIFE (CHICAGO MINUS UNITED STATES, WHITE MINUS NON-WHITE, FEMALE MINUS MALE), 1920–60

	1960	1950	1940	1930	1920
	Chicago Minus U.S.				
Males:					
White.......	−2.1	−1.1	− 0.2	− 1.4	− 1.9
Non-white...	0.0	−0.6	− 1.3	− 4.9	− 5.9
Females:					
White.......	−1.9	−1.0	− 0.2	− 0.9	− 1.1
Non-white...	0.3	1.2	1.2	− 2.4	− 3.9
	White Minus Non-white				
Males:					
Chicago......	4.3	6.9	11.6	15.0	13.2
U.S..........	6.4	7.4	10.5	11.5	9.2
Females:					
Chicago......	5.5	7.1	10.4	14.7	14.4
U.S..........	7.7	9.3	11.8	13.2	11.6
	Female Minus Male				
Chicago:					
White.......	6.8	5.8	4.5	4.1	3.0
Non-white...	5.6	5.6	5.7	4.4	1.8
U.S.:					
White.......	6.6	5.7	4.5	3.6	2.2
Non-white...	5.3	3.8	3.2	1.9	− 0.2

During the next 20 years mortality rates for white males declined less quickly,

[20] The average life expectancy—or expectation of life at birth ($\overset{\circ}{e}_0$)—is defined as the average length of life that would be lived by a cohort of persons under the assumption that they are exposed to a specified schedule of age-specific death rates throughout their lives. For example, the average life expectancy of white males in Chicago in 1950 represents the average length of life of a cohort of persons who are exposed throughout their lives, to the age-specific death rates experienced by white males in Chicago in 1950.

particularly in Chicago, where only 2.6 years were added to their life expectancy. In fact, there was no increase at all in the life expectancy of white males in Chicago during the last ten years of the period (1950–60) and, consequently, their life expectancy of 65.2 years in 1960 was again 2 years less than that of the nation as a whole.

The mortality of white females followed a similar pattern between 1920 and 1960, the chief differences being longer expectations of life for females, as well as larger gains in life expectancy during the 40-year period. For example, white females added 15 years to their average length of life during the 40-year period, as compared with 11 years for white males. By 1960, white females in the United States had attained an average life expectancy of 73.9 years.

Mortality rates are higher among non-whites than whites, although the difference diminished greatly during the 40 years from 1920 to 1960. In 1920, the expectation of life at birth was only 41.2 years for non-white males in Chicago, as compared with 54.4 years for white males. By 1960, Chicago's non-white males had attained a life expectancy of 60.9 years, as compared with 65.2 years for white males. That is, increases in longevity were much greater among non-whites than whites, especially in Chicago, where non-white males added almost 20 years to their life expectancy between 1920 and 1960, and non-white females added more than 23 years. As a result, the average length of life was only 4 to 5 years less for non-whites than whites in Chicago in 1960, whereas it had been 13 to 14 years less in 1920. By 1960, too, non-whites in Chicago had a life expectancy comparable to that of non-whites in the nation as a whole, despite a 4 to 6 years deficiency in 1920.

One of the widely discussed trends in mortality in recent years has been the increasing difference in the death rates for men and women. On the basis of

1920 death rates, for example, white women could expect to live 2 to 3 years longer than white men. By 1960, however, they could expect to live almost 7 years longer on the average, both in Chicago and the nation. Non-white women in 1920 had a small advantage over non-white men, and by 1960 they could expect to live 5 to 6 years longer than the men (Table 16).

Infant mortality rates[21] were considerably higher in Chicago than in the remainder of the nation in 1920. By 1960, however, the city's non-white rates were about 10 per cent below the nation's, and its white rates about the same level as the nation's (Table 15). In both the city and the nation, infant mortality rates decreased by one-half to three-fourths during the 40-year period, as the infant death rate dropped from the relatively high level of 64 to 122 deaths per 1,000 live births in 1920, to 20 to 48 per 1,000 live births by 1960.

Socioeconomic Differentials

The series of statistics on deaths by socioeconomic status from 1920 to 1940, compiled for the city of Chicago in the studies mentioned earlier, were analyzed in an unpublished dissertation by Mayer and summarized in an article by Mayer and Hauser.[22] With the assistance of a

21 The infant mortality rate is defined as the number of deaths to infants under one year of age, per 1,000 live births. It was also used to measure the probability of dying in the first year of life (q_0) in the abridged life tables computed for Chicago, since tests for 1930 to 1950 showed that the infant mortality rate differed by less than 1 per cent from values of q_0 obtained from the more accurate formula:

$$q_0 = \frac{(1 - f_0)\,(\text{deaths} < 1, \text{year x})}{\text{births, year x}}$$
$$+ \frac{(f_0)\,(\text{deaths} < 1, \text{year x} - 1)}{\text{births, year x} - 1}$$

22 Mayer, *op. cit.*; A. J. Mayer and P. M. Hauser, "Class Differentials in Expectation of Life at Birth," in Reinhard Bendix and Seymour Lipset, *Class, Status and Power, A Reader in Social Stratification* (Glencoe, Ill.: Free Press, 1953).

Public Health Service grant, the writers have compiled similar data for 1950. Abridged life tables and other mortality measures for 1920 to 1960 by sex and color—and for 1930 to 1950 by sex, color, and socioeconomic status—were specially computed for the present analysis, in order to utilize comparable procedures for the entire time series. Socioeconomic groups are defined on the same basis as for the fertility analysis.

Socioeconomic differentials in mortality in Chicago are summarized below under five main headings:

1. *Expectation of life at birth.*—The data of Table 17 show that in 1930, the death rates of white males and females in the highest socioeconomic group (V) implied an average life expectancy 11 to 12 years longer than that for the lowest-status group (I). By 1950, the range of life expectancy among the five status groups had shrunk to less than 6 years for white females, and to 8 years for white males. This convergence of socioeconomic differentials in mortality was due to greater increases in longevity in the lower-status than in the higher-status groups. For example, the average life expectancy of white females in Group I increased from 56.4 years in 1930 to 67.8 years in 1950, an increment of 11.4 years. During the same years, the life expectancy of white females in Group V increased by only 6.2 years, or from 67.2 to 73.4 years.

Despite a much narrower range of socioeconomic status among non-whites, the life expectancy of the highest-status group (III–V combined) was almost 9 years longer than that of the lowest-status group (I) in 1930, and still 6 to 7 years longer in 1950.

2. *Infant mortality.*—The sharp decreases in infant mortality between 1930 and 1950 were accompanied by a convergence of socioeconomic differentials, at least among the white population. In 1930 the infant mortality rate for white males and females in the lowest-status

TABLE 17

EXPECTATION OF LIFE AT BIRTH, BY SEX, COLOR, AND SOCIO-ECONOMIC STATUS, CITY OF CHICAGO, 1930–50

SEX, COLOR, AND SOCIO-ECONOMIC STATUS	EXPECTATION OF LIFE AT BIRTH ($\overset{\circ}{e}_0$)			SOCIOECONOMIC DIFFERENCES IN ($\overset{\circ}{e}_0$)[1]		
	1950	1940	1930	1950	1940	1930
White males.........	65.2	62.6	57.7	....	....	....
I (low)...........	60.8	57.8	51.2	0	0	0
II...............	64.4	61.5	56.2	3.6	3.7	5.0
III..............	67.0	64.2	59.2	6.2	6.4	8.0
IV..............	67.4	65.3	61.2	6.6	7.5	10.0
V (high)..........	68.8	65.3	63.0	8.0	7.5	11.8
White females........	71.0	67.1	61.8	....	....	....
I (low)...........	67.8	62.7	56.4	0	0	0
II...............	70.3	66.0	60.2	2.5	3.3	3.8
III..............	71.6	67.6	62.5	3.8	4.9	6.1
IV..............	72.1	69.2	64.4	4.3	6.5	8.0
V (high)..........	73.4	70.2	67.2	5.6	7.5	10.8
Non-white males......	58.3	51.0	42.7	....	....	....
I (low)...........	55.4	47.4	38.9	0	0	0
II...............	58.8	51.2	40.7	3.4	3.8	1.8
III–V (high).......	62.1	53.6	47.6	6.7	6.2	8.7
Non-white females....	63.9	56.7	47.1	....	....	....
I (low)...........	61.0	53.2	42.9	0	0	0
II...............	64.4	56.8	45.4	3.4	3.6	2.5
III–V (high).......	67.4	59.1	51.7	6.4	5.9	8.8

[1] Computed by subtracting $\overset{\circ}{e}_0$ for Group I from $\overset{\circ}{e}_0$ for each socioeconomic group in turn.

TABLE 18

INFANT MORTALITY RATES BY SEX, COLOR, AND SOCIOECONOMIC STATUS, CITY OF CHICAGO, 1930–50 (DEATHS UNDER 1 YEAR OF AGE PER 1,000 LIVE BIRTHS)

SEX, COLOR, AND SOCIO-ECONOMIC STATUS	MALES			FEMALES		
	1950	1940	1930	1950	1940	1930
White.............	26.1	30.0	61.0	19.6	24.4	48.0
I (low)..........	30.2	34.8	83.9	25.7	27.9	68.0
II..............	28.9	31.1	68.9	17.7	26.8	52.8
III	23.9	28.8	52.6	17.1	22.6	43.4
IV	25.1	27.5	49.2	20.2	20.6	36.5
V (high)	20.5	26.5	36.7	19.5	25.4	29.0
Non-white[1]........	41.9	48.0	94.7	27.5	31.7	77.1
I (low)..........	41.6	41.6	104.1	34.3	31.5	80.1
II	43.7	55.5	102.4	24.6	31.4	80.7
III–V (high).....	38.9	41.2	78.3	23.3	32.3	70.1

[1] Data for non-whites in 1930 refer to Negroes.

group in Chicago was more than 125 per cent higher than the rate for the highest-status group, while in 1950 it was 30 to 50 per cent higher (Table 18). Among the non-whites, trends in socio-economic differentials were not so consistent.

3. *Color differentials (controlled for socioeconomic status).*—Differences in socioeconomic levels between whites and non-whites in 1950 accounted for almost all of their differences in mortality. In 1930 and 1940 this was not the case, however. These findings are based on proportionate differences between the non-white and white mortality rates summarized below:

the total population. That is, one-third of the 1950 deaths in Chicago could be ascribed to socioeconomic and color differentials in mortality rates, as could 41 per cent of the deaths in 1930. Similar figures for subgroups of the population by sex and color are summarized below: Over half of the non-white deaths on

	White Males	White Fe-males	Non-white Males	Non-white Fe-males	Total Popu-lation
1950.........	22	18	50	51	33
1940.........	14	19	57	60	28
1930.........	23	25	67	69	41

PER CENT DIFFERENCE (NON-WHITE AND WHITE)

	MALES			FEMALES		
	1950	1940	1930	1950	1940	1930
Death rate (crude).........................	+ 4	+54	+75	+10	+51	+74
Standardized for age and socioeconomic status[1]	− 5	+67	+96	+ 4	+68	+99
Infant mortality rate.......................	+61	+60	+55	+40	+30	+61
Standardized for socioeconomic status[1]......	+13	+51	+41	0	+23	+44

[1] Standardized by the indirect method, using the total population on each date as the standard.

That is, in 1950 the death rate for non-white males was slightly lower than the rate for white males after standardization for socioeconomic status, while the rate for non-white females was slightly higher than the white rate when white-non-white differences in socioeconomic level were held constant. Similarly, 1950 infant mortality rates for non-whites were 40 to 60 per cent higher than white rates, but with differences in socio-economic status held constant non-white infant mortality was no higher than white infant mortality among females, and only 13 per cent higher among males.

4. *Total effect of socioeconomic and color differentials.*—One-third of all the deaths to residents of Chicago in 1950 would not have occurred if the age-sex-specific death rates for the highest-status group (V) of whites had prevailed in

each date were due to socioeconomic and color differentials, and would not have occured if the death rates of the highest-status group of whites had operated throughout the entire non-white population. The proportion of "excess deaths" in the white population varied from 14 to 25 per cent.

5. *Cause of death.*—Patterns of socio-economic differentials in mortality varied greatly by cause of death, among the white population of Chicago in 1950. Deaths from infectious diseases exhibited a very strong negative relationship with socioeconomic status. For example, among white males the mortality ratio for deaths from tuberculosis ranged from a high of 266 for the lowest-status group to a low of 41 for the highest-status group, and the mortality ratios for influenza and pneumonia ranged from 197 to 36 from the low to high

socioeconomic groups (Table 19 and Figure 1). Accidental deaths also were inversely related to socioeconomic status, with mortality ratios for white males decreasing from 172 to 54 from the low- to high-status groups. The so-called degenerative diseases, heart and cancer, varied much less by socioeconomic status and there was even a slight tendency, among white males in the three upper-status groups, for deaths from arteriosclerotic heart disease (including coronary disease) to increase as socioeconomic status increased.

Although similar data for Chicago during the period 1928–32 were ana-

TABLE 19

MORTALITY RATIOS BY SOCIOECONOMIC STATUS, FOR SELECTED CAUSES OF
DEATH, WHITE MALES AND FEMALES, CITY OF CHICAGO, 1950

SEX AND CAUSE OF DEATH	SIXTH REVISION CODE NUMBER	TOTAL		SOCIOECONOMIC GROUP				
		No. of Deaths	Ratio	I (low)	II	III	IV	V (high)
		Number of Deaths						
White Males, All Causes......	....	19,322	.....	5,033	4,227	5,392	2,839	1,831
White Females, All Causes.....	....	14,115	.....	2,560	3,062	4,412	2,401	1,680
		Mortality Ratio[1]						
White Males, All Causes......	....	*19,322*	*100*	*136*	*107*	*89*	*86*	*79*
Tuberculosis, all forms..........	001–019	645	100	266	106	53	42[2]	41[2]
Malignant neoplasms, including neoplasms of lymphatic and hematopoietic tissues.........	140–205	3,152	100	115	114	94	90	83
Diabetes mellitus..............	260	235	100	90[2]	116	107	93[2]	81[2]
Vascular lesions affecting central nervous system..............	330–334	1,308	100	108	105	95	96	99
Diseases of heart..............	410–443	8,826	100	135	103	90	88	82
Arteriosclerotic heart disease, including coronary...........	420	5,043	100	119	101	91	95	100
Influenza and pneumonia, except pneumonia of newborn........	480–493	491	100	197	122	74	56[2]	36[2]
Certain diseases of early infancy..	760–776	531	100	114	109	99	90	74[2]
Accidents.....................	E800–E962	810	100	172	112	83	69	54
White Females, All Causes.....	....	*14,115*	*100*	*125*	*107*	*97*	*91*	*83*
Tuberculosis, all forms.........	001–019	178	100	228	118[2]	75[2]	56[2]	41[2]
Malignant neoplasms, including neoplasms of lymphatic and hematopoietic tissues.........	140–205	2,647	100	106	98	102	95	98
Diabetes mellitus..............	260	431	100	131	107	103	81	77[2]
Vascular lesions affecting central nervous system..............	330–334	1,456	100	97	109	103	95	91
Diseases of heart..............	410–443	6,121	100	132	111	96	90	77
Arteriosclerotic heart disease, including coronary...........	420	2,956	100	122	109	96	89	89
Influenza and pneumonia, except pneumonia of newborn........	480–493	284	100	177	113	80	75[2]	76[2]
Certain diseases of early infancy..	760–776	373	100	135	93	88	95	98[2]
Accidents.....................	E800–E962	334	100	151	106	78	106	76[2]

[1] Ratio of actual deaths to expected deaths assuming the age-specific death rates (by 10-year age intervals) of all white males (or females) are applied to the age composition of the particular socioeconomic group.
[2] Based on less than 50 deaths.

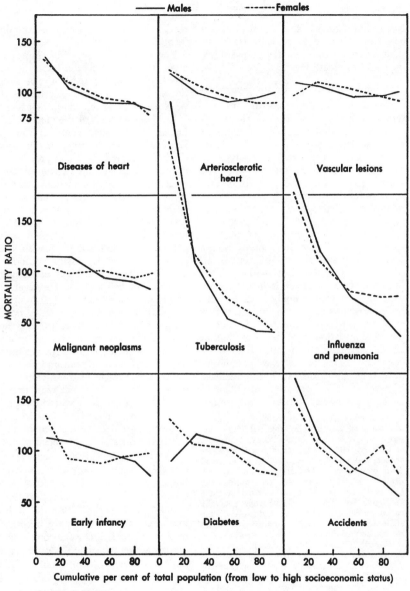

Source: Table 19.

FIG. 1.—Mortality ratios by socioeconomic status, for selected causes of death, white males and females, City of Chicago, 1950.

lyzed by Convis, they unfortunately could not be used to evaluate trends in socioeconomic differentials in mortality by cause of death.[23]

SUMMARY AND CONCLUDING OBSERVATIONS

The data and, therefore, to some extent the conclusions drawn therefrom have certain limitations in addition to those which have already been discussed. First, the fertility analysis is necessarily based on measurements of current rather than cohort fertility and may, therefore, distort certain types of relationships. That is, socioeconomic differentials in age at marriage and in spacing of births may cause discrepancies between socioeconomic differentials in current fertility and similar differentials in completed fertility. But with present data and circumstances it is impossible to achieve a cohort analysis of fertility by socioeconomic status in an urban area. An urban population is not a closed population and the combination of internal migration and the socioeconomic mobility of the population over time precludes such an analysis. The relationships reported apply, well enough, to current fertility, but cannot

[23] Lolagene Convis, "Economic Differentials in Causes of Death" (unpublished Ph.D. dissertation, Department of Sociology, University of Chicago, 1939). Analysis of trends in socioeconomic differentials in mortality by cause of death is complicated by changes in the cause-of-death classification over time. The International List of Causes of Death was revised in 1929, 1938, and 1948. The 1948 classification, generally called the Sixth Revision, was used to classify the 1950 statistics for Chicago summarized in this report. Convis' data for 1928–32 were based on the Fourth Revision (1929), and changes in the cause-of-death classification from the Fourth to Sixth Revision precluded measurement of trends from 1930 to 1950 for many important causes of death. Consequently, no attempt was made in 1950 to retain the same general cause-of-death groupings utilized by Convis. Instead, causes of death for the 1950 analysis were selected after consultation with Dr. Jeremiah Stamler (Director, Heart Disease Control Program, Chicago Board of Health), and taking account of the limitations imposed by the number of deaths occurring to Chicago residents in one year.

readily be extended to cover completed fertilities.

The second limitation of import concerns the ecological basis for defining socioeconomic status. All of the population residing in a particular census tract were assigned to the same socioeconomic level on the basis of the median family income (or median rent) of the tract. Each of the five socioeconomic groups used in the analysis, therefore, included all of the population living in census tracts for which the median family income (or median rent) fell within a specified range of values. It is not known how the socioeconomic differentials in fertility and mortality obtained by this procedure would compare with differentials obtained by assigning socioeconomic status on the basis of individual family income or rent. However, two points are worth noting: (1) While the population of a census tract is not homogeneous with respect to income or rent, there are tremendous variations among the 935 census tracts in median income and median rent, and also in the interquartile range of these values, from tract to tract. In 1950, for example, median family income varied from a low of $1,653 in census tract 539 to a high of more than $10,000 in other tracts. (2) Moreover, in studies of social stratification where the objective has been to classify the population by a small number of general socioeconomic or "class" groups, neighborhood characteristics are certainly one of the factors to be taken into account. Consequently, resort to a method of assigning socioeconomic status on a "neighborhood" (census tract) basis has some justification in itself. The important thing to remember, when utilizing this approach, is to avoid confusing the results with those that might be obtained if individuals were classified according to personal characteristics. For example, the socioeconomic differentials in fertility for 1950 described in this report should not be interpreted as direct measures of "family income" differentials in fertility.

It must also be borne in mind that the historical record of socioeconomic differentials can be reconstructed only for the city of Chicago, even though the entire metropolitan area would be more satisfactory. Accordingly, by reason of our operational definition of socioeconomic groups (which allocated the population of Chicago to socioeconomic groups in approximately the same proportionate distribution on each date), the data are undoubtedly affected by the leakage of higher-income whites to suburbia as increasing numbers of low-income non-whites became residents of the city. It may be assumed that the white out-migrants from the city tend to have more children, other things being equal, since children provide a strong motivation for moving to the suburbs. Under this assumption, the positive relationship between marital fertility and socioeconomic status obtained for the city may be an understatement of the relationship in the metropolitan area as a whole.

Lastly, conventional tests showed that reporting of births and deaths in Chicago was virtually complete as early as 1920. However, inadequate addresses on a few birth and death certificates precluded the allocation of a small number of births and deaths to census tracts and hence to socioeconomic groups. These and other deficiencies in the basic data are evaluated in the studies listed in note 2, and judged inconsequential in relation to the size and pattern of socioeconomic differentials obtained.

Despite the limitations imposed by the reliance on measures of current fertility and by the "ecological" definition of socioeconomic status, there can be no doubt that the studies summarized here add to our knowledge of fertility and mortality in a metropolitan area.

The four decades from 1920 to 1960 constitute one of the most tumultuous eras in the history of Chicago and of the nation as a whole. They witnessed recovery from World War I, the most severe depression ever experienced, World War II, and its postwar, cold-war aftermath. It was a period that encapsulates the entire history of the United States as an urban nation, for the census of 1920 was the first to record that over half the population resided in urban places. It was a period of great social upheaval and rapid social change characterized by ever greater streams of internal migration, including streams of Negroes which flowed from the South and rural areas to the metropolitan North and West. The flow of foreign immigrants sharply declined but the combination of increased internal migration and rising natural increase accelerated the rate of urbanization and metropolitanization. The period was also characterized by a rapidly increasing level of education and, except for the depression, rapidly rising per capita income and levels of living.

In broad perspective, these forty years from 1920 to 1960 brought several changes in traditional patterns of differential fertility and mortality. First, the long-standing lower level of fertility in Chicago than in the nation had disappeared by 1960, when the marital fertility of the white population for the first time was higher in Chicago. Second, Negro marital fertility overtook that of the white population between 1930 and 1950. Third, in Chicago at least, socioeconomic differentials in marital fertility had completed the transition from a negative to a positive relationship by 1950, when births per 1,000 ever-married women (standardized for age) increased consistently from the lowest- to highest-status group. Lastly, the marked convergence in mortality differentials by color and socioeconomic status during the period indicates, of course, the increasing access of all socioeconomic groups of whites and non-whites to the benefits of rising levels of living, including public health and modern medical practice.

3. City Size as a Sociological Variable

WILLIAM FIELDING OGBURN AND OTIS DUDLEY DUNCAN

A description of the circumstances attending the preparation of this paper is required by way of preface. For a dozen or so years prior to his death in April, 1959, Professor Ogburn worked intermittently on a volume tentatively entitled "Spacing the Urban Population." This work was motivated by an intense concern with the vulnerability of large cities to modern techniques of warfare. Shortly after the first military use of the atom bomb he raised the question, "Should we not study the problem of breaking up our cities into towns and villages and removing some of them from the crowded eastern seaboard into the less crowded area west of the Mississippi and further removed from the national borders?" One aspect of such a study, it was noted, should consider "the possible loss of the advantages of our urban civilization. Do the desirable products of city life come only from the big cities? With thought and planning, might they not be had from cities of fifty thousand population, especially if there was specialization by cities and adequate transportation? . . . It is possible that our urban civilization might be much better with well-planned smaller cities and towns."[1]

The dissertation[2] which occasions a contribution to the present symposium constituted one segment of the research carried out by various assistants under Professor Ogburn's direction in preparation for the writing of his volume on urban dispersal. This dissertation has been summarized in various publications.[3] The remainder of the research,[4] however, is recorded only in uncompleted manuscripts left by Professor Ogburn. Although we must, therefore, be deprived of a full statement of Professor Ogburn's thought and work on problems of cities during the last years of his career, it has seemed appropriate to make available two summary statements outlining some of his principle preoccupations. One paper, appearing elsewhere,[5] states the problem of the large modern city in terms of the technological and economic factors responsible for its growth and the inconveniences and hazards—especially that of destruction in war—resulting from population concentration and congestion and from developments in military technology.

The present paper deals with the theme of differences among cities related to their size. The outline of theoreti-

[1] William Fielding Ogburn, "Sociology and the Atom," American Journal of Sociology, LI (January, 1946), 271.

[2] Otis Dudley Duncan, "An Examination of the Problem of Optimum City-Size," unpublished Ph.D. dissertation, microfilm, University of Chicago, 1949.

[3] Otis Dudley Duncan, "Optimum Size of Cities," in Reader in Urban Sociology, ed. by Paul K. Hatt and Albert J. Reiss, Jr. (Glencoe: Free Press, 1951), pp. 632–45; James Dahir, "What Is the Best Size for a City?" American City, August, 1951, pp. 104–5; Robert M. Lillibridge, "Urban Size: An Assessment," Land Economics, XXVIII (November, 1952), 341–52.

[4] The research was supported by a grant to Professor Ogburn from the Carnegie Corporation for projects on "Social Effects of Technology."

[5] William Fielding Ogburn, "Technology and Cities: The Dilemma of the Modern Metropolis," Sociological Quarterly, Vol. I (July, 1960).

cal points and in many instances their precise phrasing come from manuscripts by Professor Ogburn; illustrative data are taken from the dissertation and later research of the junior author, who is, of course, responsible for the final form of all statements in the paper.

THE APPROACH

A knowledge of the social characteristics of cities according to their sizes

TABLE 1

NUMBER AND PERCENTAGE OF COMMUNITIES IN THE UNITED STATES LOCATED ON THE NATIONAL SYSTEM OF INTERSTATE AND DEFENSE HIGHWAYS, DECEMBER 31, 1957, BY SIZE OF COMMUNITY

POPULATION SIZE, 1950[1]	TOTAL NUMBER OF COMMUNITIES	COMMUNITIES ON THE INTERSTATE SYSTEM	
		Number	Per Cent
1,000,000 or more......	5	5	100.0
500,000 to 1,000,000...	13	13	100.0
250,000 to 500,000.....	23	23	100.0
100,000 to 250,000.....	65	65	100.0
50,000 to 100,000......	126	110	87.3
25,000 to 50,000.......	252	216	85.7
10,000 to 25,000.......	778	526	67.6
5,000 to 10,000........	1,176	706	60.0
2,500 to 5,000.........	1,557	658	42.3
1,000 to 2,500.........	3,408	1,055	31.0

[1] Incorporated places of 1,000 or more and unincorporated places of 5,000 or more, as recognized in the *1950 Census of Population.*
SOURCE: Arthur K. Branham and Florence Knopp Banks, "Common-Carrier Passenger and Freight Services Available to Communities on the Interstate Highway System," *Public Roads*, XXX (February, 1960), 276–82, Table 1.

is not only useful to the individual citizen in making choices about where he wishes to live, but such information is of value to others, as for instance, city planners. For if they know these social characteristics, it may be possible to search for their causes and, if the causes are discovered, to plan accordingly. Before the modern age of steam and scientific medicine, cities were very unhealthy with a high death rate. But as the causes of death became known, preventive

measures were taken, so that now the death rate in large cities is not very different from what it is in small places.

Many, therefore, are the uses that may be made of a knowledge of the social characteristics of cities. Of particular concern, in considering the predicament of the contemporary city, are the changes in these characteristics that might occur if the population of cities should be more scattered and if the population density should become less. If the threat of war and bombings by rockets and missiles becomes a reality, it may be that the movement of the people of the city toward the suburbs and of factories to the nearby satellite towns and cities will lead to a decrease in the size of the central metropolis along with an increase in the population of the surrounding territory. If there should be more cities of 50,000 inhabitants and fewer inhabitants of cities of 1,000,000 or more, would the citizenry be the gainer or the loser owing to the consequent change in the frequency of the attributes that are associated with communities of these sizes? Would there be more or less contentment? Would the contribution to music and literature be less? Would morality be strengthened? How would the health of the population be affected?

From this point of view, there is as much interest in the similarities between cities of different sizes as in the differences. For instance, if the ratio of pupils to teachers is the same in cities of 50,000 as in cities of 1,000,000, there would be no change in this regard if the population of cities of 1,000,000 all lived in cities of 50,000.

There is, indeed, reason to believe that there are many similarities in attributes of cities of very different sizes. One reason is the extensive development of transportation and communication between cities. By way of illustration, Table 1 shows that all communities of 100,000 inhabitants or more, and at least two-thirds of the communities no larger than 10,000 to 25,000 inhabitants, are located on or enjoy ready access to the National System of Interstate and Defense Highways. Practically all such communities have common-carrier passenger bus service and truck freight service. Under conditions of frequent travel and contacts, usages in one city spread to another. Thus a movement to have speakers at a lunch club will be found in every city. To the more or less isolated mountainous rural regions new customs spread more slowly, as they do in oriental cities, where transportation is less highly developed and where the different cities have more distinctive characteristics.

Along with extensive travel there has spread national advertising of consumers' goods manufactured under conditions of mass production. Thus all cities will sell the same makes of automobile, the same soft drinks, the same brands of shirts, the same canned fruit, the same toothbrush. These marketing conditions have led observers to wonder whether regional peculiarities will not disappear. The influence of the radio is to reduce local peculiarities of speech. This reduction of peculiarities is likely to occur along the main lines of travel and communication. It is on these main lines that cities are found. Innovations spread first along the routes of travel.

There are, then, reasons for thinking that cities of different sizes may have many traits that are the same. For the same reasons, where the frequency of an attribute differs as between a city of 50,000 and a city of 1,000,000, the difference may be so slight as to make little difference. Small differences may be of negligible importance.

To a concern with the magnitude of differences by city size and with their importance—whether as criteria of individual choice or as bases for collective action—we must add a curiosity about *why* size makes urban differences. A grasp of these reasons provides a basis

for judging whether differences observed at one time may be merely transitory and due to disappear in the normal course of events, or whether efforts to modify them may be justified by a high probability of success. Then too, many differences among cities, even important ones, may not yet be subject to measurement. Thus we lack comparative statistics on the amount of smoke pollution of the air above the cities of the United States, important though the problem is and great as the differences among cities must be. In some such cases an inference can be made about differences in traits not measured by statistics, for instance, neighborliness. Greater neighborliness in very small places can be deduced from the principle that the size of a population in a limited area affects the proportion of the population with whom an individual becomes acquainted. From such a principle there flow other characteristics, as for example less gossip and more secrecy of behavior, more anonymity and less social pressure in large cities than in tiny communities.

We are, therefore, looking for principles differentiating large places from small—principles which are basic, in the sense that clusters of other characteristics follow from these. Such principles would thus perform the functions of theory in science: explanation and prediction. They would serve to explain differences among cities by size that have been established by reliable observation and to predict still other differences that have yet to be measured.

Succeeding sections of the paper offer a selection of principles judged to meet the foregoing requirements. Illustrative applications of these principles are given, along with certain statements in qualification of their applicability. The presentation, however, falls short of meeting standards of deductive rigor that might be proposed by a specialist in sociological theory, and it will be impossible to summarize for the reader any substantial part of the empirical evidence supporting the stated principles.[6]

THE RELATION OF POPULATION TO AREA

The presence of a relatively large number of people in a relatively small space is commonly accepted as a necessary part of the very definition of a city, although it is perhaps not a sufficient criterion of urbanism. We can assume, then, a general appreciation of the fact that cities involve a special kind of relation of population to area. Not all the implications of this relation, however, may be obvious, and it may not be wholly self-evident how this relation may change, given alteration of the basic technological and organizational determinants of city structure. If, as has been argued elsewhere, most of the inconveniences and hazards of city life can be traced back to congestion,[7] it behooves us to consider some facets of urban congestion.

Under the conditions of city growth prevailing in the nineteenth and early twentieth centuries, increasing size of cities led to increasing residential densities. Thus Stewart found that the area in square miles (A) of political cities in 1940 was related to their population (P), on the average, by the formula, $A = {}^{75}/_{375}\,P$; that is, multiplication of population size by a factor of 10 was accompanied by only a 5.6-fold multiplication of area size.[8] A city of 10,000 inhabitants, for example, would have an area of 2.8 square miles as compared with 15.75 square miles for a city of 100,000. The resulting increase of density with increasing city size may be seen in figures for 1950 which, unlike those just cited, are based in part on the concept of "urbanized area." For the urbanized areas, the following densities (population per square mile) were observed for the specified population-size groupings:

3,000,000 or more	7,679
1,000,000 to 3,000,000	6,776
250,000 to 1,000,000	4,468
50,000 to 250,000	3,869

The direct relation between population size and density likewise held for the smaller urban places outside urbanized areas:

25,000 or more	3,339
10,000 to 25,000	2,721
5,000 to 10,000	2,226
2,500 to 5,000	1,765

These densities are lower than those that would be deduced from Stewart's formula primarily because a different set of areal units is employed. The urbanized areas include suburban and "fringe" components of lower average density than that of the central cities, while the groups of smaller cities exclude these same suburbs, whose average density is greater than that of places of comparable size outside urbanized areas.[9]

A counterpart to high population/area ratios in large cities is the intensive use of residential land, as indicated by the relative frequency of multiple-unit residential structures in Table 2. In cities of 500,000 inhabitants or more, over one-

[6] For more extensive presentation of evidence, see the items cited in footnotes 2 and 3; William F. Ogburn, *Social Characteristics of Cities* (Chicago: International City Managers' Association, 1937); Otis Dudley Duncan and Albert J. Reiss, Jr., *Social Characteristics of Urban and Rural Communities, 1950* (New York: John Wiley & Sons, 1956).

[7] Ogburn, "Technology and Cities," *op. cit.*

[8] John Q. Stewart and William Warntz, "Physics of Population Distribution," *Journal of Regional Science*, I (Summer, 1958), 99–123.

[9] The reader should be alert to the distinctions among various operational definitions of the urban community: urban places (incorporated and unincorporated), urbanized areas, metropolitan districts, and standard metropolitan areas. Formal criteria of each are stated in the introductory notes to the *1950 Census of Population*. Each has advantages and limitations for various analytical purposes, but it is often true that statistics are available for one type of areal unit and not the others.

third of the dwelling units in 1940 were in structures of five or more units, as compared with one-eighth of the dwelling units in such multiple-unit structures in cities of 50,000 to 100,000. The positive correlation of multiple-unit structures with city size is undoubtedly a major factor accounting for the inverse relationship of home ownership with city size (shown in the second column of Table 2). Thus we would expect the association of density with city size to be reflected in a variety of aspects of housing arrangements and family living patterns.

Unfortunately, little research has been done on temporal changes in urban densities, perhaps in part because this is a somewhat exacting and difficult research problem.[10] It is possible to infer, nonetheless, that the historical relationship is subject to change under modern conditions of local transportation. The urbanized areas of 1950 with populations of 100,000 or more were classified by the census date at which their central cities first showed a population half as large as that of 1950. Then, when the average density for an urbanized area of 100,000 and one of 1,000,000 was computed from regression equations, the following variations by age of city and size of urbanized area were noted:[11]

	100,000	1,000,000
All urbanized areas.....	3,927	5,803
1900 or earlier..........	4,459	6,370
1910.................	3,866	6,006
1920.................	4,075	5,977
1930 or later..........	3,753	4,063

[10] This problem is dealt with by Hal H. Winsborough in his Ph.D. dissertation, "A Comparative Study of Urban Residential Densities" (University of Chicago, 1961).

[11] Otis Dudley Duncan, "Population Distribution and Community Structure," *Cold Spring Harbor Symposia on Quantitative Biology*, XXII (1957), 357–71, Table 8.

Urbanized areas of the very youngest cities—those experiencing most of their growth after 1920, when the automobile was becoming important—are seen to have lower average densities than the older ones. Moreover, there is very little difference by size among these areas of recent growth, while there is quite an

TABLE 2

SELECTED HOUSING CHARACTERISTICS, BY SIZE OF PLACE, 1940

Size of Place	Per Cent of Dwelling Units in 5-Family-or-More Structures	Per Cent of Dwelling Units Owner Occupied
United States..........	10.5	43.6
Inside metropolitan districts:		
500,000 or more......	36.2	26.4
250,000 to 500,000...	19.1	34.9
100,000 to 250,000...	13.7	37.8
50,000 to 100,000....	12.7	37.3
25,000 to 50,000.....	10.1	43.3
10,000 to 25,000.....	5.5	49.3
5,000 to 10,000......	4.5	52.7
2,500 to 5,000.......	2.9	52.9
Rural non-farm......	1.5	58.3
Rural farm..........	0.2	65.1
Outside metropolitan districts:		
25,000 to 50,000.....	6.7	43.1
10,000 to 25,000.....	5.2	44.7
5,000 to 10,000......	3.6	47.0
2,500 to 5,000.......	2.6	48.8
Rural non-farm......	0.8	49.8
Rural farm..........	0.0	52.8

SOURCE: United States Bureau of the Census, *Housing Special Reports*, Series H–44 (1944–45), No. 1, Table 9; No. 2, Table 1; No. 3, Table 1.

appreciable difference for the older cities, as would be anticipated from the data given earlier.

The significance of the population-area relationship does not, however, hinge solely on the correlation of population size and density. Even if all cities had the same density, the spatial structure of large cities would no doubt be quite different from that of small cities, i.e., we would expect the spatial pattern of activity to be quite different for

25,000 people living in five square miles from that of 2,500,000 living in a compact area of 500 square miles. The radius of a city—supposing it to be shaped as a circle—is not proportional to its area, and hence to its population (on the assumption of no variation in density), but to the *square root* of its area. A quadrupling of area, and hence of population, may then be had with only a doubling of radius. Because travel is along lines, straight or curved, the ra-

3, which concern the median distances traveled by workers from their homes to their places of work. Although the comparison is merely suggestive of what the true relationship may be, it is curious that the distance traveled to work by the average person is of about the same order of magnitude as the radius of the city, computed on highly idealized assumptions. Now, this is not a *mathematically* necessary result. Conceivably, everyone might work in a shop

TABLE 3

MEDIAN DISTANCE FROM HOME TO PLACE OF WORK, BY SIZE OF CITY, IN
TWO STUDIES, COMPARED WITH COMPUTED RADIUS OF CITY AREA

SIZE OF CITY	MEDIAN DISTANCE (MILES)		COMPUTED RADIUS (RANGE, MILES)
	Study A	Study B	
1,000,000 or more........... ⎫	4.8	....	5.4 and over
500,000 to 1,000,000........ ⎬		⎫ 3.3	4.1–5.4
100,000 to 500,000.......... ⎭	2.0	⎬	2.3–4.1
25,000 to 100,000...........	1.6	1.9	1.3–2.3
5,000 to 25,000.............	0.8	1.2	0.7–1.3
Under 5,000 (incorporated)....	....	Under 1	0.7 and less
Unincorporated area.........	....	5.4	....

SOURCES: Study A, Melville C. Branch, Jr., *Urban Planning and Public Opinion* (Princeton: Bureau of Urban Research, Princeton University, 1942), question 4e. Data are from a nationally representative public opinion sample interviewed in 1942.

Study B, Thurley A. Bostick *et al.*, "Motor-Vehicle-Use Studies in Six States," *Public Roads*, XXVIII (December, 1954), 99–126, Table 9. Data were compiled by the U.S. Bureau of Public Roads from studies conducted in Arkansas, Louisiana, North Dakota, Oklahoma, South Dakota, and Wisconsin in 1951. Persons not reporting distance and those for whom no travel was required are excluded.

Computed radius, John Q. Stewart, "Suggested Principles of Social Physics," *Science*, CVI (August 29, 1947), 179–80. Radius computed from Stewart's formula relating area to population size, on the assumption that cities are circular in shape.

dius of a city is a more nearly relevant datum in considering the mutual accessibility of its parts than is the area. Hence the loss in accessibility with increasing population size is not proportionally as great as either the increase in population or in area. The heightening of density with increasing size that we have noted for older cities may well represent an adaptation that lessens the increase in radius even below proportionality to the square root of the factor of increase in area.

The significance of this abstract consideration of accessibility in relation to area is suggested by the data in Table

across the street from his place of residence and enjoy a negligible journey to work. But this is not the way our modern big cities are organized. Large-scale units of production and exchange require the assembly of many men in a small space, not all of whom can possibly reside in close proximity to the place of co-ordinated activity.

In fact, if linear accessibility were the only criterion, activities of concern to the entire urban community, or to a relatively representative segment of its population, would be located at the center of the city. But as cities become larger, the proportion of such activities that can be accommodated at the center becomes less. The three cities with populations of 1,000,000 or more included in Table 4 have central business districts (CBD's) averaging one square mile in area. Already, some parts of this district are appreciably less "central" than others; and if the CBD area were proportional to the total urbanized area it would be so extensive that much of its advantage of central location would be much greater than that of a small city, the proportion of the total trade of a metropolitan area that can be localized at the center is considerably less.

In sum, although heightening of density and the sheer geometry of city form enable the large city to compensate for its potential disadvantage in accessibility vis-à-vis the small city, the price for achieving this compensation is greater congestion of both residential and busi-

TABLE 4

AREA AND TRAFFIC CHARACTERISTICS OF CENTRAL BUSINESS
DISTRICTS OF SELECTED CITIES, BY CITY SIZE, *c.* 1950

CITY SIZE[1]	NUMBER OF CITIES IN SAMPLE[2]	AREA OF CBD		NUMBER OF VEHICLES ENTERING CBD BETWEEN 10 A.M. AND 6 P.M. PER 1,000 POPULATION	PEAK ACCUMULATION OF VEHICLES, DENSITY PER SQUARE MILE OF CBD
		As Percentage of Urbanized Area	Square Miles per 100,000 Population		
1,000,000 or more.....	3	0.4	0.08	66	22,900
500,000 to 1,000,000..	5	0.4	.09	135	27,400
250,000 to 500,000....	8	0.8	.16	168	20,700
100,000 to 250,000....	14	1.1	.24	236	15,300
50,000 to 100,000.....	5	2.4	.42	476	15,300
25,000 to 50,000......	16	2.7	.58	627	14,300
10,000 to 25,000......	16	4.2	.71	837	12,400
5,000 to 10,000.......	2	4.0	.97	942	15,100

[1] Based on 1950 urbanized area population (source does not clearly specify procedures followed for cities for which the Bureau of the Census did not delineate urbanized areas).

[2] Number varies slightly from one variable to another because of differences in reporting among surveys.
SOURCE: Robert H. Burrage *et al.* (Division of Research, U.S. Bureau of Public Roads), *Parking Guide for Cities* (Washington: Government Printing Office, 1956), Tables 2 and 4; based on comprehensive parking studies of various cities carried out in 1945–54.

lost. Consequently, we see in Table 4 that the size of the CBD, in relation to the size of the urbanized area or of its population, declines markedly with increasing city size. At the same time, although the volume of traffic entering the CBD in relation to total population is much less in large cities than in small, the density of vehicles per unit area of the CBD—and presumably the traffic congestion there—is greater in the large cities. Translating these relationships into volume of one particular type of activity, we see in Table 5 that although the absolute volume of retail trade carried on in the CBD of a large city is

ness sections. The congestion is only partially overcome by the large city's greater reliance on mass transportation: One study showed that 50 per cent of all vehicular trips in cities of 1,000,000 inhabitants or more were made by mass transit (streetcars, busses, subways, and the like), as compared with 23 per cent in cities of 50,000 to 100,000.[12] In large cities, although incomes are higher, ownership of automobiles is typically less frequent. According to a 1959 national survey, automobiles were not

[12] Frank B. Curran and Joseph T. Stegmaier, "Travel Patterns in 50 Cities," *Public Roads*, XXX (December, 1958), 105–21.

owned by 45 per cent of the households in metropolitan area centers of 500,000 inhabitants or more, as compared with only 19 per cent in smaller metropolitan centers, 13 per cent in metropolitan suburbs, and 26 per cent in urban and rural non-farm territory outside metropolitan areas.[13] Cities like Los Angeles, the bulk of whose growth has occurred during the automobile age, are exceptions, of course, as they are to the general correlation of city size and density. But such cities have compensating prob-

power, which is equal to the size of population multiplied by per capita disposable income. Neglecting income differences until the next section, we observe that a community with a large population constitutes a large local market for the sale of goods. The market for many kinds of products is not limited to a single community, of course. It may be national, as for a brand of clothing, or international, as for a cigarette or a beverage. For nearly all consumer goods, however, there must be

TABLE 5

RETAIL SALES IN CENTRAL BUSINESS DISTRICTS OF STANDARD
METROPOLITAN AREAS, BY SIZE OF SMA, 1954

SIZE OF SMA[1]	NUMBER OF SMA's[2]	PER CAPITA[1] SALES[3] (DOLLARS)		CBD AS PER CENT OF SMA
		CBD	SMA	
3,000,000 or more........	5/5	182	1,270	14.3
1,000,000 to 3,000,000...	9/9	215	1,214	17.7
500,000 to 1,000,000.....	14/19	316	1,299	24.3
300,000 to 500,000.......	20/23	307	1,277	24.1
100,000 to 300,000.......	34/95	407	1,258	32.3

[1] Based on *1950 Census of Population.*
[2] Number of SMA's for which CBD data are given in relation to total number of SMA's in size group.
[3] Excludes sales of non-store retailers (mail order, direct selling, vending machine); in SMA's with more than one CBD, sales of all CBD's are included.
SOURCE: United States Bureau of the Census, *1954 Census of Business,* Vol. I (Washington: Government Printing Office, 1957), Table 6 L.

lems of lengthy journeys to work, traffic management, and control of the smog generated from the exhaust of automobiles. The experience of such cities suggests that not all the advantages of high personal mobility, spacious residential neighborhoods, accessibility, and freedom from congestion and its effects can be realized simultaneously in a city grown large in population size.

THE RELATION OF POPULATION NUMBERS
TO MARKETS

The size of a market is measured in terms of the volume of purchasing

[13] *Automobile Facts and Figures,* 1959–60 edition (Detroit: Automobile Manufacturers Association, Inc.), pp. 34–35.

a local distributor. Distributors of an article so commonly used and of such a low price as, say, soap will be found in all communities regardless of size. But a village of 1,000 could not support a store which sold only pianos. Not many homes in a city have pianos; hence for a dealer to sell pianos largely to a local market he must locate in a large city. A person living in a small place must therefore buy from the dealer in a large city or directly from the factory either after a visit or by mail. Herein lies the attraction of large cities for the merchant. They present him with a larger market than he would have in a small city. There is competition, of course, but competition exists in the small city too.

There are many goods like pianos for which there are not enough buyers in a small community to make up a market. Hence we can forecast from the principle of the relation of population size to markets that large cities will have a great variety of specialty shops selling such infrequently bought goods as rare coins, old guns and swords, and artists' materials. Not all such goods need be sold in a shop dealing in these goods exclusively. A single store may sell a variety of goods each one of which is purchased infrequently. This is true of the modern department store, which may stock collectors' items or period furniture along with staple commodities.

This same relationship of size of city to markets applies to services and to the sale of goods used by manufacturers. Highly specialized services to individuals and families can be found in big cities that could not be rendered profitably in small places, such as animal hospitals, dental surgeons, and maritime lawyers. There are similarly specialized services for manufacturers, for example, various repair businesses.

Manufacturers likewise purchase from other manufacturers various specialties such as parts which it is not profitable for them to produce for themselves. There are many such small manufacturers supplying these specialties. Thus, although manufacturers are sometimes thought of as purchasers of raw materials, they also purchase parts and therefore constitute a local market, just as do families. Even though they may buy from suppliers in other cities it may be more convenient to trade with local manufacturers. So the idea that a big city is the most suitable place to locate outlets for specialty goods applies to manufacturers' as well as to consumers' markets, though perhaps not so extensively.

The search for systematic data bearing on this argument is handicapped in sev-

eral ways. First, very little information is published on the areal extent of the markets for various products and services. Second, census tabulations of retail sales and service trades pertain to the operations of establishments, which may have many merchandise lines or types of service. Although these data are instructive in regard to the sort of establishment specialization that is associated with city size,[14] they do not indicate directly just which items are and are not available in different sized places. For example, even though camera and photographic supply stores are rarely found in places smaller than 25,000 or 50,0000 inhabitants, the amateur photographer can get at least the most essential supplies in so-called drug stores in the smallest towns. Finally, even the kind-of-business classifications of tables showing establishments by city size are rather broad. Understandably, the census does not provide a level of detail in these tables such that most of the entries in the columns for small places would be ciphers.

The sort of rough estimates for which census data on kinds of business are suited is illustrated in Table 6, which shows the size of city at which the respective kinds of business service establishments become frequent enough for each city to have at least one. Private detective agencies, for example, are found rather rarely in cities with fewer than 50,000 inhabitants. A similar set of estimates for selected medical specialties, though based on out-of-date information, likewise illustrates that the market becomes large enough to sustain certain highly specialized activities only as population increases to 50,000 or 100,000 or even larger. The reader may perhaps be impressed with how many specialties are widely available in cities no larger than 100,000, but he should keep in mind the fact that specialties represented by ex-

[14] Otis Dudley Duncan, "Urbanization and Retail Specialization," *Social Forces*, XXX (March, 1952), 267–71.

ceedingly small numbers of establishments or practitioners are unlikely to be
presented in statistical tables with a
cross-classification by city size.

THE RELATION OF CONSUMER INCOME
TO MARKETS

Industries that must locate near consumers—notably retail trade and the per-

This difference has persisted through a
decade in which money incomes have
risen markedly in the population as a
whole. Similar differences were observed
in the years before World War II.[15] Although the educational attainment of the
labor force and its occupational distribution are more favorable to high incomes in large cities than in small, it ap-

TABLE 6

CRITICAL CITY SIZE FOR SELECTED MEDICAL SPECIALTIES AND BUSINESS SERVICES

Critical City Size[1]	Medical Specialties, 1931[2]	Business Services, 1954[3]

10,000 to 25,000.......	Eye, ear, nose and throat	Advertising agencies
		Duplicating, addressing, mailing,
		    stenographic services
		Window cleaning
		Disinfecting, exterminating
		Miscellaneous services to dwellings
		    and other buildings
		Consumer and mercantile credit; ad-
		    justment and collection agencies

25,000 to 50,000.......	Internal medicine Surgery	Outdoor advertising services Private employment agencies Telephone answering service Photofinishing laboratories Interior decorating service Sign-painting shops
50,000 to 100,000......	Pediatrics Obstetrics and gynecology Urology Roentgenology	Detective agencies Blueprinting, photocopying services Window display service

100,000 to 250,000....	Neurology and psychiatry
	Public health
	Dermatology
	Orthopedic surgery
		Coin-operated machine rental and re-
		    pair services
		Auctioneers' establishments (service
		    only)

250,000 to 500,000.....	....	News syndicates

[1] Interval in which number of medical specialists or service establishments first reaches one per city.
[2] Based on R. G. Leland, *Distribution of Physicians in the United States*, rev. ed. (Chicago: American Medical Association, 1936), Table 42.
[3] Taken from Otis Dudley Duncan, "Service Industries and the Urban Hierarchy," *Papers and Proceedings of the Regional Science Association*, V (1959), 105–20.

sonal and professional services—will pros-
per or languish according to variation in
consumer purchasing power. In considering the relation of population numbers
to markets, we should take into account
the consumer income of the population.
Hence considerable importance attaches
to the fact that the income level of the
average family is positively related to
city size. Table 7 shows that in recent
years the largest cities have had median
family incomes more than one-fifth greater than those of small cities and towns.

pears that these factors are not sufficient
to account for the city-size differential.[16]
Residents of large cities, therefore, should
enjoy higher levels of living and create a
higher level of effective demand than
those of smaller places.

The advantage of the large cities in regard to money incomes may be illusory,
however, if it costs a great deal more to

[15] Ogburn, *Social Characteristics of Cities*, pp.
4–5.

[16] Duncan and Reiss, *Social Characteristics of
Urban and Rural Communities, 1950*, pp. 105–6.

live in these cities. It is difficult to be sure that this is the case. Prices of many items, like standard brands of consumer durables, canned foods, and nationally marketed lines of clothing, may not differ greatly by community size. Average rentals per dwelling unit, however, are higher in large cities than in small towns, and other costs may well vary in the same way. The usual cost-of-living indexes are not designed to permit valid comparisons among city-size groups. An indirect indication of differences in the cost of living, however, may be obtained by comparing percentages of the budget spent for food.[17] From the work of Ernst Engel and many subsequent investigators we know that as family income increases the percentage spent for food decreases. This generalization applies to families living in the same locality at the same time. Temporal differences do not concern us here, but the factor of locality is the one at issue. Now, if families of the same size, having the same income, spend more for food in City A than in City B, it is either because food costs less in City B, or because items other than food offer greater competition for a share of the budget in City B than in City A. We have no reason to suppose that the latter condition holds as between small (B) and large (A) cities in the United States; indeed, presumably the reverse is true, if anything.

Consumer expenditure data collected in 1956[18] showed that, in central cities of metropolitan areas containing a central city of 500,000 inhabitants or more, 31 per cent of annual household expenditures were for food, beverages, and tobacco. In central cities of smaller metro-

[17] See William F. Ogburn, "Does It Cost Less To Live in the South?" *Social Forces*, XIV (December, 1935), 211–14; an elaboration of the method is given by Eleanor M. Snyder, "Measuring Comparable Living Costs in Cities of Diverse Characteristics," *Monthly Labor Review*, LXXIX (October, 1956), 1187–90.

[18] *Life Study of Consumer Expenditures* (Time, Inc., 1957), p. 35.

politan areas the percentage was 29, as it was likewise in non-metropolitan urban places. Since the large metropolitan areas had the higher average incomes, presumably the difference would be greater if the comparison involved families at the same levels of income.

Data from the 1935–36 Consumer Purchases Study permit a summary comparison with income held constant.[19] In each of twelve income classes the ratios of average outlay per family for food in mid-

TABLE 7

MEDIAN FAMILY INCOME, BY SIZE OF PLACE, FOR THE UNITED STATES, 1947, 1951, AND 1955–58

Size of Place[1]	1947	1951	1955–58[2]
United States..........	$3,031	$3,709	$4,816
1,000,000 and over.....	3,826	4,334	5,700
250,000 to 1,000,000...	3,430	4,382	5,270
50,000 to 250,000......	3,291	4,021	5,099
2,500 to 50,000........	3,119	3,583	4,624
Rural non-farm........	2,826	3,365	4,722
Rural farm.............	1,963	2,131	2,430

[1] For 1947 classification applies to urban places, size classification being based on 1940 Census; for later years, first three size classes refer to urbanized areas, while places of 2,500 to 50,000 are urban places outside urbanized areas (a few of which exceed 50,000 in population), size classification being based on the 1950 Census.

[2] Average of annual medians for the four years.
SOURCE: United States Bureau of the Census, *Current Population Reports*, Series P–60, *Consumer Income*, Nos. 5, 12, 24, 27, 30, and 33.

dle-sized cities, large cities, and metropolises to that in small cities were calculated, and these ratios were averaged with a constant set of weights, the income distribution of all urban non-relief families. On this basis, it was found that food outlays were 1.8 per cent higher in middle-sized (25,000 to 100,000) than in small (2,500 to 25,000) cities; they were 5.5 per cent higher in large (100,000 to 1,500,000) than in small cities; and they were 32.7 per cent higher in metropolises

[19] United States National Resources Planning Board, *Family Expenditures in the United States: Statistical Tables and Appendixes* (Washington, D.C.: Government Printing Office, 1941), Tables 195, 197, 199, 201, 362.

(New York, Chicago, Philadelphia, and Detroit) than in small cities. In these comparisons, although income is controlled, family size is not. But differences in average family size could affect the comparisons only slightly.

A still more refined basis of comparison is afforded by the 1951 study of consumer expenditures by the Bureau of Labor Statistics. The tables show average weekly expenditures for food purchased in stores to be prepared at home by housekeeping families.[20] The families are grouped into five size classes and nine income classes. There are, therefore, 45 possible comparisons between the aggregate of cities of 50,000 inhabitants or more (central cities of metropolitan areas) and cities of fewer than 50,000, exclusive of metropolitan suburbs. The data are also subdivided by regions, North, South, and West, so that 135 city-size comparisons within regions are theoretically possible, although with data missing in a few cells, the actual number is 126. Of these, 94 show the greater expenditure for food to be in the larger cities. With this many comparisons, to have three-fourths of them in one direction would be almost impossible if there were no true difference and the variations in the data were due solely to chance.

There seems to be little question, therefore, that living costs are somewhat higher in large places than in small towns. It may be, however, that most of the contrast is due to the very largest cities. In any event, we lack sufficient information to construct a statistical deflator that would convert money income into "real" income, making allowance for the cost of living. It is perhaps doubtful that such a deflator, if available, would wholly remove the positive correlation of income with city size.[21]

In focusing, as we have thus far, on the income level of the average family, we have neglected a point of considerable significance, i.e., the relation of community size to the number and proportion of consumers with very high incomes. The rich spend their money differently from the poor, making smaller percentage outlays for food, heat, light, and other such essentials, and larger percentage outlays for luxuries and high-quality items. The market for many products and services is virtually limited to the well-to-do, and many of these more expensive purchases are thought to represent cultural excellence—higher priced paintings, symphonies with the best paid musicians and conductors, magnificent jewelry, and fine restaurants, for example—although the rich also spend money on things that are not contributions to culture.

Wealthy families, of course, constitute but a small fraction of the total. In the United States, during the years 1955–58, families with incomes of $25,000 per annum were but 0.5 per cent, or one out of two hundred, of all families. If the same proportion held in all communities, a town of 10,000 inhabitants, or roughly 3,000 families, would include only 15 wealthy families; a city of 100,000 would include 150; and a city of 1,000,000 would include 1,500, an appreciable concentration, sufficient to support a good many markets specialized to satisfy the demand for luxuries. Actually, according to census data, in the very large cities the proportion of wealthy families is about twice as large as it is in small towns, which, in this respect, are typical of the country as a whole. The effect we are discussing is, therefore, disproportionately related to city size. Taking a somewhat more liberal definition of af-

[20] United States Bureau of Labor Statistics, *Study of Consumer Expenditures, Incomes and Savings*, Vol. XII, *Detailed Family Expenditures for Food, Beverages and Tobacco* (Philadelphia: University of Pennsylvania, 1957), Table 3, Part 4.

[21] This conclusion is supported by cost-of-living differentials reported in Margaret Loomis Stecker, *Intercity Differences in Costs of Living in March 1935, 59 Cities* (Washington, D.C.: WPA preliminary report, mimeographed, 1937), Table 63.

fluence, we note that estimates of the proportion of families with incomes exceeding $10,000 for the years 1955–58 averaged 13.7 per cent for urbanized areas of 1,000,000 population or more, 9.6 per cent for urbanized areas of 250,000 to 1,000,000, 7.3 per cent for urbanized areas of 50,000 to 250,000, 7.7 per cent for urban places of 25,000 or more outside urbanized areas, and only 5.8 per cent for urban places of 2,500 to 25,000.[22]

A considerable number of the phenomena considered unique or distinctive to large cities are no doubt due to their concentration of disproportionate numbers of families with exceptional means. By the same token, the markets of large cities have relatively more attraction for the rich than for the poor, as compared with those of smaller places. There are exceptions, of course. Large cities may offer to the general public such advantages as free summer concerts, museums with nominal admissions charges, and large libraries. Upon examination, however, even some of these facilities available to all will be found to depend for their support on local concentrations of wealth and income.

THE RELATION OF POPULATION SIZE
TO EXTREME DEVIATIONS

The larger the city the more likely it is to include within its population extreme deviations from the normal or average. If a person of extreme stature or one with a rare disease occurs once in 100,000 times, then the chances of finding such a person in a city of 1,000,000 people are much greater than in a city of 10,000 (though not, of course, than in some one of 100 cities of 10,000). Although the model of sampling with equal probabilities illustrates the principle, it is important to recognize also that the probabilities often are not equal.

[22] United States Bureau of the Census, *Current Population Reports*, Series P-60, Consumer Income, Nos. 5, 12, 24, 27, 30, and 33.

Thus we have seen that large cities have many more families with very high incomes than would be expected if such families were randomly distributed among communities. The New York metropolitan district was the residence of one-third of the persons listed in *Who's Who in American Art* (Vol. III, 1940–41) with urban or metropolitan residences, or two and one-half times as many eminent artists as would be expected on the basis of its population size. The same metropolis around 1940–42 claimed three or four times as many prominent writers as one would expect on the basis of constant probabilities.

The tendency of phenomena to occur in clusters, therefore, adds to the likelihood that large cities will be the locus of the unusual. The followers of an infrequent occupation, such as scholars, family caseworkers, oboe players, or pickpockets are likely to have some knowledge of or contact with others in the same occupation. There may be appraisals of each other's work, emulation or competition for priority. Organized or informal contacts and response to the same salient stimuli are made possible by living in proximity in the relatively small area covered by a city of several hundreds of thousands of people.

The role of many extreme types is to serve highly specialized markets. Thus there may be more demand for art works in large metropolitan areas than elsewhere. It is not clear that this would account for the aggregation of writers in and around New York. Perhaps they enjoy certain advantages from proximity to many leading publishers.

The phenomenon being described applies not only to unusual individuals but also to deviant groups. One illustration is afforded by sectarian religious groups. In the last *Census of Religious Bodies*, taken in 1936, some 256 individual denominations were recognized, of which 243 had one or more local churches in urban areas. Only 20 of these denominations had as many as 1,000 urban churches and in the aggregate this small number of denominations accounted for very nearly three-fourths of all urban churches and almost exactly nine-tenths of all urban church members reported in the census. The remaining denominations, then, can be considered "deviant"

TABLE 8

AVERAGE NUMBER OF RELIGIOUS DENOMINA-
TIONS IN CITIES OF THE EAST NORTH CEN-
TRAL DIVISION, BY SIZE OF CITY, 1936

Size of City	Number of Cities[1]	Mean Number of Denominations
1,000,000 or more.......	2	103
500,000 to 1,000,000....	2	69
250,000 to 500,000.....	4	57
100,000 to 250,000......	9	46
50,000 to 100,000.......	11	33
25,000 to 50,000........	38	24

[1] Excludes suburbs of metropolitan centers and cities specializing in functions other than manufacturing and trade. The East North Central division includes the States of Illinois, Indiana, Michigan, Ohio, and Wisconsin.
SOURCE: United States Bureau of the Census, *Religious Bodies: 1936*, Vol. I, *Summary and Detailed Tables* (Washington: Government Printing Office, 1941), Table 13.

in that they attract, singly and collectively, only a very small proportion of the population. Even a small town may have a few such deviant denominations. Table 8 shows, however, that places of 25,000 to 50,000 inhabitants have only a few more denominations than 20, while the number of denominations rises markedly with increasing city size. In a city of 2 or 3 million inhabitants, where there are over 100 different denominations, at least 80 of them must be deviants in the sense specified above. Hence there is quite a variety of unusual religions practiced by congregations in large cities.

CITY SIZE AND SOCIAL CHANGE

The principle that an extreme deviation is more likely in a large city than in a small one implies that innovations are more probable or more frequent in the former. An innovation, when it ap-

pears, though not after it becomes accepted, is a departure from the usual or the expected. Geographic differentials in the occurrence of contributions to American culture have been studied by Edward Rose on the basis of compilations of *Famous First Facts* by J. N. Kane. Although the principles on which such compilations are made are obscure and the coverage is uncertain, the ratios derived from Rose's tables which are shown in Table 9 illustrate the principle. Here the association of per capita incidence of innovation with city size may appear somewhat tenuous. Although the figure for New York is strikingly high, the rank correlation of innovations per 100,000 population with population size is only 0.17 for the 25 largest cities in 1930 (those with populations in excess of 300,000). But even if the ratio of innovations to population is a constant, a small city or town cannot expect to witness one more often than once in a

TABLE 9

INCIDENCE OF INNOVATIONS, 1900–1935,
BY CITY SIZE

City Size (1930)	Innovations per 100,000 Population	Innovations per City
New York............	2.1	146
1 to 5 million.........	0.7	14
500,000 to 1,000,000...	1.4	10
300,000 to 500,000.....	1.3	5
(Excluding Washington, D.C.).........	(0.8)	(3)
Other urban[1]..........	0.7	Under 1

[1] Computed on the assumption that all innovations are associated with urban places. If some are rural or not geographically localized, the ratio should be reduced.
SOURCE: Edward Rose, "Innovations in American Culture," *Social Forces*, XXVI (March, 1948), 255–72, Tables 1 and 5.

generation, while in the larger places, even apart from New York, innovations may come along once every two or three years on the average. Of the total of 660 innovations recorded for the period 1900–1935, slightly over half occurred in the 25 cities with populations of 300,000 or more in 1930.

To consider a class of rather less spectacular innovations, Table 10 relates the number of persons to whom patents on inventions are granted to the population of their places of residence. Metropolitan units rather than political cities were used for the larger places, because it was found that patentees have a tendency to live in suburbs of large central cities. Patents, of course, are usually granted on quite minor changes, many of which never achieve practical use. Whatever the importance of patented inventions may be as a source of change, the patentees are concentrated in the largest cities, relative to population, as is shown by indexes over 100 for the cities of 1,000,000 or more inhabitants in Table 10. Manifestly, the number of patentees per city must be far higher in the large places than in the small ones.

Innovations that are useful spread beyond the locality where they originate, sometimes indeed all over the world. The place of origin may then be called the center of dispersal, on the supposition that the spread may be in all directions with, of course, some time lag. This point of origin, typically in large communities, and the dispersal from cities are of great importance in an explanation of progress. Civilization grows and changes for the better (if it does) by virtue of desirable inventions and innovations. From this it follows that large cities are important sources of progress. To be sure, if the new is harmful, cities to that extent are obstacles to progress. The greater prevalence of writers, artists, inventors, and persons noted for achievement in great cities illustrates how gains to civilization originate in and emanate from them.

It is a significant question how far the city's prominence as an originating and dispersing center is due to a psychological tolerance of or hospitality to the new on the part of its inhabitants. It is argued that in a small community nearly everyone knows everyone else and much

of what everyone does is public knowledge. This cannot be true of the large city where a person can have privacy, isolating himself and acting anonymously. There is supposed to be a greater intolerance of eccentricity—at least of certain kinds—in small places, while in great cities where anonymity is easily attained there is a potential freedom of action not as easily restrained by the law and the police as by the intense and informal social pressure found in small communities. On this argument, there should be greater tolerance of the new,

TABLE 10

INDEX NUMBERS OF RATIOS OF INVENTIONS TO POPULATION, BY SIZE OF PLACE, 1940

Size of Place	Index[1]
Total metropolitan and urban........	100
Metropolitan districts:	
2,000,000 or more.................	130
1,000,000 to 2,000,000...........	110
250,000 to 1,000,000.............	101
50,000 to 250,000................	77
Non-metropolitan urban places:	
25,000 to 50,000.................	97
5,000 to 25,000..................	69
2,500 to 5,000...................	34

[1] Based on random sample of 554 patentees listed in U.S. Patent Office, *Index of Patents, 1940* (Washington: Government Printing Office, 1941), pp. 7–795, 879–1219. Index is obtained by dividing the percentage of inventors with residences in places of the specified size by that size group's percentage of the whole population, and multiplying the result by 100.

which is of course different, and of the innovator in large cities, and a greater acceptance of innovations there.

Some support for this line of argument may be found in the results of a public opinion study conducted in 1954. Stouffer classified a national sample of respondents on the basis of a "15-item scale of willingness to tolerate nonconformists." He reports that the proportion of the sample classified as "more tolerant" varied from 39 per cent in metropolitan areas, 30 per cent in other cities (under 100,000), and 25 per cent in small towns (under 2,500), to 18 per cent among the farm population.[23]

[23] Samuel A. Stouffer, *Communism, Conformity, and Civil Liberties* (Garden City: Doubleday & Co., 1955), p. 112.

It may be, however, that economic forces, quite apart from feelings of acceptance or rejection of change, are responsible for many important innovations associated with great cities. The concentration of trade gave rise to a need for new financial institutions, like investment banks and stock markets. Inventors may be more successful if they size of community, is roughly sketched out by the curves in Figure 1. Both radio and television audiences grew faster in large places in the initial years. As time went by and as the larger areas approached saturation, the smaller places, followed by rural areas, caught up with them. The technological characteristics and the economics of the in-

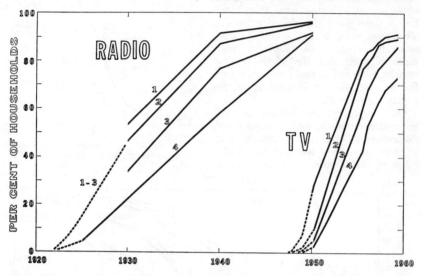

Fig. 1.—Per cent of households with radio sets and per cent with television sets, for the United States, by place of residence, 1922–59. (Place of residence code, for radio: 1 = cities of 100,000 inhabitants or more; 2 = urban places of 2,500 to 100,000 inhabitants; 3 = rural non-farm; 4 = rural farm [residence classification as of the current census]; for television: 1 = urbanized areas of 1,000,000 inhabitants or more; 2 = urbanized areas of 50,000 to 1,000,000 inhabitants; 3 = urban and rural non-farm, outside urbanized areas; 4 = rural farm [residence classification as of 1950 census]. Dashed lines represent rough estimates, controlled by national data on numbers of sets.) SOURCE: 1925 Census of Agriculture; 1930, 1940, and 1950 Census of Population and Housing; Bureau of the Census, *Housing and Construction Reports*, Series H-121, Nos. 1–6.

have large accumulations of capital with which to finance the pursuit of their ideas. There is possibly an acceleration principle as well. The more novelties that are accepted by a community, the less the resistance. As more innovations occur because of the favorable milieu of cities—whatever may be its cause—the greater is the readiness to welcome them.

The pattern of acceptance and spread of two major inventions, in relation to vention are, of course, relevant to its pattern of spread. For example, some rural areas are beyond the range of television broadcasting and may, therefore, reach saturation at a level lower than that of urban areas.

The general pattern of the diffusion process suggested by the radio and television data is sketched in Figure 2. It is supposed that the process is initiated in large cities, that the smaller places are involved at a later date, and rural areas at a still later date. (The precise timing is not specified, and could be expected to be highly variable.) If diffusion proceeds at even roughly similar rates in places of differing size, then the relative levels at any point in time, short of the attainment of saturation, will be a function of the timing of initiation. Hence the diagram suggests that large cities are at a higher level than small towns throughout the diffusion period. The time scale is not specified here, since the contrast of television with radio suggests that the whole process may be more or less rapid, depending on factors not taken into account in the present hypothesis.

One important implication of this schematic model is that cross-sectional differences in level, i.e., comparisons at a given point in time, will reflect the stage of the diffusion process. Thus at Time A and Time C the absolute difference between large and small urban places is not great, while at Time B it is considerable. This difference, moreover, will follow a predictable pattern of initial increase followed by subse-

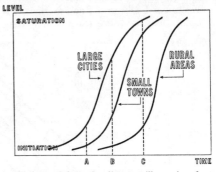
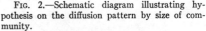

Fig. 2.—Schematic diagram illustrating hypothesis on the diffusion pattern by size of community.

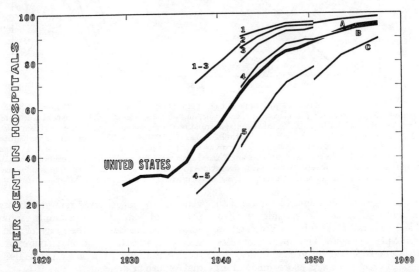

Fig. 3.—Per cent of registered births occurring in hospitals, by place of residence of parents, for the United States, 1929–57. (Place of residence code, 1937–50: 1 = cities of 100,000 inhabitants or more; 2 = cities of 25,000 to 100,000 inhabitants; 3 = cities of 10,000 to 25,000 inhabitants; 4 = urban places, 2,500 to 10,000 inhabitants; 5 = rural; 1950–57: A = metropolitan county; B = non-metropolitan county, urban; C = non-metropolitan county, rural. [For 1937–39, place of residence classification as of 1930; for 1940–49, as of 1940; for 1950–57, as of 1950.]) Source: National figures for 1929–36 are based on data collected by the American Medical Association; for remaining years, data are from annual volumes, *Vital Statistics of the United States*, issued by the Bureau of the Census and the National Office of Vital Statistics.

quent decrease. For example, the difference in level between small towns and rural areas increases from Time A to Time C, but contracts thereafter. This pattern of divergence followed by convergence is plain in the actual data shown in Figure 1. Thus in the television series the convergence of the first two size groups began early (although lack of data for the period 1950–55 makes it impossible to date the beginning of the convergence precisely), while the convergence of the second and third groups has been more recent.

In making comparisons among communities grouped by size, where it is so often true that we have data for only one point in time—usually a census date —it is, therefore, important to consider whether the variable under study is one reflecting or affected by a diffusion process. If this is the case, then extrapolations of the differences by community size, either forward or backward in time, should ordinarily allow for some eventual convergence if not complete disappearance of the differences. Assumptions about the rapidity of the diffusion process may be of use in estimating how long the community-size differences have persisted, or how long they may be expected to continue.

A final illustration suggests that the applicability of the diffusion model may be broader than the field of consumer acceptance of technological inventions. In examining the proportion of births occurring in hospitals, Figure 3, we see that a field of medical practice has been revolutionized in at least one of its structural aspects in the course of a generation.[24] Around 1930 about one-fourth of all births took place in hospitals while by 1957 the proportion was 95 per cent for the country as a whole.

[24] A more detailed analysis of this trend is being carried out by Donnell M. Pappenfort in a dissertation project at the Population Research and Training Center, University of Chicago. Mr. Pappenfort's assistance in compiling the data in Figure 3 is gratefully acknowledged.

Unfortunately, the record, particularly the detail by size of community, is fragmentary. But this provides an opportunity to illustrate the idea of retrospective extrapolations. At the time the data became available by size of community, the level for the country as a whole was approaching 50 per cent. It seems likely that this roughly coincided with the maximum difference between urban and rural areas or between the very large and the very small cities. If we imagine the curves pushed backward in time, the level for the United States would almost certainly be lower, and the urban and rural curves would come closer together. If we went as far back as the latter part of the nineteenth century, hospitalization of births, practiced mainly for the urban indigent and dependent classes, would perhaps be no higher than 10 per cent for the largest cities and even lower for other communities. The size-of-place differences at that time would have been slight, as they have become recently, with the process nearing saturation.

CONCLUSION

In summary, although frequent contacts and forces of cultural standardization may cause many differences between large and small cities to diminish or disappear, there seem to be certain theoretical reasons for expecting some kinds of city-size differences to persist. We have suggested that these have to do with the relation of population to area, the relation of population size to markets and to income, the relation of the occurrence of extreme deviations to size of population, and the conditions of social interaction that seem to make large cities often the leaders in social change. There are probably other such kinds of principles, of course, and those enumerated here are by no means unrelated one to the other.

This further consideration of city size as a sociological variable provides no reason to alter the conclusion of an earlier discussion of optimum city size that the advantages do not all lie in one direction. For the individual citizen or family, good reasons may be found for preferring either large or small cities. From the viewpoint of community and national welfare, there is cause to applaud as well as deplore the concentration of population in large cities. Whatever the ends of social policy, however —and the problem of urban vulnerability to modern techniques of war seems hardly less urgent than when this research was begun—we need an understanding of the reasons for population concentration, the factors producing important differences among cities varying in size, and the forces producing change in population distribution, if we are to make intelligent attempts to realize those ends.

4. *Analysis of Variance Procedures in the Study of Ecological Phenomena**

NATHAN KEYFITZ

Statistical theory applies probability to the drawing of conclusions from numerical data. It permits the application of a principle of economy or efficiency, which is the collecting of the minimum data for estimates of required precision. The analysis of variance is a device developed by the use of statistical theory, applicable to four general problems which arise in social science, and whose discussion will constitute this chapter.

Sample Surveys and Their Over-all Error of Estimate

Without knowledge of the error to which an estimate made from a survey is subject one cannot make proper use of the survey. Any assertion of the kind: "Unemployment stands at 6 per cent," is almost certainly wrong; without sampling theory one cannot say by how much. With a properly executed sample one can say, for example, that "Unemployment is between 5.6 per cent and 6.4 per cent," and that on the average 19 out of 20 such assertions will be correct.

Analysis of Survey Error

The second application is to break down this total survey error to find what portion of it arises in the several parts of the sample. Whereas the error of the

* This paper is an extension of ideas originally proposed in the author's Ph.D. thesis, "Urban Influence on Farm Family Size," Sociology, 1952. A portion of the thesis materials was published as "A Factorial Arrangement of Comparisons of Family Size," *American Journal of Sociology,* LVIII (March, 1953), 470–79.

over-all total is primarily of interest to users of the data, its breakdown is of special interest to data producers who in a continuing survey can apply it to re-allocate their sampling effort in such a way as to increase its efficiency. The breakdown may be among strata, stages, phases, or other parts of the sampling operation. The special advantage of variance, as against other possible measures of error, is that wherever the sources of error are independent, the sum of their variances is the variance of their sum. This fact is also helpful for one aspect of ecological description, the degree to which people resemble their neighbors; this is both of substantive interest and an aid in the design of efficient cluster samples.

Experiments Incorporated in Surveys

It is possible to incorporate experiments in a survey which is to be carried out in any case, often at trifling additional cost. If a family expenditure survey is to be undertaken, one would like to know in what degree its results will depend on whether interviewers collect information by (a) persuading respondents to keep a diary for the coming year, or (b) waiting until the end of the year and then asking respondents to recall their expenditures for the past twelve months. These two methods may be thought of as "treatments" in the language of experimental design, and if they are used in portions of the sample chosen at random precise inferences on causation can be drawn; it is possible to say how much difference in the results is due to the difference in methods of data collection. Such randomization is possible for all survey variables which are at the disposal of the survey authorities, but only to those; such variables as smoking and not smoking cigarettes are not likely to be at their disposal.

Non-randomized Contrasts

Contrasts which cannot be allocated at random include most of those with which sociology deals. But analysis of variance procedures permit precise inference on differences, if not on causes, to be drawn on a small sample; the advantage of this application of analysis of variance is to permit a degree of cross-classification (most useful for holding known extraneous variables constant) that would be impracticable to ask for on the complete tabulations of a large census. The example of this given below is part of a study of differential fertility.

It will not be possible here to develop the statistical theory for these four types of application. In presenting the first one I shall suggest the sort of thinking that has been found useful. For its further pursuit the sociologist has excellent books by Cochran, Deming, Hansen, Hurwitz, and Madow, Stephan and Mc-Carthy, Sukhatme, and Yates.[1]

SAMPLE SURVEYS AND THEIR OVER-ALL ERRORS OF ESTIMATE

Finite and Infinite Populations

Sampling theory shows how samples can provide inferences on populations, inferences which are exact in the sense that the uncertainty attaching to them is calculable. Applications in sociology often concern the making of inferences on finite rather than infinite populations. The unemployed persons in the community at the moment, the atoms in the universe, the persons in a city block, are finite populations. To estimate the differences between an interview survey and a recall survey for family expendi-tures is to work with an infinite population, or at least a situation for which the infinite population model is preferable. To use the finite population model is to play down, though one can never eliminate, the consideration of forms of distribution whose explicit discussion makes up much of the algebraically difficult part of statistics.

In our kind of sampling a number of persons are selected for interview from a large (but countable and listable) population of a country or city; the variability of persons—the degree in which they differ in their answers—in the parent population is estimated from the sample; consideration of the distribution of means of all possible samples which could be drawn in the same way as the one actually obtained (still a finite number) shows that such means have a variance inversely proportional to the sample size; unless the sample is small and the population rather unusual in the shape of its distribution, these means are distributed very nearly in the bell-shaped distribution called "normal." If the variance of the parent population can be approximated by the variance of the sample, then the variance of the sample mean is immediately available with no further approximation; approximation does however re-enter in the use of the normal distribution to draw conclusions based on the variance of the distribution of means. All this can be expressed more simply with the aid of a few symbols.

1 W. G. Cochran, *Sampling Techniques* (New York: John Wiley & Sons, 1953); W. E. Deming, *Some Theory of Sampling* (New York: John Wiley & Sons, 1950); M. H. Hansen, W. N. Hurwitz, and W. G. Madow, *Sample Survey Methods and Theory* (New York: John Wiley & Sons, 1953, 2 vols.); F. F. Stephan and P. J. McCarthy, *Sampling Opinions: an Analysis of Survey Procedure* (New York: John Wiley & Sons, 1958); P. V. Sukhatme, *Sampling Theory of Surveys, with Applications* (Ames, Iowa: State College Press, 1954); Frank Yates, *Sampling Methods for Censuses and Surveys* (London: Charles Griffin, 1953).

Estimate of Variance of a Sample Mean Drawn from a Finite Population

To draw a sample of the human population of the United States to survey incomes, or number of children, or number of months since last purchase of a car, we *imagine* a complete census in which the answers are listed as

$$Y_1, Y_2, \ldots, Y_{180,000.000}$$

in the order in which the population might be enumerated. We propose to take a random 1000 persons, whose answers are

$$y_1, y_2, \ldots, y_{1000}$$

arranged according to the order in which the sample is drawn, so that y_1 is not Y_1, but one of the 180,000,000 Y's selected at random. For compactness and generality we write n for 1000 and N for 180,000,000.

A further mental construction is needed. We go on to imagine all the possible samples of n that could be drawn from the N members of the population, and the average, $\bar{y}$, of each. If N is 180,000,000 and n is 1000, there are 10^{5000} samples, a number too big to print on one page of this book. But great though the number of possible samples may be, it is easily handled mathematically; the

$$\bar{y} = \frac{y_1 + y_2 + \ldots + y_n}{n}$$

for all of them can be averaged by elementary considerations of permutations and combinations. The average $\bar{y}$ turns out to be equal to

$$\bar{Y} = \frac{Y_1 + Y_2 + \ldots + Y_N}{N},$$

the average of the population, and we say on the standard definition that $\bar{y}$ is an unbiased estimate of $\bar{Y}$.

But one is interested less in the average of all possible samples than in what the difference between the sample mean and the true mean Y is likely to be; after all, in practice only one sample will be taken. While no internal evidence will show the error of the unique sample which is drawn, it is possible to find from the sample itself a kind of average error of all similar samples. The average ordinarily used for this purpose is the mean square difference between sample mean and true mean, and it is this which is called the error variance; its square root is the standard error. The standard error describes the distribution of means of samples in exactly the same way that the standard deviation describes the distribution of individual members of the population. It turns out once again that all possible quantities $(\bar{y} - \bar{Y})^2$ are easily averaged, and the average $\sigma^2_{\bar{y}} = E(\bar{y} - \bar{Y})^2$ *is simply and exactly*

$$\frac{N-n}{N} \cdot \frac{1}{n} \cdot S^2,$$

where S^2 is the variance of the individual members of the population, increased by the ratio $N/N - 1$ to make the resulting formula simpler. The formula for S^2 is

$$\frac{(Y_1 - \bar{Y})^2 + \ldots + (Y_N - \bar{Y})^2}{N-1}.$$

If the sample size n is large, say a few hundred or more, and the population distribution not too irregular, then S^2 may be satisfactorily approximated by s^2, the same quantity calculated from the sample.

Inference from Variance of Sample Means

We have made two imaginary constructions, one being the listing of the members of the population and the other the drawing of all the possible samples from among which our one sample has been chosen at random. The third and final construction is in effect the fitting of a normal distribution to the means of the possible samples. If the fitting is appropriate, one-third of such means would come outside the range $\bar{Y} - \sigma_{\bar{y}}$ to $\bar{Y} + \sigma_{\bar{y}}$ and 1/20 would come outside the range $\bar{Y} - 2\sigma_{\bar{y}}$ to $\bar{Y} + 2\sigma_{\bar{y}}$.

We must choose that level of precision and security we are willing to pay for, and express this in terms of two entities drawn from the imagined distribution of sample means: (1) the width of the interval that constitutes our statement from the sample of what the population mean is, and (2) the fraction of instances in which we are willing that this statement be wrong. The interval can always be narrowed, or the fraction diminished, by taking a larger sample.

The statement resulting from the *actual* observation of $y_1, \ldots, y_n$ may then be put in two ways. For simplicity in this presentation only we assume that the s calculated from the sample gives us exactly the S of the population. The two ways of expressing the inference are:

(1) The several populations, that would give the result $\bar{y}$ we have actually obtained with probability greater than .05, have means $\bar{Y}$ ranging from $\bar{y} - 2\sigma_{\bar{y}}$ to $\bar{y} + 2\sigma_{\bar{y}}$. In other words, *either* the true population mean $\bar{Y}$ is between $\bar{y} - 2\sigma_{\bar{y}}$ and $\bar{y} + 2\sigma_{\bar{y}}$, *or* a freak event of probability less than one out of twenty has occurred.

(2) If we draw many samples from the same population of mean $\bar{Y}$ the way we have drawn our one example, and from each we make the statement "$\bar{Y}$ is between $\bar{y} - 2\sigma_{\bar{y}}$ and $\bar{y} + 2\sigma_{\bar{y}}$," then 95 per cent of these statements will be correct. That is, 95 per cent of the ranges $\bar{y} - 2\sigma_{\bar{y}}$ to $\bar{y} + 2\sigma_{\bar{y}}$ (the range now being a random variable) will straddle the true $\bar{Y}$.

Use of Auxiliary Data

The collection of data is costly; if it were free there would be no reason to sample. To further the aim of securing from the sample a result of given reliability at minimum cost one seeks outside data in the form of a preceding census or an earlier sample, or even local qualitative knowledge. The ingenuity of a statistician is shown by his ability to find such outside evidence and incorporate it as auxiliary data in his survey. Such incorporation must reduce variance, but it must do so without making the sample estimates subject to possible biases in the auxiliary data.

The largest part of the books on sampling is taken up with devices such as stratification and ratio and regression estimates. Thus with outside data a population may be divided into strata which can be separately sampled; estimates are then affected not by the total variance of the population but only by the variance within strata. Analysis of over-all variance into components between and within strata is a typical analysis of variance procedure. The auxiliary data need not be in numerical form for purposes of statification, and they may be entirely subjective; all that is necessary for their usefulness is that they be related to the variable which the sample survey is designed to estimate. If one has a hunch that the west side of a city has lower unemployment than the east side, he ought to stratify the sample by east and west.

Ratio estimates take advantage of the fact that ratios—say of income to rent in a survey to estimate income—may vary less from one household to another than the object of the survey—income—itself. In phase sampling one can even convert to precise use a large sample of simple guesses on the object of survey, by "calibrating" it with a small sample of objective measurements.

Non-Sampling Error

As in any application of mathematics to real events there remains a dark underworld not covered by theory, which in our case consists of problems of definition and other sources of what is called non-sampling error. These include in an interview survey the manner of phrasing of the question and the understanding of the question by the respondent. Sampling theory enables us to say what portion of the uncertainty in the conclusion arises from the fact that a sample only of the population was examined; all other uncertainty would apply equally to a complete census taken in the same way. Sampling theory specifies, for example, the limits within which the per cent of persons answering "yes" to the question whether or not they will vote in the next election would have fallen if all of the population rather than a sample were investigated; in principle it leaves the issue of whether the interviewees responded truthfully or not exactly where that issue would stand in a complete census.

In practice the sampling outlook has had an effect on non-sampling error as well. By drawing attention to the inevitability of error in surveys and showing the relation between precision and cost, it has brought errors of every kind into the forefront of the thought of those who design surveys. It has created a rational criterion for survey management in asserting that the reduction of the several kinds of errors should be pushed to the point where returns in accuracy from the last dollar of expenditure are equal. Rational management of the survey in the face of non-sampling error requires that the non-sampling error be measured, and all good survey design makes provision for such measurement.

Sampling for a Gradient

In ecological work it is often necessary to find a percentage or other figure for each of a large number of small areas, say census tracts. The object is to discern a gradient or other pattern of income or delinquency or other ecological variable. What precision is required for each area? The answer is sometimes given as though one were intending to use the figure for each census tract by itself, and discouragingly large samples appear to be necessary. If all one wants is to know the pattern, much smaller samples will suffice. This is especially applicable where there are clear gradients in population, and the object of the sample is to estimate the gradients. The size of sample needed to "perceive" a gradient along a line, say outward from the center of a city, is a simple application of the formula for variance of a regression coefficient.

Searching for an Ecological Pattern

How to deploy a sample depends on what ecological pattern one is looking for. A method of search which is efficient for disclosing one hidden pattern may be inefficient for another. If one has no intuitive notion whatever of the spatial distribution of the characteristic, a simple random sample scattered more or less evenly over the whole area of a city or country is all one can use. But even a very small item of advance knowledge will permit a large increase in efficiency. Suppose, for example, that one suspects that within a city there is a solid area in which family sizes are large, or a certain ethnic or occupational group is resident, and the problem is to determine its boundaries. The best way to apply a given total of sampling effort is to divide the effort into a number of parts. With the first part one would do a light sampling of the whole city and secure a rough outline of the boundary. The second part of the sampling effort would be applied within a band which the first sample indicated must straddle the boundary. This second effort would define the boundary more precisely and would provide a narrower band within which a third sample could be used. It is plain that if the phenomenon really occurs within a simply connected area, such a three-part procedure will secure its delineation more precisely than would a single sample of the same total size spread uniformly over the whole area. If the advance knowledge was wrong and the phenomenon under investigation really was not in a solid area but scattered throughout the city, then the first sample would have indicated this, and there would have been some inconvenience, i.e., inefficiency, but no misleading survey result. In this the present example is typical of all proper use of hunches in the design of surveys.

ANALYSIS OF SURVEY ERROR

The discussion above assumes that sample items in the given area have been chosen independently at random. In interview surveys the demands of efficiency suggest a further restriction on selection. Spatial distribution of the item under investigation must be taken into account if the survey contains an element of cost that depends on the dispersion of the sample in space. If people do not too closely resemble their neighbors in respect of the item under survey, then an efficient design is a selection of clusters of households, possibly with sub-sampling within the clusters. The U.S. and Canadian labor force samples include up to four successive sets of clusters, each "nested" within the preceding one.

In all such sampling, decisions must be made which depend on ecological factors. These decisions include the size of clusters which shall be used and the sampling ratios at each stage. Should one use counties, parts of counties, or groups of counties as the primary sampling unit (PSU)? Once the PSU's have been described, data on them secured from a preceding census and other sources which permit their classification into strata, and a random selection made, is it efficient to enumerate all of the persons within each one that is selected? Or is it preferable to select at random within each PSU a number of the enumeration areas of the preceding census, with or without stratification? In the stratification at any given stage, does it suffice simply to take a systematic sample after numbering in sequence back and forth across the map (in what Hansen, Hurwitz, and Madow call "serpentine" fashion), or does this geographic stratification fail to produce as much homogeneity within strata as the classification of units by other data which are available? Every statistician who designs a sample gives an implicit answer to such questions as these, and to many others. There would seem to be room for their more explicit discussion, especially with the accumulation of data both by population samplers and by ecologists.

The questions which those who design samples need to address to human ecologists will receive different answers, of course, according to the topic of survey. And insofar as a sample is to collect information on a variety of facts, the answers given by the ecologist which can be incorporated in the design will have to be correspondingly general. Nevertheless, in any survey some of the facts are more important than others, and should have corresponding weight in the determination of the design.

Leslie Kish[2] has assembled from the Detroit Area Studies of the University of Michigan Survey Research Center some material which is suitable for survey design and provides as well substantive results to human ecologists on the spatial distribution of a number of characteristics. His analysis of variance was between (a) Census Tracts, (b) Blocks, (c) Homes, and (d) Persons. In the 1957 data he found at one extreme that the variance for non-white households was 72 per cent between census tracts, and only 28 per cent within tracts. At the other extreme, for "being a native of Detroit," only 8 per cent

[2] Paper given at the 1959 meeting of the American Sociological Society.

of the variance was between tracts, and 92 per cent within tracts. The variance of voting Republican was distributed 11 per cent between tracts, 9 per cent among blocks within tracts, 54 per cent among homes within blocks, and 27 per cent among persons within homes. It would seem desirable to have available this information for other characteristics and for other cities; since every area sample gathers such data whatever its object, there must be a good deal in existence. The advantage of using it to replace intuition on the quantities is clear; and one sees a trend in this direction in the design of sample surveys.

EXPERIMENTS INCORPORATED IN SURVEYS

Two methods may be proposed for a survey in close competition with each other, each with its supporters; past large-scale surveys on the two methods may not have provided clear evidence about which is better because they were taken at different times and in different circumstances, and comparisons among their results confound irrelevant matters with the point on which a decision is needed. An example of competing methods in securing family budget data is the record kept by the respondent against recall in an interview.

When a small-scale test, however skilfully designed, will be subject to too much variance to make the necessary discrimination, and no argument that can be mustered by the proponents of one method convinces the opposition, consideration should be given to designing the survey itself so that it will incidentally produce a comparison of the two methods. To carry out a large survey half on one method and half on the other will presumably provide as sensitive a test as is needed of whether there is a difference due to methods. If statistically significant differences between the two halves do not appear it is proper to average the two halves. If a significant difference does appear, av-

eraging will still be permissible if the two results may be thought of as random members of a population of methods among which there is no ground for preference. In the event that one method is shown by the survey to be inaccurate (perhaps by comparison with known outside data on certain of its totals) and the other satisfactory, then half of the survey would be discarded and half used. While no one wants to throw away half of a survey, even in this most unfavorable case the use of two methods is an insurance against the total loss which would have occurred if only one method had been used throughout and it had been the wrong one. It also provides clear guidance for subsequent surveys.

Variance of Total

In a slight modification of the usual notation, a population $X_1 \ldots X_{2N}$ is considered, and from it the values of $2n$ members $x_1 \ldots x_{2n}$ are ascertained, where x_1, etc., are randomly chosen from $X_1 \ldots X_{2N}$. The total

$$\sum_1^{2N} X_i$$

is estimated by

$$\frac{2N}{2n} \sum_{i=1}^{2n} x_i, \qquad (1)$$

an estimate whose variance is exactly

$$\frac{(2N)(2N - 2n)}{2n} S^2,$$

where

$$S^2 = \frac{\sum_{i=1}^{2N} (X_i - \bar{X})^2}{2N - 1} \qquad (2)$$

which may in turn be estimated from the sample in the usual way as

$$s^2 = \frac{\sum_{i=1}^{2n} (x_i - \bar{x})^2}{2n - 1}, \qquad (3)$$

$\overline{X}$ being the population mean and $\bar{x}$ the sample mean.

Random Split between Methods after Sample Is Chosen

Suppose that this sample has been divided at random into two halves, after selection but before the survey, the halves "treated" differently (i.e., each surveyed by one of the two methods), and survey figures $x_1, \ldots, x_n$ and $x_{n+1}, \ldots, x_{2n}$ with means $\bar{x}_1$ and $\bar{x}_2$ obtained for the halves separately. If it could be said that the two halves of the sample give essentially the same result, one could disregard the fact that there had been a division and use the estimate and its error as given in (1) and (2). It might not be easy to decide this, for the survey would presumably have secured information on a number of characteristics on some of which there would be differences which tested as significant between estimates made from the separate halves, and on some not. The test of significance for any one characteristic would be the comparison of the difference:

$$\left(\frac{2N}{n} \sum_{i=1}^{n} x_i\right) - \left(\frac{2N}{n} \sum_{i=n+1}^{2n} x_i\right)$$
$$= 2N(\bar{x}_1 - \bar{x}_2) \quad (4)$$

with its standard error, the square root of

$$\frac{(2N)^2}{(n)(n-1)}$$
$$\times \left[\sum_{i=1}^{n}(x_i - \bar{x}_1)^2 + \sum_{i=n+1}^{2n}(x_i - \bar{x}_2)^2\right], (5)$$

if we can assume homogeneity of variance. It is a fact convenient for calculation that except for the loss of one degree of freedom, and the disregard of the finite population correction, the variance for the test of significance of the difference between the totals as estimated from the two half samples is four times the estimate of variance of the total.

If enough of the characteristics test as significantly different to indicate that the two halves are measuring different entities, then the case for averaging them disappears, and each would be shown with its own variance—again formulae (1) to (3) but with n instead of $2n$.

Split between Methods within Sample Blocks

Once the sample of $2n$ items has been drawn, we can do better in the testing for a difference than dividing it into two parts unrestrictedly at random. If there are outside data, in the form of another variable Y, available for each of the sample units, then the units may be paired and the two methods allocated at random to the members of each pair. Y may be simply a measure of geographic location, in which case contiguous sample members would be paired. The effectiveness of this in increasing the sensitivity of the experiment is once again an ecological question.

The only sacrifice of such matching into more or less homogeneous blocks as compared with the preceding method of random allocation of the sample without restriction is that the number of degrees of freedom for the calculation of the error of the difference between the means of the two halves is reduced from $2n - 2$ to $n - 1$. The formula for the variance of the difference between the totals as estimated by the two halves is no longer (5) but becomes

$$\frac{4N(N-n)}{n}$$
$$\times \left[\frac{\sum_{i=1}^{n}(x_i - x_{i+n})^2 - n(\bar{x}_1 - \bar{x}_2)^2}{n-1}\right], (6)$$

the ith and $i+n^{th}$ sample members having been paired. If the difference is not significant and pooling is justified, the calculation of the mean and the variance of the mean will proceed as for the method in which no pairing is done, i.e., by formulae (1) to (3). The extent to which (6) is less than (5) is a measure of the gain in the sensitivity of the experiment through matching, obtained at no cost in the precision of the total.

Split between Methods before Sample Is Chosen

One might be willing to sacrifice some precision in the estimates of total for the sake of a gain in the sensitivity of the experiment, by matching not in the sample but in the population before the sample is drawn. This could be arranged by drawing a random sample of n households and in each case instructing the investigator that the next house on the right-hand side is to be drawn into the sample and the two methods allocated at random to the two households. The variance of estimate of the total when this is done, however, may be much larger than before, while no great increase in sensitivity of the comparison over matching would be expected if the sample is large. If there is a perfect resemblance between the members of each of the pairs into which the population is grouped, the comparison will have absolute precision and the estimate of total will contain one-half the information that would be available if the sample of $2n$ had been chosen independently at random. Thus 50 per cent is a lower limit of the amount of information that would be retained if perfect matching were secured; this is the same percentage yielded if one of the methods used turned out to be faulty in the unrestricted split of the sample between methods.

Survey Experiments in General

The experimental objective discussed above is simply to compare two methods. We may easily develop survey experiments comparing more than two methods, and the entire theory of experimental design is available for such purposes. The survey experiment may be laid out in any more or less homogeneous groups, e.g., blocks, blocks and the various "treatments" allocated within these. This may be done at any stage of a nested sample. The object may be not experimentation for future surveys but quality control in the one being taken; this may be accomplished by overlapping assignments of different workers. A special case is samples of size $2N$, i.e., complete censuses, where there is wide scope for trial of methods, as the U.S. Bureau of the Census has shown.

The experimenter in agronomy makes use of what he calls uniformity trials, that is, planting the same variety over the whole field to find out the pattern of its variation under uniform treatment. For experiments on survey methods in human populations it is ecological data which correspond to the results of uniformity trials.

NON-RANDOMIZED CONTRASTS

The studies which revealed the classical differences in human fertility have been based either on substantially complete census or vital registration records, or else on other large portions of population. When sampling error was not understood, it seemed natural to seek security for one's conclusions by bringing in as many families as possible. The nature of sampling error has been briefly discussed above, and an introduction given to the now well-established principles for making exact inferences from probability samples. Once these methods of inference are available, it is a matter of efficiency and of craftsmanship in research to use not the largest body of data that can be mustered, but the smallest that will answer the questions which are the object of investigation.

This releases energy and resources to create practical instruments with which headway can be made against other sources of error in inference, of which the most dangerous is the interference of irrelevant variables. The present section shows the use of sampling and of a simple experimental design to hold constant extraneous variables. It avoids the difficulty of the classical studies, which showed for a given population that family size falls off to a certain degree with increasing education, and to a certain degree with increasing income, but were less careful to show how much with each as distinct from the other. In simple one-way tabulations the two are confounded, in the sense of the theory of experimental design, and their separation is essential to analysis that aspires to understand causes. Cross-tabulation can separate out several variables, but to hold constant the dozen or so variables which are relevant would need far more than the three or four directions of cross-tabulation which are usually given in a census. It is possible to avoid the limitations of published census tables by the use of small samples.

The precision of a comparison based on a sample of given size is greater the less the variability, in this case the variance in number of children among families within classes of income, education, etc. The mathematical reasons for this are essentially the same as those governing the precision of estimates based on samples, referred to earlier (pp. 150–51), but with the difference that a general comparison is best thought of as an inference to an infinite population, an estimate of total as an inference to a finite population. (The numerical consequence of this difference of models is negligible.) It turns out that the variability of family size is small enough that samples comprising a few hundred families are capable of revealing all the important differentials of human fertility. The work involved in hand tabulation is trifling; the entire project described below required some

fifteen man-days of clerical work, and this included the searching of the census schedules in the stacks of the Dominion Bureau of Statistics, and the calculation of all necessary tests of significance. The complete set of original data, before summarization, appears as Table 1.

Factorial Arrangement and Its Advantages

As an example of factorial arrangement at its simplest, suppose that we have equal numbers of families (the requirement of equality can easily be removed when there are two levels, with more difficulty when there are three or more levels) in each of the four groups:

A. Wife married at age 15–19; living near city
B. Wife married at age 20–24; living near city
C. Wife married at age 15–19; living far from city
D. Wife married at age 20–24; living far from city

Then to find the contrast of age at marriage we compare $A + C$ with $B + D$; to find the contrast of distance from city we compare $A + B$ with $C + D$. This is extended in what follows to five factors: age at marriage, distance from city, income, education, and age at time of census.

It is worth noting three features of the arrangement of data in factorial form. The first is that a single set of observations tells us about the effects of all variables. In our case there are five variables, and the whole 475 families are available to report on the effect of age at marriage, and then they are available again to report on the effect of distance from cities. Without the device of factorial design one would presumably have to collect a separate set of 475 families on each of the five variables for the same precision.

Secondly, the scope of each comparison is broader than it would be if the comparisons were made separately, each with the extraneous variables controlled at a single value. Scope is a concept well known to agricultural experimenters; they want to compare variety A and variety B (of wheat, say) in such a way that irrelevant soil differences are not confounded with the comparison, but at the same time they would like to have a result which is valid over a range of soils approximately the same as that of the farmlands to which recommendations resulting from the experiment will be applied; they do not want to hold soil constant by doing the whole experiment on a single soil. In the same way one would like to be able to say that families near cities are smaller than those more distant, not only for cases in which marriage takes place at age 15 to 19, but over a wider range of ages; this is done in the factorial arrangement, in effect, by noting the difference between numbers of children of distant and near families, for cases in which marriage takes place at age 15 to 19, and also the difference for marriages of age 20 to 24, and then averaging the two differences.

The third advantage of the factorial arrangement is that if the increase of children with distance is not the same for marriages at 15 to 19 as for those at 20 to 24, then the difference of the differences can itself be measured. This quantity is called the interaction between the factors of age at marriage and distance from city. The logic of factorial design is set forth with supreme clarity in R. A. Fisher's *Design of Experiments*.

Though the advantages of factorial arrangement are as available for population research as for agriculture experimentation, we must note the difference between an arrangement of observations and an experiment. In this paper we are dealing with a sample and not an experiment; because the factors (age at marriage, distance from cities, etc.) were not allocated to individual families

at random (indeed, it is difficult even to imagine them so allocated), we have not escaped the difficulty of imputing causes to which all passive observation of nature is subject. Experiment escapes from this difficulty by random allocation of treatments, and hence of all irrelevant causes which may be operating, both those known to the experimenter and those unknown to him.

Data Used

The material of the comparisons was numbers of children born, asked by the enumerator in the 1941 Census of Canada of all women ever married. Among variables that were the subject of investigation, age at marriage and current age were reported as of last birthday. Low and high education were 0–6 years and 7 years or more respectively, measured by grade attained in the regular school system or its equivalent. Nearness was measured to the closest city of over 30,000 population. Income was also taken for the country as a whole, since no data were available to classify individual families; the measure used was net farm income divided by number of farmers and their family workers. In respect of income and distance from city the highest and lowest quartiles were used. Within these categories a random selection of individual families was made. The procedure yielded 475 families, for each of which children born are shown in Table 1. The cell averages, the numbers of cases on which the averages are based, and the fact that the variance within cells is 8.41 estimated with 443 ($= 475 - 32$) degrees of freedom provide all the information needed in this analysis.

In addition to the five variables mentioned above, thirteen variables were held constant. For a family to qualify it was required that (1) both husband and wife be of Protestant religion, British origin (i.e., English, Irish, or Scottish ancestry) and English mother tongue,

TABLE 1

NUMBER OF CHILDREN EVER BORN IN 475 ONTARIO PROTESTANT FAMILIES, FROM 1941 CENSUS

	PRESENT AGE OF MOTHER							
	45–54				55–74			
	Age of Mother at Marriage							
	15–19		20–24		15–19		20–24	
	Years of Schooling of Mother							
	0–6	7+	0–6	7+	0–6	7+	0–6	7+
A. Low income, near city	14	0	2	3,4,3	6	1,1	0	10,5,5
	13	4		0,3,5	5	2	1	3,2,3
	4	0		2,4,3	7	6	5	3,0,4
		2		5,4,6		3	2	0,14,0
		3		3,2,2		6		3,1,1
		3		2,2,3		3		1,2,0
		0		2,3		4		8,3,6
		4				6		5,9,0
		7				5		1,0,9
		1				0		5,4,4,4
No. of families...	3	10	1	20	3	11	4	31
Av. children.....	10.3	2.4	2.0	3.0	6.0	3.4	2.0	3.7
B. Low income far from city	14	9	6,7	1,4,3	4,9	3	6,9	5,9,3
	10	4	3,8	1,6,2	7,7	2	5,5	4,9,2
	2	3	6,6	0	9,4	4	0,7	6,8,7
	16		2,10		9,7	6	4,10	3,5,6
	13				14		10	9,7
No. of families...	5	3	8	7	9	4	9	14
Av. children.....	11.0	5.3	6.0	2.4	7.8	3.8	6.2	5.9
C. High income, near city	5	3	7	9,3,0,2	2	2	3,6	3,0,4,2
	0	2	5	5,4,3,3		7	8,1	7,3,2,0
	0	16	3	3,1,3,9		5	9,2	8,2,6,3
	13	6	6	1,7,1,3		4	6,2	5,6,3,2
		0	4	6,12,2,1		5	3,9	4,2,1,5
		13	3	2,7,5,5		11	8,3	4,2,5,1
		2	1	3,6,2,5		4	5,5	2,0,2,6
		6	3	0,4,2,5		3	10	6,5,6,0
		6	4	4,1,1,8				3,6,6,10
		5	4	3,6,0,4				2,1,1,2,2
				2,6				
No. of families...	4	10	10	42	1	8	15	41
Av. children.....	4.5	5.9	4.0	3.8	2.0	5.1	5.3	3.4
D. High income, far from city	3	9	7,4	7,3,4,5	3	6	5,11	1,6,1,9
	9	10	8,0	4,3,1,3	5	8	1,1,3	1,1,11,1
	2	5	1,3	5,7,5,6	2	10	6,7,3	5,4,1,3
	10	4	4,3	0,1,1,2	2	6	6,12	2,1,10,5
	11	3	6,4	1,10,1	7	6	9,9,8	7,3,8,6
	13	3	6,4	2,2,7,4	5	3	8,1,5	1,4,5,2
	5	5	0,3	4,5,3,3	10	4	5,2,6	8,4,5,10
	14	2	6,4	5,2,3,4	2	8	2,3,2	2,6,1,3
		3	4,3	2,2,2,1			4,0,4	5,1,7,3
		5	3,3	4,4,2,0			2,2,1	6,8,8,3
		15	10,6	3,7,9,5			9	8,7,3,4
		5	1,6	1,4,1,3				4,4,4,1
			3	3,1,0,4				12,3,4,2
				3				6,4,1,3
								5,10,2,3
No. of families...	8	12	25	52	8	8	29	60
Av. children.....	8.4	5.8	**4.1**	3.3	4.5	6.4	4.7	4.5

SOURCE: Nathan Keyfitz, "A Factorial Arrangement of Comparisons of Family Size," *American Journal of Sociology*, LVIII (March, 1953), 470–79.

(2) both be born on a farm, now living on a farm, and living in the same municipality since childhood, (3) the husband be a farm operator, either working by himself or employing labor. These 13 census variables, six applying to the wife and seven to the husband, are of course correlated with one another and together describe a fairly large part of the population of rural Ontario.

Calculation Exemplified for Two Cells

A difficulty presented by Table 1 is the unequal number of observations in the several cells. We could apply the standard analysis of variance by rejecting observations at random, or with much more labor we could fit least squares constants. Instead, however, we use Yates's[3] extremely simple method for dealing with unequal subclass numbers, which is applicable in the case of dichotomous variables. What follows is an attempt at non-mathematical exposition of a part of Yates's argument.

The unit comparison for the effect of distance from cities may be exemplified by the group which has had 0–6 years of schooling, was married at age 15–19, is at present aged 45–54, and has low income. In this group, the three families in which the place of residence was close to a city had 14, 13, and 4 children respectively, while the five families in which the place of residence was far from a city showed 14, 10, 2, 16, and 13 children (Table 1). Thus we divide the variation among the eight families into just two parts, one the difference between the two means of the two cells,

$$\frac{14+10+2+16+13}{5} - \frac{14+13+4}{3}$$

$$= 11.0 - 10.3 = 0.7 ,$$

[3] F. Yates, "Analysis of Multiple Classification with Unequal Numbers in the Different Classes," *Journal of the American Statistical Association,* XXIX (1934), 51.

and the other the deviations of orginal sizes from the means within cells,

$$3, -1, -9, +5, +2, +3.7, +2.7, -6.3 .$$

By squaring each member of the last line, summing and dividing by 6, the number of degrees of freedom within classes, we estimate the within-cell variance as 30.1.

To complete the comparison we must calculate the variation to which the difference of the means would be subject if it was affected only by the same causes that operate within the two groups. Suppose the true variance within groups of the population from which family sizes $x_1, x_2, \ldots$ are drawn is σ^2, then the variance of

$$\tfrac{1}{5}(x_1 + x_2 + x_3 + x_4 + x_5)$$

$$- \tfrac{1}{3}(x_6 + x_7 + x_8) \text{ is } \frac{\sigma^2}{5} + \frac{\sigma^2}{3}.$$

The standard deviation of the difference of our sample means on the hypothesis of no population difference is thus

$$\sigma\sqrt{\frac{1}{5}+\frac{1}{3}} .$$

If we substitute for σ its estimate from the within-cell variation, i.e.,

$$\sqrt{(30.1)} ,$$

we obtain a denominator for a t-test of significance of the difference which amounts to 0.7, and we have

$$t = \frac{0.7}{5.5\sqrt{0.53}} = 0.17 .$$

Since the theoretical distribution of t in the null-case for a normal variate is known,[4] we can find the probability of a chance deviation as large as the one observed. It turns out that there is a large probability of t being greater than 0.17, and we therefore can only conclude either that there is no population difference, or that there is such a differ-

[4] R. A. Fisher, *Statistical Methods for Research Workers* (New York: Hafner Publishing Co., 1958), p. 174.

ence but that the sample is too small to reflect it.

Weighting To Use Information in All Cells

This calculation, however, uses the information on only 8 of the 475 families of Table 1. The next step must therefore be to calculate the difference in average family size for families living at different distances from cities for the remaining fifteen comparisons for which data are provided in Table 1, and then to find the appropriate combination of the six-

dom variable with variance 8.41/5 and the figure of 10.3 as a similar drawing with a variance 8.41/3. The difference between the averages (0.7) is a drawing with variance

$$8.41(1/5+1/3) = \frac{8.41}{1.88},$$

and we may therefore say that the difference is subject to the same sampling error as an estimate of average family size within a cell which may be imagined as based on 1.88 families. Thus a set of numbers such as 1.88 will in the absence of interaction between dis-

TABLE 2

ESTIMATES OF FERTILITY DIFFERENCES FOR FIVE CONTRASTS AND THEIR SIGNIFICANCE

Contrast (1)	Weighted Average of 16 Differences in Average Children Born = Estimated No. of Children Associated with Contrast (2)	Equivalent Number of Observations N (3)	Estimated Standard Error of (2) $\sqrt{\frac{8.41}{N}}$ (4)	$t = (2)/(4)$ (5)
Far minus near...................	0.699	105.5	0.282	2.5[1]
Low minus high income..............	0.175	90.2	.305	0.6
Present age 55–74 minus 45–54.........	−0.297	115.6	.270	−1.1
Age at marriage 15–19 minus 20–24.....	1.498	77.7	.329	4.6[2]
Schooling 0–6 years minus 7 and over....	1.013	91.0	0.304	3.3[2]

[1] Significant at .05 level.   [2] Significant at .01 level.   SOURCE: Same as Table 1.

teen differences. It happens that where there are a number of blocks in each of which two treatments are compared, the whole of the information on the difference due to treatments contributed by a block is calculable from that block itself. (This is not true when three or more treatments are compared within a block.) It follows from this fortunate circumstance that we need merely calculate the difference in each block and weight it by the variance to which it would be subject on the null hypothesis. As the pooled variance of individual family sizes within cells is 8.41, the figure of 11.0 obtained in what we now think of as the first treatment in the first block may be regarded on the null hypothesis as a single drawing of a ran-

tance and other factors constitute the proper weights to apply to the differences. We find

$$\frac{(1.88)(0.7)+(2.31)(2.9)+\cdots}{1.88+2.31+\cdots}$$
$$= \frac{73.72}{105.47} = 0.699$$

for the estimate of the additional number of children associated with distance. The denominator for a *t*-test is the square root of the unit variance, 8.41, divided by the equivalent number of cases, 105.5, hence $t = 2.48$, which is significant at the .05 level.

Substantive Results

Table 2 gives results for the five variables investigated. It will be seen that the largest difference (1.50 children) is that for age at marriage, the second largest that for schooling (1.01 children), the third distance from cities (0.70 children), while the two remaining are not significant.

The analysis of variance for a test of significance is derived from a model in which the variable is normally distributed. Since family size is truncated at the lower limit of zero it cannot be a normal variable. However, it can be made very nearly normal by a logarithmic transformation of the original data. This involves replacing each family size x in Table 1 by $\log_e (1 + x)$; thus 0 children transform to 0, 1 child to 7, 2 to 11, 3 to 14, etc. All calculations are repeated with the transformed children, and when this is done the same three variables appear as significant.

The difference due to distance in a similar study carried out for French farm families in Quebec[5] was 1.28 ± 0.28 against Ontario's 0.70 ± 0.28; the difference between the two differences is

$$0.58 \pm \sqrt{(0.28)^2 + (0.28)^2}$$
$$= 0.58 \pm 0.40 ,$$

which is not statistically significant. It would tie in well with other facts to be able to say that the friction on the spread of secular city influences is greater in Quebec than in Ontario; income and mobility are undoubtedly higher in rural Ontario than in rural Quebec. There may indeed be greater friction in Quebec, and it may show itself in a larger differential in favor of distant farm families, but this would require larger samples for its demonstration.

[5] N. Keyfitz, "A Factorial Arrangement of Comparisons of Family Size," *American Journal of Sociology*, Vol. LVIII (March, 1953).

We can say that for Ontario as for Quebec there is a diffusion of small family patterns outward from large cities. It has long been known that the small family associated with the industrial revolution came first to rich rather than poor, more educated rather than less, etc. There has been some uncertainty about whether *in addition* a spatial differential existed; whether for given income, education, etc., families living near the city had fewer children than those farther away. At least for two Canadian provinces the question is resolved.

The differential of family size with distance, like other features of family size, is to be thought of as a passing historical phenomenon rather than a permanent feature of civilized social life; during the past twenty years there has been a tendency to convergence of family sizes among the several statistically identifiable groups of the population. For example, twenty-five years ago the province of highest birth rate had double the births per thousand of the lowest; today the highest has only 20 per cent more than the lowest. The trend to a uniform family can be conveniently measured by calculating the variance in birth rates among provinces from year to year, although such a use of variance has no relation to its use for tests of significance. If the convergence, however measured, is due to the permeation of all social groups by the attitudes of the industrial revolution, then it presumably also applies to the spatial differential, distance from cities.[6]

[6] Section "Non-Randomized Contrasts" of this chapter is a condensation of the article by N. Keyfitz, "Differential Fertility in Ontario," in *Population Studies*, Vol. VI, No. 2 (November, 1952).

5. *Cityward Migration, Urban Ecology, and Social Theory**

RONALD FREEDMAN

This thesis deserves to be read in its original complete text, for it is an example of focusing a wide range of sociological theories upon a body of evidence accumulated by the "ecological method." The concept of "mental mobility" proposed here is especially deserving of theoretical as well as research attention.

Data corresponding to the special tabulations from the 1940 census, made for this study, can be made available for more than 150 cities from the 1960 census. The editors hope that this study will be widely replicated.

PROBLEM OF STUDY: THE IMPACT OF MIGRATION UPON THE CITY

Since the end of the great migration from Europe to America the problems of internal migration have attracted increasing attention in this country. The earlier interest in the problems created by foreign migration to the great cities of America has been shifted to the newer problems arising from redistribution of population within the country, particularly from rural to urban areas. Part of this interest has resulted from the recognition that the maintenance of urban population growth depends in part upon a continual net gain of migrants from rural areas.

Since the early part of the last decade there has been an increasing recognition that urban migrants (migrants from one urban place to another) are also a sig-

* Abstracted by the editors from Ronald Freedman, *Recent Migration to Chicago* (Chicago: University of Chicago Press, 1950).

nificant part of the cityward migrant stream. Migration has frequently been discussed in connection with alleged problems arising out of residence requirements for relief benefits and voting. These problems as well as larger problems of assimilation and community organization have involved urban-to-urban as well as rural-to-urban migrants.

The redistribution of the urban population associated with migration into and within the city is related to many urgent problems of urban life. For example, problems of the stability of the electorate and the ability of political machines to control the political life of local areas are closely related to the rate of turnover of the local population and to the educational and economic level of in-migrants. Similarly, the number and economic status of the migrants in various local areas is related to the urban pattern of land values, which is in turn of central importance in determining location of various urban functions. Problems of housing, urban redevelopment, and city planning are also closely related to changing population settlement patterns. The nature of the settlement pattern of different types of migrants within the city has more or less direct relevance to almost every type of problem with which the student of urban life is concerned.

One approach to evaluation of the problems created in urban life by internal migration has been that of the students of "differential" or "selective" migration. In attempting to evaluate the

92

effects of internal migration upon the areas at either end of the migration process, sociologists have necessarily found themselves concerned first with the problems of what kind of people the migrants are and how they differ from non-migrants in the sending and receiving areas.

Most studies of selective migration have been concerned with differentials in the sending area. However, it is the differentials in the urban receiving area which are of significance for that area. The fact that migrants are a selected group in the source area does not necessarily indicate that they will be differentiated in the same or in any other respect in the urban receiving area. Of course, for comparisons centered in the receiving area, it is neither necessary nor desirable to ignore variations in the types of places from which the migrants have come. Comparisons of migrants from each type of place with non-migrants in the receiving area are probably the most useful for the students of urban life.

"Selective migration" studies of the role of the migrant in the city have been deficient even when they have dealt with differentials in the urban receiving areas, because each city has been treated as if it were a single homogeneous area. However, for the sociologist, the city is not a homogeneous unit but a complex organization of heterogeneous subareas, each with its distinctive institutions, characteristics, and population types. It is mainly in terms of the organization of these heterogeneous subareas within the city that the nature of social life in the urban environment has been analyzed.

When the importance of the differentiation of the city into distinctive subareas is recognized, it is not unreasonable to take as the receiving area in cityward migration the particular neighborhood in the city in which the migrant makes his home, rather than the city as a whole. The subarea in which the migrant lives may be considered to be among the social characteristics which define his status in the city.

Viewed as one of the currents of movement within the city, the selective distribution of internal migrants in the city is relevant to theories concerning the relation of mobility to urban social disorganization. Explicitly or implicitly, most students of urban life have related the incidence of social disorganization in urban subareas to the rate of mobility in these areas. The fact that indices of social disorganization decrease with distance from the center of the city has been related to a postulated decrease in the rate of mobility with distance from the center of the city.

In the light of the basic importance attributed to mobility in urban social organization, the pattern of selective distribution of the internal migrants takes on additional significance. Study of this pattern appears to be one of the necessary first steps in any program of fundamental research to investigate the role of mobility of various types in creating the distinctive structure and problems of the urban community. Thus, an adequate definition of the role of the internal migrant cannot stop with a statement of migration differentials on a city-wide level. It must continue with an analysis of the selective distribution of migrants within the subareas of the city, for the distinctive concentration of migrants in particular urban areas in itself constitutes an important migration differential and is relevant to many urgent problems of urban life.

The United States census enumeration of 1940 included for the first time a question about migration during a fixed period of time. The question: "In what place did this person live on April 1, 1935?" appeared on the census population schedules. On the basis of replies to this question it is possible to classify the 1940 population of the United States by "migration status" with further subclassification by place of origin (residence in 1935) and place of destination (residence in 1940). This was the first time that data of this character had been available in the United States. The present investigation utilized these data to answer some of the significant questions about migration to Chicago.

The central problem of this study is whether different types of migrants to Chicago between 1935 and 1940 were differentiated from the non-migrant population and from each other in systematic manner with respect to significant social characteristics, including distribution within the city.

One fundamental theory to be investigated is that despite variations in the type of place of origin, different types of migrants tend to have in common certain characteristics, including a tendency for concentration within distinctive areas. The basis for this theory is the idea that mobility is such an important characteristic that it tends to determine many other aspects of the life of the mobile person.

The migrants have in common the experience of making the transition from a familiar to an unfamiliar environment. The magnitude of this transition will vary with the type of place from which the migrants come, but even those migrants who come from urban centers similar to Chicago must leave behind them the matrix of familiar associations and interpersonal relationships which have defined their daily round of life. As compared with non-migrants, all migrants to a greater or lesser degree face a break in routine and the challenge of new experience and relationships in terms of which mobility is defined.

One part of the theory is the hypothesis that different types of migrants will have in common a tendency to locate within a distinctive group of common areas. The basis for this hypothesis is the fact that distinctive areas of the city have been identified as "mobile" by students of urban life. Insofar as there

are areas in which mobile populations and living arrangements conducive to mobility are segregated, these areas may be expected to be congenial to migrants. Individuals who have the social attitudes favorable to migration may be expected to seek out in disproportionate numbers the areas of the city in which mobility and personal freedom from social restraints are at a maximum. The result would be to create a "migrant zone" as a distinctive part of the urban ecological pattern.

Insofar as the hypothesis of the migrant zone is valid, a significant test may be made of certain aspects of the widely held hypothesis that there is a relationship between mobility and social disorganization. If migrants are concentrated in distinctive "mobile" areas, these areas should be characterized by high rates for indices of social disorganization. At least, a test may be made of the specific hypothesis that local areas with a high rate of in-migration, either from outside or inside the city, are characterized by high rates of specific types of social disorganization. One object of this study is to discover whether such "problem" migrants constitute the dominant element among each type of migrants and among migrants in general. Insofar as they do, or insofar as migrants are concentrated in disorganized areas of the city, there will be additional evidence that the movement of "problem" migrants to the city is an element in urban disorganization. Insofar as such "problem migrants" constitute only a small part of the total migrant stream it may be necessary to reformulate present theories about the relationship of mobility and social disorganization.

One other aspect of the problem requiring brief consideration is the distinctive status of the Negro migrants. With respect to migration differentials as well as other aspects of his life, the Negro's color is more important than his place of origin in determining his social characteristics, and his color is more important than his social characteristics in determining his areal segregation.

Age as a Factor in Other Migration Differentials

The extent to which age differentials account for the differentials in other social characteristics is of considerable importance. For example, the fact that rural migrants to Chicago have a lower rate of unemployment than the non-migrant populations is of some significance in itself, but it is important to know whether the relatively low rate of unemployment is a function of age differences. Unfortunately, the only social characteristics for which the age-specific distributions are available for both migrants and non-migrants are sex ratio and educational status.

In the absence of age-specific distributions for most of the social characteristics, an indirect standarization method is used to discover whether migrant-non-migrant differentials can be attributed to the age differences alone.

MIGRATION DIFFERENTIALS IN THE CITY AS A WHOLE

One of the methods of studying the role of the migrant in the life of the city is to study on a city-wide basis the relationships between the migrant status and the social characteristics of the population of Chicago. This is the method customarily employed by students of differential migration. By comparing the non-migrants in the city with the different types of migrants to the city a conception may be developed of the place of each type of migrant in the demographic, social, and economic structure of the city.

In this section the over-all purpose is to discover, as far as possible from city-wide census data, what kind of person the cityward migrant is and how his characteristics are related to his place of origin.

Age Differences

From every type of evidence the selection of the migrants with respect to age was related to the cultural level of their place of origin. All the migrants were highly concentrated in the young adult years as compared with the non-migrants, but the concentration in the youngest of the adult years was greater the more rural the background of the migrants. For Negro migrants the rural-urban continuum does not apply in the same manner as for the white migrants. Rural Negro migrants, whether farm or non-farm, have among their number relatively more children and old people than the urban migrants. This probably indicates that the Negro rural migrants are more likely to migrate in family groups. The distinctive rural-urban differentials noted for Negroes are mainly attributable to migration from the South.

Significant implications are attached to the age differentials just summarized. First, the "excess" of young adults among every group of migrants indicates that the migrants are potentially a very productive group both from the economic and demographic point of view. The youth of the migrants indicates that large numbers of them are at the beginning of their productive occupational careers and have a full span of working years to contribute to the economy of the city. Relatively few of them are members of those groups above 45 years of age which sometimes encounter difficulty in securing employment in our economy. Among the white migrants the relatively small numbers at either extreme of the age distribution indicates relatively small numbers of persons dependent for economic or other forms of assistance. From the point of view of population growth, the youthfulness of the migrants to the city indicates that they are on the threshold of family life and parenthood and may be expected to contribute more than their proportional share of births to the population.

Sex Differences

The findings with respect to the sex ratio (males per 100 females) of migrants to Chicago may be summarized as follows:

1. Migrants from each rural-urban cultural level, whether white or Negro, had a lower sex ratio than comparable non-migrants.

2. There were significant regional variations in the sex ratios. For white migrants the low migrant sex ratios were mainly attributable to migrants from the regions near Chicago but outside the inner suburban region. For Negroes the low migrant sex ratios were mainly attributed to Southern Negro migrants.

3. The lowest sex ratios for white migrants were in the late adolescent and young adult age groups. However, only a small part of the low over-all migrant sex ratios can be attributed to concentration in these age groups, since each of the major types of migrants had relatively low sex ratios even when age was held constant.

4. The variations between the migrant sex ratios were not related consistently to the rural-urban cultural continuum nor did the sex ratios of the suburban migrants tend to be similar to those of the non-migrants.

Age and proximity to Chicago appear to be the significant factors underlying the low sex ratio of the whole migrant population of Chicago.

Work Status Differences

1. The work status of migrants compared favorably with that of the non-migrants. As compared to non-migrants, most migrant groups were willing to work, as evidenced by the high proportion in the labor force, and they were able to find and hold employment, as evidenced by the low unemployment rates of those migrants in the labor force. While the differences between migrants and non-migrants with respect to

proportions in the labor force can be attributed to age differences, this is not true for the differences in unemployment rates. The migrants as a whole cannot be characterized as an urban labor reserve. This description properly can be applied only to a limited group of migrants—the Negro rural and urban migrants from the South and the white rural migrants from the South. These "problem" migrants from a "problem" area were unusual among migrants in having a high unemployment rate.

2. For both male and female migrants work status, particularly as denoted by unemployment rates, is associated with the rural-urban cultural level of the place of origin, but the relationship is opposite in direction for males and females. For males, the more rural the background of the migrants the more unfavorable was the work status as indicated by high unemployment rates. For females, the more rural the background of the migrants the more favorable was the work status, as indicated by low unemployment rates. Some evidence which was presented indicated that the high rate of unemployment found for the urban-to-urban female migrants may be a function of higher standards of what constitutes suitable employment rather than inability to find work. It was not a function of age.

3. The data on variations in work status of migrants from different regions have indicated that: (a) high unemployment rates characterized the Southern migrants, while the migrants from other regions tended to have lower unemployment rates, with those for migrants from the east north central and west north central regions most consistently low; (b) high proportions in the labor force tended to be most characteristic of migrants from the west north central region and east north central region as compared to other regions. This was particularly true for female rural migrants.

Occupational Differences

An analysis of the migrant occupational differentials should give a precise indication of the migrant's role in the economy by specifying the nature of his employment. Particularly, it should indicate whether the relatively good adjustment of the migrant in the urban labor market in terms of finding employment is a function of his willingness to take poorly paid and poorly esteemed unskilled jobs. The comparative occupational distribution of the migrants not only indicates their functional position in the economic structure but also reflects aspects of their social status.

Compared to non-migrants, male migrants, as a whole, were highly concentrated in the service-production occupations and particularly in those service-production occupations of white-collar status. *They were also concentrated in high-status occupations.*

The concentration of migrants in white-collar occupations is attributable to the migrants from other urban places. The difference between urban migrants and non-migrants is particularly marked for the professional workers. Sixteen per cent of urban migrants are professional workers as compared with 6 per cent of the non-migrants. Thus, the urban-to-urban migrants are clearly concentrated in the service-production occupations and particularly in those of high status.

It is not possible to designate the occupational status of the rural non-farm migrants as being "higher" or "lower" than the non-migrants. They have about the same proportion of white-collar workers as the non-migrants, with concentrations at both extremes of the occupational scale—that is, among professional workers and laborers.

The occupational status of the rural farm migrants is clearly lower than that of the non-migrants. The rural farm migrants are relatively more numerous than the non-migrants only in the two

lowest-status service-production occupations (domestic service workers and other service workers) and in two physical-production occupations involving least status and skill (operatives and laborers). They are relatively less numerous than non-migrants in every one of the white-collar occupations and among the craftsmen. Their occupational status is clearly lower than that for either non-migrants or any other migrant group. The rural farm migrants are the only male migrant group concentrated in the occupations considered typical of the low-paid, unskilled workers on the margins of the urban labor market.

It is significant that although both rural farm and rural non-farm migrants had relatively large numbers of workers in some of the physical-production occupations, neither group had as large a proportion of craftsmen as the non-migrants.

Rural white migrants and both urban and rural Negro migrants from the South are unusually concentrated in low-status occupations, whether service-production or physical-production. This is consistent with the previous characterization of these groups of migrants as "problem" migrants on the fringe of the labor market.

As compared with non-migrants, female migrants were concentrated in the occupations providing professional and personal services. Urban, rural non-farm, and rural farm migrants were each relatively more numerous than non-migrants in professional work, domestic service work, and other service work. They were relatively less numerous in all other occupations.

It is difficult to designate any of the female migrant groups as being of "higher" or "lower" status than the non-migrants, since each group of migrants is concentrated at both extremes of the occupational hierarchy.

Region of origin had very little effect on the nature of the occupational differentials between the female migrants and the non-migrants.

The more the cultural level of the place of origin resembled that of Chicago (the more urban), the higher was the occupational status of the female migrants.

Regional variations in migrant occupational status were as follows:

1. The regions sending physical-production workers to Chicago in greater than average numbers (as compared with comparable migrant groups) are either Southern regions or Northern regions near Chicago, mainly the surburban or East North Central regions. The Southern regions send semi-skilled or unskilled physical-production workers in relatively large numbers, while the Northern regions near Chicago send relatively large numbers of physical-production workers at all skill levels. Skilled physical-production workers (craftsmen) are drawn in significantly large numbers only from the regions immediately surrounding Chicago (suburban and East North Central regions).

2. The more distant Northern regions (especially Northeast and West) send disproportionate numbers of workers only in white-collar occupations.

3. The Southern migrants, especially those from the Border States and the Deep South, tend to be concentrated in the low-status occupations, both service-production and physical-production. Although concentrated in some of the low-status occupations, the migrants from the South Atlantic region are, in general, of higher occupational status than other Southern migrants.

4. The surburban migrants, especially the females, tend to be concentrated in the occupations in which non-migrants are relatively most numerous. This is consistent with the expectation of similarity between non-migrants and suburban migrants.

Educational Differences

The relation of educational attainment to migrant status is important as an indication of whether Chicago selected as in-migrants persons who were better prepared for life in terms of formal education than the permanent residents of the city. There is a general belief that migrants with more than average formal education are an asset to a receiving area.

In this section the educational attainment of the migrants is evaluated in terms of data on the years of school completed by persons 25–34 years old. Data for the other age groups are not available. However, there is considerable value in the data for this particular age group alone. It excludes most of the persons who have not completed their formal education. Since the data are limited to a specific age group, age differences will not affect the educational differentials to any substantial amount. The data refer to "cohorts" who have recently completed their education. This age group includes a substantial number —30 per cent—of the migrants. The educational comparisons made then are between young adults who have presumably completed their formal education.

The migrants as a whole were better educated than the non-migrants. Except for the male rural farm migrants, each male and female migrant group was found to be better educated than the comparable non-migrant group. The average migrant, male or female, had completed about two more years of school than the average non-migrant. Furthermore, more than three times as many migrants as non-migrants had completed the four years of college generally considered the equivalent of college graduation. Every migrant group, including even the male rural farm migrants, had a higher proportion of such college graduates than the corresponding non-migrant groups. If college graduates are an asset to a city, Chicago gained a disproportionate number of valuable citizens among its migrants.

The selective influence of rural-urban background with respect to educational attainment is evident for both male and female migrants. Urban migrants were best educated, rural non-farm less well educated, and rural farm migrants least well educated. Rural farm and foreign migrants, both male and female, had a higher proportion of persons who had completed less than seven years of school than corresponding non-migrant groups.

Except for rural migrants from the Deep South and Border States, both rural and urban migrants of either sex and from every region were better educated on the average than comparable non-migrant groups.

The low educational attainment of the Southern migrants is mainly attributed to Negro migrants. The white rural male migrants from the South had a somewhat lower median educational level than the male non-migrants, but the difference was relatively small. All other white migrant groups from the South had a higher median educational attainment than the non-migrants.

Differences in Economic Status

The relative economic status of the migrants to Chicago was consistent with their occupational and educational status. Insofar as median rentals are an index of economic status for each group, migrants as a whole were of higher economic status than the non-migrants. However, when each migrant group is compared separately with the non-migrants, it appears that only the urban migrants were of higher economic status than the non-migrants. The rural non-farm migrants were of approximately the same economic status as the non-migrants, and the rural farm migrants were of lower economic status.

Differences in Family Status

The comparative family status of the migrants and non-migrants is of great importance, since family relationships are one of the basic determinants of the life pattern of the individual. Persons who live apart from other members of their families are relatively free from the customary restraints and responsibilities of family life. Similarly, persons who live in small families, particularly those who live in two-person families without children or older relatives, are likely to share, in some measure, the relative freedom from customary familial social controls of persons who live alone. The person who is free from customary familial restraints is typically depicted as a mobile individual whose freedom may lead either to the sophistication or to the disorganization typical of different areas of urban life. Since family status is considered to be such a basic factor in creating the distinctive life organization of the urban dweller, it is desirable to describe migrant family status differentials.

On the average, migrants of every type belonged to smaller families than non-migrants. Migrants of every type were found to be much more likely to be living as members of one-person or two-person families than non-migrants.

Data on living arrangements also indicated that every type of migrant was more likely than the non-migrant to be living under extrafamilial living arrangements. Among the non-migrant population only 8 per cent of the males and 6 per cent of the females were resident in extrafamilial living arrangements. The comparable proportion for all migrants was 27 per cent for males and 26 per cent for females. The greater concentrations of migrants than non-migrants in non-familial living arrangements cannot be attributed to age differences.

The relatively unstable character of the migrant living arrangements is further indicated by the fact that the overwhelming majority of all types of migrants were tenants rather than homeowners. Twenty-five per cent of the non-migrants but only 4 per cent of the migrants lived in homes they owned. Thus, as compared to non-migrants, migrants of every type were concentrated in families whose size and living arrangements are generally associated with a maximum of personal freedom and a minimum of family restraints or responsibilities. A very large proportion of the migrants were either unattached individuals or individuals whose family and home responsibilities were likely to be relatively few. The significance of the concentration of migrants in extrafamilial living arrangements and in very small families is that these are characteristics frequently associated with the ideal-typical urban person.

The extent to which migrants were concentrated in extrafamilial living arrangements is related to the rural-urban cultural continuum. For both sexes rural farm migrants were most concentrated and urban migrants least concentrated in extrafamilial living arrangements with the rural non-farm migrants again in the intermediate position. This would appear to indicate that the rural farm migrants, who presumably faced the greatest adjustment problems in the city, were likely to be living under arrangements in which the freedom from family controls is at a maximum. However, the significance of this relationship is not clear, since the rural migrants were most concentrated as lodgers in private households, but not in the quasi-public households.

Summary of Migrant Differentials for the City as a Whole

The migrants as a whole had either equal or higher rank than the non-migrants with respect to those characteristics for which "high" and "low" rank have some meaning in the urban en-

vironment. Thus, either male or female migrants as a whole had achieved a higher educational attainment and were more frequently in the labor force and less frequently unemployed. Male migrants were of higher occupational status than the non-migrants, while the female migrants were not distinctly either higher or lower than non-migrants in occupational status. Migrant families were generally of higher economic status than non-migrants insofar as rental is an indication of economic status. The migrants as a whole may be described as having had the characteristics associated with a relatively favorable economic and social position in the city.

In addition to the characteristics for which rank evaluations are meaningful, the migrants had other distinctive characteristics as a group. As compared to non-migrants, both male and female migrants were predominantly young adults. They were concentrated in typically urban service-production occupations. They were relatively free from primary group controls in that relatively large numbers of them were living alone or in small families and were living under mobile extrafamilial types of residential arrangements. Migrants as a group also had a relatively low sex ratio.

Although migrants tended to resemble each other in some respects as compared to non-migrants, the characteristics of different types of migrants have been found to vary in relation to the rural-urban cultural level of their place of origin. Among three major types of internal migrants only the male rural farm migrants were found to have characteristics indicative of low social and economic status. Thus, with respect to occupational status, employment, educational attainment, and economic status, the male rural farm migrants were found to be in a lower position than non-migrants. The urban migrants were found to be in a better position than the non-migrants in each of these categories, while the rural non-farm migrants were either of about equal or higher status than the non-migrants.

In comparing migrants from different regions with the non-migrants only the migrants from the Southern regions were found to have the relatively low status in specific characteristics noted for the rural farm migrants. Migrants from the Southern regions, particularly the Deep South and the Border States, tended to be of lower occupational, educational, and work status than migrants from any other region. In large part, this is attributable to the large numbers of Negroes among the migrants from the South. However, even white rural migrants from the South were found to compare unfavorably with Chicago non-migrants in some respects.

The role of most migrants as indicated by their social characteristics has not been found to be that encompassed in the stereotype of the "problem" migrants. Only the rural farm male migrants or migrants from the Southern regions have been found to have the low occupational, educational, or economic status associated with this stereotype, and even among these groups a substantial share had "non-problem" characteristics.

One significant aspect of the role of the migrants which emerges from the analysis of the different characteristics is that in many respects the migrants, other than a few small low-status groups, have the characteristics of the ideal-typical urban dweller. The concentration in service-production occupations, high educational status, small families, the extra-familial living arrangements which characterized almost every migrant type are the characteristics frequently associated by urban sociologists with the ideal-typical urban mode of life. Even the male rural farm migrants, the most disadvantaged in most respects, share some of these characteristics.

SELECTIVE DISTRIBUTION OF MIGRANTS WITHIN THE CITY

The Subareas of the City

Since one important aspect of this study is the selective distribution of internal migrants within local areas of the city, it is necessary that the whole city be divided into local areas which are relatively homogeneous but which include a migrant population large enough to make analysis of migrant characteristics and rates significant.

To meet the need for local areas relatively homogeneous, yet large enough to include enough migrants to justify analysis of their characteristics, Professor Louis Wirth and Ernest W. Burgess divided the city into 24 convenient areas of migrant settlement which were combinations of local communities wherever possible and, in some cases, combinations of local communities and census tracts. These 24 residential areas were used by the Census Bureau as the units for the tabulation of the detailed migration data. They are admittedly a compromise between the small areas desirable for homogeneity and the large areas desirable for the inclusion of adequate numbers of migrants. Most of the 24 residential areas consist of combinations of census tracts or community areas readily identifiable with distinctive areas treated in some of the Chicago studies.

Hypothesis To Be Tested

The distributive pattern of the migrants is examined in relation to several hypotheses concerning the selective factors which locate the migrant within the city.

The initial hypothesis is that migrants of different types and of different social characteristics will tend to be segregated together in disproportionate numbers in certain areas of the city, designated as a migrant zone. This hypothesis is based on the idea that members of all groupings of migrants will tend to be attracted in disproportionate numbers to a common zone, because they have in common the minimum of *mental mobility* required to undertake the migration to Chicago. The hypothesis of a migrant zone involves the assumption that certain kinds of areas are more receptive or congenial than other areas to intercity migrants and other mobile types. On the basis of previous studies it may be expected that these areas will be characterized by living arrangements conducive to a maximum of personal freedom from social controls and a minimum of responsibilities or physical possessions tying the individual to the home or neighborhood. Apartments, especially small furnished apartments, furnished rooms in rooming houses, and hotel rooms have usually been described as typically urban living arrangements which meet these specifications. For ease of reference, such types of living arrangements will henceforth be designated as "urban living arrangements." Areas in which these types of living arrangements prevail have usually been described as having a minimum of "neighboring" and primary personal relations, and a maximum of secondary social relations with considerable freedom from social controls. Such areas may be expected to select migrants.

If the hypothesized migrant zone consists of areas with urban living arrangements, it should follow the spatial location pattern of these areas. Areas with urban living arrangements have frequently been described as extending out from the central business district in long narrow lines along the rapid transportation routes. Aside from the living arrangements themselves, access to rapid transportation should be an attraction to a population with mobile propensities. In any particular city, then, a migrant zone may be expected to consist of areas with urban living arrangements, lying along the lines of rapid transportation. A second main hypothesis to be tested

is that migrants of each type are segregated in the subareas of the city in such a manner that their distribution by social characteristics tends to resemble that of the non-migrant population. This hypothesis arises out of the frequently repeated observation that there is a selective process in urban life which sifts and distributes the population within the city in terms of social and demographic characteristics. To the extent that such a process exists, its operation should be observable in the distribution of migrants into areas in which their characteristics resemble those of the resident population.

On the surface, it may appear to be inconsistent to hypothesize at the same time a segregation of migrants in terms of their social characteristics and a concentration of migrants in a zone irrespective of type or social characteristics. However, these hypotheses need not be inconsistent, if the degree of concentration in the areas of high concentration varies for different kinds of migrants in such a manner as to produce a population structure tending to resemble that of the non-migrants.

Location of a Migrant Zone

A first step to investigating the possible existence of a migrant zone in Chicago is the determination of those residential areas in which there is a disproportionate concentration of migrants, without initial reference to their social characteristics. Areas were considered to be migrant concentration areas when the percentage of migrants in the population was greater than average.

The migrant zone is defined as consisting of the group of 13 contiguous residential areas in which any or all of the major migrant types are concentrated. The migrant zone is indicated by the shaded areas in Figure 1.

The economic status of an area has

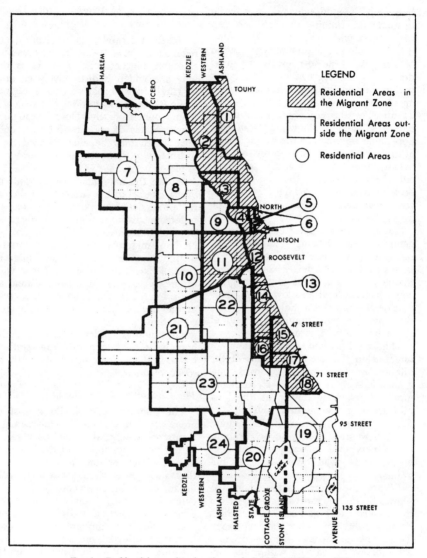

Fig. 1.—Residential areas in migration analysis, City of Chicago, 1940

frequently been designated as a basic
factor in determining the nature of the
segregation within the area. Therefore,
it is desirable in this preliminary location
of a migrant zone to consider the gross
differences in segregation that occur
within the zone and outside the zone on
an economic basis. For this purpose, the
24 areas of the city have been designated as "high" or "low" areas of rent
depending on whether the average rental in the area is higher or lower than the
average rental for the city as a whole.
All of the areas may then be classified
on a fourfold basis as high-rent or low-
rent areas and as inside or outside the
migrant zone.

The greatest and most consistent concentration of migrants is in the high
rental areas of the migrant zone. There
is a significant but lesser concentration
in the low rental areas of the migrant
zone. In both high and low rental areas
outside the migrant zone there are less
than proportionate numbers of any of
the major migrant groups.

The only marked concentrations of
migrants in the low-rental areas of the
migrant zone is that of the rural migrants. The ratio of urban to rural migrants is relatively low in all the low-
rent areas of the migrant zone.

In the high-rent areas of the migrant
zone, there are significant concentrations
of every type of migrant, but the concentration is greatest for the urban migrants.

Within the migrant zone, then, the
segregation of migrants is most clear cut
in the series of high-rental areas which
lie in a solid tier along the lake front.
These may be considered to be primary
areas of concentrations within the migrant zone. In addition, there are a few
low-rent areas on the periphery of the
zone in which the migrant concentration
is mainly rural in character. This may
be considered to be a secondary zone
of migrant concentration.

Concentration of Migrants from Differ-ent Regions in the Migrant Zone

Urban and rural migrants from every
region are concentrated in the areas inside the migrant zone. Area 11 is the
only one which is distinctively an area
of rural migrant non-suburban region,
while it has concentrations of urban migrants only from the Deep South and
Border States. It appears to be the only
area which may be characterized as a
distinctive port of entry for rural migrants.

Within the migrant zone, migrants of
every characteristic (except female rural professional workers) are concentrated in disproportionate numbers in
the high-rent areas. Many, but not all
kinds of migrants are also concentrated
in the low-rent areas of the migrant
zone. This distinction is consistent with
the designation of the high-rent areas as
the primary areas and the low-rent areas
as the secondary areas of migrant concentration.

The findings tend to substantiate the
hypothesis that migrants are concentrated in the migrant zone irrespective of
social characteristics.

The Characteristics of the Migrant Zone

The migrant zone should consist of
areas whose location and living arrangements are congenial to mobile persons.
In the initial statements of the hypothesis of the migrant zone, it was suggested
that such areas should have typically
urban living arrangements and be located on or near transportation routes
affording easy, rapid access to the Loop.

In Figure 1 the migrant zone is shown
to consist of a contiguous group of areas
oriented along the lake front in a north-
south line running through the Loop
with a second orientation line running
westward out of the Loop perpendicular
to the north-south line. These are precisely the lines of the principal rapid
transportation routes in Chicago. It is

apparently not inaccurate to characterize the migrant zone as located along the principal fast transportation lines to Chicago.

The migrant zone is also characterized by typically urban living arrangements. In the introduction to this section typically urban living arrangements were designated as those which involve a maximum of freedom from family or neighborhood social controls and a minimum of responsibilities or possessions

the tenant, so that the residence in such homes involves responsibilities or possessions discouraging to mobility. Finally, an area with typically urban living arrangements will generally be one in which a relatively large proportion of dwelling units are vacant at any given time. Except under such conditions as a wartime housing crisis the rapid turnover in urban type living accommodations necessarily involves periods of vacancy between tenants. A tabulation of the

TABLE 1

HOUSING CHARACTERISTICS FOR CHICAGO, THE MIGRANT ZONE, AND THE NON-MIGRANT ZONE

HOUSING CHARACTERISTICS	CITY TOTAL	NON-MIGRANT ZONE	MIGRANT ZONE		
			Total	High Rent Areas	Low Rent Areas
Percentage of occupied dwelling units:					
In single-family detached structures.......	16.2	23.4	5.3	6.1	3.9
In apartment buildings, containing 5 or more units................................	31.2	21.6	45.7	56.6	25.3
With roomers........................	5.2	3.7	7.4	5.8	11.3
With one or two rooms...................	11.3	4.3	21.2[1]	[2]	[2]
Percentage of tenant-occupied units:					
Rented furnished.......................	13.0	4.3	22.9	25.0	18.1
Percentage of dwelling units:					
Vacant..............................	3.8	2.5	5.8	6.0	5.5
Tenant occupied.......................	71.9	69.1	75.9	74.6	83.6
Owner occupied.......................	24.3	28.4	16.4	19.4	10.9

[1] Based on data for community areas all or part of which are included in migrant zone.
[2] Data not available for these areas.

tying the individual to his home. It is fairly well accepted that the types of living arrangements most likely to meet these specifications are apartments, especially small furnished apartments in multiple-unit structures, and furnished rooms in rooming houses. Because of the very nature of units of these types, most of them are likely to be tenant-occupied. On the other hand, these areas should have a relatively small proportion of detached single family homes, which are generally indicative of more stable neighborhoods. They are more likely than other living arrangements to be owner-occupied or at least to be furnished by

characteristics of housing (Table 1) shows that the migrant zone has a disproportionate number of those types of dwelling units which have been characterized as ideal-typically urban, in comparison with the rest of the city.

It is significant that the zone in which the migrants are concentrated has characteristics customarily associated with the most distinctively urban areas of the city. Areas with the living arrangements found in the migrant zone have usually been described as the locus of the secular social relations, the anonymity, and the relative freedom from group restraint typically associated with urban life. The migrants are apparently attracted to areas in which are found at least the externals of the ideal-typical urban modes of life.

Segregation of Migrants by Social Characteristics

The second basic hypothesis to be investigated is that migrants are segregated in urban subareas on the basis of their social and cultural characteristics in the same manner as non-migrants. Many students of urban life have called attention to the fact that populations tend to be segregated in distinctive areas according to their cultural characteristics. If such a process of segregation exists, it should be one of the factors operating to determine where the migrants make their homes within the city. The distribution of migrants with any specific social characteristics should be similar to that of the non-migrants with the same characteristics.

The applicability of the segregation process to the distribution of migrants is analyzed in this section by correlating the percentage of migrants having specific characteristics in each of the 24 residential areas with the percentage of non-migrants in each area with the same characteristics. Separate series are presented for the correlations of the urban and rural migrant distributions with each other and with the non-migrant distributions. For example, a typical correlation involves the relationship between the percentage of urban migrants "employed" and the percentage of non-migrants "employed" in each of the 24 areas. Table 2 lists these correlation coefficients for all the social characteristics for which data were available. Separate series of correlations are presented for males and females, since sex will be an important variable in many of the classifications employed.

In interpreting the battery of correlation coefficients in Table 2 the fact that

each correlation is based only on 24 areas must be considered.

In general, the correlations of the rural and urban migrants with each other and with the non-migrants are high and significant, indicating that non-migrants and different types of migrants do tend to be segregated by social characteristics in the same manner. In any area where a relatively high proportion of the migrants has a specific characteristic a relatively high proportion of the non-migrants tend to have the same characteristic. There are some important exceptions to this generalization which will be considered in some detail.

The correlations with respect to work status and occupation indicate that populations are segregated on the basis of functional roles in the economy. For males, these correlations are uniformly significant and high. Of 24 correlation coefficients for male occupations only 1 is lower than $+.77$ and that one correlation (for non-migrant and rural migrant domestic servants) is $+.64$. For females the occupation correlations are considerably less consistent and less significant than for the males. Eight of the 24 coefficients for females are not significant at the .05 level. In addition, of the 24 occupation correlations, 22 of those for the females are lower than those for the males. This is not to dismiss as insignificant the segregation of females in terms of occupational types; 16 of the 24 occupation correlations for females are significantly large. However, it is clear that segregation of the female migrants on the basis of occupation is less consistent and less far-reaching than for males.

Two interpretations of this difference suggest themselves. In the first place, it may be a reflection of the fact that while the status and location of the male is determined by his own occupation that of the female is more likely to be determined by the occupation of her husband or father. The woman's occupation is less likely to be a central fact in the organization of her life than the occupation of her husband. On the other hand, the discrepancy is unquestionably due in part to the fact that the location of certain nurses' training institutions and the nature of census definitions have resulted in a statistical "segregation" of female migrant professional workers in areas where non-migrant professionals are relatively few.

With respect to work status, both male and female rural and urban migrants are segregated within the city in the same manner as the non-migrants. In this case the correlations for females are all significant at the .05 level of significance or higher. The correlations for males are also significant at this minimum level except for one significant at the .10 level. This exception is the correlation between the proportion of rural migrants and non-migrants "not in the labor force."

The correlations for work status and occupational categories are evidence

TABLE 2

CORRELATIONS[1] OF SELECTED SOCIAL CHARACTERISTICS OF THE NON-MIGRANT, URBAN MIGRANT, AND RURAL MIGRANT POPULATION IN THE 24 MIGRANT AREAS, BY SEX, CHICAGO, 1940

SOCIAL CHARACTERISTICS	MALES			FEMALES		
	Correlations between			Correlations between		
	Non-Migrant and Urban Migrant	Non-Migrant and Rural Migrant	Urban and Rural Migrant	Non-Migrant and Urban Migrant	Non-Migrant and Rural Migrant	Urban and Rural Migrant
Per cent of employed persons who are:						
Professional and semi-professional workers...	+.86	+.84	+.85	−.09[2]	−.12[2]	+.79
Proprietors, managers, and officials..........	+.86	+.88	+.94	+.64	+.34[2]	+.09[2]
Clerical, sales, and kindred workers..........	+.86	+.87	+.96	+.54	+.54	+.85
Craftsmen, foremen, and kindred workers....	+.79	+.87	+.82	+.02[2]	+.53	+.33[2]
Operatives and kindred workers..............	+.88	+.91	+.86	+.85	+.85	+.93
Domestic service workers....................	+.77	+.64	+.87	+.71	+.41[2]	+.87
Service workers, except domestic............	+.91	+.89	+.86	+.68	+.75	+.57
Laborers...................................	+.91	+.89	+.94	−.15[2]	+.69	+.07[2]
Per cent of persons 14 years old and over:						
Employed.................................	+.83	+.79	+.89	+.81	+.84	+.81
Unemployed..............................	+.86	+.81	+.92	+.94	+.92	+.94
In emergency work........................	+.71	+.84	+.91	+.88	+.65	+.60
Seeking work.............................	+.87	+.74	+.87	+.88	+.88	+.88
Not in labor force........................	+.51	+.27[2]	+.77	+.85	+.81	+.77
Per cent foreign born........................	+.89	+.73	+.84	+.90	+.77	+.86
Median years of education of persons aged 25–34 (25 and over for non-migrants).............	+.84	+.89	+.80	+.68	+.81	+.95
Per cent of white population aged:						
5–13.....................................	+.88	+.84	+.92	+.89	+.87	+.93
14–17....................................	+.76	+.43	+.23[2]	+.79	+.76	+.67
18–19....................................	+.69	+.08[2]	+.08[2]	+.33[2]	+.06[2]	+.67
20–24....................................	+.03[2]	−.31[2]	+.76	+.18[2]	−.33[2]	+.62
25–29....................................	+.27[2]	+.07[2]	+.63	+.37[2]	+.09[2]	+.38[2]
30–34....................................	+.43	±.0	−.34[2]	+.62	+.17[2]	+.33[2]
35–44....................................	+.58	−.01[2]	+.61	+.76	+.26[2]	+.18[2]
45–54....................................	+.80	+.54	+.73	+.78	+.35[2]	+.58
55–64....................................	+.82	+.56	+.67	+.48	+.36[2]	+.63
65 and over..............................	+.15	−.04[2]	−.24[2]	+.30[2]	+.15[2]	+.63

[1] See Appendix X of the dissertation for t-values for estimating level at which correlations in this table are significantly different from zero.

[2] Not significantly different from zero at the .05 level.

that both non-migrants and different migrant types tend to be segregated together in urban areas on the basis of their functions in the economy. Since occupational role and economic status are closely related, there is no question that occupational segregation and economic segregation are closely related processes.

Although segregation in terms of economic roles is sometimes regarded as the primary basis for segregation, other cultural factors, not unrelated to economic roles, are known to operate in the process. Education and nativity represent two such factors. The high significant correlations for both education and nativity indicates that the migrants are attracted to areas where the non-migrant population has a similar background and nativity status.

Age is the characteristic in terms of which there is the least indication of similar segregation of migrants and non-migrants. For both sexes the correlations are least significant in young adult age groups, in the 65 years and over categories, and particularly in the correlations between rural migrants and non-migrants.

The lack of correlation in the young adult age groups in which migrants are relatively most numerous makes the consistently high correlations in terms of functional and cultural characteristics even more significant, for they cannot be explained as functions of correlations in the age distributions. Apparently, young adult migrants to the city distribute themselves in the city on the basis of their functional and cultural characteristics rather than in terms of age.

There is also some possibility that the young adult non-migrant is more likely than the migrant to be living in his parent's home, which is not necessarily located with reference to his own functional or cultural characteristics. The older adult, whether migrant or non-migrant, is more likely to have found his place in the city in relation to functional

or cultural role. As compared with young adult migrants, there may be a lag for the young adult non-migrant within the process by which his cultural and functional roles determine his location in the city. The young adult non-migrant has more ties to home and neighborhood not immediately connected with his cultural or functional role.

The preceding correlation analysis supports the hypothesis that migrants are segregated in urban subareas in such a manner that in each area the different migrant and non-migrant populations tend to resemble each other with respect to important social characteristics.

RELATIONSHIP OF MIGRANT DISTRIBUTION
TO SOCIAL DISORGANIZATION IN CHICAGO

The ecological settlement pattern of migrants to Chicago in the period 1935 to 1940 did not correspond with the gradient pattern frequently found for indices of social disorganization and also attributed to mobility. Studies in Chicago and elsewhere have found that indices of social disorganization show a decrease with distance from the center of the city. Either explicitly or implicitly this gradient pattern has been related to a similar gradient in mobility. The highly disorganized areas near the center of the city are customarily depicted as areas of high mobility. Decrease in the incidence of the phenomena of social disorganization with distance from these areas is frequently postulated as associated with a decrease in mobility. Recognition is sometimes given to the somewhat greater extension of social disorganization along radial transportation routes.

Area-rate maps for intercity and intracity migrants in Chicago between 1935 and 1940 do not show the consistent gradient pattern found for social disorganization and postulated for mobility. Although the migrant zone includes some of the central disorganized areas, it extends far beyond these areas. On the other hand, some of the disorganized areas close to the Loop, especially those in the angles between the two main radial routes, have low migrant rates. Insofar as migration is an index of mobility, the inconsistency between the spatial distribution of migrants and the phenomena of social disorganization indicates either that there is no consistent relationship between mobility and social disorganization, or that there may be several distinctive kinds of mobility, all of which do not have the same relationship to each type of social disorganization.

The relationship between specific types of social disorganization and mobility, as represented in migration, may be tested more exactly by correlation analysis. For the 75 community areas of Chicago the rate of juvenile delinquency (1934–40) has been correlated (by the rank method separately with the intracity and intercity migrant rate). The correlation of juvenile delinquency rates with the intercity migrant rate is not significantly different from zero (−.03 ±.12). There is a small but significant rank correlation (+.31 ±.12) with the intracity migrant rate. If the 10 community areas with large Negro populations are eliminated, the rank correlations between the juvenile delinquency rates and the migrant rates in the 65 "white" community areas are not significant. The correlations were +.15 (± .12) between the juvenile delinquency rates and the migrant rates and −.18 (±.12) for the correlations between the juvenile delinquency rates and the intercity migrant rates. Whatever relationship exists between area-rates for migration and delinquency is attributable to intracity migration, and even this small correlation is reduced to a non-significant level when only "white" areas are considered.

The relationship of the mobility in ecological areas to rates of mental disorders is of special interest, since Faris and Dunham have advanced the hypothesis that mobility is one factor which may account for the differences in the distribution of different types of psychoses. In his introduction to the Faris and Dunham study, E. W. Burgess has suggested the desirability of studies of the relationships of different types of mobility and migration to the incidence of mental disorders.[1]

Unfortunately, data for insanity rates are not available for the same period as the migrant rates. The principal body of data in the Faris and Dunham study is for the period 1922–34. Since it is unlikely that the basic pattern of distribution of psychoses changed radically from this period to the 1935–40 migration period, these data have been correlated with the migrant rates despite the time discrepancy.

Faris and Dunham found that schizophrene rates were lowest at the periphery of the city and highest in the central disorganized areas, especially in the rooming-house districts and other types of areas characterized by excessive mobility. On the basis of this data and various theoretical considerations Faris and Dunham advanced the hypothesis that schizophrenic disorders are a function of the social isolation associated with excessive mobility. On the other hand, they found no significant ecological pattern for manic-depressive rates, although they did not deny that such a pattern might exist. Although there were actually considerable variations among the manic-depressive rates in different areas of the city, this pattern was characterized as "random" because the variations did not fit into the typical ecological or any other apparent pattern. On the basis of this "random" pattern, Faris and Dunham advanced the hypothesis that manic-depressive psychoses are psychoge-

[1] Faris, Robert E. L., and H. Warren Dunham, *Mental Disorders in Urban Areas* (Chicago: University of Chicago Press, 1939).

netic in orgin, that the social factors precipitating the onset of the psychoses are distributed at "random" in the city, and that excessive mobility is presumably not a relevant factor. On the basis of this interpretation of the differences between the schizophrenic and manic-depressive distinctive patterns, the expectation is that migrant rates should be positively correlated with rates of schizophrenic disorders and not correlated at all with rates of manic-depressive disorders.

The actual correlations are not consistent with the expectations. There are no significant correlations between the schizophrene rates and either migrant rate, but there are substantial correlations between the manic-depressive rates and both migrant rates. For the 46 areas, including the Negro areas, the correlations for the schizophrenic rates are +.12 (±.15) with intracity migrants and +.06 (±.12) with the intercity migrant rates. For the 43 "white" areas the correlations for the schizophrenic rates are +.11 (±.12) with intracity migrants and −.02 (±.15) for intercity migrants. On the other hand, for all 46 areas the correlations for the manic-depressive rates are +.68 (±.15) with intracity migrants. For the 43 "white" areas the correlations of the manic-depressive psychoses are +.72 (±.15) with the intracity migrants and +.60 (±.15) with the intercity migrants. Insofar as either intercity or intracity migrant rates are indices of mobility in an area, these correlations are inconsistent with the expectations based on the Faris and Dunham study.

This does not, by any means, invalidate the hypothesis that schizophrenic mental disorders are functionally related to the social isolation produced by excessive mobility of certain types. It does again indicate, however, that in attempting to validate such a relationship it will be necessary, as Burgess suggests in his introduction to the Faris and Dun-

ham study, to differentiate between different types of mobility and migration.

Insofar as the distribution of venereal disease cases is an index of the distribution of vice and socially unacceptable sex behavior, it may be considered to be another type of index of social disorganization which may be compared with the migrant distribution. The correlation between the syphilis rate for 1937 and the intercity migrant rate is +.22 (±.12). The correlation of the syphilis rate with the intracity migrant rate is +.39 (±.12). These small correlations are largely a function of high Negro syphilis rates. When the 10 community areas with large Negro populations are eliminated, the rank correlations between the syphilis rates and the migrant rates in the 65 "white" community areas fall to +.07 (±.12) for the intercity migrants and +.23 (±.12) for the intracity migrants. Neither of these correlation coefficients indicates any substantial relationship between the distribution of migrants and syphilitics. However, the relationship is more marked for the intracity migrants. This is consistent with a similar finding for juvenile delinquency rates.

Another type of social disorganization is that which centers about family disintegration. This may be interpreted to be especially relevant to the present problem, since the migrants have been shown to be concentrated in extrafamilial living arrangements. The latest period for which adequate data are available for the 75 community areas is 1929–35. Family disintegration rates are based on a combination of divorce cases and nonsupport cases.

For the 75 community areas, the correlation of the rate of family disintegration and the intercity migrant rate is +.26 (±.12). The correlation with the intracity migrant rate is +.57 (±.12). If the 10 "Negro" areas are omitted, the correlations between migrant rates and family disintegration rates are +.10 (±.12) for the intercity migrants and

+.46 (±.12) for intracity migrants. For all 75 community areas the correlations are small but significant for both types of migrants; for the "white" community areas, only the correlation with intracity migrant rates remains significant.

Discussion

The correlations between various indices of social disorganization and the migrant rates have not been found to be consistent. In some cases (e.g., schizophrenic psychoses) where correlations were expected on the basis of previous studies in ecology none were found. In at least one case (manic-depressive rates) where no correlation was expected, a significant correlation was found. In some cases a significant correlation was found between an index of social disorganization and the intracity migrant rate, but no significant correlation was found between the index of social disorganization and the intercity migrant rate (family disintegration, syphilis). In almost every case the correlations with the intracity migrant rates were greater than with the intercity migrant rates.

How can these findings be reconciled with each other and with the customary generalization that mobility and social disorganization are positively related? The first possibility to be considered is that change in residence, whether intracity or intercity, is not an index of mobility at all and that therefore nonconsistent relationship may be expected between these indices and indices of social disorganization. Mobility has already been defined several times in this study in terms of change, new experience, new stimulations. It involves a minimum of routine and a minimum of control of conduct by rigid community standards. The argument may be made that residential changes do not necessarily involve mobility in this sense.

It is true that some residential changes may change the daily routine of the migrant very little. However, on the average, changes in residence, particularly those which involve intercity migration, may be expected to disrupt the daily routine of the migrant. Even where the migrant moves into a house or a neighborhood similar to that which he left, there is an irreducible minimum break in routine, a minimum of new experiences, and at least temporary freedom from many social restraints. This is particularly true if the individual leaves part or all of his family behind him. Prior to the establishment of a matrix of new social relationships in the community, the migrant is to some extent a stranger. Social controls are relatively ineffective until he is known and located socially as well as spatially in the community. Intracity migrants may be considered to be somewhat less mobile than intercity migrants, since, presumably, a move within the city involves a lesser dislocation of established habit patterns.

A second possible explanation of the inconsistencies found is that different types of mobility or mobility of persons of different types do not necessarily all have the same relationship to each type of social disorganization. As has been indicated, the early statements of theories and findings relating social disorganization and mobility to the classical ecological gradient pattern were based on the settlement pattern of the immigrants of the late nineteenth and early twentieth centuries. This was a pattern based on the entry of the unskilled, low-status foreign-born at the center of the city and their gradual movement outward to the periphery after a period of assimilation and acculturation. These migrants were unaccustomed to the mobility and to the general cultural pattern of Chicago.

The migration pattern of the period 1935–40 is fundamentally different in character from this earlier immigration. The economic, educational, and social status of these later migrants is considerably higher than that of the earlier foreign migrants. The types of social disorganization associated with the mobility of such a group might be expected to differ from those associated with the mobility of the earlier immigrants.

The "newer" mobility represented by the intercity migrants also may differ fundamentally from the "older" immigration in that the intercity migrants are more likely to be accustomed to the mobility of city life than the "older" foreign migrants. This difference involves a consideration of a basic contradiction in the theories of urban sociology.

Urban sociologists attempt to explain both the nature of urban social organization and the phenomena of social disorganization in terms of the same concept —extreme mobility. On the one hand, mobility is used to explain social disorganization and psychopathic behavior. On the other hand, mobility is used to characterize the mode of life of the typical urban apartment-dwellers who may be living at considerable distances from the central disorganized areas. The concept of mobility is, in fact, frequently used to characterize the ideal-typical urban personality, the sophisticated rational personality which at its best is associated with intellectual and scientific achievements and genius for rational organization. Intelligence and inventiveness are frequently related to mental mobility. Yet, the same concept of mobility is used to explain the disorganization of personality and social life. To characterize mobility, per se, as a "cause" of social disorganization is to raise the question of why the typical urban dweller is not socially disorganized. It poses a further question of how the urban community continues to function at all, if the social process which is central in urban life is disorganizing and disrupting.

The hypothesis is advanced here that it is not the *amount* of mobility alone which distinguishes disorganized from normal urban areas but also the extent to which the population is *mentally mobile*—the extent to which it is *adapted* to mobility, and an established part of its culture. The ideal-typical urban dweller is usually characterized as a socially mobile person. He is a person who is adjusted to a relatively high rate of change and new experience as a normal part of daily life. He accepts change and assimilates it to his life organization. To the experienced urban dweller change in routine is in itself routine. If this were not the case, it would be difficult to conceive of the continued mobile urban environment. The adjusted urban dweller must be conceived to be one who has worked out a more or less stable pattern of life in terms of a moving equilibrium rather than a stable set of norms. To such a person and to the groups to which he belongs mobility is not necessarily disorganizing. It is a basic part of the structure of personal and social organization. On the other hand, to those persons who are unaccustomed to mobility, to whom frequent change is in itself a new experience, the mobility may well be disorganizing and demoralizing. The hypothesis advanced here assumes that in the mobile disorganized areas there is a concentration of people who are either unaccustomed to mobility or constitutionally unable to adjust to it. On the other hand, in such outlying apartment-house areas as Hyde Park the amount of mobility may be great, but the population consists largely of persons accustomed to urban life to whom mobility itself is routine and less likely to be disorganizing.

According to this formulation, the central disorganized areas should contain many population groups which are not yet fully adjusted to the urban mode of life. These may be regarded as the mentally immobile in the urban environment. Thus, in Chicago, the concentration in the central disorganized areas of foreign-born and Negro populations, subject to intense cultural conflict, has frequently been noted. Such groups are subject to intense mobility in the form of new experiences without having the typical urban life organization as a mode of adjustment. In some central slum areas with large foreign-born or Negro populations, there may even be a higher rate of social disorganization with relatively little residential mobility.

This relatively brief treatment of the manner in which mobility and social disorganization are related is by no means exhaustive. A detailed study of the incidence of specific types of social disorganization is not within the scope of this study. The intent has been to indicate, first, that the pattern of settlement of recent migrants to the city is not consistent with previous theories of the relationship between mobility and social disorganization. It is not consistent with the classical ecological gradient pattern. Secondly, this inconsistency has been related to a basic inconsistency in the use of the concept of mobility in urban sociology. These inconsistencies point to a need for reformulations of existing theory. As one step in this direction, a high rate of mobility has been postulated to be a normal component of urban life, not necessarily disorganizing in its effect on persons habituated to urban life. The hypothesis has been advanced that insofar as the types of social disorganization typically concentrated in central areas are related functionally to mobility, the relationship involves inexperience with mobility and not the quantity of mobility alone.

NEGRO MIGRATION DIFFERENTIALS

The analysis of the limited indirect data available on Negro migrants has indicated that although they are concentrated within the migrant zone both their distribution and their social char-

acteristics are distinctive. The specific findings may be summarized as follows:

1. In work status, occupational status, and educational status, the position of the Southern Negro migrants is not as favorable as that of white migrants as a whole compared to the general non-migrant population. With respect to occupation, migrants from each Southern region are heavily concentrated in the domestic service or other service work occupations.

2. With respect to each of these characteristics, the migrants from the Deep South have a lower status than either non-migrants or any other migrant groups.

3. Although all of the Negro migrant groups are overwhelmingly concentrated within the Negro zone, those from the North and West have relatively larger numbers on the white zone than any other Negro migrant group. Of the Southern migrants, those from the South Atlantic region have the greatest concentration in the white zone.

4. Inside the Negro zone the same groups of Negro migrants relatively most numerous in the white zone are relatively most numerous in the best Negro residential area. In the relatively low-status area of the Negro zone the Negro migrants from the Deep South are concentrated most consistently and in greatest numbers.

In general, Negro migrant differentials are distinctive from those of the whites. In terms of his social characteristics, the Negro migrant appears to have a different role from that of the white migrants. He is more likely than the white migrant to fit the stereotype of the "green" migrant whose socioeconomic status in the city is relatively low. The Negro internal migration of this period is comparable in some respects to the immigration of the late nineteenth and early twentieth centuries. The Negro migrant is taking the jobs at the bottom of the occupational pyramid which were formerly held by the immigrant.

SOME IMPLICATIONS OF THE FINDINGS

From the point of view of the city planner or the citizen who wishes to assess the effect of the migration to Chicago upon the human resources of the city the implications of the findings are that, on the whole, the city appears to gain desirable citizens in its migrants. At least with reference to the period 1935–40 the migrants tended to be relatively well-educated young adults on the threshold of their productive years, ready and willing to work, and able to find employment. These are characteristics which presumably would be judged desirable in a population by most citizens.

Insofar as a few specific migrant groups have been found to depart from this high standard, they have been identified as coming from areas whose cultural development and opportunities have lagged behind those of the nation as a whole. Although migrants of this type represent only a small part of all the migrants, their presence in Chicago is an indication that the stream of cityward migration is one aspect of the national interdependence which gives a great city a stake in the development of every part of the country.

A second implication of these findings is that theories of the growth and changes of the structure of American cities based on the migrant settlement pattern of the great period of foreign immigration may need to be modified. The evidence in this study has indicated that the settlement pattern of recent migrants, whether internal or foreign, is essentially different from that of the great mass of foreign immigrants of earlier periods. Therefore, it may be expected that the impact upon the structure of the city of the newer migration will be different in at least some respects from the earlier foreign immigration. Both the characteristics of the migrants and their "port of entry" within the city appear to have changed. Examination of the recent migrant distribution pattern strengthens those theories of urban growth which emphasize intensive development along fast radial transportation lines as a modification of purely concentric growth patterns.

Finally, the findings suggest the need for a revaluation of sociological theories concerning the relationship of mobility and personal or social disorganization. It well may be that mobility is not disorganizing to a population accustomed to a mobile life pattern or at least that in such a population social disorganization will take distinctive forms. In any event, there is evidence of a need to distinguish types of mobility and types of persons subject to mobility in using mobility as a central concept in urban sociology.

PART 2

Urban Social Organization and Mass Phenomena

Perhaps the set of insights which have come most belatedly to urban sociologists have been those concerning social organization in the urban setting. Because urban society differs in so many ways from rural society, which social philosophers had come to regard as the normal or most moral state, there was a tendency to deny that social organization existed in the city, or to claim that if it did it was inferior and lacking in fundamental respects. Consequently, everything rural was interpreted as "normal" and "good" and things urban were abnormal and bad by comparison. Evidence to justify this was amply provided by the boisterous and bawdy behavior in the cities that mushroomed in the American wilderness without benefit of the tradition of urban life already developing on the Continent. Science, learning, art, and aesthetics were small and comparatively insignificant forces in the total social life of American cities peopled primarily by recent frontiersmen or European peasant villagers. The exploitation of natural resources, processing of agricultural products, and a developing manufacturing dominated political and social as well as economic life. City life shocked and irritated many social philosophers of the early twentieth century, with the result that many sociologists had a distinctly negative view on many aspects of urban life.

Under these conditions, early observations concerning social organization in the city tended to emphasize disorganization or lack of organization. The huge and rapidly growing population, aggregated from the four corners of the earth, seemed to be an amorphous mass through which simple emotional responses of a contagious type, analogous to crowd phenomena, could sweep. Mass communication, mass movements, mass psychology attracted a great deal of comment and observation. Realization that the urban community is a highly intricate social as well as ecological and economic organization has come only gradually. That the social structure of the city includes all of the simpler forms of social organization (such as primary groups) found in rural societies, plus some distinctly new forms, also has been appreciated only rather recently. The contributions of this section are a part of this gradual unfolding of comprehension.

Despite the substantial nature of the contributions reported here, and the growing amount of research under way in many parts of the world, it remains true that the study of social organization in the city is still a lagging branch of urban research. Empirical data concerning complex organizations are difficult to obtain. The modern metropolis is such a very large and multidimensional topic for organizational study that it is difficult to subdivide it meaningfully into manageable research projects. Also, until recently there was a tendency for this branch of soci-

115

ology to be based on informal, impressionistic observation—a kind of social philosophy of contemporary city life. Within the last decade the systematic study of formal and informal social organization in the city has become an important field of social research, so that the next decade or two should see very significant strides forward.

6. The Function of Voluntary Associations in an Ethnic Community: "Polonia"*

HELENA ZNANIECKI LOPATA

Voluntary associations are social groups organized for the purpose of reaching one or more goals through co-operative, normatively integrated activity. The voluntary joining of an existing association or the formation of a new one indicates a positive evaluation of the goals, of the means proposed to attain them, and of fellow members. Voluntary associations are characterized as having a purpose, a division of labor, a hierarchy of statuses, associational norms, qualifications and tests for membership, property, and an identifying name and/or symbol.[1]

The present study of voluntary associations is limited to a particular ethnic community—the Polish-American community, or "Polonia."[2] It tries to answer the question: "What are the functions of the voluntary associations of Polonia in 1959 in the light of the developments and changes in these functions throughout the history of this community?"

Thomas and Znaniecki, in their study of *The Polish Peasant in Europe and America* (1914–18), devoted considerable attention to the functions of voluntary associations among Polish immigrants living in America and predicted that these associations would cease to exist in the 1920's. A cursory glance at Polonia in the 1950's indicates that this

prediction has not been borne out. We must therefore assume that either the interests and identifications of Polish Americans which make the functions of their voluntary associations important to them have remained unchanged since World War I or that over this interval of time the associations have been able to modify their functions so as to keep their membership intact or gain new members to replace those who have withdrawn.

My three-year study of the voluntary associations of Polonia was based on a hypothesis that any association of participants in such a community would have to perform three basic functions:

1. The formation and preservation of the community as a distinct, though not necessarily unchanging, unit;
2. The formation, development, and active manifestation of a close relationship between this community and the national culture society from which its members emigrated;
3. The formation, development, and active manifestation of a relationship between this community and the national culture society within which it now exists.

To discover the actual performance of these and other functions by the associations of Polonia, the following steps were taken:

1. A survey of sociological literature dealing with the assimilation of ethnic groups, with particular attention to factors facilitating or hindering this process.

* Based on the author's Ph.D. dissertation of the same title, Sociology, 1954.

[1] See chapter on "Social Groups" in Robert Bierstedt, *The Social Order* (New York: McGraw-Hill Book Co., Inc., 1957).

[2] A term used by Polish Americans.

117

2. A historical and comparative analysis of the functions of various voluntary associations in Polonia.[3]

3. An analysis of pertinent background information, especially membership in other Polish-American associations, as given in biographical sketches in *Who's Who in Polish America* and *Poles in Chicago, 1837–1937.*

4. An analysis of associational life in Chicago as described in *Dziennik Zwiazkowy* (The Alliance Daily), one of the two Polonia dailies in Chicago.

5. Presentation of questionnaires to five hundred members at meetings of twenty different associations in Chicago and analysis of their answers.

6. Interviews with residents of the community and with leaders and participants in local and superterritorial associations.

THE FOUNDING OF POLONIA

The Poles came to this country in large waves relatively late in the history of European migrations. The heavy immigration did not start until 1880, gaining momentum up to the peak year of 1912–13, which brought 174,365 Poles to the United States.[4] A frequent estimate of the number of persons of Polish birth and parentage who were living in America in 1920 is 3,000,000.

Those who migrated during the period of sizeable movement were primarily peasants from the rural, non-industrial areas of Poland. Upon arrival in the United States, however, they settled mainly in urban, industrialized centers. Since they lacked the knowledge and skills which could be utilized there, they obtained only the lowest-paying positions within its economic structure.[5] They lacked the economic resources to command any but the lowest-rental housing, located in areas of the city which were considered undesirable by the economically more successful dominant groups. The lack of education and of familiarity with urbanized, industrialized life had the further effect of creating a wide social gap between the peasant migrants and the dominant segments of society. On the part of the peasants, it resulted in bewilderment and confusion about the strange and often hostile and deprecatory world in which they found themselves.

In addition, both they and the dominant group were affected by the differences in culture. The Polish language is very different from English; and Polish culture at the time of the migration was primarily feudal, patriarchal, Catholic, and characterized by *Gemeinschaft* relations, especially in the more isolated rural areas. The peasant came from the strata of Polish society in which strong kinship ties and in-group control were accompanied by a more or less unified, single pattern of behavior resistant to change. This made the learning of a new culture more difficult for the peasant than for the more cosmopolitan middle- and upper-class migrants. Although lacking biological traits which would make for visible hereditary differentiation from the dominant American society, his culturally acquired characteristics prevented the first generation from easily assimilating into American society and helped create a physical stereotype of the Pole.

All these factors, combined with family and even village migration, resulted in a tendency of the Poles to desire, or to be forced into, living in close physical proximity to each other. Gradually, the need for services and activities not available for satisfying the wants peculiar to the Poles led to the growth of a service

---

[3] Based on primary sources, records of meetings and speeches, and secondary sources, histories of the community and of specific associations.

[4] R. A. Schermerhorn, *These Our People* (Boston: D. C. Heath & Co., 1949), p. 265.

[5] Robert E. Park and Ernest W. Burgess, *The City* (Chicago: University of Chicago Press, 1925).

industry[6] and a multiplicity of voluntary associations among them. Thus, a real community arose in the ecologically distinct settlements of Poles in America. By the year 1919, it was possible for a person to live, work, shop, go to church, send the children to school, and spend leisure time within the confines of such a community, never needing to speak English or come into primary contact with members of the dominant group.

Purposeful assimilation is undertaken only when there is a desire for membership in the dominant society and knowledge of the means by which this can be gained; and it can be gained only with the help of the dominant society. The presence and functioning of a community which satisfactorily meets all the needs of its residents is a deterrent to both the desire and acquiring of knowledge necessary to join the dominant society. In the case of the Polish immigrant, the desire for immediate acculturation was comparatively weak. Also, because of the development of Polish nationalism, identification with American society was relatively slow in its development.

Additional factors which played a role in slowing up the rate of assimilation of Poles in America can be briefly summarized as follows:

1. Formation of numerous ethnic voluntary associations whose chief function was the preservation of the community as a distinct entity;

2. Ability to transmit the culture and identification of the community to new generations through schools, the church, and associations, in isolation from American culture;

3. Recent revival of interest in Polish culture, due partly to the arrival of displaced persons.

[6] Everett C. Hughes and Helen MacGill Hughes, *Where Peoples Meet* (Glencoe, Ill.: Free Press, 1952).

Nevertheless, changes did occur, and the shift of the community from Polish to Polish-American orientation reflects a gradual moving away from Polish society and the formation of an intermediate, marginal product.

Certain factors have assisted the gradual assimilation of Polish Americans into the main stream of American culture:

1. Settlement in this country for a period long enough to permit the birth and growth of a second and even a third generation without direct contact with the mother country;

2. Lack of hereditary physical differences between Polish Americans and members of the dominant society;

3. Abstinence from use of forcible means of assimilation on the part of the dominant group;

4. Lack of marked discrimination and prejudice;

5. Contact with American culture through schools, mass communication media, and economic activities;

6. Appearance of other migrant groups (Southern white, Negro, and Latin American) at the bottom of the socio-economic hierarchy;

7. Bad economic and social conditions in the mother country;

8. Increase in similarity of experiences with the rest of American society;

9. Satisfaction with life in America;

10. Economic and geographical dispersal;

11. Immigration of displaced persons who accentuate the increasingly American character of the Polish-American community.

THE FUNCTIONS OF POLISH-AMERICAN VOLUNTARY ASSOCIATIONS WITHIN THE COMMUNITY

In referring to "Polonia," Polish Americans indicate a consciousness of the existence of a unity which is marginal to both Polish and American societies. The original immigrants, as Thomas and

Znaniecki pointed out, did not form a self-conscious, unified group. There were no strong bonds connecting those who came from different parts of Poland or who settled in different parts of America. The consciousness of a bond between all persons of Polish birth or descent living in America grew up gradually as a result of the efforts of a number of different leaders.

The initial broadening of communication between several groups in the same area was due to consciousness of the bond of Polish Roman Catholicism, as contrasted with the English-speaking version of that religion. The Polish Roman Catholic Union, founded in 1880, tried to bring together only Roman Catholics in the United States who were identified with Polish culture. Within a relatively short time, however, several other voluntary associations whose emphasis was entirely or at least primarily upon the development and preservation of national culture consciousness arose among Polish Americans.

The programs of these early associations called for complete identification of the membership with the mother country, but this lost its appeal for Polish Americans in the 1920's. As a result, the existing voluntary associations were faced with the problem of finding a new orientation sufficiently strong to prevent their own and the community's dissolution. At the time Thomas and Znaniecki made their study (1918), the Polish associations had not yet found new functions—hence the prediction of their early death.

In the 1920's, Polish Americans turned their attention to the prejudice and discrimination which persons identified as Poles allegedly faced in contacts with the dominant American society. Desire for a better status of Poles in American society presented community associations with a dilemma which took over a decade to resolve. If prejudice against the Poles was keeping them from economic and social equality within the larger community and if they desired this equality, then one of the ways it could be acquired was by resigning "Polishness," i.e., by acculturation and assimilation of individual Poles into the dominant society. However, if the associations, by encouraging assimilation and providing means for it, undertook the function of helping their members, they would naturally be working for their own eventual dissolution.

The assimilation solution was unacceptable to Polonia in the 1920's and 1930's. In the first place, for many individuals such a change of identification and culture was psychologically too difficult. In the second place, Polish Americans felt that it would correspond to an admission of the inferiority of their own cultural background. In the third place, the very nature of the community and the life of its associations lay in the performance of a distinctive function based upon the existence of a group feeling of separation from the larger society. Accordingly, the people who had vested social, psychological, and economic interests in the life of the community sought in the 1920's and 1930's to find justification for the continued existence of Polonia.

The task which the associations faced was twofold: first, the formulation of an ideology which would satisfactorily explain a continuing need for their existence; second, the addition of activities which would appeal to the interests of the changing Polish American and prevent him from searching for associations outside the community.

The ideological basis for the voluntary associations in Polonia since 1938 assumes that their continued existence and active functioning are necessary not so much for Poland as for all persons of Polish birth and descent living in America. It assumes further that the life of the American society is determined politically, socially, and economically by the successful pressure of powerful and well-organized ethnic subgroups.

Acceptance of this view of American society would lead to the conclusion that strong support of Polish-American voluntary associations on the part of every person of Polish birth and descent is indispensable for his or her own welfare. It is to his best interest to work for the betterment of the status of the whole subgroup of which he is irrevocably a member. The only way Polish Americans can obtain some of this power pressure is by organizing and using the same types of pressure as other ethnic minority groups do.

This ideology has led to the development and intensification of two functions. One is that of crystallizing those aspects of Polish and Polish-American culture common to all subgroups of Polonia and of imparting this culture to old and young alike, so that their co-operative contribution can be secured and their self-image made more prestigeful. The second is that of improving the status of the unified group by protecting its "rights" against other groups, by applying all sorts of pressures on its behalf and "educating" the rest of American society to its importance and growing influence.

The Educational and Cultural Functions of Polish-American Voluntary Associations

The educational functions of organized groups in Polonia before World War I were dual: first, education of the adult peasant immigrants about Polish national culture by intellectual and political leaders both here and in Europe; and second, the formal imparting of this culture *in toto* to their descendants. The second function required a voluntary effort on the part of the Poles in America to build and finance formal schools in which their children could learn their own culture. Most of these schools were formed within the Polish Roman Catholic parish and were taught by religious personnel.

Statistics on the number of schools supported privately or parochially by Polish Americans are contradictory. If we accept Roucek's authority, there were in the 1930's approximately 560 Polish-American parochial schools with 276,286 pupils, 27 seminaries and normal schools, and 3 colleges plus one college and one seminary of the Polish National Catholic Church.

Rev. Francis Bolek listed fewer students in 1948 than Roucek in 1937, although more schools were mentioned by him. Considering the natural multiplication of Polish Americans and the increase through immigration over these eleven years, the relative number of schools had not kept up with the population increase. This means that increasingly large percentages of children of Polish birth or descent are attending public schools. Furthermore, the geographical movement of Polish Americans to new city areas leads one to suspect that frequently the schools which formerly served Polish Americans exclusively are still listed, although most of the students now come from other ethnic groups. The dispersal involved in individual family mobility further increases the number of children not under the influence of parochial schools. Two conclusions can be drawn from this material on Polish parochial schools: one, that Polish Americans have supported a rather high number of parochial schools throughout the history of their settlement; and, second, that the proportion of children attending these schools, as compared with the public schools, is steadily decreasing.

The very function of the parochial school has undergone changes. Started originally as an attempt to transmit Polish culture *in toto* as well as the Catholic religion, teaching was done entirely in the Polish language, with stress on the literature and history of Poland. Gradually an increasing number of graduates from these grade schools wished to enter public high schools. It then became necessary to prepare these students by means of a curriculum resembling that of the public grade schools. In recent years, some of the parochial schools have even dropped the teaching of Polish, and the schools themselves are more like American schools than like the former Polish-oriented centers of ethnic culture.

Simultaneously with the functioning of the parochial schools have been the efforts of all Polonia associations to educate the youth. As in the parochial schools, at first the effort was directed to preservation of the whole of Polish culture through its total transmission to the youth. In their early years, the larger, multipurposed associations in Polonia had "culture and education" sections,[7] e.g., the Polish Women's Alliance and especially the Polish Falcons. Almost every group had and continues to have "completing" schools for the purpose of teaching the Polish language and the literature and history of Poland to those children who attend public schools where these subjects are not taught. As late as 1959, a new series of such "completing" schools was opened in Chicago by the Illinois Division of the Polish American Congress.[8]

A change, however, has occured in the

educational programs for the youth. Instead of trying to transmit total Polish culture, the associations are now stressing those aspects of the national or Polish-American culture which deal with literary and artistic achievements and especially with contributions to world or American culture. The purpose behind this selective education is to make the youth "proud of their Polish heritage," and it is dependent upon increasing Americanization of the younger generation and the new ideology.

The same emphasis can be found in the "cultural clubs" among Polish Americans which have evolved, particularly in the last two decades. Such groups concentrate on the preservation, study, and "development of appreciation" of certain aspects of Polish culture. Composed primarily of adults, many of whom are Poles of the second or even third generation, they build the self-confidence of these people by stressing the "superiority" of Polish culture.

A number of institutes devoted to the study and preservation of Polish culture have been organized by the "new emigration," that is, the political refugees and displaced persons who have come to the United States since 1939. These are being gradually joined by the more educated of the "old emigration" and their descendants.

Polonia's interest in acquiring knowledge about artistic aspects of Polish and Polish-American culture can best be exemplified by the Polish Arts Clubs. The first of these was formed in Chicago in 1926 with the following purposes:

1. To broaden our knowledge, appreciation, and enjoyment of serious music, art, and literature;

2. To render moral and material aid to promising writers, musicians, and artists;

3. To make Polish music, art, and

---

[7] "The Polish Roman Catholic Union added a Youth Division in 1939 to supplement its already existing educational department. Its activities are typical: it arranges choir competitions, dramatic circles, schools of Polish language and spelling contests in both Polish and English for the children of Polish parochial schools. Its 'scouts' and 'daughters' participate in essay contests and courses about Poland. The Division of Educational Aid which used to support a Polish professorship at De Paul University furnishes stipends to students at Weber High School. The Union itself assumed in 1941 the $109,000 mortgage of the Seminary at Orchard Lake." (Quoted from Mieczyslaw Szawleski, *Wychodztwo Polskie w Stanech Zjednoczonych Ameryki* [Warsaw, Zakladu Narodowego Imienia Ossolinskich, 1924], p. 143.)

[8] *Dziennik Zwiazkowy*, Chicago, October 1, 1959.

literature better known in the United States.[9]

In 1947, the various cultural clubs in the different Polish-American communities combined to form the American Council of Polish Cultural Clubs, which serves as a clearing house for news and arranges annual national conventions. Development of "appreciation" and knowledge about the artistic and literary aspects of Polish culture on the part of Polish Americans and diffusion of this appreciation and knowledge to the rest of the American society is the specific function of many local cultural clubs which have multiplied in the past two decades. Throughout all their announcements, both oral and written, runs the same refrain: "We should be proud of being Americans of Polish birth or descent. Look at the world-famous writers, composers, musicians, and artists Poland has contributed." It is this very refrain which the *Polish Review* repeated, as it attempted to renationalize the Poles in America during World War II.

Those groups which do not actually participate in the creation or re-creation of art consider it their function to encourage Polish and Polish-American artistic creation or expression. They arrange for concerts by known performers, exhibit artistic objects, and in other ways either help persons who are new contributors or publicize the works of known culture developers. The tours of Polish artists in the United States have been made possible through the co-operative efforts of the many groups devoted to cultural activities and to the multipurposed associations.

A number of groups in Polonia participate actively in the expression of artistic aspects of Polish culture. Such are the relatively numerous choirs who present

Polish programs. They perform at almost every important social event in Polonia. In each large community, a number of "orchestras" or "bands" specialize in playing typically Polish music. Having a Polish name familiar to the community, knowing the national songs, and contributing to the "we" feeling of an event, they have a virtual monopoly at the numerous dances given by the associations of Polonia. The very formal "Night in Poland" ball, organized yearly by the Legion of Young Polish Women and attended by Polonia "society," makes a great point of having a Polish orchestra.

The two recently initiated weekly TV programs devoted to Polish folk music and dancing, conducted by Polish Americans, have, however, been greeted ambivalently. Some Polish Americans object to them because they consider them of "low" level and fear that Americans will be still further reinforced in their conception of Polish culture as peasant folk culture. This ambivalence demonstrates the conflict in Polonia between two segments interested in preserving different aspects of Polish culture: those who enjoy certain elements of the folk culture, such as dances, costumes, songs, and holiday observances, are frequently criticized by those who want to stress only the "intellectual" national cultural achievements, such as the music of Chopin. Both groups resort to class-conscious descriptions of themselves and "the others."

An organized professional theater has several times been attempted in Chicago. In 1906, a group of actors was collected, a business manager hired, and a theater rented, but they survived only a few years. Another group, formed in 1912, tried to revive Polish theater. Again the attempt failed because of inability to draw sufficiently large and sustaining audiences to cover expenses.[10]

[9] Thaddeus Slesinski, "The Development of Cultural Activities in Polish American Communities," *Polish American Studies*, V, Nos. 3–4 (July–December, 1948), 100.

[10] Karol Wachtl, *Polonia w Ameryce* (Philadelphia: by author, 1944), p. 212.

During the 1920's and 1930's, sporadic productions appeared in Polonia, due mostly to the efforts of one community leader. In the last two decades, however, the number of productions and theatrical groups have increased considerably. Professional actors residing in Chicago have formed the "Theater Reduta" and "Towarzystwo Scena Polska." In the fall of 1959, productions appeared almost monthly. Frequently, internationally famous Polish actors come to Chicago and take leading roles. The productions are attended by two groups: The social elite of the old emigration with their descendants and the "new emigration."

Religion and the Polish-American Associations

Thomas and Znaniecki found the Roman Catholic parish to be one of the major social forces in Polonia. It performed not only the function of the parish in Poland, but also that of the "commune." As a result of migration and settlement in a foreign land, the early Poles in America centered most of their organizational and social life around the church, its institutions, and building, to which they devoted great efforts and sums of money. Thus, the parish was the first organized institution of the Polish American.

Polish Roman Catholics have over the centuries developed a very strong tie between their religion and their national culture. The close affiliation of religious with nationalistic feelings developed during the long years of political occupation of "Polish lands," when attempts were made to repress Catholicism as a means of denationalizing Poles.

The immigrant Polish peasant in the United States was faced with an existing American Catholic hierarchy and a parish system different from the one to which he was accustomed. He resented the attempted imposition of leadership from priests who did not understand his language or the variations to the ritual which he valued. Therefore, one of his first steps was to obtain Polish priests and to form national parishes. Another feature of American Catholicism heightened the resentment against its hierarchy. Parishes had to be built and maintained by residents of each particular geographical area, although the resulting structures and possessions then became part of the superterritorial religious property. The Polish immigrants did unite and work hard to build their own churches and parochial schools, old-age homes and orphanages, but their resentment against the hierarchy grew and spread even against Polish priests.

This resentment broke into open conflict with the American version of Roman Catholicism in 1904. In that year 147 clerical and lay representatives of 20,000 church members in five north central states of America met and officially broke away from this church, forming the Polish National Catholic Church.

The majority of Poles did not join the National Church, but remained within the Roman Catholic Church. However, their early voluntary associations formed for the purpose of building and maintaining a church and related institutions were usually organized and led by Polish priests. In fact, at first, the clergy formed the chief source of leadership even of groups whose primary functions were other than direct support of the church. Gradually, secular leaders became trained by parish-located groups, and they took over the leadership. Religious emphasis has been declining in many of these groups as their members found other interests, though a hard core of associations whose function is to help the religious personnel in the performance of their roles still remains in each parish. But other groups have tended to separate from the parish, with frequently expressed dissatisfaction over clerical attempts to control their activities.

Attempts to unify all Polish-American Roman Catholics with primary emphasis upon religion have been numerous, but not so successful as intergroup associations which relegate religion to a secondary place. The Polish Roman Catholic Union had much difficulty in the early years and much more after the formation of the purely nationalistic Polish National Alliance, which has continued to be the more successful of the two. A number of groups broke away from the PRCU in the 1880's and 1890's because they objected to the regulations giving almost dictatorial power to the Roman Catholic Church. The PRCU saved its associational life by the addition of other functions besides religion, especially insurance and a stronger emphasis upon Polish nationalism, in conjunction with its continuing interest in religious preservation.

Other attempts to organize interassociational groups for Poles with main emphasis on religion were abortive. Several Catholic congresses were held, but they did not produce any lasting association. Even the Union of Polish Chaplains in America, an organization for professional religious men, was short-lived.

Despite the decrease of emphasis in Polonia upon the religious function as primary motivation of many groups, loss of members of formerly national parishes, decline in parochial school enrolment of Polish Americans, and hostility to strong clerical leadership, the connection between the religious aspect of Polish national culture and the other aspects remains. Most of the multipurposed associations, with the exception of the socialistic and some professional groups, do emphasize education in and preservation of Roman Catholicism as a secondary function. Even the Polish National Alliance, which originally refused to include in its constitution any religious qualification, did so later.

The Economic Function of Polish-American Voluntary Associations

The function of providing economic aid to members had an early start in Polonia. Thomas and Znaniecki found during World War I a proliferation of mutual-aid groups, frequently united into federated insurance organizations. This led many observers to conclude that the peasant was incapable of maintaining interest in idealistic associations and, therefore, the large fraternal associations were based on local mutual-aid groups.[11]

However, certain qualifications must be kept in mind to avoid overemphasis on this one function. In the first place, mutual-aid societies have never limited themselves to the economic function alone, as shown by the extent of their activities and the frequency of interaction among members. Second, many of the federated associations started out with idealistic functions and only later added insurance to provide themselves with a broader base and more working capital, offering the already formed mutual-aid groups a service by taking over the performance of the economic function. Third, if the economic function were the only important one, then many associations would have limited themselves to that function alone, whereas none of the Polish-American fraternal groups have done so, becoming, instead, multipurposed centers of the community. Finally, many associations having idealistic bases without any insurance program have existed in Polonia and are constantly being formed in recent decades.

Nonetheless, the economic function has played an important role in the life of the major Polonia associations. It was frequently introduced to save already existing organizations from inevitable death. The strongest and oldest associations, such as the Polish National Alli-

11 Szawleski, *op. cit.*

ance, the Polish Roman Catholic Union, the Polish Alma Mater, the Polish Falcons, the Sea League, the Polish Women's Alliance, the Polish unions, and the Spojnia of the Polish National Catholic Church are federated, multi-purposed groups with insurance programs. "Social memberships," not involving insurance, are given by some groups but are small in number compared to insurance memberships.[12]

None of the more recently formed associations have developed insurance programs. Factors acting as deterrents to new insurance programs are: the popularity of the established insurance structure; decrease of interest in such programs with improvement in the economic position of Polish Americans; a tendency to utilize American insurance companies by the more Americanized younger generations who are not interested in other functions of these groups and do not want to be bothered with repeated contacts with the societies; geographical dispersal; and increase of interest in more culturally oriented, idealistic associations. Nonetheless, the "new emigration" (those who came over after the outbreak of World War II, most of whom were displaced persons) has added insurance to other functions of its own groups, thus repeating the pattern of the early life of the old emigrations. Many groups in Polonia, of course, do not and never have had insurance programs or directly economic functions.

A quasi-economic function seems to be performed by the Polish professional associations. Polonia has groups of doctors and of lawyers which are identified by the prefix "Polish-American." As Hughes and Hughes point out in *Where Peoples Meet*, the professional man with

12 In 1959, the PNA had 222 social members, as compared to 337,635 insurance members. The Polish Falcons listed the largest proportion of social members: 5,153 to 22,364 insurance members (*Polish American Journal*, XLVIII, No. 21 [October 10, 1959], 1).

a non-visible minority group background must decide whether to identify himself with this minority and thus attempt to obtain a monopoly over possible clients who also identify themselves with it, or to break relations with it and seek clients within the general society. Not only professional, but other occupational groups tend to be formed in Polonia for the benefit of those who share not only the occupational interest, but Polish-American background. The Polish-American Federal Employees organization is an example of this tendency.

The Function of Meeting Special Interests within the Community

The Polish-American community contains within it persons who share certain interests. Occupational groups belong, of course, to this type of special-interest associations. So do the clubs which bring together persons interested in the same activity, such as sewing, sports, or card playing. The sport clubs have multiplied in recent years, indicating an Americanization of interests; bowling, for instance, is unknown in Poland. Their purpose is to carry on activities of a specific type with the co-operation and often in competition with other members and sometimes with other groups. The singing societies are of this type, with the additional function of co-operative performances for non-members.

Other associations, such as political clubs, show more basic divisions of the community, for they are mutually exclusive. It is only in recent years, however, that Republican Party clubs have been organized among Polish Americans.

A number of groups for veterans of the armed forces exist in Polonia. These have the multiple function of providing companionship for those who shared similar experiences in the past, "protection" of their interest, and care of members who are no longer able to be active participants. In the past years there have been two main veterans' associations in Polonia, the Society of Veterans of the Polish Army and the Polish Legion of American Veterans. Only those who fought with the Polish armies can join the former group. A recent development within this group was the breaking away of some members and the formation by them of the Society of Combatants of Polish Armies of World War II. The parent organization had been composed of veterans of World War I until the entrance of Polish displaced persons. The new veterans were, on the average, much younger, more nationalistic toward Poland, and more fully trained in modern warfare. When other members attempted to maintain control over the group by passing a bylaw that officers of the association had to be American citizens, the "new emigration" veterans formed their own association.

The conflict between the "new" and the "old" emigration is further suggested by the fact that most persons arriving after 1939 formed separate groups rather than joining established Polish-American associations. The Mutual Aid Society of the New Emigration, for example, is composed of about 1,000 persons, all of whom came to America after 1939. Meetings are held in Polish, and that is also the language of informal communication. The DP's tend to have a higher educational background than the early settlers; they come from all social classes; and they have a strongly developed national consciousness. Considering themselves political exiles, they regard the "old emigration" and its descendants as completely "Americanized" and "denationalized."

In the first years of the settlement of DP's who had been sponsored by Polish Americans, a great deal of hostility sprang up between these two groups, and the presence of the fresh arrivals seemed to have increased the Americanization of the original Polonia residents by showing them how non-Polish they had become. In more recent years, however, there has been greater co-op-eration, especially on occupational and educational levels which have cut across "degree of Americanization" lines. Furthermore, the new emigration Poles tend to be more conscious of Polish culture and more "proud" of its various aspects. Coming into contact with descendants of Polish peasant immigrants who are frequently ashamed of this background, the new emigrants have tended to increase the interest of Polonia in Polish literary culture. Thus, the presence of new migrants seems, in the long run, to have reinforced the interest in various aspects of Polish culture which is characteristic of the new ideology adopted by Polonia's associations.

The Welfare Function and Care for Deviants within the Community

Thomas and Znaniecki found, in 1918, a complete absence in Polonia of associations concerned with the prevention of individual or neighborhood disorganization or with care of members of the community who were unsuccessful in their adjustment and labeled as deviants by the outside society. Extreme interest in Polish rather than in local problems, lack of group cohesion, and the absence of a past history of group responsibility for the behavior of its members prevented community activity along these lines. A slow reorganization of attitudes and the development of completely new techniques to meet the needs of life in urban, industrial America were necessary before any attempt at "caring for our own" or taking responsibility for the unsuccessful and deviants began to be undertaken, and this move is still so new that only a few attempts have been recorded.

In reviewing the history of Polonia and its present activities, the investigator is struck by the enormous sums of money and the concentration of effort still directed toward Poland. In particular, the relief of war victims has been and still is receiving co-operative and intensive support from almost all the voluntary associations. Until recent years, assistance given to Polish Americans in the form of economic aid was made to members of each group separately. In spite of a high delinquency rate among second-generation Polish Americans, in spite of slum and near-slum conditions in which many immigrants lived and are continuing to live, very little co-operative effort is directed toward alleviation of these problems. In fact, hardly any reference to such problems can be found in any of the literature.[13]

One of the explanations for the lack of community-wide co-operative efforts to meet the problems of adjustment to American life is undoubtedly connected with the conflict and strife within Polonia. Very rarely has any form of co-operative interorganizational activity been possible, and then primarily only for crises in Poland. The question naturally arises: Why have community problems not been a strong unifying link among Polish Americans? A survey of the life and orientation of the community suggests the hypothesis that Polish Americans have never even admitted the existence of deep problems within the community. Such an admission would lead to further loss of prestige. Co-operative efforts to help deviants would involve publicity and awareness of such problems. In its constant striving for prestige in both Poland and America,

the community has chosen to direct its activity toward relief of Poland and toward political pressure and cultural activities which would gain internal and American recognition of Polonia. And it has tended to reject or at least ignore those members of the community who do not contribute to the effort to raise the status of Polish immigrants and their descendants.

The Function of Providing Polite Companionship[14]

The "social hour" follows most meetings in Polonia. The function of providing members with the companionship of those of similar background and/or interests and of arranging social gatherings for their enjoyment is performed by all groups whose participants meet in face-to-face relations. The Legion of Young Polish Women plans at least three large-scale social events for Polonia each year, including the "Night in Poland" ball.

INTERNAL ORGANIZATION OF ASSOCIATIONAL LIFE IN POLONIA

A glance at the association life of Polonia over the years discloses two trends: (*a*) the combination of numerous local groups into fewer multipurposed, superterritorial organizations, and (*b*) conflict and disunity within and among these organizations.

A federated, multipurposed organization in Polonia, such as the Polish National Alliance, the Polish Roman Catholic Union, the Polish Alma Mater, the Polish Women's Alliance (and ten other groups of this type) usually developed in the following order:

1. With the increase in immigration at the end of the nineteenth century, numerically small local groups were formed

[13] One of the few references to this subject was made in the *Polish American Journal* of March 28, 1953. Editor Len Porzak quotes with agreement the Chicago Society Forum: "Our prestige is low in the USA. Our 'Polish' organizations should be criticized for stressing Polish culture to the absolute exclusion of basic social and economic problems, such as Employment Bureaus for our youth, proper scholarship, housing programs, delinquency and Bureau of Information" (p. 2). Harold Finestone of the Institute for Juvenile Research in Chicago is now preparing a comparison of the attitudes toward the deviant and their consequences in Italian-American and in Polish-American communities.

[14] Florian Znaniecki, in his last unpublished work on *Social Roles*, has a chapter dealing with the culturally structured relations of "polite companionship" (1957).

in various communities at the time of their settlement, and these multiplied.

2. Individuals or small groups of leaders developed plans for uniting these local groups and called together conferences of representatives of as many geographically scattered groups as they could contact and influence.

3. Representatives did attend the conference and accept the idea of a federated organization. A charter was drawn up, officers were elected, and plans were made for expansion.

4. Expansion occured through:

a) The addition of already existing "societies"—the term used for member groups;

b) The formation of new groups where none existed or existing ones did not wish to join.

5. A complex organizational system was developed, providing for centralization, but also delegation of power, usually a central body, regional, district, and smaller area groups of member societies, and national congresses for policy formation and/or support for policies centrally developed.

6. New groups performing specialized functions or consisting of special categories of members, frequently lacking a local basis, were gradually added and old ones dissolved as the interests of members changed.

The two main problems involved in the formation of federated groups were definition of functions with a sufficiently broad, yet significant appeal to large numbers of Polish Americans, and establishment of an organizational structure that met all the requirements satisfactorily. Centralization of authority was frequently opposed by a desire for greater autonomy and/or voice in policy-making on the part of member groups.

The organizations succeeded in solving the first problem by stressing Polish nationalism until the early 1920's and then by changing to the new ideology, and by the addition of many functions, such as insurance, to their orginally stated purposes as the interests of Polish Americans changed.

The problem of the organizational distribution of power continues to plague Polonia associations, resulting in frequent schism, complete withdrawal, and formation of new groups. Relatively frequent resort has been taken to outside authorities by referral to American courts to settle disputes over power. Most existing federated groups developed strong central bodies, which were absolutely essential for those with insurance programs. Conflicts most frequently occured during national congresses over election of officers, policy-making, and especially dues and representation. The smaller groups have attempted to set up limitations of power on the part of the larger societies.

At the present time, the Polish National Alliance is the leading group in Polonia, both numerically and in the amount of activity its members and leaders undertake. Its Chicago Society is one of the most prestigeful and active in the community. Its president is the acknowledged spokesman of Polonia and has been able to organize an interassociational group, the Polish American Congress, of which he is also the president. Besides the PNA, the women's associations are the only ones which have been able to maintain their membership. Even the Polish Roman Catholic Union is steadily decreasing. The total number of persons having memberships in the fourteen fraternal associations in 1959 is 779,639, with a total decrease since 1958 of 3,595. In addition to these, Polonia has federations of groups without insurance, such as the Polish Singers Alliance, the Alliance of Malapolska (a region in Poland) Clubs, the American Council of Polish Cultural Clubs, etc.

The various local and federated associations of Polonia have at various times attempted to organize interorganizational associations. There have been at least eighteen of these in the history of the community, each of them aiming to combine the efforts of various groups along a certain line of activity and especially to act as spokesman for Polonia in its relations with Poland and America. Some of these have lasted only as long as it took to plan and conduct the first conference. None has lasted throughout the history of Polonia.

The various attempts met with failure mainly for two reasons: the lack of goals sufficiently strong to appeal to large numbers of groups and the constant struggle between existing organizations for control of these associations. The endorsement of an interorganizational association by one faction of Polonia's groups usually meant its ultimate death because of the opposition of other factions. An exception exists at the present time, when the unifying link is not so much the political situation of Poland, but the increasing interest in political pressure upon the American government for status recognition of Polish Americans.

Polish Americans are now conscious of their past failures to unify under a group composed of representatives of their associations which would co-ordinate their efforts in relation to outside societies. They frequently attribute this lack of unity to "Polishness." In fact, they state that Poles are too individualistic to do anything but fight each other. But the development and acceptance of the new ideology of American society and Polonia's place in it provide a sufficient basis for some co-operation through the Polish American Congress, which has survived since 1953 despite some conflicts.

Thus, the Polonia of this time is quite well organized. The majority of active Polish Americans do have knowledge of the activities of others and co-operate in many events. This awareness and co-operation is probably true for most of the relatively decreasing number of Americans of Polish birth and descent.

It is obvious that Polish-American associations are continuing to meet the needs of sufficient numbers of persons to keep themselves going. Their organization and activities frequently resemble those of American associations more than those of the original Polonia groups. However, for economic, companionate, and prestige purposes, the Polish-American associations still provide the satisfaction of certain needs in ways not duplicated by American associations. As one of the active participants in Polonia associations summarized for me: "I'd rather be a big fish in here than a nobody out there." And, believing at least partially in their image of American society, such persons continually concentrate their attention on the "greatness" of their cultural heritage and on the importance of "Poles sticking together" in order to "get our own" from the Irish, Italians, Jews, Germans, *et al.* who compose the United States.

The Polish Mass Media and Voluntary Associations

In the city of Chicago there are approximately 500,000 persons of Polish birth or descent. The majority of them are settled in the near northwest and on the south side of the city (towns of Lake and Russell Square) and in the steel community of Hegewish. Within these four areas, an undetermined number of associations perform their multiple functions. Most of them have monthly meetings, a varying number of "parties," and an annual banquet. They are concerned with the collection of money for the relief of Poland, church activities, educational stipends or grants. Their members are, more frequently than not, holders of insurance policies. District and other regionally federated meetings draw representatives from the local groups, and their social events are usually open to all residents of Poland. Throughout the year, a number of theatrical productions are given in church or school auditoriums. The Polish Arts Fair in Chicago draws hundreds of persons. The main social event is the "Night in Poland" ball which takes place in February. Polish national holidays are celebrated with parades and speeches. Sports competitions occur with regularity.

News about all these associations is communicated in the Polish language by Polonia-directed press and radio. This is how the activities which require community co-operation are publicized by the groups which are sponsoring them. The Polish press, however, performs more complex functions than just those of a local newspaper. The Polish press has helped Polish-American associations and Polonia as a whole to develop, crystallize, and even change their basic orientation toward the two national culture societies. The press has served a multiplicity of functions: it gives local news; formulates and spreads community ideology; unifies geographically dispersed groups; evaluates and publicizes activities of the leaders; and also reflects internal conflicts. It is so edited and orientated that the individual Polish-American reader gets a feeling of the great value and importance of community life. In recent years, especially, he is reminded of the positive aspects of Polish culture, of the importance of identifying himself with Polonia, of the life and work of persons with the same background as his who have gained a prestige status in various societies. He is informed of the existence of multitudinous associations which have interesting meetings and pleasurable activities. He is shown the significance of the community to the world at large by being given items of news in which reference to it is made. He is appealed to as a person who can contribute time and money to help other people less fortunate than he. He is reminded of his political role by appeals to vote and suggestions for sending letters, telegrams, etc. Varied groups compete for him as a desirable potential member. The continued existence of these publications indicates that they are still serving a need not met by American periodicals. Evidently sufficiently large numbers of persons or relatively strong social groups consider them worth supporting for many years. The Polish language radio serves similar, if less important functions. Its continued operation shows that news, music, and even advertisements in the Polish language serve a need for persons who either do not understand English or prefer to hear Polish and who are especially concerned with events and their local interpretation within Polonia.

The Function of Relating Polonia to Polish Society

The second major function of Polish-American voluntary associations has been and remains the crystallization, active manifestation, and adjustment of a close relationship of this community to the Polish national culture society. As Thomas and Znaniecki pointed out, Polish peasant immigrants kept in contact with relatives and friends in Poland, sent them money, and expressed homesickness. They maintained the customs, the language, and the general outlook of that particular region of Poland with which they were familiar.

However, they were relatively unaware of the existence of a Polish national society which, though politically controlled by three foreign states since the 1790's, had a common and distinct secular literary culture and an independent organization functioning for the preservation, growth, and expansion of this culture.[15] It was the upper, educated classes, however, who were developing, preserving, and unifying this culture. At

---

15 Florian Znaniecki, *Modern Nationalities* (Urbana, Ill.: University of Illinois Press, 1956), p. 21.

the time of the great migrations to America, nationalism had already been absorbed by the urban population but had not yet penetrated into the relatively isolated rural areas. Because of their political activities, some nationalistic leaders had to flee from the mother country, and many came to the United States. Having themselves a strong consciousness of a common cultural heritage and identification with it, they attempted to communicate this consciousness to the locally orientated Polish peasant immigrant through the formation of social organizations and the Polish press. This they succeeded in doing before World War I, and thus Polish nationalism became the main force unifying the many Poles living in America.

This building up of a nationalistic orientation toward Poland was a gradual process. The first step was the formation of the Polish Roman Catholic Union in 1880. As its name implies, this association functioned primarily as a means for stressing, identifying, and preserving Roman Catholicism among Poles in America. Under the influence of nationalistically conscious leaders in Polonia and Europe, the Polish National Alliance was formed eight years later with the single purpose of promoting nationalism.

The following decade was characterized by bitter strife within the community between those who considered nationalism as the primary goal of associational life and those who were religiously oriented. In the meantime, other associations stressing Polish culture were founded. Each group started a "fund," collecting money to be used by political leaders in the "fight for independence." Political leaders from Europe were greeted with enthusiasm in every community in America as they toured and made speeches. Paderewski became one of the Polish-American heroes.

In the first fifteen years of the twentieth century, the number of appeals and the intensity of effort in response increased steadily. Polonia directed all its attention toward Poland, and this activity gave it a feeling of excitement and importance. It became known as the "Fourth Province of Poland," the others being those under Russian, German, and Austrian domination. Interassociational organizations were soon formed to coordinate all the efforts to help Poland. The peak of this identification with the mother country national culture society was reached during and immediately after World War I. William C. Boyde, a commissioner of the Red Cross, estimated that at that time the Poles in America sent approximately $20,000,000 to Europe through various groups, including the Polish War Victims Relief Fund.[16] In addition, after September, 1917, 28,000 Polish-American men enlisted in the Polish Army on French Soil and fought for political liberation in Europe.[17]

Withdrawal of Identification with Poland

Even during the period of heightened Polish nationalism and concentrated orientation toward that national culture society, conflict and dissatisfaction prevailed in Polonia, reflecting the political problems of the mother land. Throughout the period preceding World War I various political parties in occupied Poland and refugees living in England, France, and Switzerland were not united in their efforts for Poland. Each party wanted to be considered the official "government in exile," to act as co-ordinator of all efforts for the liberation of Poland, and thus to have the dominant political power over the republic, once it was created. Each party naturally attempted to get the backing of as many Poles as possible, particularly of the great numbers in America.

[16] Wachtl, *op. cit.*, p. 365.

[17] *Ibid.*, p. 324.

As long as the goal of political liberation was uppermost, these conflicts were pushed into the background. Once the Republic of Poland was formed, however, the already present frustrations were increased by other events and resulted first in the anger of Polonia toward Poland, then in apathy and withdrawal of identification. This process can be summarized in the following way:

1. The goal of Polish liberation had unified Polish Americans without, however, eliminating internal conflicts in Polonia. When the goal was accomplished, internal tensions again came to the fore.

2. A psychological letdown succeeded the extreme nationalistically based concentration of attention, and people became more interested in their own problems.

3. The Polish national society no longer needed the manpower provided by the Polish Americans, and its need for money steadily decreased. It now turned its attention to the problems of setting up a new state. The Polish Americans felt rejected, ignored, no longer part of a group striving for common goals.

4. The vague, idealized Poland of nationalistic heroes and poets who sang of an "oppressed" land which could not be blamed for the conditions forcing emigration now became a concrete political state which failed to live up to expectations:

a) The only contact Polish Americans had with this state was through delegates from Poland who came for money.

b) These delegates were met with personal demands which they were unable to fulfil, and their presence took prestige away from local leaders by emphasizing their inadequacies.

c) Polish Americans did buy $18,472,800 worth of bonds issued by the Polish government, with some consequent loss of money. In addition, large

sums were lost by private investors in business and industry in Poland. Osada estimated the loss at $6,000,000 in the period from 1919 to 1923.[18]

d) Political campaigns in Poland were accompanied by "mud-slinging" which had the dual effect of disillusioning the Polish American, who had thought of his motherland as a harmonious whole, and making him suspect that his money was being used in these campaigns. A motto became popular in Polonia during the 1920's: "Close your pocket, boy, your money is going for political purposes."

e) The Polish government and society resented the interference in their internal affairs by Polish Americans who, in turn, felt they had a right to voice their opinions because of their financial contributions.

f) Many Polish Americans had emigrated to the newly formed republic, only to become dissatisfied not only with living conditions there, but also with their own status in Polish society.

g) The soldiers who had fought in France and Poland returned to America with bitterness against the government for having demobilized them during the war with Russia—an implication that they were not an important part of the army—and for not having paid their transportation all the way back to their homes.[19]

5. Increasing, though at that time unrecognized and unconscious, Americanization, especially of the younger generation, had taken place in the decades while attention had been directed toward Poland.

The result of the lessened identification with Poland was dual: the turning of attention inward toward the Polish-American community itself, and an in-

18 Osada, *Jak Sie Krztalcowala Polska Dusz Wychodztwa w Ameryce* (Pittsburgh: Sokoli Polskie, 1930), pp. 170 ff.

19 Wachtl, *op. cit.*, p. 365.

creasing effort to obtain prestige from the American society.

From 1934 until World War II, contact with Poland involved mostly travel by individuals and association representatives, personal communication, and some cultural exchanges. The new ideology of Polonia gave increasing attention and appreciation to Polish culture as a subject of study and as the cultural background of those who were identified as Polish Americans, but this did not involve identification with Polish society. However, after the invasion of 1939, Poland again became the center of international attention. Political refugees again attempted to revive nationalism among the Polish Americans. However, the type of appeal used and the response Polonia made to it were quite different. During World War II, Polonia was not treated and did not treat itself as the "Fourth Province of Poland." Emphasis was placed upon developing the pride of Polish Americans in past and present contributions to the war effort.[20]

Polish Americans responded to these appeals on two levels: humanitarian and political. During the war and in the years since, although with less frequency in the late 1950's they sent money, but chiefly packages, to assist the Polish victims of the war. At the same time, they increased their political pressure upon the American government on behalf of Poland. Thus, as active American citizens they attempted to raise the international prestige of the nation with which their background was connected. The content of their communications, however, did not reflect identification with a distant national culture society. Likewise, an attempt to form a division of Polish-American soldiers to join the European armies failed during World

[20] *The Polish Review,* published in New York with the support of the Polish government in London, emphasized "the glorious past" and "the gallant present."

War II. Polonia newspapers showed equal interest in the progress of American war efforts on both fronts.

After World War II, Poland became one of the communist satellites of Russia, and Polonia's interest in it continued on both the humanitarian and political levels. Most of the support for the government-in-exile came from the displaced persons, or "new emigration," who are more politically oriented toward Poland than the "old emigration" and its descendants.

The humanitarian interest of Polish Americans is reflected in their activities on behalf of Polish DP's. The Polish American Congress made considerable efforts to bring such persons to the United States. Having obtained permission from the American government to allow non-quota numbers of DP's to enter this country, it helped in the screening process in Europe and obtained guarantees of home and employment from Polish Americans.

The Function of Relating Polonia to American Society

Polish-American voluntary associations have performed a third major function, that of defining, crystallizing, and changing the relation of Polonia to American society. Starting with the late 1920's, Polish-American voluntary associations concentrated their attention on the development and utilization of methods by which *community* participation in American society could be increased. None of the efforts of the larger associations have been directed to encourage individual assimilation, i.e., complete identification and participation in the life of the American society. On the contrary, they have striven to act as a unified interest group in their relations with American society.

The function of relating the self-conscious unit of Polish Americans to the general society, as visualized by their ideology, has been dual:

1. Making Polish Americans better qualified to take part in American society by making them conscious and "proud" of their national and cultural background, and by giving them the knowledge and skills which would insure their success as representatives of the Polish unit within American society;

2. Increasing the prestige and power of Polish Americans as a group by direct pressure upon organized American groups, especially the government, and public opinion.

The first of these functions has been performed through educational activities of all groups and has had a dual nature: the teaching and development of Polish and Polish-American culture among both children and adults; and, second, encouragement of education in certain aspects of American culture on the part of members. The latter activity includes the granting of student stipends, fellowships and loans, the adjustment of the parochial school curriculum to that of public schools, and the encouragement of literary, professional, and artistic achievements. It also includes the transmission to Polish Americans of knowledge about American laws and business practices. A latent function of the numerous voluntary associations has been the training of leaders in organizational work and the opening of avenues of upward social mobility.

Besides their interpretation of American culture, the great contribution Polish-American associations are making toward participation of their community in American life is in the political field. The size of the Polish-American group and its concentration in areas where it is the primary ethnic group might lead an observer to assume that these people have been able to exert considerable political pressure upon the American local, state, and national governments. The amount, direction, and effectiveness of the participation of Polish immigrants

and their descendants in American political life was slowed by two factors: In the first place, desire to participate in American society was lacking because of identification with the Polish national culture society. In the second place, the immigrants, lacking knowledge of democratic political behavior and of the means which could be utilized to influence it, frequently did not establish their status as citizens.

Organization of effective political action is dependent upon the ability of a relatively large group of persons to form a central association which can act as spokesman for the group in its relation to the state. In the past, the Polish Americans have been unable to agree upon the goals and means for the formation of such a group. Each of the existing associations tended to view itself as the representative of the community and to resent the formation of any interassociational organization to which it would have to delegate authority. Only in recent years did one of the voluntary associations in Polonia reach such proportional size and power as to become the leader in founding an interassociational organization, the Polish American Congress. This intergroup association directs its activities primarily toward political pressure upon the American state and its propaganda toward the American society. Led by the president of the Polish National Alliance, it unites representatives of other associations in its chief offices.

The second problem which faced Polish-American associations in their attempt to organize effective action has been that of agreeing upon the type of action or policy of the government they want to support or discourage.

A third problem of political action which has delayed the effectiveness of Polonia has been the need to transform whatever agreement could be reached by Polish-American leaders into action on the part of many persons in the form of votes, communications, etc. The slow, but definite increase in the education of Polish Americans has assisted in gradually overcoming this problem.

There is a definite increase in the uniformity and effectiveness of political pressure on the part of Polish Americans. This is evidenced by the increasing number of persons identified as of Polish descent who are now obtaining elected or appointed political posts on the local scene, as, e.g., in Chicago, and on the national level.

Several means have been utilized by Polish Americans in their efforts to influence the policies and actions of the American government. The most frequently used method has been to send all kinds of communications and correspondence to governmental groups and influential persons, referring to general situations in which Poland or Polonia has been placed or to specific events or actions. In addition to written communications, Polish Americans have established personal contacts with persons in governmental positions who could influence policy or action deemed important to Polonia associations. Congresses and conventions of associations attempt to secure important governmental officials as guests, speakers, and participants in discussions as a means of impressing these officials with their strength and ideas. All social or nationalistic events in the larger communities of Polish Americans also try to draw American governmental witnesses. Finally, influential persons are asked to become members of Polish-Americans associations, especially of those devoted to relief and the propagation of Polish culture and, in recent years, to anticommunist efforts.

Polish Americans have staged a number of "protest meetings" which are socially interesting phenomena. Any "protest" meeting is supposed to serve one or more of the following four functions: (1) to draw attention to the "wrong" or "injustice" of a policy or action of a group of people and to induce a change voluntarily out of "shame" (by appealing to the humanitarian values of the offending group);[21] (2) to win the sympathy of other influential groups which could apply pressure to the offending group, thus forcing it to change; (3) to show strength of numbers and of feeling and to serve as a threat of the use of other, less peaceable means of forcing a change; and (4) to serve as a psychological release for participants, giving them an opportunity to express their emotions and to feel that they are "doing something" to alleviate the situation.[22]

Pressure groups can best attain their goals by establishing their own representatives in influential governmental positions. This most effective means has only recently been successfully utilized by Polish Americans, as mentioned before.

Realizing that the functioning of a democratic government is based upon the attitudes and actions of a majority of its citizens, Polish-American associations have been concentrating their efforts toward influencing public opinion in the society at large. Publicity is given to all accomplishments and activities of members of the community and its associations which the community assumes will be positively evaluated by the society. Thus, the cultural contributions of artists and educators are constantly sent to

21 Polish Americans held numerous protest meetings against the Yalta agreement. They served the first, third, and fourth functions more than the second. Attempts were made to force the U.S. government to retract those pacts. Voting records of all Congressmen were publicized and communications sent to Washington threatening a loss of votes to those who did not support the Polish-American stand.

22 In 1906, Polish Americans protested the Russian reprisals against the 200,000 Poles who had participated in demonstrations in Warsaw. See Zwiazek Narodowy Polski, 60th Rocznica: *Pamiatek Jubileuszowy 1880–1940* (Chicago: Dziennik Zwiakowy, 1940), p. 113.

American newspapers and other mass communication media. So are commentaries about the contributions of Polish Americans to American history (Kosciuszko, Pulaski, the "first settlers," etc.) or to contemporary life. The Polish press publishes pamphlets, leaflets, and books for distribution to American audiences dealing with the national culture or individual achievements. Efforts are made to induce American press representatives to cover various functions and events in Polonia, and these are supplemented by the attendance of Poles at non-Polish occasions.[23]

Polish Americans have often tried to exert pressure on the Roman Catholic hierarchy to obtain positions of prestige and power for priests identified with the community. These attempts are complicated by the fact that the priests are dependent upon their non-Polish superiors and thus cannot themselves take part in such activities, and also by the image of the Church as not subject to pressure. With the increasing numbers and wealth of parishes identified as Polish American, there has come a gradual, though delayed, increase in the number of persons with Polish names in the higher echelons of the Roman Catholic hierarchy.

SUMMARY AND CONCLUSIONS

Since 1880, the voluntary associations of Polonia have undergone considerable changes in the functions they have been performing. Starting as representatives of the "Fourth Province of Poland," they have become a marginal product

[23] The American press is always asked to attend the White and Red Ball of the Legion of Young Polish Women, and especially to photograph the debutantes.

combining identification with Poland and America. At the present time they reflect not so much identification with the Polish national culture society as identification with American society, as a distinct subgroup. Except for the relatively few remaining un-Americanized economic immigrants of the first immigration and the relatively recent political migrants (since 1939), it is not possible to treat Polonia as an ethnic Polish community.

In the American political field, Polish Americans operate as interest groups. But primarily they function as status-seeking groups. Within the community, they serve as an in-group status-sifting device. All their attention is centered on the development of internal pride in their cultural and societal background, coupled with the development of "out-group" recognition of the bases for such pride. This function necessitates continued contact with the Polish national society, but of a limited type involving identification not with the present, but with the past. It also necessitates education and cultural activities directed toward the preservation not of Polish culture *in toto*, but only of certain positively evaluated aspects of it. It implies relations of Polish Americans with American society, not as completely assimilated individual Americans, but as a unified group.

The recent geographic and economic dispersal of Polish Americans from the ecologically isolated Polonia communities is a fact of deep concern to the voluntary associations. Their continued existence into the 1960's will depend upon the effectiveness of their prestige-raising function; and this is in itself destructive to their perpetual activity.

7. Some Factors Affecting Participation in Voluntary Associations*

HERBERT GOLDHAMMER

Voluntary associations are those more or less formally organized groups whose membership is by choice or individual volition. Social clubs, interest groups, professional associations, and the like are well-known examples. The family, the state, the church are non-voluntary in that the choice of whether to belong or not to belong seldom is confronted as a real life situation.

The voluntary association has played and continues to play an especially important role in American society. The associative and contractual elements in the corporate forms of organization that led to the founding of the Virginia, Massachusetts, and Plymouth settlements are pronounced enough to lend at least some touch of actuality to a doctrine of political genesis based on man's capacity for formal association and collective action. Observers of American life found voluntary associations to be one of the most striking characteristics of American social organization. Following his visit to the United States in 1831, De Tocqueville observed: "In no country in the world has the principle of association been more successfully used, or applied to a greater multitude of objects, than in America."[1]

The voluntary association flourishes in a social setting in which the community can no longer function as an all-inclusive social group. When a community is small and each member is known and accessible to the other, and when racial, national, religious, and economic differences are absent, the voluntary association can have but few functions. There is in such a community too insufficient specialization of interest, too little social exclusiveness, too great a degree of direct communication to provide a basis adequate for its existence. It was the growth of the great urban centers during the last century that produced conditions most fertile for the extensive development of associations. In the city the forms of social differentiation are not only magnified a hundred-fold, but the sheer numerical effect of large urban aggregates is alone sufficient to necessitate social formation of a much smaller size.

The role of the voluntary association can scarcely be appreciated without an understanding of its relation to other major group formations. The family has increasingly lost many of its economic, protective, educational, and recreational functions. The church has also very directly felt the effect of the competition it has had to meet from voluntary associations for the time of its members. The churches themselves have now taken a leading role in initiating group activities and thus have been able to compete with voluntary associations by themselves providing similar organizations under their own auspices. These services have in large part been assumed by other agencies—by commercial establishments, by

* Abstracted by the editors from the author's Ph.D. dissertation of the same title, Sociology, 1942.

[1] Alexis de Tocqueville, *Democracy in America* (London: Longman, Green, Longman & Roberts, 1862), I, 216.

the state, by the school, and by voluntary associations.

Transformations in the structure of the state have also given a tremendous impetus to the organization of associations. Democracy in the sense of an active and direct participation of the people in the governmental process has long ceased to exist. Voluntary associations have developed in order to act as communication belts between different sectors of the population and governmental agencies that are removed from them. It is precisely the functions of crystallizing, expressing, and enforcing the wishes of its members or leaders ("lobbying") that has throughout the greater part of American history characterized the activities of large numbers of voluntary associations that do not have a purely convivial or recreational interest.

Participation in group activities, especially leisure-time organizations, assumes the availability of time not required for the productive activities involved in the major business of getting a living. The movement toward shorter hours of work and the technological improvements introduced into the home have increased the amount of leisure time for both the gainfully occupied and the housewife. Despite the growth of individualized recreational activities many leisure-time interests are convivial in character. The satisfactions provided by participation in group activities often arise more from the emotional sustenance provided by satisfactory human relationships and the sense of social solidarity and personal security that such relationships inspire than from the specific nature of the activities thus jointly engaged in. Commercial and individualized recreation can scarcely provide these satisfactions, and in an urban civilization the segmenting of human relationships often renders it difficult to develop and sustain the purely informal friendship group. Consequently both leisure time and even many types of instrumental associations

have been increasingly relied upon to provide the conviviality and human relationships that formerly were provided by the family, the kinship group, and the informal friendship circle and the neighborhood group.

The growth of voluntary associations has been regarded as one of the major indices of the "disintegration" of American communal life. The confusing picture presented by hundreds of warring, mutually jealous, and exclusive associations is made to act as witness for the social atomization of urban existence. Justifiable as this may be, it must nevertheless be recognized that the presence of these associations equally indicates a form of integration and cohesion operating in a large number of circumscribed spheres of urban life and that without the integrative and often very highly rationalized functions of these societies working in their own distinct spheres, the large urban community could scarcely exist.

There are a number of major areas of sociological analysis that are much illuminated by the study of voluntary associations. Three may be briefly examined: social stratification, social control, and the division of labor.

An analysis of social stratification derived by classifying the individuals of a community according to certain attributes such as occupation, wealth, education, and social esteem and on this basis arranging them in a pyramidal form which is intended as a direct representation of the social structure neglects an essential aspect of social stratification, namely, the form of stratification as it actually manifests itself in the social intercourse of individuals and groups in terms of their inclusion in or exclusion from spheres of social contact. This latter problem gives special relevance to the study of voluntary associations. For the latter play an increasingly important part in the urban system of social interaction; and thus the social "co-ordinates" that establish the "place" of the individual in the social structure of the community derive increasingly from his affiliation with such groups.

The relation of voluntary associations to social stratification is carried to a further stage in the analysis of their role in social control, both in stabilizing and disrupting a given social structure. In urban investigations there has been an appreciable tendency to emphasize automatic and unconscious equilibrium. This is particularly true of the older ecological studies of the urban community. It is necessary, therefore, to place emphasis on the manipulatory activities of particular or specific individuals or groups which occupy given positions or roles in the social structure and not merely to assume as given the presence of human agents in general as necessary to mediate the processes of urban life which are supposed to run their course by themselves by virtue of some inner principle. In this process of conscious manipulation and control voluntary associations play a paramount part.

With respect to division of labor it may be pointed out that four centers of enterprise provide the services available in any community; these are: (1) individual and corporate commercial enterprises; (2) individual and unorganized group (informal) non-profit action; (3) the non-voluntary associations—the family, state, and church; (4) voluntary (non-profit) associations.

The study of associational participation has a very considerable interest independent of its contribution to the general field of associational analysis outlined above. Man is a social animal; he lives in groups. It would be inexcusable to repeat so truistic a statement were it not for the desirability of pointing out that trite as our knowledge may be that man "lives in groups," it is apt to be meager and unsatisfactory when we ask what types of men live in what types of groups, to what extent and why. The study of man's participation in voluntary associations constitutes a particular aspect of this larger problem.

The number of factors that in all probability may be associated with differential rates of participation in associations is rather large. It costs money to belong to most associations; physical mobility is required for participation; shy, introverted personalities find it difficult to make social contacts; persons who have recently moved will not be "rooted" in the community; association contacts are useful to persons who from a career standpoint are "on the make"; married persons have more responsibilities than single persons—all of these differences plausibly could affect participation in voluntary associations. Hypotheses formulated deductively (that is, on the basis of deductions from other types of sociological knowledge) often permit contradictory yet equally plausible hypotheses.

The present study concentrates on an intensive study of the relationship between these factors and participation in voluntary groups: age, education, and personality (neurotic score developed by Thurstone).

RESEARCH PROCEDURE

The data of this study were secured primarily through the distribution of a one-page questionnaire to approximately 5,500 Chicago residents; in addition supplementary material was made available from a study of 1,000 engaged couples conducted by Ernest W. Burgess and Paul Wallin. The majority of the schedules were distributed to the working personnel of a considerable variety of Chicago business concerns through the co-operation of the managers, personnel managers, and proprietors of these concerns. Factories, wholesale houses, retail establishments, and business offices are represented. A much smaller number of schedules were distributed to educational institutions; the remaining schedules were distributed, through the co-operation of officers, to the members of associations. It would have been preferable to avoid the distribution of schedules to associations, but it was not an easy task to secure the co-operation necessary to obtain an adequate number of schedules. Of the 5,500 schedules 78 per cent were obtained through contacts other than associations. Since the major aim of the study is to investigate the relationship between specified attributes of individuals and their amount of associational participation, the derivation of 22 per cent of the schedules from persons who were known to be members of at least one association is not a serious drawback.

The schedule was anonymous. In order to determine the location of the respondent's residence he was asked to give his present address in terms of the street intersection nearest to the place where he lived. The schedule was distributed under the joint name of the Chicago Recreation Commission and the University of Chicago.

Respondents were asked to record the names of all organizations to which they belonged. These lists were then used to classify memberships according to type. The major difficulty with this procedure lay in distinguishing between social and cultural clubs, and some had to be classified as "type unknown." Many organizations, such as labor unions, do not confine themselves to a single type of activity, but may have cultural, social, and political activity. The classification was necessarily based on the major emphasis of the organization being dealt with.

The questionnaire requested the person to record other pertinent facts about himself, in addition to membership in associations. Among them were:

sex
age
nativity
religion
education
marital status
residence status (living alone, with parents, etc.)
length of residence at present address
length of residence in Chicago
rental level
occupation
church attendance
social status
income
neuroticism (Thurstone)

Although the following analysis will deal primarily with age, education, and neuroticism, other variables are employed in the analysis.

PRELIMINARY CONSIDERATIONS OF THE DATA

Contrary to the popular notion that almost every American belongs to four or five societies, clubs, or associations, the present study found that the number of persons without any organizational affiliation was considerable, and the number of associations is far fewer than the stereotype would suggest. Because of sampling limitations, the present study is not intended as a sample census of Chicago, with respect to membership in voluntary associations, but it may be pointed out that approximately 30 per cent of the men and 40 per cent of the women in the sample reported no affiliations at all. Since part of the sample was secured through associations, these figures almost unquestionably represent the minimum possible number of urbanites without any affiliations.

The widespread impression that most Americans belong to at least one association probably is a consequence of the heavy concentration of memberships among relatively few people. Membership distribution is very similar to income distribution. We find that a small proportion of the sample holds a very considerable proportion of the total memberships. Persons holding five or more memberships constitute a little more than 4 per cent of the sample but hold almost 20 per cent of the total memberships.

It was found that persons who belong to more organizations attended more association meetings, but the relationship is not linear. The more associations an individual belongs to, the fewer times he attends per membership held. This seems to reflect the principle that the more organizations an individual belongs to, the smaller is the amount of time available for participation in any one organization. Men who were holding or had held office in a particular association had been members for an average of more than two years longer than non-officers. Officers and ex-officers attended meetings more frequently than non-officers, if they were men; for women there was no significant difference in frequency of attendance of officers and non-officers.

AGE AND ASSOCIATIONAL
PARTICIPATION

The general pattern of the relationship of age to membership frequency is one that would be represented graphically by a U-curve. For the total male sample the lowest point of participation is reached in the low age group 20–25; for the total female sample there is low participation for a longer span, from age 20 to 31. Thus, high participation is found in the late teens and in mature adulthood and after. There were only a few exceptions to this general pattern. Foreign-born young people did not exhibit high participation, and this is probably due to their unassimilated status. Also, the young Jewish respondents tended to have participation rates that were no higher in the teens than in the twenties. With these minor exceptions it is concluded that there is a clear inverse relationship between age and membership frequency in the younger age groups and a direct relationship between age and membership in the older age groups, with the age 25 being roughly

the turning point in the relationship. For lower income groups the U-shape seems to cover a longer span, and the point of inflection occurs in the late 20's. Closer examination of the data suggests that there is a tendency for membership frequency to decline again as old age approaches. Also, there must be a pattern of rising participation from adolescence to young adulthood. It would appear, then, that if we had data permitting an extension of the distribution through the very late and very early years of life, the U-pattern would become the central portion of a distribution having an M-shape.

Single (never-married) men deviate from this pattern in that they have below-average participation level for later adult years. Married men and women and single women follow the general pattern rather regularly.

The pattern of frequency of attendance by age follows very closely the distributions for membership frequency. If we compare the two high points in each U-distribution (the high rate of the younger age group and the high rate of the older persons) we find that the youngest age group tends to have a higher rate than that of the older persons in the case of the males; the reverse was true in the case of females.

The type of association joined varied somewhat with age. Older persons showed a preference for fraternal and mutual benefit organizations. Older men also joined labor organizations and are active in them more than younger men. Social clubs, hobby clubs, and (of course) athletic clubs are joined more frequently by younger than by older persons. Apparently, as persons grow older, they tend to become less interested in group recreational activities purely for the sake of conviviality, especially of the type provided by social clubs that have no serious purpose. Instead, membership in civic, property owners', service, and business associations tends to increase with age. Among women partictpation in patriotic, military, political, and reform associations increases with age with only a minor irregularity until old age.

The marked U-pattern in the age curve of participation in voluntary associations is hypothesized as resulting from the damping effect in the early 20's of courtship, getting established vocationally, and bearing the first child.

EDUCATION AND ASSOCIATIONAL PARTICIPATION

The greater the level of education, the higher the rate of participation in voluntary associations. This relationship was very strong for women and moderately regular for men. In all cases, persons who had attended college had substantially higher level of participation than those who had not, and those with postgraduate education had extraordinarily high levels of participation. This positive correlation between participation and education was found not to be caused solely by higher income resulting within each education group, for a significant direct association persisted within income groupings.

Occupation accounts for some of the frequent participation of better educated men. Those in professional and semiprofessional occupations had very high rates of membership, whereas in the manager-proprietor-official groups and skilled and worker groups, the correlation is only mild, and participation rates are lower.

Contrary to the Protestant and Catholic respondents, participation rates among Jewish respondents were higher among those with low education than among educated Jews. This was interpreted as being due to the popularity at the time of Zionist, mutual aid, and region-of-origin societies among workingclass Jews.

The relationship between attendance frequency and education is similar to that for education and membership frequency. Moreover, the more highly educated a person is, the more frequently will he exercise leadership roles in associations.

Highly educated persons were found to be much more inclined to join professional and scientific associations. The lower educational strata show a preference for fraternal, mutual aid, and labor organizations. Interest in cultural organizations increased with increasing education, with the exception of low-education foreign-born groups, which also had high participation rates. Many of these groups are devoted to the maintenance of national art forms, dance, music, and literature. Preference for civic, service, business, and improvement associations increased fairly steadily with increasing educational level in the case of men; but there was found to be little variation among women below the postgraduate level.

What is there in the nature of educational attainment that accounts for its direct relation with participation in associations? This question cannot be answered on the basis of the present data, but the hypothesis is ventured that renewed investigation may reveal that educational level operates not by any exclusive means but a considerable extent through its influence on the degree to which the individual possesses a certain sense of social importance, social responsibility, and a desire to maintain an appropriate place in the community. Education, the hypothesis would state, functions here partly through its relation to the individual's sense of his social status or a social status to which he aspires.

NEUROTICISM SCORE AND ASSOCIATIONAL PARTICIPATION

From the relevant data from Burgess and Cottrell's study of married couples it was possible to secure the number of association affiliations and Thurstone Neurotic Inventory scores for a limited sample.[2] Similar data, together with information on past and present offices held in associations were obtained from the Burgess and Wallin study of engaged couples. Although there are some slight irregularities in the distributions, there is a distinct tendency toward an inverse relationship between total neurotic score and membership frequency. This is especially evident for married women. Other studies confirm this finding. Burgess and Cottrell found that more men with good marital adjustment were members of associations than men with poor marital adjustment. Divorced and separated men and women have been found to belong to fewer organizations than single, married, or widowed persons.

To explain this finding, it is hypothesized that the deviant personality is much less likely to find the degree of sympathy, understanding, and indulgence that he usually desires in the more formal framework of association relationships. Nor does he so often possess the desires, initiative, or capacity to exploit such relatively formal settings for the cultivation of human relationships. It is pointed out that patterns classified by the Thurstone Inventory as "neurotic" do in most instances refer to the presence of characteristics that are usually socially disesteemed and often personally distressing.

With respect to the holding of official posts, it was found that the chances individuals will become officers in organizations of which they are members are greatest when their total neurotic score

² See Ernest W. Burgess and Paul Wallin, *Engagement and Marriage* (New York: J. B. Lippincott Co., 1953).

are either very low or are very high, and are smallest when their neurotic scores are moderately high. This surprising finding that persons with very high neurotic scores tend to be officers was explored in detail through factor analysis. The results suggested that persons with marked feelings of inferiority and lack of confidence in general, or to variability of mood (especially of depressive rather than euphoric states) act as a driving force for a reaction formation or compensation which takes the form of striving to hold office. This minor variation should not overweight the much larger differential which throughout most of the total neurotic score range showed an inverse relationship between frequency of office holding and neurotic score.

CONCLUSION

It seems pretty clear from the data of this study that in dealing with participation in voluntary associations we have to do with an aspect of behavior whose determination is the consequence of a relatively large number of factors whose influence on participation depends very much on the particular combination of values of each variable that exist in the case of each individual. In this study it was not possible to find one or two basic factors that would account for or explain all of the deviation. Age, education, and personality factors were shown to be statistically significant, but singly each explains only a modest share of the variation, and jointly they leave much unaccounted for. The present experiment needs to be replicated on representatives of both urban and rural populations and making use of a great many sociological as well as psychological variables.

8. Urbanization and the Organization of Welfare Activities in the Metropolitan Community in Chicago*

ARTHUR HILLMAN

Twenty years have elapsed since this dissertation was written, and its wide-ranging inquiry into many aspects of welfare institutions may now seem overly ambitious. Its scope is accounted for in that it was a unit of study within a metropolitan research program, directed by the late Professors Merriam and Wirth. Studies in depth in the Chicago area by them and their students were designed to supplement various facets of their work on urbanism for the National Resources Committee. Its reports, notably *Our Cities*,[1] helped bring urban problems to public attention at a time of expanding national governmental programs.

Some of the data presented in the dissertation record effects upon welfare activities of the great depression of the 1930's which was a turning point in the organization of social work in the nation. A review of the major findings of this study will be followed by a brief statement of subsequent trends with reference to the organization of welfare services in the Chicago metropolitan community.

The detailed analysis of welfare institutions in Chicago was intended to be more than just a recitation of metropolitan history. Similar analyses for other metropolises will lead eventually to general theories based upon comparative research. The selected data, the simple generalizations, and the theoretical framework provide background for suggestions for further studies. The pointing up of research possibilities is appropriate because the original study was intended to be exploratory rather than exhaustive, and because a new and mature interest in the sociological study of social work is developing. Practitioners and social work educators are increasingly ready to receive insights and help in ordering their observations from the theory and research of sociologists. As a result, sociologists now are more free to study welfare activities as they do other social processes and institutions without having their roles misunderstood.[2]

URBAN ATTRIBUTES: SOCIAL WORK AS RESPONSE

The major finding of my study was that the complex of organized welfare

* Based on the author's Ph.D. dissertation of same title, Sociology, 1940.

[1] National Resources Committee *Our Cities: Their Role in the National Economy* (Washington: Government Printing Office, 1937).

[2] The recent rapprochement of sociology and social work serves to sharpen rather than to lessen the importance of the basic distinction between the two disciplines. The distinctiveness of each can best be appreciated where there is not defensiveness on either side. See Arthur Hillman, *Sociology and Social Work* (Washington: Public Affairs Press, 1956), p. 11, including bibliography of recent articles discussing relationships between social sciences and social work, pp. 71–72. See also Herman D. Stein and Richard A. Cloward, eds., *Social Perspectives on Behavior: A Reader in Social Sciences for Social Work and Related Professions* (Glencoe, Ill.: Free Press, 1958) and the review of it by Hillman in *Social Problems*, VI (Spring, 1959), 376.

activities in the Chicago community (and by implication in any modern metropolis) can be understood as a response to the rapid growth of the city and as a function of its industrial and social characteristics. Social work in Chicago is in large measure a product of urbanization, not only in the volume and nature of problems, but also in the fact of organization and in the methods adapted. These latter are in accord with the more impersonal social relationships of urban life as compared with rural life.

The greater impersonality and more tenuous social relations, higher incidence of economic insecurity and greater prevalence of personal and social maladjustments incident to the rapid growth of the city, with the presence of surplus wealth and vigorous leadership in the specialization of metropolitan life, have combined to give occasion and form to organized social work. Since living in large cities makes individuals more interdependent and at the same time more impersonal in their relations with each other, there develops a tendency toward greater formality and system in social organization. Organized and professionalized social work is a part of this development. It is the typically urban way of assuming responsibility for social problems and of undertaking to meet them as a communal obligation rather than as a multiplicity of personal obligations. It is thus an integral part of urban society and not merely an amplification of deep-rooted rural or familial customs of inter-individual sympathy and kindness. This is not to deny that there are historical antecedents of social work in simpler communities and that some of these survive in the city, but to emphasize its new forms and the unprecedented occasions for organized assistance.

In my thesis, these broad conclusions were supported by chapters which summarized the rapid growth of Chicago, the adjustment problems of its many immigrants and the perennial and periodically critical economic insecurity of the people. The city's hundred years of history had seen an over-all change from "mutual aid and informal assistance in the frontier and village to organized relief and welfare services." Some of the oldest agencies now active have antecedents dating from the 1850's. Aided by mergers and institutional transformations, there was considerable evidence of continuity of agencies while steadily evolving to more complex and more secular forms. Notable also was the development of specialized services within multipurpose agencies and by the creation of new organizations.

CONTROL AND PLANNING OF SOCIAL WORK

Private Welfare Agencies

In the purest form of voluntary person-to-person assistance the individual donor or helper usually can control what is given. In the urban community this prerogative gradually is lost by being transferred to formal agencies or weakened by forces of social control. It is characteristic of urban life that one part of the community does not know how the other part lives and that such help as is extended by voluntary efforts becomes the responsibility of special agencies. Under such conditions, the financial contributor nominally has a veto power which he may exercise by refusing to give to an agency, but he soon finds that he is the object of an organized campaign and also that his personal influence can act only in a limited way to control what is offered in service. Chicago's experience illustrates this well.

At the turn of the century when Chicago was already a city of nearly two million people, the field was wide open for organized, voluntary efforts. Some agencies were sponsored by religious or ethnic groups, others had a leadership of strong personalities like Jane Addams and her associates at Hull-House. There were also appeals made on behalf of possibly dubious and many new enterprises whose sponsors were unknown, and businessmen found they needed to know more in order to protect themselves from fraud. Accordingly, within the Association of Commerce the Subscriptions Investigating Committee was organized in 1911. This was the beginning of community control, or auditing in a simple sense, of voluntary or private agencies which made an appeal for financial support.[3] Before approving an agency the Association's Committee required that minimum standards be maintained in such matters as licensing and accounting for funds. It also looked for evidence of co-operation with other social agencies as a test for endorsement.

The Council of Social Agencies dates from 1914 and has provided constituent agencies a medium for mutual stimulation and for planning, not only to avoid duplication of services but also to consider gaps in the total community social work program. Its staff has grown from one full-time person at its inception to more than 40 professional workers and their assistants at the end of 1959.[4] The member agencies are organized in divisions—Family and Child Welfare, Health, Recreation and Informal Education—and it also carries on research and other interagency service functions. Co-ordination and planning is achieved by a combination of staff consultation with agencies, of studies—both of community conditions and of agency practices, including the geographic spread of serv-

[3] The oldest form of co-ordination between agencies in Chicago is the Social Service Exchange, whose antecedents go back to 1886. Through the registration of cases under care by each agency, duplication of effort could be reduced to a minimum and the knowledge of various agencies pooled in dealing with a particular case.

[4] The name of the council was changed to the Welfare Council of Metropolitan Chicago in 1949 in order to emphasize both the broader scope of its interests and its area of responsibility.

ices—and considerable discussion in committees in which professionals and laymen participate.

The Community Fund of Chicago, another controlling agency, was organized in 1934 as an outgrowth of experience with a special appeal for unemployment relief. The agencies felt a need for a federated appeal, if only to hold their own in competition with requests for funds to meet emergency relief needs. The emphasis on voluntary assistance to the unemployed came in the early 30's before large-scale governmental assistance was organized. The Community Fund of Chicago came into being much later than similar organizations in other cities, which date back to about World War I. The existence of numerous large and autonomous welfare organizations in the nation's second largest city and the risk of conflicting interests involved in joint fund-raising, had made Chicago leaders hesitant before the depression in starting a community fund. The fund in Chicago was set up to provide only a part of the deficit of agencies and almost never more than 50 per cent, whereas, in other financial federations, agencies expect to stake everything on one joint appeal and do not need to do any additional fundraising as Chicago agencies have continued to do.

There is a close tie-up between the Community Fund and the council and a significant form of community control in the process of the review of budgets of member agencies of the fund. Staff specialists from the council prepare reports summarizing the service of the agencies and giving their evaluation and recommendations, which the committees of the Community Fund can use in bringing pressure on agencies in matters of building, professional standards, and other qualitative aspects of service. Moreover, the Community Fund, and some local foundations, also ask the Welfare Council, through its staff and committees, to review the extension of services either by the addition of new departments or branches or by the actual founding of new agencies. This provides an opportunity to review what is proposed in the light of existing services, and possibly to prevent needless duplication, undue concentrations in agency programs, or false starts which may prove difficult to maintain.

The Welfare Council includes within its membership the major public agencies active in providing health, welfare, and educational services. Their participation is on a voluntary basis and brings into the planning discussions consideration of the bulk of services in terms of numbers affected and financial outlay. The membership of public agencies and of about 100 additional voluntary agencies distinguishes the council from the Community Fund. Included in the latter are sectarian groups such as the Catholic, Jewish, and Lutheran charities which have their budgets reviewed in their totality by the fund. However, in the main, Catholic agencies do not participate in the council, although Jewish and Protestant agencies do, despite their having separate financial federations.

The example of Chicago illustrates the process of institutionalization of control and planning in social work with increasing urban growth. One of its special facets is the tie between this control and the local community social structure, via the link of social agency boards of private citizens.

Board Member Study

A special study of the composition of social agency boards and some measures of their participation in the control of social work were included in the dissertation. Despite their participation in the council or fund, the individual agencies have autonomy, and boards have more responsibility than in other cities because of the need for raising a part of their funds independently. Board members act in some cases as representatives of the sponsoring groups and generally as responsible persons in the community.

A total of 4,786 persons serving on the boards of 290 agencies in 1937 were included in the setting. A few public agencies were included but most of them were voluntary in nature. The agencies included were members of the Council of Social Agencies or were endorsed by the Chicago Association of Commerce or both, and thus were a part of the recognized community program of welfare services.

Eighty-seven per cent were members of one board only. A total of 58 persons were members of four or more boards including some officials who serve in an ex officio capacity. An effort was made to identify board members by their affiliations with other organizations. There were 1,002 members of the Chicago Association of Commerce committees of whom 14 per cent were also members of social agency boards. About half were members of only one board and one committee, but one banker was a member of six committees and six boards. The Commercial Club of Chicago, a much smaller and more limited membership group, had 117 of its 188 members on one or more social agency boards.

Men and women were represented almost equally on boards. The occupational distribution of board members or of the husbands and fathers of board members, showed as might be expected, a concentration among professional people and among managers and proprietors in the commerce and industry group. Lawyers, clergymen, and physicians were most numerous among those in professions.

Using the ecological approach, as had often been done in studies of social organization as well as disorganization, a map of the residential distribution was prepared. About 30 per cent lived outside of the city but within the immediate Chicago region. The largest number of these suburbanites was in Evanston, 283, or a rate of 57.6 per 10,000 population. The highest rate was in Lake Forest with 317.0 per 10,000—a total of 173 board members. Within the city a heavy concentration in wealthier residential areas was found, and 14 of the 75 community areas (those with less wealth and lower status residents) had no board members residing therein.

These data tend to show not only the kind of people identified with the support of particular agencies but also those associated with the over-all control of the Community Fund and Welfare Council since activity on committees in the latter is more likely to be drawn from people who are identified with some agency.

Governmental Programs

The effect of the Social Security Act had not been felt in the late 1930's but the federal government had helped finance large-scale unemployment relief and work relief programs in the Chicago area. These had greatly expanded the public social services which had previously been organized as local governmental responsibilities. The Cook County Bureau of Public Welfare had been reorganized in the late 1920's to provide a comprehensive program of "normal" services under professional direction. However, in the early 30's it was dispensing grocery orders to those on relief, until the federal regulations specified that assistance should be given in cash rather than in kind. This rule was made in deference both to the desire to keep open normal channels of trade and to respect the client's right to make his own decisions. It illustrates a control effect of federal financial participation in welfare programs, even when combined with state and local administration.

Public expenditures for income maintenance and other welfare services in the depression years, and since then, have been markedly greater than those for voluntary services, although the latter are pace-setters in various ways and also tend to be better publicized. With the rise of governmental expenditures, private agencies were sometimes put on the defensive as people asked why they should be giving voluntarily when there was so much tax money being used for welfare purposes. Family welfare agencies were able to differentiate their work from that of public relief services, especially after the latter were organized on a large scale. Thus, agencies emphasizing casework deal with the more complex family problems and do not attempt to provide financial aid unless economic assistance is necessary temporarily and incidentally, or in emergencies to people who are not eligible because of residence requirements for public relief.

Working out such complementary roles on the part of public and private agencies is one of the central questions in community planning. It applies also to recreation services where large-scale programs have been developed under public auspices, and the Park District, the Board of Education, and the numerous voluntary agencies have had conferences to acquaint each other with the scope of their services and to plan to avoid duplication or any working at cross-purposes. It poses a major problem of urban community organization, the solution to which seems to be an uneasy equilibrium that changes almost continuously as new programs unfold in either the public or private spheres.

RECENT TRENDS

Professionalization

The trend toward professionalization which had been noted in the 1930's continued with the demand for professionally qualified workers exceeding the supply. (One of the current projects of the Welfare Council is the sponsoring of a recruitment program for social work.) Specializations within practices continue to be recognized, such as medical social work, psychiatric social work, social group work, and others, but a major development was the formation in 1955 of a unified professional association. The Chicago area chapter of the National Association of Social Workers had 1,585 members in November, 1959. It was primarily concerned with questions of practice, but it had active committees on civil rights and public social policies. Thus, it was prepared to take action on city and state matters and, as part of the national organization, to express itself on legislation affecting welfare policies.

The trade union movement within social work which was born during the depression did not gain ground although several agencies continued to have contracts with unions of their employees.

The local professional schools of social work at the University of Chicago and Loyola University were augmented by the establishment of a branch in the city of the University of Illinois school of social work. The latter began its work with the training of group workers but has since expanded its offerings in the Chicago area. The University of Chicago, the oldest and largest school, added a professor of group work in 1958 and began to provide field work instruction, thus supplementing its previous emphasis on casework and public welfare services. In general, the professional schools have strongly bolstered the professionalization trend not only by turning out professional welfare workers but also by moving toward a more generic type of training of future workers.

Participation in Planning

Leaders in the social work field have been concerned about broadening the participation in community planning, motivated by democratic considerations of representativeness and perhaps also by a fear of inbreeding of ideas or of being out of touch with actual sentiments in the community. From the professional viewpoint, the matter of early case finding, or an emphasis on preven-

tion through the detection of problems, has also entered into the interest in opening up new channels of communication. In Community Fund circles the increase of participation in planning processes is associated with more effective interpretation and fund-raising.

In 1945 the Council of Social Agencies established the social work labor planning project, the aims of which were twofold, (a) to make welfare services more fully known and used as needed by workers, and (b) to secure active participation by representatives of labor groups in community planning of health and welfare services. It was staffed at first by a director and by representatives of the AFL, CIO, and the Railroad Brotherhoods. The latter were jointly responsible to the council and to their labor bodies who had to approve the appointments.

This project was an outgrowth of wartime development, particularly labor's participation in fund-raising and the consequent interest on both sides in having representation on planning committees and agency boards. The CIO, starting with the work of the United Automobile Workers in Detroit, developed a program of union counseling, that is, the training of union members who could help their fellow workers to know where to turn for help. This was not counseling in any technical sense, but it was a kind of problem-spotting and referral service in which the interests of social work practitioners and union people coincided. The work of the union counselors, and indeed the whole labor project, provided the main impetus for the establishment of the Community Referral Service which was set up in 1945 to help people find their way among the growing mass of agencies and services available.

Some of the early work of the project included, in addition to the training of union counselors, interpretation through labor newspapers and through speeches at meetings, and consultation in order to help newly appointed union members take their places on boards and committees. Relationships between unions and public agencies were developed and strengthened, but much of the interest centered on voluntary participation in the work of private agencies.[5] Other staff representatives from organized labor were working with the Community Fund, and after a few years the labor relations work of the fund and council were unified.

Another expression of interest in broadening participation in community planning[6] was the beginning of staff service by the Welfare Council to local community councils, also starting in 1945. At first only one person was employed in Area Welfare Planning and even at the most there has not been a large enough staff, never more than three or four, to provide service to neighborhood and district councils. But the emphasis was placed on helping some get started in problem areas and on co-ordinating the work of those which were either in existence or were getting under way with various kinds of staff help. There was formed the Association of Community Councils, with staff service from the Welfare Council, which acts on a city-wide or metropolitan basis on problems which might arise in any locality. A program of action on health, housing or urban renewal, or the like, might be developed centrally, discussed, and passed back to local units for further attention. The association has annual conferences and monthly meetings and numbers several

[5] Arthur Hillman, "Labor Joins the Chicago Council," *Community, Bulletin of Community Chests and Councils,* XXII (November, 1946), 48–49, 52.

[6] There were similar developments in other cities in the 1940's. See Arthur Hillman, *Community Organization and Planning* (New York: Macmillan, 1950), pp. 247–48. In the 1950's welfare councils in several major cities largely withdrew from this type of service.

hundred among its year-round participants.

An adjunct of the Area Welfare Planning Development is the suburban program of the Welfare Council, which began with one full-time community organization specialist in the fall of 1955. Provision was made for two additional staff members in 1959. They serve the suburban area of Cook, Du Page, and Lake counties, Illinois. The program has three major purposes: (1) developing and strengthening social planning organizations throughout the metropolitan area, of which some are well established but others are only in a beginning stage; (2) advising and assisting communities to secure new health and welfare services (this is done wherever possible by "purchasing" services from a nearby agency, or encouraging a new unit to merge with an older established agency in an adjacent area); (3) providing staff services to the Suburban and Chicago Committee on Fund Raising and Welfare Services. This committee came into being in 1958 sponsored by the Suburban Community Chest Council, the Community Fund of Chicago, and the Welfare Council of Metropolitan Chicago. The committee was set up to deal with the friction generated in the suburbs by the money-raising efforts of the Community Fund–Red Cross joint appeal.

The competition each fall for the voluntary welfare dollar in the metropolitan region develops sore points which take months to heal. Lack of communication and understanding between Chicago and suburban fund raising groups aggravates this problem. . . .

Leadership offered by Chicago centered agencies is looked upon with suspicion in many suburban communities and new ideas are likely to be rejected without careful examination. The same suspicion is expressed to a lesser degree between neighboring communities when assistance or advice is given. Older communities are inclined to ignore the potential for a cancerous social condition in an adjacent area to spread and in time also affect their community life.[7]

The kind of problem referred to is obviously only a part of the difficulty of creating metropolitan community-wide co-operation on matters of common interest. Improved communication, at least, and joint planning and programs become imperative in many fields to cope with the effects of rapid and sometimes sprawling growth of new residential areas together with industry in the outlying parts of the metropolitan region. The suburban program of the Welfare Council has given particular attention to emergent human needs in the south end of Cook County as new workers and their families move in because of the St. Lawrence Seaway.

These comments on recent trends serve to illustrate again the basic thesis that the organization of welfare activities in a metropolitan community represents an adjustment to rapidly changing needs and that as the nature of the social problems and their context changes, the organization must undergo change also.

OTHER CHANGES: SUGGESTIONS
FOR STUDIES

The twenty years since my first research in this area provide a fresh opportunity to look for other forces in the city affecting the content, the organization, and the support of welfare activities. They are listed here together with suggestions for further studies, which in some cases would be only of a descriptive or historical sort, but in others there is the possibility of a research design.

1. A Gallup poll in April, 1939, asked a cross-section of persons in the United States, exclusive of farmers, "If you lost your present job or business and could not find other work, how long do you think you could hold out before you

[7] Report on the Suburban Program of the Welfare Council of Metropolitan Chicago, October 1, 1959, prepared by Wade T. Searles, Associate Director. Five pages mimeographed.

would have to apply for relief?" Nineteen per cent said they could hold out one month or less and an additional 16 per cent from one to six months, according to their own estimates. A follow-up study might reveal only differences in the feeling of security following a period of relatively full employment compared with that of the depression. However, the availability of unemployment insurance and of old age benefits might realistically alter the answers. This question might be regarded as a kind of political weather vane.

2. The early history of social work in Chicago was marked by the relief activities of ethnic groups, including many which were church-sponsored. Have these diminished in importance as the groups have become assimilated? Have newcomers, particularly displaced persons or Spanish-speaking peoples, created similar institutions?

Other questions of interest are connected with the church sponsorship of social agencies. There has been an increasing acceptance in Protestant bodies of professionalization and of public programs, and a consequent necessity for redefining traditional roles. The line between welfare services which are "religious" in a sectarian sense and those which are similar to what is done by secular agencies is not easily drawn, but new attempts at definition of the distinctive social work of the church have been made in recent years with some reaffirmations of interest in the field.[8]

3. Studies might be made of different responses to Community Funds appeals, comparing industries and employee groups organized in various ways. Doubt-

[8] E. Theodore Bachman, *The Emerging Perspective*, Report of First National Conference on the Churches and Social Welfare, 1955, Volume III (New York: National Council of the Churches of Christ in the U.S.A.). Also, P. Mathew Titus, Ph.D. dissertation, "Study of Protestant Charities in Chicago with Special Reference to Neighborhood Houses and Social Settlements," Chicago Theological Seminary, 1939.

less pertinent data are available which could be analyzed fruitfully by social scientists interested not only in campaign methods but also in community structures.

The role of corporations as pace-setters would be of interest in Chicago. In an intensive Indianapolis study, the factor of dependency on corporate gifts was used as a factor in intercity comparisons.[9] Students of corporations generally might make a historical and comparative study of their evolving policies with respect to philanthropic gifts, which would include interpretations by board members and officers of stockholders' short-run interests as over against the purchase of community good will or the corporate self-interest involved in contributions to local welfare.

4. Sociological theories of causation are being tested and refined in new approaches to prevention and treatment of juvenile delinquency. The need for interdisciplinary and interagency co-operation in this field is being steadily recognized.[10]

5. Further study might be made of the social characteristics and, by depth interviews, of their motivations of board members and other volunteers. "Time and motion" studies could be made of what they actually do as compared with professionals, both practitioners and administrators.[11]

6. The revived interest in citizens' or-

9 J. R. Seeley and others, *Community Chest: A Case Study in Philanthropy* (Toronto: University of Toronto Press, 1957) pp. 169-71.

10 Oliver Moles and others, *A Selective Review of Research and Theory on Delinquency* (Ann Arbor, Michigan: Survey Research Center, University of Michigan, 1959); *Neighborhood Centers Today* (New York: National Federation of Settlements and Neighborhood Centers, 1960), pp. 97-140; *Breaking through Barriers* (Chicago: Welfare Council of Metropolitan Chicago, 1960).

11 Cf. Bernard Barber, "Bureaucratic Organization and the Volunteer" in Herman D. Stein and R. A. Cloward, eds., *Social Perspective on Behavior* (Glencoe: Free Press, 1958) pp. 606-9.

ganizations—organized usually on a delegate basis—in relation to "urban renewal" attempts to cope with physical and social changes of cities, might be recorded in case studies and analyzed with reference to types of demographic situations, organizational structures, leadership and participation, including the part played by economic and institutional interests.

7. The students of cultural history and of organizational processes might find common interests in accounting for innovations in practice or in administrative arrangements. To what extent is there independent invention of new cultural elements in social work, and can the alternative or concomitant process of diffusion be traced, through conferences, personal contacts, professional publications, and the like? This can be done historically for such ideas as the social settlement, and more recently for union counseling, or the current interest in special services to the multiproblem family. Resistance to or readiness for change at a given time would need to be culturally analyzed to account for the acceptance of innovations.

THEORETICAL CONCLUSIONS

The principal characteristics of the organization of social work under urban conditions, which are evident from this study, are specialization, co-ordination, and professionalized administration. Specialization, both in method and in type of problem treated, is a product of the volume and great variety of welfare services needed to be performed in a large city as well as of the refinements in knowledge and skill which are applied in the practices of social work. The necessity for some co-ordination of social services arises from the development of specialization and also from the need for systematizing the exchange of information and establishing regular procedures if collaboration (and communication) is to take place in a large city. Much of the co-ordination which has been achieved

depends on voluntary co-operation between agencies, and there is never a
complete departure from a system of free
enterprise.

The division of labor and the developments
of techniques in social work with the interests
in economy and efficiency in administration,
are an expression in the field of human relations of the rationalization of modern, industrial life. Thus it has come about that to say
that a social worker shows impulsiveness or
sentimentality is indulging in opprobrium.[12]

Orderliness and efficiency as social values are reflected in the planning process,
and in the related and supporting functions of research as carried on by the
Welfare Council and other agencies for
the central control of programs which
extend throughout the metropolitan community.

The growth of research as a part of organized social work seems to epitomize
the drive toward rationality, but it does
not provide an escape from value considerations or the need for a philosophy to
give meaning to the techniques and programs developed. The measurement of
results requires that goals be stated, and
thus the interest in objectivity, rather
than sentimentality or spontaneity, leads
to the careful formation of criteria or
purposes against which measurements
can be made. However, much planning
is in terms of specific projects, or services, and the evaluative research is correspondingly partial or segmental within
the broad field of social work. Therefore,
only limited objectives need to be stated
for particular programs or agencies and
there is in general a lack of a coherent
philosophy to animate the field, beyond
the pragmatic tests, such as the avoid-

ance of waste and duplication, on which
there tends to be general agreement.

Rationalization is also reflected in
greater attention to the decision-making
process, particularly in the conscious efforts to broaden the community base of
participation, as has been noted in some
of the recent trends, and through advance preparations to economize on time
spent in meetings. Perhaps the search for
consensus in the community, even if
reached in terms of specific choices, is
the most that can be expected in a rationale—that is, working agreements from
time to time, in the light of evidence at
hand, tentative and subject to review,
with many compromises and unresolved
conflicts rather than a comprehensive
philosophy within terms of which decisions can be made consistently. This
view of a dynamic equilibrium, of prob-
lem-solving from which may accrue a
body of principles, is in keeping with the
nature of urban society in which change
is "the norm instead of the occasional,
the extraordinary and often the fearful."[13]

The Power Structure

Decisions about welfare services, like
other public decisions in the urban community, are made within a community
structure in which some persons or
cliques or segments have more influence
than others. Attention to concentrations
of power, or its general distribution, has
been greater since Floyd Hunter's study
of a southern city. His concept of a power structure has been provocative but
there is a danger of applying it broadly
without regard to the particular community context or to the type of decisions
being made. "Not all communities are as
tightly structured as that studied by
Hunter. One can find in other large cities

[12] Dissertation, pp. 230–32. See also Bradley
Buell and others, *Community Planning for Human Services* (New York: Columbia University
Press, 1952) for an elaborate statement of the
case for "coherent planning and action," for new
designs for administration of services as needed
for economy and efficiency. This was reviewed by
Hillman in *Social Work Journal*, XXXIII (July,
1952), 154–55.

[13] Peter Drucker, *Landmarks of Tomorrow*
(New York: Harper & Bros., 1959), p. 24. See
also S. Kirson Weinberg, "Social Disorganization
Theory," *Social Problems*, V (Spring, 1958),
339–45.

more of a balance between political forces, more competition between newspapers perhaps, and generally more fluidity in power relationships."[14]

Chicago's very size—and its economic diversity—makes for some unpredictability in community behavior and leads one to look for a plurality of power structures. Examples can be cited of the force of the Chicago *Tribune*, or the Catholic hierarchy, or the Democratic political machine, or of Protestant groupings; the power of each may be only that of veto on specific issues. One can expect occasional coalitions of power and common denominators of agreement within which such agencies as the Community Fund may operate. Chicago undoubtedly has a power structure, but compared with smaller communities its voice seems to be more muffled, at least with respect to welfare matters.

Leadership: A Professional Elite

The influence of leading professionals cannot be entirely separated from others who help make decisions, but there seems to be a special, disciplined role. Associated with them are semiprofessional volunteers whose service on boards and committees is a function of their knowledge and experience rather than their means or general power in the community. The leadership of this combined

[14] Hillman, *Sociology and Social Work*, p. 46.

group is exercised in the step-by-step, year-by-year kind of planning; part of the fascination for those engaged in such decision-making is that the goals are not static.

Social workers, particularly in administrative or community planning positions, act as brokers or mediators, as an elite corps of specialists in maintaining an equilibrated social system. Controlled social change generally demands special skills from the managerial group.

The leadership role of professionals is largely limited to a top-level group, but their power is not one of gross manipulation. In social work as in other forms of large, modern organization, there is a highly elaborate specialization of tasks, with initiative expected at several levels, and ideas or innovations flowing upward for co-ordination. The work of the administrator and planner is not to give orders but to be sensitive to what is happening, to keep the parts of the total operation moving and in balance, and to help articulate a consensus in a dynamic sense.

The most active in leadership positions in the welfare field know how incomplete is the co-ordination and how imperfect the teamwork. But given the voluntary character of much of the rest —and compared with large institutions like corporations, churches, or the military—the degree of organizational unity is impressive.

9. *On* Street Corner Society*

WILLIAM FOOTE WHYTE

Since the study *Street Corner Society* explores a wide range of topics, any neatly organized commentary is difficult. In reviewing this work, I shall consider the following four questions:

1. What did the book contribute to a sociology of slum districts?
2. What does the book contribute to the theory of (*a*) group processes, (*b*) the relations of individual to group, and (*c*) the relations of groups to larger organizations?
3. What are the possibilities of the methods used in such a study?
4. What light may a study done in the years 1936–40 cast upon the human problems of slum life today?

Before facing those questions, I should sound a note of caution. *Street Corner Society* was my first but also my last effort in the field of urban sociology. All my subsequent work has been in industrial sociology. Therefore, I can no longer claim to speak as a specialist in the field under discussion. These remarks are the impressions of a man who has left home, can remember what it was like back there, and has tried to keep in touch, but might not recognize the place if he went home again.

ON THE SOCIOLOGY OF SLUM DISTRICTS[1]

The Cornerville study may be viewed first in the historical context of the devel-

opment of this sector of the urban sociology field. The main trend I see here is from a moralistic to an objective or scientific approach.

Charles Booth's *Life and Labour of the People of London* is representative of the moralistic approach. While the study contained a wealth of data on the people and their living conditions, the point of view may be represented by this paragraph upon the relations between rich and poor in a London parish:

. . . their poverty has met with compassion, and those who visit in the name of Christianity seek to relieve the distress they find. The two duties seem to be naturally, and even divinely, combined. The heart is softened, gratitude is felt, and in this mood the poor are pointed to God. Sin is rebuked, virtue extolled, and warning words are spoken against drunkenness, extravagance, and folly. Advice, assistance, and rebuke are all accepted, and the recipient is urged to turn to where alone the strength can be found and to no longer neglect the observances of religion.[2]

This point of view would be regarded as quaint and naïve in sociology today as indeed it was when I made my study. However, it is my contention that basically the same point of view persisted for thirty or more years after Booth but found expression in different words. The people were no longer called sinful; they and their institutions became "interstitial."[3] This was by no means universal. For example, the writings of Robert A.

* Based on the author's Ph.D. dissertation, "Street Corner Society: The Social Structure of an Italian Slum," Sociology, 1943.

[1] The argument of this section is presented in more detail in my article, "Social Organization in the Slums," *American Sociological Review*, VIII, No. 1 (February, 1943), 34–39.

[2] *Religious Influences* (Third Series, London: Macmillan & Co., 1904), VII, 45.

[3] For example, this point of view is found in Harvey Zorbaugh's *The Gold Coast and the Slum* (Chicago: University of Chicago Press, 1929).

Woods, Robert E. Park and H. A. Miller, and Louis Wirth[4] seem to me to represent the objective, non-judgmental approach. Nevertheless, at the same time these men were pursuing their research, others hewed to the moralistic line.

The middle-class normative view gives us part of the explanation for the long neglect of social organization in the slums, but it is hardly the whole story. Some sociologists saw slums in this way because they were always in the position of outsiders. The life of the district is hidden from the outsider. This can be documented by the following experience:

Once, after I had been many months in Cornerville, I went to look up a man whom I knew quite well. He lived in a part of the district where I was not generally known. When I did not find him on his corner, I looked for him at his home. I knew the building but was not quite sure which flat it was. I knocked on several doors—including his own—and got the same answer everywhere. Nobody had ever heard of him! Nobody had any idea of where he lived! Of course, they all knew him, as he later told me, but none of them knew me. Thus, a stranger-sociologist can learn from his own experience of asking questions that nobody knows anybody else in a slum district.

Some students of urban life also failed to make any clear distinction between rooming-house districts and slums where people live in family groups over a long period of time. While rooming-house districts in general are much less highly organized than the kind of area I was describing, even here, people do not always live in anonymity. Margaret Chandler[5] found a very active group life among the taverns of Woodlawn in Chicago. However, it was highly unstable. An acquaint-ance of a week might be described as an old friend, so rapidly did the ties shift.

Street Corner Society found that Cornerville had its own social organization. It also had its own norms of behavior. Behavior that seemed to the outside middle-class world disordered and unregulated conformed to definite standards within the community. For example, this proved to be the case even in the field of sex behavior.[6] A corner boy had definite standards as to the desirability of females, according to their previous sexual experience (or lack of it), physical attractiveness, and social status. The most desirable in all of these categories were also the most unattainable—the two facts certainly not being unrelated. However, a virgin turned out to be not only the most desirable of women but also the one with whom sex relations would be a violation of the code of corner boys. The same corner boy who would think nothing of cheating a prostitute would go to great lengths of self-restraint to protect the sexual status of a virgin. No doubt fear of the consequences of intercourse with a virgin had been a force in the establishment of this norm, but it seemed apparent that corner boys were not simply reacting to possible sanctions. They had internalized this norm and would have felt extremely guilty in violating it, quite apart from the fear of consequences.

This emphasis upon social organization in Cornerville is not intended to give the impression that the slum is necessarily a homogeneous, tightly integrated community with a uniform set of social norms. There certainly were groups in conflict with differing sets of social norms, and some of this variety and conflict are described in *Street Corner Soci-*

[4] Woods, *The City Wilderness* and *Americans in Process* (Boston: Houghton Mifflin Co., 1898 and 1902); Park and Miller, *Old World Traits Transplanted* (New York: Harper & Bros., 1921); Wirth, *The Ghetto* (Chicago: University of Chicago Press, 1928).

[5] Margaret Chandler, *The Social Organization of Workers in a Rooming-House Area*, unpublished Ph.D. dissertation, University of Chicago, 1948.

[6] See my "A Slum Sex Code," *American Journal of Sociology*, XLIX, No. 1 (July, 1943), 24-31.

ety. But even the conflict was organized. To be sure, there were individuals in Cornerville who were social isolates, but they were the exception, not the rule.

The man who looks at slum districts through the glasses of middle-class morality is not, in fact, studying the slum district at all but only noting how it differs from a middle-class community. He seeks to discover what Cornerville *is not.* My study was undertaken to discover what it was. One can learn much more that way.

The social anthropologists, and particularly Conrad M. Arensberg, taught me that one should approach an unfamiliar community such as Cornerville as if studying another society altogether. This meant withholding moral judgments and concentrating on observing and recording what went on in the community and how the people themselves explained events.

GROUP AND ORGANIZATIONAL
PROCESSES

The Individual and Group Structure

Throughout, the study placed great emphasis upon studying the relations of the individual to the group and the structure of informal groups or gangs. These group studies seemed to tell us something about the relation of group structure to leadership, performance, and mental health. I certainly was not the one to discover that street corner gangs have leaders. This was known before my time,[7] and Frederic Thrasher's book on *The Gang*[8] presents voluminous data on the point. My own contribution consisted

of working out the structure of the gang in considerable detail: not only does each gang have its leader—or its leader and lieutenants—but also each gang has an informal hierarchical organization in which each individual has a definite place, from top to bottom. Positions might shift, to be sure, but they tend to be relatively stable, and my work showed how the position of individuals in the gang might be determined through observation and interviewing.

The study also showed how the structure depended, in part, upon an exchange of personal favors in which each man was expected to do favors for every other man, but in which higher-ranking individuals did more for their followers than they allowed the followers to do for them. The higher-ranking individuals conformed more closely to the norms of the group than did the lower-ranking ones, and this seemed to have something to do with the placement of individuals in the hierarchy. These ideas have been elaborated upon and systematized by George Homans in his study of *The Human Group.*[9]

Group Structure and Performance

The relationship between performance and group structure, which I first noted at the bowling alleys, has seemed to me one of the most exciting ideas to come out of the study. The general statement can be put in this way. There tends to be a correlation between the *performance* of the members and their *ranking* in the informal group structure when the following conditions obtain:

1. The members *interact frequently* together.
2. The group *participates frequently* in some kind of competitive activity.
3. The activity contains an important element of *skill.*

[7] However, let us not overestimate how long this was known. For example, in their classic study of *The Polish Peasant in Europe and America* (Boston: Richard C. Badger, 1920), W. I. Thomas and Florian Znaniecki wrote ". . . there is a large proportion of immigrant children—particularly in large cities—whose home and community conditions are such that their behavior is never socially regulated, no life organization worthy of the name is ever imposed on them" (V, 295).

[8] Chicago: University of Chicago Press, rev. ed., 1936.

[9] New York: Harcourt Brace, 1950.

4. The activity is *highly valued* (considered important) by the group.

The significance of these conditions may require this explanation. I assume first a relationship between frequency of interaction and fixity of individual rankings in the group structure. If members seldom interact, their relative positions are likely to be unclear and unstable. As members increase their frequency of interaction, a more definite patterning of positions tends to emerge.

The competitive activity must also be frequent for us to expect a pattern to emerge here. Skill is important, for a game of pure chance would yield chance rankings of individual members.

If the activity is thought of little consequence, then it is unimportant how the members perform. Only in a *highly valued* activity is it important how the members score and do we expect to find the ranking-performance relationship.

The members do not just sort themselves out passively in response to these conditions. On the contrary, the conditions bring forth social pressures that influence performance. Everyone is razzed by members of an opposing team, but the nature of the razzing is unconsciously adjusted to the ranking of the individual at whom it is directed. When the high-ranking man runs into a poor streak, opponents try to tell him that this is his natural form, but they find it hard to conceal their surprise, and the yelling has the ring of insincerity. Furthermore, the volume of shouting is relatively low compared to the situation in which a low-ranking member is in a streak of superior performance. The opponents then verbally pile onto the upstart, yelling loudly that he is performing "over his head." If anything, this is even more true of low-ranking opponents than it is of high-ranking ones. Of course, the man's teammates try to encourage him, but even they are inclined to mutter to each other that the fellow is "getting lucky."

No such mixed feelings interfere with the cheering of the teammates of the high-ranking member. Their cheers are based upon the assumption that good performance is to be expected and that any stretch of inferior performance must be a temporary lapse.

These pressures sound intangible, and yet they are felt. How can the low-ranking man have confidence in his ability when nobody else in his group does? In experimental situations, O. J. Harvey and Muzafer Sherif[10] have shown that high-status group members tend to overestimate their future performance more than do low-status members. Predictions of performance of others are more overestimated for high-status members than for low-status members—whose performance may even be underestimated.[11]

Group Structure and Mental Health

My study of the Norton Street gang also suggested the possible relationship between group structure and mental health. There I observed that a marked

[10] "An Experimental Approach to the Study of Status Relations in Informal Groups," *American Sociological Review*, XVIII, No. 4 (August, 1953), 357–67. The article is by Harvey, and the research was part of a program conducted by Sherif.

[11] This aspect of the Cornerville study suggests the possibility of the development of a field of the "sociology of sports." I have often wondered why few, if any, people are interested in such a development. Perhaps it is because academic research is traditionally associated with serious aspects of life, whereas sports seem to be on the frivolous side. From a scientific point of view, this neglect is certainly unjustified. Professional baseball would particularly lend itself to sociological study. The research man who undertook a study of a team would be able to relate the social structure of the team to a wealth of statistical data on individual and group performance—batting averages, runs batted in, runs scored, earned-run averages, and so on. Today many sociologists are trying to do *hard* quantitative analyses of *soft* data: the attitude responses people give to questionnaires. The student of the baseball team would be able to get the attitude data, but he would also be able to build upon statistical indices of *performance*.

change in the structure of the Nortons, which left Long John without social support, apparently brought on both a drastic drop in Long John's performance at the bowling alleys and marked neurotic symptoms. Similarly, I found that when Doc did not have the few dollars needed to enable him to take the initiative in social activities in the manner to which he had been accustomed, he, too, fell victim to neurotic symptoms.

In the cases of both men, it was possible to make something of a clinical test of the relation between group structure and mental health through applying therapy along the lines indicated by the theory. When Doc was able to re-establish for Long John a position quite comparable to the one he had occupied in the Nortons, his neurotic symptoms disappeared—and his bowling performance improved so dramatically that he won the prize money in the competition to end that season. As soon as Doc was getting a regular, though small, income from a recreation center project, he was able to re-establish his customary social pattern, and he had no more trouble with dizzy spells.

This should not suggest that any disruption in an individual's customary position in a social group will lead to mental health problems. Most of us are more or less intimately involved in a number of different social spheres. When we find ourselves thrown into an unsatisfactory position in one of these spheres, we are often able to compensate for the disturbance by channeling more of our social activities and interactions into one or more other spheres. My assumption is that it is only when the individual, for whatever reason, is unable to compensate for a marked disruption in his social spheres that we can anticipate mental health problems for him. In the case of the Nortons, a disruption of the relations of a member to the group could be expected to have a severe impact because such a high proportion of the individual's total social interactions was concentrated within that group. These Cornerville findings seem to fit in with current trends in exploring relations between social life and mental health.

The Social Role of the Settlement House

Outsiders have often assumed that the settlement house in a slum district is in touch with the life of that community. I found, at least in Cornerville, that the settlement house was highly selective in its contacts and influence. Most of the social workers thought in terms of a one-way adjustment of the slum community to their own middle-class standards. They showed in many obvious and subtle ways that they considered themselves superior to the people of the community. This served to cut them off from the rank and file of the district and to attract only those with strong urges toward social mobility, the very people who were moving up and away from the district.

These findings may well have a significance far beyond slum districts and settlement houses. We may be dealing here with patterns of behavior to be observed all over the world where officials of government or private agencies are trying to "uplift" members of a community representing a lower social status and a different culture from that of the officials. This idea was first suggested to me by the late Scudder Mekeel[12] as he paraphrased an article of mine on "The Social Role of the Settlement House,"[13] so as to apply it to the relations between Indian service personnel and the American Indians. He claimed that one only needed to change "social worker" into

[12] "Comparative Notes on the 'Social Role of the Settlement House' as Contrasted with That of the United States Indian Service," *Applied Anthropology*, III, No. 1 (December, 1943), 5–8.

[13] *Applied Anthropology*, I, No. 1 (October–December, 1941).

"Indian service agent" and "corner boys" into "Indians," make a few minor adjustments, and everything else in the article would apply just as well to the Indians as it did to Cornerville.

The Strains of Social Mobility

The study of the Italian Community Club seems to me representative of the dilemmas and conflicts faced by men who are trying to advance themselves socially, to rise from lower-class to middle-class positions. The explicit purpose of the club, as announced at its founding, was twofold. On the one hand, the members were to contribute to the betterment of the local community. On the other hand, they were to carry on activities that would improve their own social standing. The story of the club is a history of an unsuccessful attempt to reconcile these two objectives. At point after point, members had to choose between these objectives. Their choices reflected their varying desires and capacities for social mobility. The choices also served to mark their progress, or lack of it, on the mobility ladder.

While this is a case study of a single group, I suspect that it is broadly representative of a social process.

The Decline and Fall of the Ward Boss

The Cornerville study casts light upon a change that was then taking place throughout the country, the decline and fall of the ward boss.

Cornerville had earlier had a ward boss in the classic style. For purposes of the present account, it will be necessary to identify the district, and surely 20 years after the completion of the study, such identification can do no harm. Cornerville was the North End of Boston, the historic section which contains the old North Church and Paul Revere's home. For many years, the North End had been dominated by the Hendricks Club under the leadership of one of Lin-

coln Steffens'[14] favorite political bosses. The Hendricks Club was located in the West End, but the West End and the North End were parts of the same ward.

In the course of my study, I was witnessing a shift in political power within the ward from the Irish to the Italians, but the changes went far beyond this.

The old ward boss had built his power upon the patronage he could control through the city government and the state government, through jobs he could offer in the building of tunnels, subways, and other municipal and state projects, and even through placing people in private companies who needed favors from local government.

The termination of the major construction projects in an old city and the depression together destroyed the foundations of the power of the old ward boss. Now it was only the federal government that had jobs and important favors to give out, and such political influence as could be helpful in these fields tended to gravitate to those who represented much wider constituencies than a single ward. At the same time, the racket organization developed within the city wards to build up a source of influence and money that was not dependent upon the ward politician.

When I first undertook to review *Street Corner Society*, I assumed that this process of political change had been well documented by now in the literature of political science. A look at the literature suggests that this is not the case.[15] To be sure, it is now well recognized that the

---

[14] *The Autobiography of Lincoln Steffens* (New York: Harcourt Brace, 1937).

[15] I have been able to find only scattered references. See, for example, the chapter by John P. Dean and Edward A. Suchman on "Social Institutions: The Political Role of Labor Unions and Other Organizations," in *Voting: A Study of Opinion Formation in a Presidential Campaign* (Chicago: University of Chicago Press, 1954). I am indebted to Andrew Hacker and Wayne Thompson for advice on this area of studies.

old ward boss is no longer with us and that the forms of political control have changed. However, no one seems much interested in tracing out this process of change. Why not? Wayne Thompson suggests that the explanation is the same as the one I have applied to the political change itself. As political power shifted away from the ward and city and up to state and particularly federal levels, so has the interest of students of politics shifted. So we find the ward boss buried indeed but without any ceremonial appropriate to signalize the significance of his passing.

ON RESEARCH METHODS
The Role of the Participant Observer

Throughout the Cornerville study, I played the role of participant observer. I shall not describe this role here, for it was not original with me, and it has been described elsewhere. However, some remarks about the particular application of this role to the Cornerville study will be relevant.

It seems to me that the role of the participant observer is particularly appropriate in an exploratory study. If I had gone into the field with highly structured research methods, I would necessarily have been limited to the conceptions of slum districts that already existed in the literature. As I have indicated, some of these conceptions were highly misleading. Acting as a participant observer, I was not bound by the preconceptions. I could feel my way along, learning as I went. The role then offers the researcher the advantage of flexibility.

It also offers possibilities of penetration to depths that are difficult to reach by some other methods. Here, we necessarily speak impressionistically because there is no scientific means of measuring the depth of a given study. I can only report that, as I went on, I had the impression that I was peeling off successive layers of Cornerville life. This impression was reinforced as I looked back upon my earlier ideas. It seemed to me then that many of the ideas I had had, the questions I had asked, and the answers I had received were on quite a superficial level. Critics will certainly differ over the depths of understanding I did reach regarding Cornerville, but I feel that whatever penetration I achieved must be credited in large part to the participant observer role I played.

The role also offers the advantage of introspection. This sounds like a highly unscientific asset, and yet I feel that introspection can be of invaluable aid to social science.

I am not suggesting that the participant observer need only look within himself to discover the meaning that his associates find in life. I am suggesting that the research man may find in introspection valuable leads to analysis of social data. Many of the ideas subsequently developed in the book had their inception in introspection. In most cases, this would be difficult to document, for the introspection was interlaced with observation, interviewing, and discussions of the study with Doc and others. However, at one point the connection is clear. My analysis of the social structure of bowling grew directly out of introspection. If I had not become intimately involved in the bowling activity of the Nortons, if I had not participated in the prize contest, if I had not reflected over how I felt in this social process, then it is very unlikely that I would have grasped the connection between the bowling scores and the structure of the gang.

The participant observer role also offers possibilities for carrying out field experiments. Perhaps "experiments" is too strong a word, for the participant observer seldom achieves the degree of control implied by the word. On the more pedestrian level, as his position becomes well established, he often says to himself, in effect: "If X were changed in this way, then I would expect Y to change in that way." And sometimes he is in a position to introduce the change in X and to check the prediction regarding Y. Such was the case with Long John's neurotic symptoms. I suggested a diagnosis to Doc and indicated the conditions necessary for a cure. Doc took the steps to re-establish a viable position for Long John, and the neurotic symptoms disappeared.

A Community Study?

I began my work on Cornerville with the idea that I was making a community study. It followed from this conception that I must somehow describe and analyze the behavior of something over 20,000 people. It was obvious that I could not interview 20,000 people or any large fraction thereof. How then was I to present to the public something that could be properly called a community study? The Lynds' studies of *Middletown* and *Middletown in Transition*[16] provided one possible model. They divided their studies up into areas of human activities, which meant writing chapters on making a living, leisure time activities, religion, and so on. There were no individuals or groups who figured as characters in the studies, with the exception of the chapter on the town's leading family in the second volume.

Another possibility would have been to use a questionnaire on a sample of the population. I must confess now that the questionnaire was hardly a realistic possibility at the time because I had no familiarity with the instrument nor respect for its powers. However, it now seems perfectly clear that, while I might have used the questionnaire to advantage perhaps in some aspects of my research, I could not have used it as a primary research tool in making a study of the nature of Street Corner Society.

For studies of this type, the question-

naire has severe limitations. In the first place, it is not very well adapted to studies where the social structure is important, although now efforts are being made to increase its utility in this respect.[17] It does not get at actions but concentrates primarily on attitudes. The observational data seem to me the very foundation of my study. Finally, at least on any sensitive issue, few Cornerville people could have been counted on to give dependable answers to questions put to them by strangers.

As I have noted in more detail in the *Street Corner Society* Appendix (in the enlarged 1955 edition), I began with the assumption that I was making a community study much like that of the Lynds. I saw my membership in groups such as the Nortons and the Italian Community Club simply as a means of gaining the personal acceptance that would enable me to gain a more intimate picture of the various broad segments of life of Cornerville people.

It was only 18 months after the field work began that I came to realize that group studies were to be the heart of my research. I could study the community through intensive examination of some of its representative groups.

A group study carried me in two directions: to the role of the individual in the group and to the place of the group in relation to the political organization, the racket organization, and the social agencies.

While I speak of selecting representative groups, it is clear that they were not representative in any statistical sense. While it might be possible to select corner gangs on this basis, the problems of gaining acceptance are such that the field worker can hardly afford to sample but must move in where he can most readily gain entrée.

16 New York: Harcourt Brace, 1929 and 1937.

17 See James Coleman, "Relational Analysis: The Study of Social Organizations with Survey Methods," *Human Organization*, XVII, No. 4 (Winter, 1958–59), 28–36.

As it turned out, I never made studies of other corner gangs that were anywhere nearly as intensive as that of the Nortons. However, I did gather sufficient data on four other corner gangs to be able to say with some confidence that the routines of life I described, the structure and organization of the groups, and the patterning of activities in the Nortons was broadly similar to what was to be found elsewhere. I confirmed this also by interviews with several corner boy leaders who had broad contacts in the community as well as valuable experience to report to me on their own gangs.

The Nortons provided me with some opportunity to observe the connections between the corner gang and the political organization. However, when Doc dropped out of the political campaign, it became evident that I would never gain a really inside view of the political organization through concentrating my attention upon the Nortons. It was this realization which led me to seek out Senator George Ravello and work closely with his organization through two political campaigns.

Similarly, the Nortons provided me with some orientation toward the significance of gambling and racketeering activities in the district, but they did not provide an inside view of the racket organization itself. It was for this reason that I sought out Tony Cataldo, a "middle management man" in the rackets of Eastern City. While I never did become as intimate with Tony as I had hoped—for reasons on which I have speculated in the Appendix to the book—my failure in this personal approach led to what turned out to be probably a more fruitful effort. By joining a local club of which Tony was a member, I was in a position to make direct observations on the role and influence of a racketeer in a Cornerville group.

This research strategy enabled me to place individual in group and group in some of the structures of the larger community. I cannot claim to have presented a total community study. Readers of *Street Corner Society* will find there little about Cornerville families or of the problems of adjustment between first- and second-generation Italian-Americans, except as these areas of life are refracted off my group studies. The same may be said of the role of women in Cornerville. We see them as they affect the lives of the men with whom we are concerned. We do not see them in their own right. Perhaps the most important gap of all is the field of religion. While the church seemed much more important for the women than for the men of Cornerville, the institution was of obvious importance for the men as well.

On these neglected areas, I did indeed gather fragmentary data. I could have reported impressionistically upon them, but I preferred to concentrate where I had intensive data. I wish now that I had gone further in these neglected areas, but I am not sure that it would have been possible for me. If time was not the main limitation, what then was it? While my answer is only speculative, I am inclined to think that the answer lies in the emotional load on the participant observer in such a study. The observer carries with him through the period of study those groups in which he participates. They are with him even when he is not with them bodily. Away from the group, he reflects about what he has seen, heard, and done. And then there are times when he needs just to lie fallow and recharge his batteries. Very occasionally, and even in late stages of the study, I would find myself setting out to interview someone with whom I was only vaguely acquainted and then turning back before I had even made the contact. I would then blame myself for a failure of nerve. As I look back on it, I don't think that was the proper diagnosis. Perhaps it was rather that my social-emotional circuits were fully loaded, and

I was unconsciously avoiding an overload. I realize that an explanation depending upon vague electronics analogies is most unsatisfactory. But it is the best I can do in trying to recreate for readers the way I felt at the time.

The Time Dimension

I was learning my field research methods as I went along. If I had been an experienced field worker in the beginning, would it have been possible to gather the same quantity and quality of data in a much shorter time? I have often asked myself that question, and have always come out with the same answer: yes and no. Had I begun the study with experience and a good sense of direction, much of the necessary data certainly could have been gathered and analyzed in a shorter period. However, there seem to be limits to this potential increase in efficiency. As I look back on the study, it seems to me that my most valuable findings depended upon following a group through time.

It would have taken only a few weeks to gain acceptance in the Nortons and make a systematic study of the structure of that group—for that particular time period. However, that would not have revealed the changes that took place in structure and individual behavior over time.

It is exceedingly difficult for me to talk meaningfully about the structure of a group or organization without utilizing the time dimension. A static picture may show the placement of the parts in relation to each other, but it does not show the forces that are holding these parts together. Only as we observe the group through time and note the changes that take place in it and in its relation to the outside world are we in a position to observe the pressures and counter pressures bearing upon the individual members and upon the group. Perhaps this is a justification for what is now often

called a structural-functional approach. It argues that you cannot properly understand structure unless you observe the functioning of the organization—which necessarily involves a time period. How long? Long enough to observe some change processes.

SLUMS YESTERDAY AND TODAY

What, if anything, does the book have to tell us about present-day slums in the United States and their problems?

While methods for the study of groups have advanced notably since my study, I assume that, if the findings were valid then, they are valid today. Of course, the obverse of that statement is also true. If they were invalid then, they can hardly have improved with age.

If we go beyond the study of groups, we face quite a different problem. At the community level, we deal with a pattern of culture and social organization which may well not apply to the North End of Boston today or to the slums of Manhattan, and so on.

If we compare Cornerville of the 1930's with, for example, the areas of Negro and Puerto Rican slums in New York City, there does seem to be an impressive difference in the realm of violence. *West Side Story* shows two boys' gangs not only fighting it out with their fists but also with knives and even, finally, guns. This picture is confirmed in newspaper accounts of gang fights. By contrast, in my three and a half years in Cornerville, I saw not a single gang fight and only one very brief fist fight between two teen-agers. No one reported to me any gang fights in that period. Why this difference?

The comparison seems to call for a little historical perspective.[18] Corner-

[18] The discussion of the history of the district is presented in much more detail in my "Race Conflicts in the North End of Boston," *New England Quarterly* (January, 1940). The use of the word "race" in the title is, of course, erroneous. However, this was the way the Italian-Americans referred to their clashes with the Irish-Americans.

ville, as I saw it, had arrived at a period of relative calm and peace, but in earlier years there had been frequent outbreaks of violence.

The Irish had populated and dominated the district before the entry of the Italian immigrants. Apparently, the young Irishmen were just as keenly attached to their street corners as the Italian-Americans I observed.

In the early days of Italian settlement, the newcomers had to run the gantlet of teen-age Irish gangs that controlled the street corners in the district. Many young Italian-Americans learned to fight the hard way, getting beaten up by the Irish.

The Genoese and other North Italians were not accustomed to the use of the knife. The Southerners knew no other way of defending themselves. Most of them had been peaceable people in Italy, but when a fight arose, they settled the matter with knives. It was either a serious fight or no fight at all. The Irish had quite a different outlook upon fighting. To them, street fighting was a sport which was governed by certain unwritten but clearly understood rules. Accepted weapons were fists, feet, knees, brass knuckles, blackjacks, sticks, stones, bricks, bottles, and other blunt instruments. Knives and guns were strictly banned. The purpose of the sport was to beat up the opponents, and bruises and welts of all kinds were legitimately dealt out and received, but it was against the rules to kill or seriously injure an opponent.

Under these circumstances, it is natural that the Irish were shocked when the Italian defended himself with a knife. In some cases when this happened, and they were able to disarm the Italian, they gave him a much more serious beating than he would otherwise have received. This provided an opportunity to give vent to outraged feelings and to give the rule-breaker a good lesson. More frequently, however, the brandishing of a knife served to ward off the impending

conflict. I have heard it said many times that "you can chase six Irishmen with a knife, but if you only swing a club, nobody will run."

The Irish and the Italians did not fight in all parts of the North End. At any period there were fairly well defined Irish areas and Italian areas. An Italian or an Irishman could keep out of trouble by remaining in his own area, particularly at night. The most bitter battles were fought along the advancing frontier of the Italian settlement where sovereignty was still undecided.

As the native-born generation grew to maturity, the young Italian-Americans adopted the Irish-American norms of fighting. With members of your own gang, you engaged in "rallies" against the Irish gangs. These were good, clean fights—with fists, banana stalks, rocks, and so on, but no knives.

As the Irish moved out of the North End, the ethnic clashes were fought upon sectional lines. There was a long tradition of fighting between the Italian North End and Irish Charlestown. For years it was not considered safe for a young Italian to set foot in Charlestown, and the young Irishman who ventured into the North End found himself in similar jeopardy. The North End boy who was seen in Charlestown would make for the bridge and try to outrun his pursuers until he reached his own territory. Many rallies were fought out on neutral ground —in the middle of the Charlestown Bridge—and some of these went on, with interruptions, for days. A boy could go home for lunch or supper and return to find the rally still in progress. Most of those involved were in their teens, but sometimes when word of a big rally went around, men in their twenties would join in battle, and gangs from many corners would march onto the bridge.

The Irish were not the only enemies. For years, there were frequent "rallies" between Italian gangs representing different street corners. However, as the ethnic population shift became complete, fighting gradually died down. So far as I could determine, the last gang rallies in the North End were fought around 1930.

If we compare the North End of Boston today with some sections of Manhattan, the differences are striking. However, if we compare the North End of 1910 to 1920 with these sections of Manhattan, the similarities are equally striking.

The comparison suggests that gang fighting is related to shifting populations with attendant struggles for control of territory. When the population stabilizes, when the same people live for long periods of time in the same places, we can expect to see a decline in gang fighting.

Territory provides one important key to the problem. While I did not see North End gangs fighting each other, this was perhaps because it was clear to everybody concerned which gang belonged on which corner. Nevertheless, I could observe the sentiments toward territory which must underlie these gang fights. The younger men of Cornerville seemed to feel that the corner really belonged to them. Furthermore, they were at home on their corner, and only there. Doc commented to me that most of the corner boys felt extremely insecure when they ventured very far away from their corners.

These attachments to territory arise, of course, in an environment where there is relatively little territory in relation to the population. When the population is then shifting, the crowded conditions provide ample opportunity for small frictions that quickly build up into large-scale clashes.

Can the recurrent outbreaks of gang violence in New York City today be attributed to the shifting populations and to the consequent obscurity of the allocation of scarce territory? I suggest this as a possible explanation. At the same time, we should note that the parallel I have drawn is not complete. As the North End Italian-Americans became acculturated, they abandoned knives and took to fighting with fists and blunt instruments. Knives and even occasionally guns figure in the clashes reported in New York. It would be comforting to believe that this is simply a stage in the evolution of "rumbles," as they are called there. However, I know of no evidence for a trend away from lethal weapons. It is indeed possible that a real change has taken place in teen-age culture in that area so that knives have become perfectly acceptable weapons.

CONCLUDING REMARKS

Whenever a student undertakes to describe and explain Society B in terms of how it differs from Society A, he runs the risk of overlooking the structure and processes of Society B. To explain what a society *is not* does not tell us what it *is*. *Street Corner Society* undertakes to present Cornerville in its own right. This non-judgmental approach is now taken for granted, but it was not at all common in the literature on slums when the Cornerville project began.

The methods used in the research no longer seem fashionable today. We seem to be in the era of large-scale quantification and statistical analysis of questionnaire data. The "case study" is considered by many to be of value only in the exploratory phase of research where it is to be followed by a more rigorous approach. The participant observer, being a non-standardized instrument, has gone out of style.

I do not intend any broadside against questionnaire studies. I have used questionnaires in the past and expect to do so in the future. I object only as does any workman whose methods are declared to be technologically obsolescent.

A "case" proves nothing by itself. It assumes scientific meaning only as it is related to (*a*) other cases and (*b*) some theoretical framework. Thus, the structure of one corner gang becomes significant as we look for, and find, similar structures on other corners. The problems of a single individual, Doc or Long John, take on general significance as we examine the relations between individual and group and develop theoretical ideas about the role of the individual in the group and the pressures the group puts on him. A study of one group, the Italian Community Club, becomes significant as we relate it to the class structure of the larger community. Examination of the changing nature of political control suggests both country-wide trends and propositions about relationships between local leaders and political powers at higher levels.

To be sure, there are problems of personal bias in the role of participant observer, but failure to immerse one's self in the situation may simply mean that the researcher retains the biases he started with—as we see in some of the earlier slum studies. Furthermore, as long as the participant observer concentrates on observing and reporting what happens, the data he brings in provide some protection against bias. While the problem of bias is not unimportant, the participant observer has to try to cope with his biases every day in his field work, and this seems to me an important part of the training of any sociologist.

What light does the book cast on slum problems today? Presumably, the analysis of the structure of the gang and of the role of social agencies may be equally applicable today. Some of the differences we see seem to be accounted for by different stages in the historical evolution of slum districts. However, we would need new slum district studies carried on today before we could speak with confidence of such historical trends.

10. The Police: A Sociological Study of Law, Custom, and Morality*

WILLIAM A. WESTLEY

The city policeman in the United States often feels himself to be a pariah. The public views him with suspicion and distrust, and he tends to see the public as his enemy. At least this was true of the community which we studied; it was hard to find anyone who would put in a good word for the police and the favorite comment of policemen themselves was "We are only a hundred and forty *against* a hundred and forty thousand."

These reciprocal attitudes are the product of the history and peculiarities of policing in North America. When the municipal police forces of the United States were first established in the middle of the nineteenth century they were a rough and lawless group.[1] Even today they are only beginning to detach themselves from political domination and its accompanying corruption. This is a major reason for the attitude of the public toward the police. This attitude has in turn, a great deal to do with the way in which policemen act and how they see themselves. It helps explain why policemen withdraw from others, stress secrecy, are abnormally and almost pathologically status conscious, and sanction behavior forbidden in the larger community. It is the theme in terms of which we will explain the development, nature, and function of police norms.

Originally many police departments consisted entirely of political appointees and experienced a high turnover in personnel with every change of party. During recent years this system has been rapidly replaced by civil service. Yet this has not happened in all cities and in many where it seems to have developed, police promotions and careers still depend on political influence. Where this is true, the police remain an instrument of the dominant political group and law enforcement has a highly partisan and often profitable character. This, of course, supports public suspicion of the police.

These difficulties are aggravated by the fact that while the police are ordinarily men of low status both in terms of background and because of their occupation they must, in the words of some, discipline their betters. As a result their judgment is often challenged and their dignity undermined.

These then are the general conditions which the metropolitan police of North America face and which are responsible for the attitudes and norms peculiar to their occupation. The nature of these norms and attitudes, the function they serve and the way they have developed are the subject of this paper.

DATA AND TECHNIQUES

The data are drawn from a case study of a single police department in a small midwestern industrial city. The study was made in 1949. Like many industrial cities this one held a tolerant view of prostitution and gambling and had a

* Based upon the author's Ph.D. dissertation of the same title, Sociology, 1951.

[1] Raymond B. Fosdick, *American Police Systems* (New York: Century Co., 1920), pp. 61–69.

169

long-standing reputation for municipal corruption. Since it had a sizable proportion of unattached males, a rapidly growing and generally impoverished Negro minority, and a large slum neighborhood, it faced many of the problems of the larger cities in the northern United States.

The study was made in two phases: the first consisting of a period of observation and completely non-directive interviewing, and the second of systematic interviews with a quota sample of the men in the department. The first period functioned to acquaint the researcher with the nature of the special milieu in which he would work and enabled him to formulate meaningful questions. Part of this period was spent with the police department of a neighboring metropolis. Since this was not the department where the study would finally be carried out, it gave us the freedom to ask blunt questions in sensitive areas without endangering the study. At the same time it gave us the comparative data necessary to the differentiation of those characteristics which were generic to policing as an occupation and those which were particular to the community in question.

The remaining part of the first phase was spent with the department to be studied. During this period, which lasted for several months, the researcher rode in squad cars and walked the beat with policemen for full shifts and around the clock; he sat in the detective bureau and the records office and behind the desk for weeks on end. He tried to observe all the duties and all the contingencies of the work of the department. The result was an over-all view of the men at work, a sense of the culture of the police, and a set of hypotheses about their norms and how they developed.

The second phase of the field work consisted of organized interviews with approximately 50 per cent of the men in the department, who were chosen so as to be representative of all ranks and di-

visions. Each man was interviewed about a predetermined series of areas of his work, background, and attitudes, but they were not asked specific questions except those necessary for face sheet data and for special purposes. The validity of the respondents' replies was judged by the researcher's knowledge of the department and the internal man-to-man consistency. The data were then subjected to a rough form of statistical analysis to test the primary hypotheses.

The purpose of this study was to investigate the way in which the contingencies of work would give rise to work norms which in turn would influence individual morality. Other studies of occupations and professions had demonstrated both that every occupation has its special problems which the people so employed must solve individually or collectively and that each tends to maintain some control over its members.[2]

This perspective influences the research in the following ways: first, we were interested in identifying work norms and the functions they served for the members individually and collectively. To us this meant finding the problems which the work norms solved. This involved a detailed description of the round of work, and how policemen responded to different tasks. Secondly, we wanted to see how and why policemen internalized these norms. To do this, we gathered occupational life histories which concentrated on how the occupational role was learned, what experiences had the greatest emotional impact, and how the man learned to deal with these experiences. The net result was a case study of a single police department which described its organization and duties, the

[2] It is impossible to give credit to all the workers in this field. Many were my fellow students or colleagues. However, the guiding hand behind much of this work was that of E. C. Hughes, and fortunately, some of his papers have been collected in a volume entitled *Men and Their Work* (Glencoe, Ill.: Free Press, 1958).

social norms and the function they played, and the way in which new policemen were socialized into the occupation, accepting its norms and integrating them into their morality.

POLICING AS AN OCCUPATION

The distinctive properties of policing as an occupation lie in its relationship to the community or public, its bureaucratic, quasi-military type of organization, and its legal monopoly over the use of violence.

We have already mentioned that the public views the police with suspicion and that the police tend to see the public as an alien and perhaps an enemy. This became obvious in the early phases of the research, for, when we talked to policemen, they were deeply concerned with their relationship to the public and many of them described this with an identical phrase, "We are only a hundred and forty against a hundred and forty thousand." The longer we worked with them, the more it became apparent that this felt hostility of the public was the most pervasive and important influence on the conduct of the police and seemed to underlie almost everything they did. At work it was responsible for their emphasis on secrecy and their intense concern with status and reputation; at home it meant that they tended to isolate themselves from any but policemen, feeling that their neighbors criticized them for their odd hours and unsavory associations and picked on their children for the assumed sins of their fathers. Many of them told stories to this effect.

The fact of public distrust of the police is, we feel, not to be disputed. A survey of the attitudes of social workers, union stewards, Negro leaders, and lawyers made by students drawn from a criminology class in the local college indicated that the vast majority thought the police to be ignorant, corrupt, and brutal. Whether or not these results are representative of the attitudes of the people in that community, they certainly were representative of how the police thought the people felt about them. Thus, when approximately half of the men in the department were asked how they thought the public felt about the police, some 73 per cent *stated* that the public saw them as racketeers, power crazy, parasites, etc., and only 13 per cent said that the public liked the police. If it is recognized that many of the policemen distrusted the interviewer, these proportions grow in significance.

It is clear that these policemen felt themselves to be social pariahs. They felt that others saw them as despicable. This was an ever present threat to their occupational reputation and self-esteem. It colored their perceptions and memories, and they became sensitive to slights and remembered and told of insults. To some extent they got involved in a vicious circle in which, because they suspected the attitudes and motives of others, they often reacted in ways which engendered these attitudes. Thus, the policeman may see more behind the blow of a drunk than is the case, and defend himself with an enthusiasm which the bystander sees as brutality. In fact, many policemen told the observer that it was all right to rough a man up if he were acting in such a way as to make the public lose respect for the police.

Many of the day-to-day duties of the police are such that they continually re-experience the impact of these public attitudes, for the public frequently resents the appearance of the police. Areas in which the police are required to restrain or arrest, such as traffic violations, brawls, public disorders, domestic disputes, minor legal violations (e.g., obstructing the sidewalk), tend to elicit resentment. Furthermore, since interactions arising from police intercession tend to be highly charged with emotions, these are the experiences which the police tend to remember.

Supplementing this source of aggravation is that arising from the way in which the public imposes collective responsibility on the police. For the policeman this means that the sins of his fellows are visited upon him. Let one man in the department get drunk or brutal, and every man in the department feels himself condemned and hears open remarks to that effect.

The fact that policemen wear a uniform undoubtedly contributes to the tendency of the public to see them as replaceable and collectively responsible. Unfortunately, this uniform sometimes symbolizes incompetence and brutality, and many of the men are highly sensitive to this fact. Rookie policemen are sometimes so conscious of this that they refuse to wear their uniforms to and from work.

Public distrust is, therefore, the major occupational problem of the police. It is the basis for two of their most important norms: the maintenance of secrecy, and the maintenance of respect for the police.

Organization

The police have a quasi-military type of organization with a strict hierarchy of offices and a tendency to appointment and promotion by means of an impartial system of examinations. In addition, like the military man the policeman wears a uniform and is considered to be on duty twenty-four hours a day. This means that he takes on a way of life rather than a job. Both the department and the public seem to feel that for the policeman the call of duty is expected to come before self and family. The effect of these definitions and type of organization is to detach the policeman further from the rest of the community. It also has the effect of promoting a solidarity and ingroup character among them. This in turn makes the individual man highly dependent on his fellows—for he cannot escape.

The Monopoly of Violence[3]

The most unusual quality of policing as an occupation is its use of violence in support of occupational ends. The police are legally entitled to use force to make an arrest, to maintain public order, or to protect themselves. They often need force to meet and restrain its illegal use by others. Thus, the fact that they use force is understandable. But they don't confine their use of force to the ends for which they are entitled; they also use it to support private and occupational ends, and, what is more, they actually feel that they are entitled to this extracurricular usage. Thus, it was found that policemen characteristically approve the use of force if it has the effect of maintaining respect for the police. Naturally they have their own ideas of what makes for respect. They feel, for example, and perhaps with some justification, that in the slums people respect a rough, tough approach. They also feel that people who attack the police verbally or especially physically should be taught respect with strong methods.

Policemen also feel that it is legitimate to use violence to make a good arrest or extract a confession. Public revulsion against the third degree has restrained but not eliminated their enthusiasm in this area. To some extent this is because the police are seldom seriously criticized for their "misuse" of violence when it results in the solution of an important crime. The net effect of the criticism has been to make the police restrict the illegal use of violence to groups who have little or no recourse to the law: principally criminals and the politically impotent.

Where there is great pressure from the public to get the police to restrict the incidence of some crime (as is always the case for some sex crimes) or to solve

[3] For a fuller treatment of how the police use violence, see William A. Westley, "Violence and the Police," *American Journal of Sociology,* LIX, No. 1 (July, 1953), 34-41.

a big case the police tend toward the illegal use of violence to meet these demands. Thus, in some cases the police find that they cannot control the incidence of crimes except by the illegal use of violence. If a rapist or an exhibitionist is at large, they can often identify the offender, but they can't get the victims to testify. In situations of this kind violence may be used to obtain a confession or to drive the criminal out of the community.[4] The sex criminal is likely to be driven out of town; the man with a record is fair game for the third degree. In circumstances of this kind it may be said

TABLE 1

BASES FOR THE USE OF FORCE
NAMED BY 73 POLICEMEN

Type of Response	Frequency	Percentage
a) Disrespect for the police......	27	37
b) When impossible to avoid......	17	23
c) To obtain information.........	14	19
d) To make an arrest.............	6	8
e) For the hardened criminal......	5	7
f) When you know a man is guilty.	2	3
g) For sex criminals.............	2	3
Total.....................	73	100

that violence is a way of adjusting the difference between the requirements of the job and the means for achieving it.

It should be clear from the arguments we have been advancing that the study of how the police use and misuse violence illuminates the character of their occupation. Violence is, after all, one of the ultimate means of coercion and whoever can use it should be sorely tempted under sufficient provocation. That the police will have this provocation from time to time is not surprising, but that they should experience such continuous

[4] A police captain in a large city told the author that he was able to drive pickpockets out of his city by simply pulling them into the station and splashing acid on their clothes. Thus, he was able to put an end to a crime wave which he couldn't stop with legal means.

provocation that they almost cease to recognize when they are using violence illegally indicates that the provocation is also a part of their way of life. However, once they have widened in their minds the area for which violence is legitimate, they will of course use it to support their own ends. This became starkly apparent when 73 policemen, representing a 50 per cent sample of the men in the department, were asked when they thought a policeman was justified in roughing a man up. Characteristically they mentioned occupational ends before legal ends. Table 1 describes their reasons by and in order of frequency. In 69 per cent of the cases (a, c, e, f, g) the policemen are legitimating their use of violence in terms of occupational but illegal ends. The full significance of these replies can only be understood if it is realized that these policemen did not feel the observer to be a member of their in-group. Thus, they thought that these reasons would justify the illegal use of violence even to the outside community. Obviously, they had come to think of the police norms as true moral norms and for them an occupational rule had become a moral principle.

NORMS

The city police tend to be both an occupational and a social group. This latter characteristic is not true of many other occupations because their members are widely dispersed and they seldom see each other. The police are always in contact with each other and because they feel themselves an out-group with a high degree of collective responsibility they come to share perspectives and develop rules of conduct.

The department we studied had three general norms which we could identify. Each had a persistent effect on the conduct of the men in the department, and each was functionally related to the social problems which the police department faced. The norms were identified through observation as persistent prescriptive statements by policemen and as regularities in conduct. They were checked in interviews by asking the men to legitimate some unpopular or illegal form of behavior by policemen. Here it was assumed that norms would be used to legitimate conduct, or in other words any shared definitions of proper action would function as moral justifications.

Three norms were identified: the maintenance of secrecy, the maintenance of respect for the police, and the acceptance of the fact that in the case of an arrest the end justifies the means. The first two were prescriptive, the third permissive.

Secrecy[5]

The maintenance of secrecy is the most important of the norms. It is carefully taught to every rookie policeman; it is observed by all the men, and there are powerful sanctions against its violation. All social and occupational groups probably believe in some degree of secrecy, for the stool pigeon, or squealer, is everywhere an anathema. However, among urban police the rule has the force of life, and the violator is cut off from vital sources of information and the protection of his colleagues in times of emergency.

Secrecy means that policemen must not talk about police work to those outside the department or gossip within the department. Naturally the last is not as stringently observed as the first. Yet it is observed, for some policemen told the researcher that others sometimes planted a juicy item of gossip just to find out whether one did talk. Policemen carry secrecy a long way and with true professional integrity will perjure themselves before revealing secrets. At least this was true of the policemen in the department studied, for when questioned about whether they would first report and then

testify against a fellow officer who committed a felony, 75 per cent of the men interviewed declared that they would not.[6]

Secrecy is a direct product of public distrust of the police on the one hand, of police corruption on the other. In turn the two are related. Since policemen feel that they are despised by the public and since naturally they don't like being disliked they do all they can to prevent the public getting evidence against them. This is best done by sticking together and keeping mistakes within the department. The man who talks too much is a threat to everyone. As a partner he is likely to reveal mistakes and what policemen consider innocent foibles, e.g., small graft. As a member of the department he talks about things which give the department, and therefore every man in it, a bad name; and he may even bring on an investigation. A stress on secrecy prevents this kind of thing. The verbally uninhibited rookie has a short and unpleasant career. The old hand knows that he must keep his mouth shut.

The Maintenance of Respect for the Police

This is a strange rule. Normally it would be taken for granted. The fact that it is a rule is indicative of the extreme sensitivity of the police to public criticism and their need for prestige. We first perceived its existence as a kind of explanation for certain incongruities in police accounts of their interaction with the public. They were all aware of the fact that the public and, therefore, the researcher were critical of violence. Ordinarily they talked the formal line and

---

[5] See William A. Westley, "Secrecy and the Police," *Social Forces*, XXXIV, No. 3 (March, 1956), 254–57.

[6] We obtained an unusual kind of corroboration for this statement. When my paper on secrecy was read in Berkeley, one of the San Francisco newspapers had its reporters interview the chiefs and some of the patrolmen in seven nearby cities and ask them the same question. Six out of seven of the chiefs denied our allegation, but all the patrolmen supported what we had to say.

maintained an aversion to its use. Yet there were times when they advocated it unabashedly. For example, there were many accounts of that unpleasant public character the "wise guy," the fellow who talks back to the police or *speaks to them disrespectfully*. They maintained that it would be a good thing to teach a fellow like that a little respect, and some men told of occasions when they did.

We put our hunch to a test in asking the men to legitimate violence. As can be observed from Table 1, disrespect for the police was the reason most frequently advanced to justify its use. Remember too, they were not legally entitled to use violence for this end; yet they gave this reason to an outsider. The implication is clear. They had so thoroughly accepted the maintenance of respect for the police as a collective end that it had assumed the proportion of a moral sanction.

The "Good Pinch"

Policemen use this term to refer to an arrest which will stick and which will bring them credit without political repercussions. The norm is that policemen believe that the good pinch is an end that justifies almost any means. Thus, even policemen who have a personal aversion to the use of violence will approve its use by others if it results in a good pinch. As in the case with the maintenance of respect for the police, the good pinch and steps leading up to it are considered a moral legitimation for the illegal use of violence. Thus, Table 1 reveals that 37 per cent of the men interviewed gave the good pinch or steps leading up to it (categories c, d, e, f) as justification for the use of force.

The importance of the good pinch in the ideology of the police can be explained by the functions it performs for the individual policeman and for the department as a whole. We have already pointed out that the police feel themselves to be despised by the public and that they are very sensitive to criticism and manifestations of disrespect. However, despite their withdrawal and secrecy they cannot disregard or accept this negative definition of their occupation and, therefore, themselves. They have a great need to justify their work. This is the function of the good pinch. It silences criticism and brings credit. It gives prestige to the man, may help him get a promotion, and certainly bolsters his self-respect. It enhances the reputation of the department and assures the public that it is on the job.

Certain consequences of this emphasis on the "good pinch" are dysfunctional to the department. It promotes competition between men and particularly between divisions at the expense of co-operation and smooth functioning. Thus, it is the source of a rather typical conflict between the detective and patrol divisions. In the department we studied it was the responsibility of the detective division to follow up leads which might be provided by the patrol division. Naturally the patrolmen resented this, since it meant that the detective got the credit for the good pinch. They often tried to get around this unpleasant prospect by trying to investigate the crime themselves or by using any tactic they could get away with in order to get a confession or dig up evidence. Police chiefs ordinarily have to give a lot of attention to this problem if they want to maintain the morale of the patrolmen.

SOCIALIZATION

So far we have tried to delineate the norms of the police, the work experiences which generate these norms, and the functions of the norms for the men and the department. This then has been a kind of functional analysis of police norms and at the same time a limited description of a police department as a kind of social system. To complete this analysis, it is necessary to show how recruits are socialized into this system, becoming part of the group, and internalizing norms.

The socialization of a policeman is exemplified in the experience of the rookie, who is in the process of moving from the world outside into the police department. We gathered accounts of their experiences with the police department from 50 per cent of the men who were rookies at the time of the study. We also interrogated experienced men about the qualities desirable in a rookie policeman.

We found that the socialization of the rookie consists of three general stages: the recruit school, training by the older men on the job, and personal contacts with the public. The first stage, the recruit school, functions principally as a kind of *rite de passage* between the status of citizen and policeman. In it the rookie is sharply separated from the world in which he has been previously committed; he is thoroughly indoctrinated with the idea of being a policeman, and he is taught the rudiments of his job. However, his real training begins when he is assigned to an older man, usually in a patrol car.

The Role of the Recruit

The success of this next stage in the recruit's training is directly dependent on the skill with which he plays the recruit role. The older man must somehow be encouraged to pass on his knowledge and to help the younger man. He does this when he finds what he considers a willing and intelligent listener. In fact he usually wants to talk, for he feels that he has a lot stored up and there are long hours in the patrol car in which there is little else to do. If the rookie gives him half a chance, he will tell him all he knows.

The older men, hungry for an audience, see in the rookie a chance to talk about themselves as policemen. Having long been bottled up, the older man, who

is insecure about himself and the worth of his job and who faces from day to day an unfriendly world, craves a chance to reassure himself by persuading someone else. Thus, the rookie can be a psychological asset. However, he must play his part, he must listen, he must be appreciative, and he mustn't learn too fast and be one of those "smart ones." This is vital. Each rookie will normally work with several different experienced men, in different areas of police work. With these men he builds his reputation, and it had better be a good one.

Insecurities about Action

The rookie who plays the recruit role soon comes to accept the policeman's attitudes and ways of acting. The day-to-day contingencies of his work are often unfamiliar. Family quarrels, irate storekeepers, impudent teen-agers, taunting drunks, all pose problems which he cannot solve with his previous experience or what he has learned in the police school. Yet he must do something, for this is his job. At the same time he must not make mistakes, for he is both the representative of the law and in a probationary status. As a result he tends to do as his partner does and to accept his partner's definition of the situation. "See that fellow over there. . . . He's a drunk but he won't give you any trouble. . . . Just tell him to go and he'll go quietly. . . . Most of them are that way, but you'll get a bad one now and then. . . . You don't have to take anything from them though. . . . Just pull them in. . . . If there's one thing I hate, it's a guy who is too soft. . . . That sort of thing never does the force any good." It is in this way that the police lore, both formal and informal, and the policemen's attitudes are passed on to and accepted by the new man.

Knowledge About vs. Acquaintance With

In his contacts with his colleagues, through his work with his partners, the new policeman shapes his conception of the policeman's role and his relationship to the group. The fact that he is always warmly received by the experienced men, the repeated assertions of the necessity of sticking together, and pointed references to the difference between the policeman and the public—"Everybody hates a cop" and "You gotta make them respect you"—amalgamate the rookie into the force and separate him from the rest of the community. He learns the informal rules, the limits of acceptable discussion, and when to break the law. He becomes familiar with the policeman's idea of law enforcement and of when and how it is to be applied. He becomes aware of the pressures working on the police and the channels of influence within the department. All these things he learns, but his relationship to them is what William James called knowledge about rather than acquaintance with. The latter is acquired differently.

The Reality Shock

The older men have all told the rookie how tough it is, but when he experiences it himself, it comes as a shock. It is when he himself has the experiences which are responsible for the norms that he comes to accept them emotionally. They then become truth.

E. C. Hughes has called this process of finding out "reality shock." Evidently it happens in many occupations. Our interviews with the police rookies indicate that for them, at least, it is cumulative. The basic experience is one of rejection and hostility from the people of the community in which he works. He finds that sometimes when he is in a fight, the bystanders are more sympathetic to the man he is trying to arrest than they are to him. He finds himself condemned for something one of the other fellows in the department has been accused of doing. He is taunted and jeered at. In many of the areas where he has to work he is greeted with silence and evident hostility. Although neither all of his experiences nor even most of his experiences are of this kind, these are the ones that hurt and which he seems to remember. Furthermore, they are the experiences which substantiate what the experienced men have told him. To protect his own feelings and to maintain his self-respect, he must reject these accusations, and one of the most convenient ways to do this is to reject the people who make them, i.e., the public. With these experiences he comes to need the rule that "You gotta *make* them respect you" and to value the stress placed on secrecy. When these things have happened to him, he has truly passed from the community into the police force. He has acquired new commitments, a new self-conception, and a new morality.

CONCLUSIONS

Law enforcement is the policeman's job. On the one side is the law, a system of statutes, regulating conduct and imposing sanctions. On the other side is the law in force, which is both more discretionary than the statutes and at the same time goes beyond them. Between them stands the policeman, who interprets and applies the law but modifies it to meet what he sees as right and what he sees as the needs of the community. Many of the modifications the policeman makes are based on his own customs, which can then be said to shape the law.

The customs of the police are in fact occupational norms, a collective and cultural response to the social problems which they face as an occupational group. Among the urban police in North America the most important of these problems is the critical, unco-operative, and often hostile public with which they have to deal. They find the public a threat, both to their occupational goals and to their self-esteem. They respond by stressing secrecy, by insisting that policemen do whatever is necessary to enforce respect by the public, and by condoning any means which will result in a prestigeful arrest. Policemen obey and enforce these norms because of the sanctions supporting them and because they see them as morally right.

The norms, then, can be seen as part of the policeman's morality. They are internalized as a part of the policeman's socialization into the police force. This occurs because on the one hand they are explicitly taught to the rookie by the older man and because on the other hand the rookie, when he experiences the hostility and what he sees as the injustice of the public, develops an emotional need for them. They protect him from threats to his dignity and self-esteem; they offer him a prescription for added prestige and a balm for his wounds.

PART 3

Ethnic and Racial Groups in Urban Society

When the program of urban studies began at Chicago, the city was gorged with immigrants from all of the nations of Europe. The inflooding immigrants from Eastern and Southern Europe had aroused public concern to such a point that quota restrictions to immigration had just been imposed. Native-born Americans whose parents had been immigrants were concerned about preserving "the American way." Prejudice against Italians, Poles, and other ethnic groups was high and often bitter. Many civic leaders condoned this prejudice, claiming that the immigrant horde was culturally so alien that it could not be assimilated. The fact that each ethnic neighborhood had its own community institutions, its churches, schools, newspaper, and recreational and associational facilities, was widely interpreted to mean that a century or more might be required to break down the self-imposed cultural isolation. During those years the Negro community was just beginning its first rapid growth, under the stimulus of economic opportunity created by the immigration quotas. Jobs at the lower end of the socioeconomic scale that could no longer be filled with immigrants were being opened to Negroes.

The discovery that the ethnic community was a gigantic sociological defense mechanism which facilitated the survival and adjustment of immigrants but which the second generation sought to modify and escape was a major research accomplishment of urban sociology during the 1920's and 1930's. Because it was a heated public issue, and because ethnic neighborhoods in the city were colorful and distinctive in their variety, sociologists were fascinated by urban ethnological research. Almost none of this work was solely descriptive, in the tradition of folk anthropology of the time. Instead, it was analytical and concentrated on exploring the behavior patterns and processes of adjustment and change as the immigrant adapted to the new economic environment, and prospered. Stonequist's article on the marginal man is protoypical of the search that was made for theoretical formulations. Wirth's study of The Ghetto set a superb pattern for the sociological study of ethnic contrasts and cultural change. Hostility and tension between ethnic groups were treated as objective phenomena to be explained rather than a battle to be joined.

The Chicago school of urban sociology pioneered in this branch of social research and, under the direction of Louis Wirth as well as of Robert E. Park, maintained a continuous program of ethnic and race research, working through Hull-House and numerous other neighborhood centers undertaking to serve and hasten the adjustment of immigrant ethnic groups. A regular program of research training in the sociology of race relations was established and maintained for several

179

years, until about 1954. The contributions presented here represent, in each instance, a new departure and a unique set of new insights in this field. Although some of these studies now are several years old, they still stand as examples of original thinking and study worthy of continued reading.

The tradition that was begun with these studies recently has been revived. A study now is under way at the Community and Family Study Center, the goal of which is to chart the degree and nature of the eventual adjustment made by the European immigrants and their children and to study more closely the problems of adjustment and assimilation now exhibited by Negroes and Puerto Ricans. Monographs based on the materials of this study are now in preparation.

11. An Approach to the Measurement of Interracial Tension*

SHIRLEY A. STAR

INTRODUCTION

The Problem and Its Background

This research, carried out in the spring of 1949, was designed to investigate the impact of actual and impending Negro residential movement into their neighborhoods upon the attitudes of residents of hitherto exclusively white areas. At the time the study was undertaken, heightened tension and repeated episodes of anti-Negro violence had been and still were accompanying Negro movement from their primary areas of residence (the "Black Belt") into the immediately surrounding white neighborhoods (Kenwood, Hyde Park, East Woodlawn, Greater Grand Crossing)—a movement necessitated in any case by high Negro migration from the South to Chicago's already overcrowded Black Belt over the preceding decade, but facilitated and much accelerated by the removal (through the United States Supreme Court's invalidation of restrictive covenants) of the legal barriers maintaining the boundaries of the Black Belt.[1] Practical concern to avert interracial violence conjoined with a period of renewed theoretical interest in sharpening the conceptual tools employed in the analysis of intergroup relations[2] to suggest that measurement of interracial tension might prove useful in anticipating or predicting the occurrence of such outbreaks. With-

in its broader context of interest in the invasion process, the present research therefore incorporated an attempt to develop and test in a preliminary way an instrument that would reflect changes in community levels of interracial tension.

[1] For a less abbreviated account of the growth of the Chicago Negro community and the conflicts accompanying it, see Chicago Commission on Race Relations, *The Negro in Chicago* (Chicago: University of Chicago Press, 1922); St. Clair Drake and Horace R. Cayton, *Black Metropolis* (New York: Hartcourt, Brace & Co., Inc., 1945); Metropolitan Housing and Planning Council, *The Changing Pattern of Negro Residence in Chicago* (Chicago: Metropolitan Housing and Planning Council, 1949). More general accounts of the essentially similar development of Negro residential segregation in northern urban areas can be found in Maurice R. Davie, *Negroes in American Society* (New York: McGraw-Hill Book Co., 1949); E. Franklin Frazier, *The Negro in the United States* (New York: Macmillan Co., 1949); Charles Johnson, *Patterns of Negro Segregation* (New York: Harper & Bros., 1943).

[2] See Susan Deri, Dorothy Dinnerstein, John Harding, and Albert P. Pepitone, "Techniques for the Diagnosis and Measurement of Intergroup Attitudes and Behavior," *Psychological Bulletin*, XLV (1948), 248–71, for a discussion of lack of conceptual differentiation, clarification, and precision in the terms of intergroup relations analysis as a major factor then impeding the development of adequate measuring devices; and Louis Wirth, "Research in Racial and Cultural Relations," *Proceedings of the American Philosophical Society*, XCII (1948), 381–86, for a major contribution to the development of a systematic frame of reference for the study of race relations. It should be acknowledged that the conceptual usage on which the present research is based is a direct outgrowth from Wirth's original efforts to establish needed conceptual distinctions.

* Adapted from Shirley A. Star, Ph.D. dissertation, "Interracial Tension in Two Areas of Chicago: An Exploratory Approach to the Measurement of Interracial Tension," Sociology, 1950.

It is the latter, technological aspect of the study with which this chapter is concerned.[3] And it is important to emphasize at once that this research was neither a systematic study of the causes of interracial tension nor an attempt to demonstrate that measures of interracial tension can actually have predictive value in anticipating interracial violence. It was, rather, the necessary research preliminary to either of these larger purposes, and as such, was solely concerned with developing a measure of tension and demonstrating that this device had sufficient validity to justify further research efforts with it. Accordingly, after a brief presentation of the details of the study design, the sections of this chapter successively take up the concept of tension on which the tension scale is based, a brief description of the scale itself, and the empirical data bearing on its validity. The chapter closes with a discussion of some theoretical and practical considerations that affect further use of the tension scale, and particularly, though not exclusively, its use as a predictive device.

Design of the Research

The design of this study was essentially that of an opinion survey in which the attitudes of two community areas of Chicago, differing only in their relation to the course of Negro residential expansion, were to be compared. In other words, it was looked upon as a quasi-experimental study, the "experimental" community to be one into which Negroes had moved to the accompaniment of a good deal of interracial tension and sporadic violence; the "control," an otherwise comparable community removed from the path of Negro residential expansion, in which there had been no history of interracial violence and little or no interracial tension. With "all other things being equal," differences in racial

attitudes between the communities could be presumed to be attributable to the communities' differential experience with reference to the invasion process, and any measure of attitudes which purported to measure interracial tension must indicate a difference in tension levels between the two communities.

In practice, this basic scheme could not be fully implemented, as a brief description of the two community areas in which the research was carried out will make clear. As an instance of an "invaded" community, Greater Grand Crossing was selected. This area of the South Side of Chicago—bounded, roughly, from the north, clockwise, by Sixty-third Street, Cottage Grove Avenue, Seventy-ninth Street and Halsted Street—lay just to the south of the main Negro community. (See Fig. 1.) Negro residential movement into Greater Grand Crossing had been going on since the early forties, when Negroes began moving into the northern portion of the community, frequently called Park Manor, in which the restrictive covenant cases arose. In 1948, shortly before this study, the northernmost census tract in Grand Crossing had over 10 per cent Negro households, and both this tract and the one immediately south were judged to have had a "significant" increase in the number of Negro households since 1939.[4] Negro movement into the area had been accompanied by a number of interracial incidents—house burnings, stonings, crowds collecting around Negro residences. There were over twenty such incidents in the eighteen months preceding this research, and they continued as Negro movement in the community proceeded southward, with four or five occurring within a month or two after this study.[5] In summary, then, Greater Grand Crossing was, in fact, a community where changes in

[3] The broader aspects of community attitudes in the face of Negro residential expansion are fully reported in Star, *loc. cit.*, 24–77.

[4] *The Changing Pattern of Negro Residence in Chicago.*

[5] Data from Reports of the Chicago Commission on Human Relations.

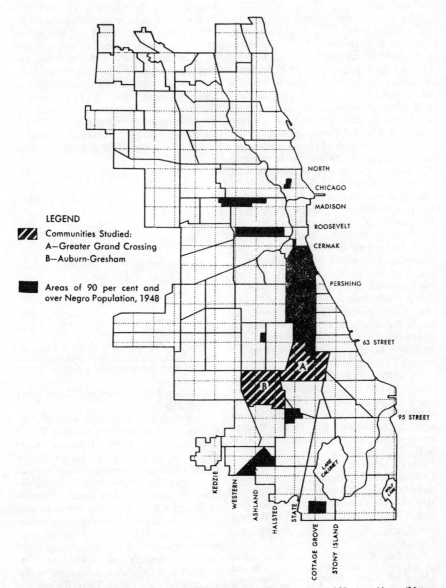

LEGEND

Communities Studied:
A—Greater Grand Crossing
B—Auburn-Gresham

Areas of 90 per cent and over Negro Population, 1948

Fig. 1.—Map of Chicago, showing communities studied in relation to areas of Negro residence (Metropolitan Housing and Planning Council of Chicago, June, 1949).

racial composition were taking place with some degree of interracial tension and violence.

The case of the control community, Auburn-Gresham, was less clear-cut, however. Auburn-Gresham is located immediately to the southwest of Greater Grand Crossing, lying between Seventy-fifth and Eighty-ninth streets on the north and south and between Halsted and Western avenues on the east and west. The southeast corner of Auburn-Gresham touched the northwest corner of a secondary area of Negro settlement, running from Ninety-first Street south to Ninety-seventh Street and from Stewart Avenue east to South Park Avenue. A stretch of non-residential land separated the two, however, and there had been no movement of Negroes into Auburn-Gresham at the time of the study. In 1948, there was no census tract in Auburn-Gresham which had as much as 1 per cent of Negro households, and no tract showed any significant change in this respect since 1939.[6] So, in comparison with Greater Grand Crossing, at least, Auburn-Gresham was an area of stable racial composition, in which there had been no Negro residents and no interracial violence.

In terms of available 1940 Census data,[7] the two communities were alike in many respects: median educational attainment of the adult population, median age of population, sex ratios, marital composition, and proportion foreign-born. There were, however, genuine differences between Auburn-Gresham and Greater Grand Crossing, as well. Most notably, Auburn-Gresham was a community of somewhat higher economic level than Greater Grand Crossing, as is illus-

[6] *The Changing Pattern of Negro Residence in Chicago.*

[7] All data referred to here, with the exception of religion, are drawn from Louis Wirth and Eleanor H. Bernert (eds.), *Local Community Fact Book of Chicago* (Chicago: University of Chicago Press, 1949). Religion is derived from the findings of the survey.

trated by median rentals of $45.25 and $38.85, respectively, and further confirmed by similar differences in such other economic indices as median earnings, occupational distribution and proportion of dwelling units in need of major repair. In addition to its higher economic circumstances, Auburn-Gresham was more an area of single-family homes than was Greater Grand Crossing (35 per cent of the dwelling units in the former area, but 24 per cent of the dwelling units in the latter were of this character), and a larger proportion of the Auburn-Gresham

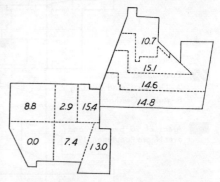

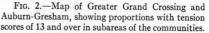

Fig. 2.—Map of Greater Grand Crossing and Auburn-Gresham, showing proportions with tension scores of 13 and over in subareas of the communities.

population (55 per cent vs. 43 per cent) were Catholic.

It is thus apparent that, even though the two communities of Greater Grand Crossing and Auburn-Gresham were chosen in an attempt to vary only the racial situation, they did not correspond in composition as closely as could be desired. Moreover, since it bordered Greater Grand Crossing at the northeast and an area of Negro settlement at the southeast, Auburn-Gresham was not as completely insulated from contacts with the Negro community and its residential expansion as its use as a contrasting racial situation should imply. Nevertheless, the population patterns of Chicago were such, that no other pair of communities could be found to approximate the basic research design as closely as did Greater Grand Crossing and Auburn-Gresham.

Within these two communities, area-probability sampling methods were used to sample the white population aged eighteen and over. In Auburn-Gresham, one-eighth of all blocks containing dwelling units were randomly selected, and one-twelfth of all dwelling units in these blocks were chosen; or, in other words, one household in every 96 was selected for inclusion in the sample. The same method was employed to secure a representative sample of Greater Grand Crossing, where one-eleventh of the dwelling units in a random one-quarter of the blocks was selected, for a sample of one household in every 44. Within these households, individuals to be interviewed were selected randomly.

Since Negro residential invasion was not going on simultaneously throughout the whole community of Greater Grand Crossing, which is, after all, an area of two and one-half square miles with a population of over 60,000, this community was sub-divided into four sections with reference to its experience with Negro residents. These sections are referred to as:

Zone I. The invaded section of the community. As it will be used in this report, this zone contains only those sample blocks in which Negroes and whites were living.[8] Essentially, however, it may be thought of as the section of the community north of Seventieth Street. This was the part of the community in which most of the pre-study interracial violence had occurred.

Zone II. The "threatened" section of the community. This area of Greater Grand Crossing just south of Zone I to about Seventy-third Street, was immediately contiguous either to the old Negro community or to the section invaded at the time of the study. It has been invaded since the date of the study and was the area in which the immediate post-study incidents occurred.

Zone III. The "intermediate" section of the

community. As its name implies, this section of the community lay between the threatened area and the outer section of the community, or, roughly, it was the band lying between Seventy-third and Seventy-sixth streets.

Zone IV. This is the section of Greater Grand Crossing most remote from the Negro residential areas.

In order to be able to treat these sections separately, supplementary samples of Zones I, II, and IV were randomly drawn. When these supplementary samples are combined with the cases in the community cross-section, approximately equal representative samples of the four zones are obtained.

Details of sample size are shown in Table 1. As may be seen there, 788 interviews were originally assigned, of which 619 were obtained, giving a rate of loss of 21.4 per cent over all. If the "ineligibles" (i.e., interviews assigned to non-existent dwelling units, dwelling units occupied by non-whites or dwelling units occupied by non-English-speaking families) are excluded from consideration, the loss rate drops to 18 per cent of eligible respondents—12 per cent who refused to be interviewed, 3 per cent who were never found at home after nine calls at various times of day and week, and 3 per cent who were legitimately unavailable (i.e., out of town or hospitalized during the entire survey period). The sample was examined for biases which might result from these losses, and these biases were found to be negligible. The sample was, however, adjusted to correspond to the age-sex distribution of the 1940 Census, and all results presented are based on the adjusted sample.[9]

DEVELOPMENT OF AN INTERRACIAL
TENSION SCALE

The Concept of Interracial Tension

If the variable of tension was to be thought of as having possibly predictive significance, it had to refer to phenom-

[8] The fact of Negro residence was determined by a canvass of the sample blocks.

[9] For further details on sampling, see Star, *loc. cit.*, 167-94.

ena observable prior to the actual occurrence of overt interracial violence and subject to more rapid variation than the underlying, slow-to-change attitudes expressed or implied by such concepts as antipathy, prejudice, discrimination, and segregation.

The distinctive qualities of interracial tension as a concept in the general area of intergroup conflict were most immediately suggested by two quite brief definitions. First, Drake and Cayton parenthetically defined racial tension as "that latent uneasiness which occasionally

With respect to interracial tension, the situation is apparently one in which intergroup relations are strained, are being stretched so tight that it is feared or expected that they will break.

Tension, then, was thought of as the emotional concomitant of conflicts whose outcome is in doubt, at least to the participants in them. Change, in the sense of any challenge to the *status quo*, appeared to be the central factor in the emergence of tension, for, given a social arrangement more or less accommodating a situation of intergroup antagonism,

TABLE 1

NUMBER OF INTERVIEWS ASSIGNED AND OBTAINED IN
EACH SAMPLE SEGMENT, APRIL–MAY, 1949

	NUMBER OF INTERVIEWS					
	Assigned			Obtained		
SAMPLE SEGMENT	Community Cross-Section	Supplementary Zone Sample	Total	Community Cross-Section	Supplementary Zone Sample	Total
Greater Grand Crossing...	380	231	611	294	183	477
Zone I..............	35	117	152	21	97	118
Zone II.............	88	63	151	70	45	115
Zone III............	159	....	159	121	....	121
Zone IV.............	98	51	149	82	41	123
Auburn-Gresham........	177	....	177	142	....	142

bursts forth into violence";[10] second, the dictionary said that tension is: "1. The act of stretching; the condition of being stretched tight. 2. Mental strain. 3. Any strained relation, as between governments."[11]

These definitions together suggested that tension is the emotional concomitant of something else, for the "uneasiness" and "mental strain" must have a source, and something—presumably "relations"—must be "stretched" or "strained" to give rise to the conflict and uncertainty implied by the emotional reaction.

[10] *Op. cit.*, 93.

[11] *College Standard Dictionary* (New York: Funk & Wagnalls Co., 1940).

any disruption of stable expectations with reference to intergroup conduct can be expected to lead to an increase in tension. Whenever one group ceases to acquiesce or presses for a change in previously accepted social patterns while the other group wishes to maintain them without being sure of their ability to do so, there exists the typical setting in which conflict and the possibility of violence emerge. The doubt, strain, uncertainty, and concern over the outcome of the conflict, the uneasiness experienced over the possible course of events, make up the subjective experience of the conflict referred to as tension.

The importance of tension is precisely that it is an indicator of the existence of this sort of conflict. For, where relations are strained, they may snap altogether, and there may be an outbreak of violence. Tension, then, may be regarded as a warning signal, an indication that there *may* be storms ahead. This is not to say that every instance of high interracial tension invariably eventuates in violence. It is known, in fact, that many other factors intervene to make the relationship less than exact. But the fact that violence, when it occurs, usually has developed out of a tension situation makes tension a symptom which cannot be disregarded, even though it is not by itself conclusive evidence of impending violence.

If this formulation of interracial tension is tenable, then research into reactions accompanying Negro residential expansion into white neighborhoods afforded an almost classic framework for its investigation. Here, indeed, was a situation in which the conflicting interpretations of the two groups—white demands for containment and *de facto* segregation of the Negro community confronted by Negro efforts to break out of the confines of the traditional Black Belt —clashed without prior certainty of the outcome. Tension was subjectively perceived and reported; the potential for violence appeared to be continuously present and had, repeatedly, eventuated in overt hostile action.

Construction of an Interracial Tension Scale

This approach to the measurement of interracial tension began with its identification with the kind of subjective uneasiness just discussed. Informal interviews, followed by analysis of the forms in which uneasiness was expressed and the kinds of evidence people had in mind when they said that the interracial situation of a community was "tense" or "getting more tense," indicated that there were five main signs of uneasiness or tension over race relations:

1. An increase in *incidents* of interracial friction.
2. An increase in *awareness* of incidents of interracial friction and rumors about them.
3. An increase in *expectations and predictions* of impending trouble and violence.
4. An increase in *dissatisfaction* with the current situation in race relations and, especially, with recent developments.
5. An intensification of *hostile attitudes*.

Of these signs of tension, only the first entailed objective phenomena, while all of the others were subjective, referring to the thoughts, feelings, beliefs, and attitudes of the people of a community. Thus, the very nature of interracial tension suggested that techniques of attitude measurement could be employed for its assessment.[12]

The tension-measuring instrument developed for testing in this research is a Guttman-type intensity scale.[13] Since Guttman scales are unidimensional, the tension scale was based, not on all the signs of tension just enumerated, but on the last of these, the single dimension of intensification of hostile attitudes.[14] More

---

[12] Use of the objective criterion of increase in number of incidents of interracial violence as an index of the amount of tension existing in a community is also theoretically possible, but both require information difficult to collect accurately and make the measurement of tension in advance of occurrence of some degree of overt violence impossible. An interracial barometer of this type was used for a time by the city of Detroit, but was abandoned as inadequate. See City of Detroit Interracial Committee, *Annual Report* (Detroit: City of Detroit Interracial Committee, 1946).

[13] Samuel A. Stouffer *et al.*, *Measurement and Prediction*, Vol. IV of *Studies in Social Psychology in World War II* (Princeton: Princeton University Press, 1950), pp. 3–361.

[14] It would, of course, have been possible to construct scales for each of the four subjective signs of tension separately, after which they might have combined into a composite index of tension. Since the goal was a relatively simple measuring device, it seemed more useful to omit the other signs from the tension measure itself, so that their relationship to the measure could be employed as a first test of its validity.

specifically, within this category, it is a scale of degree of resentment directed toward Negroes, especially as these resentments may grow out of the kinds of contacts residential mingling entails. The final scale contains nine questions, which are, together with the weights assigned to answer categories, presented below in order of increasing frequency of "most tense" (i.e., score of 2) answers.[15] The actual distribution of answers to the in-

[15] This ordering of questions from most to least extreme item in the scale is based on mean frequencies for the two communities studied, with each community weighted equally. It is, thus, a *general* ordering of the items, used in order to construct *one* scale to describe all the areas studied, but it is not the best order for any one of them, as indicated by the following large but less than perfect rank correlations between this general item order and the actual item orders observed in each area:

Greater Grand Crossing

Community cross-section	.983
Zone I	.917
Zone II	.967
Zone III	.917
Zone IV	.954
Auburn-Gresham	.967

dividual items in the two communities studied are presented in Table 2, while scale scores will be found in Table 7. The items are:

1. On the whole, would you say you like or dislike colored people?
    a) (*If "Dislike"*) Are your feelings about colored people very strong, pretty strong, not so strong, or not strong at all?

Like	0
Dislike, feelings are:	
Very strong	2
Pretty strong	1
Not so strong	1
Not strong at all	1
Don't know	1
No special feelings	1
Don't know	1

2. When you see colored people shopping in the same stores that you do, does it bother you or not?
    a) (*If "Yes, bothers"*) How much does it bother you—very much, pretty much, or only a little?

Yes, bothers:	
Very much	2
Pretty much	0

TABLE 2

DISTRIBUTION OF ANSWERS TO THE INTERRACIAL TENSION SCALE ITEMS

ITEM NUMBER AND CONTENT	PERCENTAGE OF GREATER GRAND CROSSING RESPONDENTS WHOSE ANSWER WAS:[1]				PERCENTAGE OF AUBURN-GRESHAM RESPONDENTS WHOSE ANSWER WAS:[1]			
	Anti-Negro and		Neutral or Indeterminate (Wt. of 1)	Pro-Negro (Wt. of 0)	Anti-Negro and		Neutral or Indeterminate (Wt. of 1)	Pro-Negro (Wt. of 0)
	Most Intense (Wt. of 2)	Not Most Intense (Wt. of 1)			Most Intense (Wt. of 2)	Not Most Intense (Wt. of 1)		
1. Liked or disliked	10	24	46	20	6	18	64	12
2. Shopping in same stores	11	16[2]	2[2]	71	11	10[2]	4[2]	75
3. Working in same jobs	17	16[2]	6[2]	61	15	20[2]	8[2]	57
4. Over-demanding	19	31	12	38	14	32	12	42
5. Eating in same restaurants	29	19	8	44	24	17	15	44
6. Living in same neighborhoods	36	41	21	2	31	37	31	1
7. Pushing in	38	51	6	5	30	52	8	10
8. Rude in public	37	14	10	39	37	14	12	37
9. Attending same schools	40	16	11	33	40	18	14	28

[1] The sum of each row is 100 per cent, based on 294 cases in Greater Grand Crossing and 142 cases in Auburn-Gresham.

[2] These answer categories were, atypically, given a weight of 0 in scaling.

Only a little 0
Don't know 0
No, does not bother 0
Don't know 0

3. If a colored person had the same kind of job as you in the place where you worked, would it be all right with you, or wouldn't you like it?
   a) (*If "Wouldn't like it"*) How much would this bother you—very much, some, or not at all?
   All right 0
   Wouldn't like it; bothers:
   Very much 2
   Some 0
   Not at all 0
   Don't know 0
   Don't know 0

4. As you see it, are colored people today demanding more than they have a right to, or not?
   a) (*If "Yes, they are"*) Does this make you feel pretty angry, or a little angry, or don't you feel strongly about it?
   Yes, they are; feel:
   Pretty angry.............. 2
   A little angry 1
   Don't feel strongly 1
   Don't know 1
   No, they are not 0
   Don't know 1

5. When you see colored people eating in restaurants that white people go to, does it bother you or not?
   a) (*If "Yes, bothers"*) Does this bother you very much, some, or hardly at all?
   Yes, bothers:
   Very much 2
   Some 1
   Hardly at all 1
   No, does not bother 0
   Don't know 1

6. When you hear about colored families moving into white neighborhoods, do you like it, dislike it, or don't you care very much one way or the other?
   a) (*If "Dislike"*) Are your feelings about this very strong, pretty strong, not so strong, or not strong at all?
   Like 0
   Don't like; feelings are:
   Very strong 2
   Pretty strong 1
   Not so strong 1

Not strong at all 1
Don't know 1
Don't care 1
Don't know 1

7. Do you think colored people today are trying to push in where they are not wanted?
   a) (*If "Yes, are trying"*) Does this bother you a good deal, a little, or hardly at all?
   Yes, are trying; bothers:
   A good deal 2
   A little 1
   Hardly at all 1
   Don't know 1
   No, are not 0
   Don't know 1

8. Some people say that colored people go out of their way to be rude to white people on streetcars and places like that. What's your opinion on this—do you think colored people try to be rude or not?
   a) (*If "Yes, try"*) How angry does this make you—very much, a little, or hardly at all?
   Yes, try; angers:
   Very much 2
   A little 1
   Hardly at all 1
   Don't know 1
   No, do not try 0
   Don't know 1

9. Do you approve or disapprove of white and colored children being in the same schools together?
   a) (*If "Disapprove"*) Do you object to this very much, a little, or hardly at all?
   Approve..................... 0
   Disapprove, object:
   Very much 2
   A little 1
   Hardly at all 1
   Don't know 1
   Don't know 1

As is apparent above, the items are, in general, scored trichotomously, with the most intense answer to each *sub*-question (e.g., "very strong," "pretty angry," etc.) forming one extreme; the least prejudiced answer to the *main* question (e.g., "like colored people," "approve of white and colored children attending the same schools," etc.), the other extreme; and all other possible answers, in an intermediate position. In two cases (Questions 2 and 3), patterns of scale error required dichotomous scoring, and intermediate answers were combined with the least prejudiced extreme.

In the first trial of the tension scale, five of these questions—Questions 1, 2, 3, 5, 8—were included in a pretest of one hundred interviews. When scored as above and with the use of the item order actually observed, the five questions scaled with a reproducibility of 94 per cent. The four additional questions were added to the scale for the main study in an effort to increase both the number of intervals in the scale and its reliability. In the final study, the added questions proved to belong to the same universe of content, and the entire set of nine questions scaled with a reproducibility coefficient of .894, which was taken as an acceptable level in view of the number of questions used, the preservation of trichotomous answer categories, the random patterning of scale errors, and the use of a generalized item order.[16]

VALIDITY OF THE INTERRACIAL
TENSION SCALE

The study design employed permitted three main types of checks on the meaning of the interracial tension scale. In the first place, the scale was based on only one of four theoretically expected subjective signs of tension, while the interview gathered data on all four; as a very minimal test, it could reasonably be expected that the scale should correlate positively with these other signs. Second, the study included three ways of measuring tension apart from the scale, with the

[16] It should be observed that because of variations in item order, the items scaled better for either community separately or for a single zone within Greater Grand Crossing than they did in this combined test, but it would have been impossible to compare the scale scores of community areas or zones if variable item orders had been used.

thought that—whatever the merits or disadvantages of these alternatives as practical measures—the tension scale should, again, be positively correlated with them, if they all indexed the same phenomenon. Finally, the scale could hardly be said to be a measure of community levels of interracial tension unless it proved capable of distinguishing between more and less tense communities. The results of each of these tests of the scale will now be described in turn.

Relation to Other Signs of Tension

On the basis of the scores they received on the tension scale, respondents were divided into three approximately equal groups representing the highest, middle, and lowest tension thirds of the population, respectively. These groups were then compared with respect to differences in attitudes selected to represent subjective signs of tension that were not employed in the scale.

These comparisons, shown in Table 3, clearly indicate that high race tension scores in contrast to low race tension scores were associated with more frequent hostility toward Negroes, with more frequent awareness of incidents or rumors about incidents of interracial friction in the community, with more frequent dissatisfaction with the race relations situation, and with more frequent expectations and predictions of impending conflict between Negroes and whites. While the data in Table 3 are, for simplicity, limited to the results for Greater Grand Crossing, much the same sort of relationship obtained in each of the zones of Greater Grand Crossing considered separately and in Auburn-Gresham as well.

In the general area of intensified hostility, for example, 70 per cent of the highest tension group in Greater Grand Crossing wished to exclude Negroes from the community, while 46 per cent of the middle tension group and 40 per cent of the lowest tension group expressed this attitude; in Auburn-Gresham the corresponding figures were 92, 65, and 46 per cent, respectively. In comparison with the lowest tension group, over twice as many people in the highest tension group in each sample segment endorsed the prejudiced view that Negroes are not as intelligent as whites. Also indicative of the greater hostility toward Negroes on the part of the highest tension group was the fact that people in this group were far more likely to oppose a state Fair Employment Practices Commission law than were people in the lowest tension group.

With regard to dissatisfaction with the current situation, the highest tension group was much more inclined to dislike the community because of the Negro invasion. In fact, when tension scale scores are combined with distance from the invasion, the complete range of variation occurred; dissatisfaction over Negro movement into Greater Grand Crossing varied regularly from 100 per cent of the highest tension group in the invaded zone to 0 per cent of the lowest tension group in the section most remote from Negro in-movement, as the following data make clear:

proportions favoring deterrent action among the three tension groups from highest to lowest were 84, 63, and 33 per cent, respectively.

Awareness of incidents or rumors of interracial friction followed the same pattern: the highest tension group was more likely to say there had been trouble between Negroes and whites in the community and more likely to know of plans to combat Negro movement than was the low tension group. And finally, with regard to predictions of friction and violence between Negroes and whites, the highest tension group was most likely to predict a worsening of Negro-white relations in the next year or so.

In the light of these data, there can be little doubt that the tension scale, though limited in its content, is a measure reflecting all the subjective signs of tension.

Relation to Other Tension Measures

Three indices which might themselves be regarded as measures of interracial tension were included in the study in addition to the tension scale. These were:

The preoccupation index.—This measure is based on the observation that, when people are tense about some sub-

GREATER GRAND CROSSING RESPONDENTS LIVING IN:	PERCENTAGE MENTIONING NEGRO IN-MOVEMENT AS A REASON FOR DISLIKING COMMUNITY OF RESIDENCE AMONG RESPONDENTS WHOSE TENSION SCORES WERE:		
	Highest	Middle	Lowest
Zone I ("Invaded")	100	65	45
Zone II ("Threatened")	63	45	21
Zone III ("Intermediate")	44	22	11
Zone IV ("Remote")	29	23	. . . .

Quite similarly, dissatisfaction with the current situation, as expressed in a desire for action that would hinder Negro movement into the community, was far more frequent in the highest tension group, whatever community is examined. On Auburn-Gresham, for example, the

ject, they will be preoccupied with it and refer to it at the first opportunity. In order to obtain this index, the interview deliberately did not touch on Negro-white relations explicitly until the seventh question, while the third through sixth questions were so phrased that the preoccupied respondent could introduce the subject. The preoccupation index, then, is a measure of the immediacy with which respondents turned to the subject of Negro-white relations.

"Self-rating" of tension.—One way of finding out whether people are tense or not is simply to ask them directly. As close as possible an approximation to this self-rating measure was made by

Interviewers' ratings of tension level of respondent.—Interviewers were asked, "What degree of tension about race problems did respondent exhibit during interview?" In making this rating, they were instructed:

This item is the place where you report to us your observations on the respondent. During the course of the interview you will have noticed things which are not completely

TABLE 3

RELATION OF INTERRACIAL TENSION SCALE SCORES TO OTHER SUBJECTIVE
SIGNS OF TENSION: GREATER GRAND CROSSING CROSS-SECTION

SUBJECTIVE SIGN OF INTERRACIAL TENSION[1]	PERCENTAGE EXPRESSING INDICATED ATTITUDE AMONG RESPONDENTS WHOSE TENSION SCALE SCORES WERE:		
	Highest (10 and above)	Middle (6–9)	Lowest (5 and below)
Awareness of incidents and of rumors about them:			
a) Know of actions being taken to make it harder for Negroes to move into the community	31	19	17
b) Think there has been trouble between Negroes and whites in the community	33	19	17
Expectation of impending trouble or violence:			
c) Think Negro and white people in the community will get along worse in the next year or so; *or* Expect violence if Negroes move into the community[2]	58	34	35
Dissatisfaction with current situation and recent developments:			
d) Dislike living in Chicago because of presence of Negroes	8	2	
e) Dislike living in community of residence because of presence or nearness of Negroes	43	24	13
f) Favor action to make it harder for Negroes to move into the community	82	60	46
Hostile attitudes:			
g) Think Negroes are not as intelligent as whites	46	37	17
h) Oppose a state FEPC law	60	41	36
i) Don't want Negroes to live in their neighborhood	70	46	40
Number of cases	101	95	98

[1] For exact wording of questions asked, see Star, *loc. cit.*, 235–47.

[2] The first of the two questions implied was asked if respondents believed their community to be racially mixed; the latter, if respondents believed there were no Negroes living in their community.

asking people who believed Negroes were already living in their community, "On the whole, are you bothered about the fact that colored people live around here or not?" People who regarded their community as all-white were asked the comparable question, "Would it bother you if colored people moved into (name of community) or not?"

reflected in the respondent's words when they are written on paper—his gestures, his tone of voice, etc. What you are to do here is to rate your respondents *not* on what they said, but on the manner in which they said it. Did the respondent get very excited, heated about what he was saying about Negroes, was he agitated, "jumpy," "fearful," about race relations, did he gesticulate, raise his voice, express hostility toward Negroes very decidedly: In short, was he tense about race relations, and if so, how tense?[17]

Of these three indices, interviewers' ratings showed rather large differences between the communities. As presented in Table 4, 49 per cent of the people of Greater Grand Crossing received ratings of moderate or higher tension, while only 31 per cent of the Auburn-Gresham residents were so rated. Within Greater Grand Crossing, the percentages rated as rather tense about race relations were 51 per cent in the invaded area, 55 per cent in the threatened area, 54 per cent in the

[17] National Opinion Research Center, "Specifications for Survey S-93" (March, 1949), p. 11.

intermediate area and 40 per cent in the more remote area.

The preoccupation index also indicated a difference between communities, if only differences in percentages raising racial questions in the context of dissatisfaction with their community or earlier are considered. Such immediate spontaneous mentioning of interracial problems in the community context occurred 28 per cent of the time in Greater Grand Crossing, while it was only 4 per cent in Auburn-Gresham. Differences within Greater Grand Crossing were large and closely related to distance from the invasion, running from 64 per cent in the invaded area to 14 per cent in the more

TABLE 4

COMMUNITY DIFFERENCES IN THREE INDICES OF INTERRACIAL TENSION

INDEX OF INTERRACIAL TENSION	GREATER GRAND CROSSING					AUBURN-GRESHAM
	Cross-Section	Zone I	Zone II	Zone III	Zone IV	
Preoccupation index:						
First Spontaneous Mention of Negroes at:						
Question 3: Dissatisfaction with living in Chicago.................	3	5	3	4	4	....
Question 4: Dissatisfaction with living in the community...........	25	59	40	23	10	4
Question 5: People in the community who don't get along.............	2	1	8	1	....	....
Question 6: People not wanted in the community....................	33	12	22	38	37	60
No spontaneous mention...........	37	23	27	34	49	36
Total per cent.................	100	100	100	100	100	100
"Self-rating":						
Are bothered.....................	19	56	32	15	1	1
Would be bothered.................	60	6	32	66	79	75
Would not be bothered.............	11	1	6	16	9	21
Are not bothered..................	8	37	28	2	1	1
Don't know.......................	2	....	2	1	10	2
Total per cent.................	100	100	100	100	100	100
Interviewers' rating:						
Extremely high....................	8	6	12	7	4	4
High.............................	12	11	18	11	9	11
Moderate.........................	29	34	25	36	27	16
Little............................	30	22	27	24	33	19
None............................	16	25	10	18	22	47
Can't rate........................	5	2	8	4	5	3
Total per cent.................	100	100	100	100	100	100
Number.........................	294	118	115	121	123	142

remote area. Yet, when this immediate preoccupation is combined with the secondary preoccupation indicated by reference to Negroes in the context of undesirable people, there were no differences between Greater Grand Crossing and Auburn-Gresham (63 per cent as against 64 per cent), though the differences within Greater Grand Crossing remained.

Data pertaining to community differences in self-ratings of tension are also presented in Table 4. It may be noted that Auburn-Gresham did not differ significantly from Greater Grand Crossing in the proportions rating themselves as tense and that, in the latter community, residents of the invaded area were least likely and the residents of the more remote areas most likely to admit to tension over the Negro invasion. This reversal of the usual relationships resulted largely from the tendency of persons who were making hypothetical self-ratings—how they *would* feel if there were an invasion—more often to assume they would be disturbed by it than was the actual case among respondents who made current self-ratings.

There are major objections to each of these three indices as a practical measure of tension. In the case of self-ratings, as was just mentioned, reliability decreases with remoteness from the experience being rated. Interviewers' ratings are not really independent judgments; despite all instructions to the contrary, they were, no doubt, at least in part based on the information available to the interviewer making the rating from the content of the interview and from the knowledge that Greater Grand Crossing was invaded and Auburn-Gresham was not. The preoccupation index has the defect that, by the way it was defined, people living in uninvaded areas could not receive the highest preoccupation rating, which, essentially, required a reference to the invasion.

For reasons such as these, none of

the three indices is offered as a workable alternative to the tension scale, even though, as will be seen in the next section, two of them at least, appear to offer greater discrimination than does the tension scale. Rather, they were included in the study for what light they could throw on the meaning of the tension scale.

TABLE 5a

RELATION OF INTERRACIAL TENSION SCORES
TO OTHER TENSION INDICES

(Greater Grand Crossing)

INDEX OF TENSION	PERCENTAGE WITH INDICATED RATING AMONG RESPONDENTS WHOSE TENSION SCALE SCORES WERE:		
	Highest (10 and above)	Middle (6–9)	Lowest (5 and below)
Preoccupation index:			
Immediate (Q's. 3 or 4).	44	26	15
Secondary (Q's. 5 or 6).	37	37	30
None revealed........	19	37	55
Total per cent......	100	100	100
Self-rating:			
Tense..............	94	79	62
Not tense...........	6	21	38
Total per cent......	100	100	100
Interviewers' rating:			
Extremely high or high	45	11	3
Moderate............	36	34	33
Little or none........	19	55	64
Total per cent......	100	100	100
Number........	101	95	98

The relationships among the several indices of tension revealed rather high associations. In Table 5a, it is shown, for example, that only 19 per cent of the highest tension score group in Greater Grand Crossing revealed no preoccupation with interracial problems while 55 per cent of the lowest tension score group showed no evidence of preoccupation. Similarly, over 90 per cent of the highest tension score group gave themselves self-ratings indicating tension, while only three-fifths of the lowest tension score group rated themselves in this manner. Finally, while two-thirds of the lowest tension score group in Greater Grand Crossing received interviewer ratings of little or no tension, in the highest tension score group only 19 per cent received low tension ratings from interviewers. Comparably large differences were found in each of the zones of Greater Grand Crossing and in Auburn-Gresham, as summarized in Table 5b.

All four of these indices of tension— the tension scale, the preoccupation index, the self-ratings, and interviewer ratings—are interrelated, as is indicated by the coefficients of contingency shown in Table 6. Typically, the closest relationship was between the tension scale and interviewer ratings, with correlations running from .42 in Auburn-Gresham to .67 in the threatened area, but each of the other possible pairs of indices also showed significant relationship.

Of more importance, perhaps, than the *degree* of relationship among these four indices is the *kind* of relationship. For these four indices of tension together form a Guttman scale, a fact which clearly indicates that *they are all measuring one simple variable.* The scale pattern, for which the reproducibility coefficient is .93, indicates that (except for scale errors) anyone whose tension scale score was in the range of the highest third was also rated by the interviewer as at least moderately tense, made some spontaneous reference to Negro-white problems, and classified himself as actually or potentially tense about them. Similarly, when interviewers rated respondents as tense the last two conditions generally obtained. Thus the four indices of interracial tension afford merely different points along the way of a single continuum, with the tension scale, itself, permitting the finest gradations.[18]

The evidence presented in this and the preceding section would seem most conclusive: by every criterion that is available, the tension scale appears to measure what is commonly understood by the term "interracial tension."

TABLE 5b

RELATION OF INTERRACIAL TENSION SCORES TO OTHER TENSION INDICES

(Zones of Greater Grand Crossing and Auburn-Gresham)

INDEX OF TENSION	PERCENTAGE WITH INDICATED RATING AMONG RESPONDENTS WHOSE TENSION SCALE SCORES WERE:		
	Highest (10 and above)	Middle (6–9)	Lowest (5 and below)
Preoccupation index (none revealed):			
Greater Grand Crossing			
Zone I	8	26	36
Zone II	9	31	43
Zone III	22	33	51
Zone IV	24	54	64
Auburn-Gresham	19	35	55
Self-rating (not tense):			
Greater Grand Crossing			
Zone I	29	35	80
Zone II	9	40	60
Zone III	29	44	57
Zone IV	20	68	71
Auburn-Gresham	44	77	75
Interviewers' rating (little or no tension):			
Greater Grand Crossing			
Zone I	96	54	29
Zone II	85	67	36
Zone III	95	84	63
Zone IV	93	75	73
Auburn-Gresham	93	74	60
Number of cases:			
Greater Grand Crossing			
Zone I	41	39	38
Zone II	34	43	38
Zone III	46	34	41
Zone IV	38	40	45
Auburn-Gresham	47	52	43

[18] Experimentation indicated that the four indices scaled with the scale score and the five-point interviewer rating subdivided in many different ways, dichotomously, trichotomously, and even quatrochotomously, an outcome which still further confirms the notion that sheer differences of degree are involved. Perhaps the most interesting of the tenable scale patterns is one which divides scale scores at the point which maximizes inter-area differences. In this scale, the most extreme tension type is defined by scale scores in the upper, "critical" range, followed by interviewer ratings of "high" or "extremely" high, and the other two indices of tension.

Community Differences in Tension Scores

Community comparisons of scores received on the tension scale may be regarded as another sort of test of the validity of the scale. For if it is as good a measure as it thus far appears to be, then it should be able to distinguish a community which was generally agreed to have a high level of interracial tension from one in which the level of tension was low.

The communities used in the study

as indicated earlier (see Fig. 1), not completely insulated from contacts with Negro areas, but it appeared to be remote from the kind of immediate threat that is usually thought of as generating tension. These impressions were confirmed by race relations observers, so Auburn-Gresham was regarded as less tense than Greater Grand Crossing.

The assumption, then, was that if the tension scale measured tension, it should show a difference between Greater Grand Crossing and Auburn-Gresham,

TABLE 6

INTERRELATIONS AMONG FOUR INDICES OF TENSION

| COMMUNITY AREA AND SUB-ZONE | CORRECTED[1] CONTINGENCY COEFFICIENTS BETWEEN: | | | | | |
| | Tension Scale and: | | | Preoccupation Index and: | | "Self-rating" and: |
	Preoccupation Index	"Self-rating"	Interviewers' Rating	"Self-rating"	Interviewers' Rating	Interviewers' Rating
Greater Grand Crossing...	.39	.43	.56	.31	.52	.39
Zone I	.35	.70	.53	.62	.32	.52
Zone II	.43	.52	.67	.30	.40	.62
Zone III	.32	.47	.46	.44	.51	.31
Zone IV	.46	.28	.55	.37	.54	.31
Auburn-Gresham	.34	.40	.42	.46	.32	.33

[1]Because of the small number of cases, the contingency coefficients were computed for 3 × 3 tables, except in the cases of tables involving the "Self-Rating" where only 3 × 2 tables were possible. Since the value of a perfect correlation is .816 in a 3 × 3 table and .707 in a 3 × 2 table, the values presented here are the original values divided by .816, and .707, respectively, to bring them into a .00–1.00 range.

were selected with just this purpose in mind. Greater Grand Crossing was partially invaded, threatened by further invasion, and had seen a good deal of interracial violence both before and after the study. The threatened zone, particularly, appeared to be an area of high tension, an assumption at least partially borne out by the occurrence of violence there shortly after the conclusion of the study, while the invaded zone seemed to be a section of subsiding violence and tension. There was, then, little doubt in classifying Greater Grand Crossing as a tense community. The case of Auburn-Gresham was, however, less clear. It was,

and, especially, between the threatened zone of Greater Grand Crossing and Auburn-Gresham.[19]

One other point should, perhaps, be

[19] It should be emphasized again that this comparison is in no sense based on the assumption that the tension scale should predict outbreaks of violence and thus should distinguish areas in which there is more likelihood of violence from areas in which violence is less likely. If this were to be assumed, it would mean leaping to the prediction problem without pausing for adequate validation of the tension scale. Moreover, it would be vastly oversimplifying the problems involved in predicting outbreaks of violence, if it were assumed that they could be predicted from any single factor. Further discussion of this point will be found in the final section.

disposed of before turning to the empirical data, that is, the question of the sense in which summaries of the scores *individuals* received on the tension scale can be considered measures of *community* tension. While community tension is not here *defined* in terms of the number of individuals within the community who show signs of tension, yet the fact is that interracial tension for reasons having fundamentally little to do with their racial attitudes. But, among communities of roughly similar social and cultural backgrounds, the number of such persons should be relatively constant, and any large differences in tension scores will, therefore, reflect community differences in tension levels.

TABLE 7

DISTRIBUTION AND CUMULATIVE FREQUENCY OF SCORES ON THE INTERRACIAL TENSION SCALE

SCORE[1]	PERCENTAGE RECEIVING GIVEN SCORE						PERCENTAGE RECEIVING GIVEN SCORE OR HIGHER					
	Greater Grand Crossing					Auburn-Gresham	Greater Grand Crossing					Auburn-Gresham
	Cross-Section	Zone I	Zone II	Zone III	Zone IV		Cross-Section	Zone I	Zone II	Zone III	Zone IV	
18	2.9	3.6	1.4	2.0	5.6	3.4	2.9	3.6	1.4	2.0	5.6	3.4
17	4.5	0.7	3.4	4.0	3.7	0.6	7.4	4.3	4.8	6.0	9.3	4.0
15	4.0	2.1	6.2	4.6	1.2	1.1	11.4	6.4	11.0	10.6	10.5	5.1
13	3.2	4.3	4.1	4.0	4.3	2.3	14.6	10.7	15.1	14.6	14.8	7.4
12	6.6	8.6	6.9	7.3	5.6	10.2	21.2	19.3	22.0	21.9	20.4	17.6
11	7.2	10.7	4.8	11.9	4.3	10.2	28.4	30.0	26.8	33.8	24.7	27.8
10	6.1	5.0	4.8	5.3	3.7	4.0	34.5	35.0	31.6	39.1	28.4	31.8
9	7.2	7.1	8.3	5.9	7.4	10.8	41.7	42.1	39.9	45.0	35.8	42.6
8	6.9	3.6	6.9	5.9	6.2	2.8	48.6	45.7	46.8	50.9	42.0	45.4
7	10.3	14.3	10.4	9.3	13.0	13.6	58.9	60.0	57.2	60.2	55.0	59.0
6	8.5	7.9	10.4	7.3	8.6	9.6	67.4	67.9	67.6	67.5	63.6	68.6
5	8.7	11.4	6.9	9.3	14.2	7.4	76.1	79.3	74.5	76.8	77.8	76.0
4	4.8	2.9	6.2	6.0	3.7	3.4	80.9	82.2	80.7	82.8	81.5	79.4
3	11.4	10.0	11.0	8.6	11.7	12.0	92.3	92.2	91.7	91.4	93.2	91.4
2	6.6	6.4	6.9	6.6	5.6	8.0	98.9	98.6	98.6	98.0	98.8	99.4
1	0.8	1.4	1.4	1.3	1.2	0.6	99.7	100.0	100.0	99.3	100.0	100.0
0	0.3			0.7			100.0	100.0	100.0	100.0	100.0	100.0
Total per cent	100.0	100.0	100.0	100.0	100.0	100.0						
Number	294	118	115	121	123	142						
Mean score	8.04	7.88	7.86	8.22	7.81	7.69						

[1] Scores of 16 and 14 were impossible by virtue of the scale pattern obtained and are therefore omitted.

community tension does manifest itself as increased tension on the part of individuals or as a greater number of tense individuals in the community. It follows that summaries of individual scores will *reflect* community tension levels.

As with any social measure so far devised, the interracial tension scale is not perfect, and there will be some misclassification of individuals. That is to say, a certain number of persons will, for example, receive scores indicative of high

With these qualifications in mind, the community comparisons may now be examined. The distribution of scores on the tension scale is presented in Table 7.[20] As shown there, the mean scores were 8.04 in Greater Grand Crossing and 7.69 in Auburn-Gresham, a difference which is not significant. When score distribu-

[20] It should be noted that individuals were scored by assignment to nearest scale type rather than by summation of the weights given individual answer categories.

tions are dichotomized at the point at which differences between the communities are maximized, however, 14.6 per cent of the Greater Grand Crossing section received scores of 13 or above, while only 7.4 per cent had such scores in Auburn-Gresham. This difference of 7.2 percentage points is significant at the .98 level.[21] All four of the zones within Greater Grand Crossing showed an excess of these highest scores as compared with Auburn-Gresham, though only for the last three zones did the differences approach the level of statistical significance.

These differences, while statistically significant, may seem disappointingly small. Yet, it should be recalled that the comparison is not precise. For example, the northeast section of Auburn-Gresham adjoins Greater Grand Crossing and may to a certain extent identify its problems with those of Greater Grand Crossing, while the southeast section of the community adjoins an area of Negro settlement and might, therefore, feel more threatened. In fact, when these sections are excluded from the Auburn-Gresham data, then, for the remaining three-fourths of the community, only 4.8 per cent had tension scores of 13 or higher. In the northeast section, adjoining Grand Crossing, 15.4 per cent had tension scores at this level; and in the southeast section, adjoining a Negro area, 13.0 per cent did. (See Fig. 2.)[22]

In other words, Auburn-Gresham cannot be considered as a pure instance of a community with little interracial tension. Between sections of Auburn-Gresham which have some relation to the likelihood of subjective perception of threat, there was, in fact, at least as much variation in tension levels as between Auburn-Gresham and Greater Grand Crossing. Elimination of the more tense portions of Auburn-Gresham increased this latter difference by more than a third, from 7.2 per cent (7.4 per cent vs. 14.6 per cent) to 9.8 per cent (4.8 per cent vs. 14.6 per cent).

These data should serve to indicate the relativity of the concept of tension. Though there was reason to regard Auburn-Gresham as less tense than Greater Grand Crossing, the fact is that there was also every reason to believe that the entire city, or, certainly, the whole South Side, of Chicago, of which these two communities are a part, was characterized by a high degree of tension over the expansion of the Negro community.[23]

The obvious conclusion is that intracity comparisons cannot be relied upon to determine the maximum degree of discrimination of which the tension scale is capable. Rather, comparative studies of other cities, especially cities with varying patterns of race relations, are needed. Fortunately, one such study has been made which permits comparison, in a partial way at least, with the results obtained in two community areas of Chicago.

In a community relations survey of a small city in upstate New York, three of

[21] Since the point of dichotomization was determined by the samples used in the study, there is a possibility that we are capitalizing on sampling error and overstating somewhat the difference between Auburn-Gresham and Greater Grand Crossing. But the fact that the point selected for dichotomization is consistently the point of maximization of difference in comparing Auburn-Gresham with each of the subsamples of Greater Grand Crossing as well gives somewhat greater reliability to the point selected. Needless to say, a replication of the study is necessary before any final conclusions about the reliability of the cutting point can be made.

[22] The geographic divisions made in Auburn-Gresham are arbitrary, based primarily on the number of cases available in the section.

[23] In a review of interracial violence in Chicago published in *New Republic* for January 9, 1950 (William Peters, "Race War in Chicago," pp. 10–12), for example, the statement is made that: "Reliable observers have said for two years that a race riot of major proportions is in the cards unless preventive action is taken—and soon. . . . From the viewpoint of the profession in race relations, Chicago is sitting on a powder keg. . . . A cruel kind of warfare is going on in the no man's land around Chicago's Black Belt."

the questions comprising the tension scale were included.[24] This community had a population of about 60,000 in 1950, with a Negro population of 2.5 per cent. In the decade 1930–40, the Negro population had grown gradually from 1.8 per cent to 2.5 per cent, part of the increase being represented by a decline in the white population for that period. This city was found, upon study, to have some degree of prejudice and discrimination against Negroes. There were, however, rather stable patterns of race relations, and such friction as arose from them was not sufficient to create in the white population generally the sense of conflict and threat to the *status quo* that is the precondition of interracial tension. It seemed, then, that this community offered a better example of low tension levels than did Auburn-Gresham.

Comparisons between Greater Grand Crossing and Auburn-Gresham, on the one hand, and the upstate New York community, on the other, can be made by means of a three-item subscale of tension.[25] The cumulative score distributions presented in Table 8, make clear that the proportion of individuals characterized by tension over interracial relations was significantly higher in either Greater Grand Crossing or Auburn-Gresham than in the New York community, no matter what scale point (other than zero) is selected. If scores are dichotomized at the point which maxi-

TABLE 8

DISTRIBUTION AND CUMULATIVE FREQUENCY OF SCORES ON THE
THREE-ITEM INTERRACIAL TENSION SUBSCALE

	PERCENTAGE RECEIVING GIVEN SCORE							PERCENTAGE RECEIVING GIVEN SCORE OR HIGHER						
SCORE	Greater Grand Crossing					Auburn-Gresham	City in Upstate New York	Greater Grand Crossing					Auburn-Gresham	City in Upstate New York
	Cross-Section	Zone I	Zone II	Zone III	Zone IV			Cross-Section	Zone I	Zone II	Zone III	Zone IV		
6........	8.5	8.5	8.9	8.6	6.2	5.1	2.5	8.5	8.5	8.9	8.6	6.2	5.1	2.5
5........	10.9	8.6	11.8	13.2	7.4	8.5	2.3	19.4	17.1	20.7	21.8	13.6	13.6	4.8
4........	17.0	23.6	15.8	17.9	15.4	16.5	4.0	36.4	40.7	36.5	39.7	29.0	30.1	8.8
3........	32.0	25.0	34.5	31.1	38.4	34.1	22.7	68.4	65.7	71.0	70.8	67.4	64.2	31.5
2........	20.7	23.6	19.3	17.9	22.2	26.2	18.4	89.1	89.3	90.3	88.7	89.6	90.4	49.9
1........	9.6	9.3	8.3	9.3	8.6	8.5	27.0	98.7	98.6	98.6	98.0	98.2	98.9	76.9
0........	1.3	1.4	1.4	2.0	1.8	1.1	23.1	100.0	100.0	100.0	100.0	100.0	100.0	100.0
Total per cent.....	100.0	100.0	100.0	100.0	100.0	100.0	100.0							
Number...	294	118	115	121	123	142	529							

mizes the difference between this stable community and each of the other samples (scores of three and above vs. scores of two or less), the proportion of tense

[24] We wish to express our gratitude to the Department of Sociology and Anthropology, Cornell University, for their co-operation in including these questions in their study and in making their data available to us.

[25] The three questions for which data from the upstate New York community are available are those numbered 1, 4, and 7 in the tension scale. Since they are drawn from a larger set of items proved to scale, the three items may be treated as a kind of subscale of tension, even though three items would not ordinarily be regarded as sufficient to test the hypothesis of scalability. When scaled with the same trichotomous scoring of the items as was previously indicated, the data for each community yielded an acceptable scale, coefficients of reproducibility being .91, .94, and .93 for Greater Grand Crossing, Auburn-Gresham, and the New York community, respectively.

individuals in each of the zones of Greater Grand Crossing and in Auburn-Gresham was well over twice that in the small eastern city. Differences between the New York community and the other samples all exceed 30 percentage points, in fact.

In contrast, differences between Auburn-Gresham and Greater Grand Crossing were quite small at this cutting point, the difference being only 4.2 per cent and not statistically significant. Though these differences are statistically insignificant taken individually, the consistent though small excess for each of the four zones of Greater Grand Crossing over Auburn-Gresham in proportion with scores of three or higher suggests that some real difference existed. This likelihood is increased if the comparison is shifted to extremely high tension scores —scores of five or six. Here the difference of 5.8 per cent between Auburn-Gresham and Greater Grand Crossing approached more closely an acceptable significance level, its probability of nonchance occurrence being .89.

Because of the invariant ranking property of Guttman scales, scores on the subscale can be translated into their equivalent scores on the full scale[26] and attention transferred back to the full score distributions in Table 7. For this full distribution it is clear that at the point at which the scale so sharply discriminated between the Chicago and the upstate New York situations, there was no significant difference between the Greater Grand Crossing and Auburn-Gresham situations, and this is true no matter whether the lower limit of scores most indicative of tension is set at 5, 9, or any point between. At the upper end of the range of scores, indicative of extremely high tension, there does appear to be a difference between the two communities; as we have previously indicated, the difference in scores of 13 and over is significant.

Other intercity comparisons, based on

the full scale, are needed, before the discrimination of which the tension scale is capable can be fully described. The data presented here are, however, sufficient to indicate that the tension scale will show large contrasts between situations which differ substantially in the degree of interracial tension prevailing. The relatively small differences between Auburn-Gresham and Greater Grand Crossing which the tension scale indicates appear to be more a function of lack of difference in the tension levels of these two communities than of insensitivity in the scale.

[26] The exact translation, for perfect scale types, is as follows:

Scale Type on Sub-Scale	Equivalent Scale Types on Full Scale
6	18
5	13–17
4	10–12
3	5–9
2	3–4
1	2
0	0–1

Since individuals were scored "to scale type" rather than by weight summation, use of this table of equivalents is inexact only to the extent to which the principle of scoring non-scale types toward middle types whenever possible leads to a different assignment of the same non-scale type individual when his full set of answers to the nine questions is considered as over against his assignment on the basis of the three items in the subscale. The magnitude of differences resulting from procedures with respect to non-scale types can be seen by comparing the actual tension subscale score distribution with the distribution to be expected from the equivalent full scale scores, as is done below for the two Chicago community areas:

SCORE	PERCENTAGE RECEIVING EACH SCORE			
	Greater Grand Crossing		Auburn-Gresham	
	Sub-Scale	Equivalent Full Scale	Sub-Scale	Equivalent Full Scale
6 (or equivalent)..	8.5	2.9	5.1	3.4
5 (or equivalent)..	10.9	11.7	8.5	4.0
4 (or equivalent)..	17.0	19.9	16.5	24.4
3 (or equivalent)..	32.0	41.6	34.1	44.2
2 (or equivalent)..	20.7	16.2	26.2	15.4
1 (or equivalent)..	9.6	6.6	8.5	8.0
0 (or equivalent)..	1.3	1.1	1.1	0.6
Total per cent..	100.0	100.0	100.0	100.0
Number......	294	294	142	142

NEXT STEPS IN RESEARCH ON THE MEAS-
UREMENT OF INTERRACIAL TENSION

This research has demonstrated that it is possible to construct an instrument that measures, in relative terms at least, the amount of interracial tension existing in a white community, while adhering rather closely to the usual denotative and connotative implications of the concept of tension. Although further research, to be described, is needed for the full establishment of a tension scale in social research technology, it now appears to offer great promise of ultimately providing a tool by means of which other studies of intergroup hostility, tension, and conflict—their causes, mitigation, and control—can be made more precise. It may also prove to be of administrative usefulness as well, since a fully established device of this kind could furnish periodic readings to interest agencies, and thus provide them with a sense of the way in which events are moving: rises and declines in intergroup tensions, indications of possible "trouble spots," measures of the effectiveness of ameliorative action, etc.

Since a major interest in the tension scale derives from the potential usefulness in the prediction of interracial violence, it may be well to discuss explicitly the problems involved in adapting it to this use. Then the kind of research which is still to be carried out before the tension scale can be used in any substantive fashion may be dealt with more directly. Finally, some explicit attention should be given to the advisability and implications of limiting either research on or measurement of *inter*racial tension to only the dominant group, as has been done in this study.

The Problem of Prediction of Interracial Violence

Obviously, many variables are involved in the causation of any incident of interracial violence, of which the tension level of the community is only one.

As the minimum elements in violence, Dr. Williams has offered the following hypothesis:

Mass violence (e.g., race riots) is most likely under the following conditions: (a) prolonged frustration, leading to a high tension level; (b) presence of population elements with a propensity to violence (especially lower class, adolescent males in socially disorganized areas); (c) a highly visible and rapid change in intergroup relations; (d) a precipitating incident of intergroup conflict.[27]

And, in any concrete instance, the causal factors are likely to be much more complex. By way of illustration, Dr. Williams may again be quoted:

To take a hypothetical case, we may suppose that the causal factors in an urban race riot can be shown to include at least the following: (1) a high level of frustration arising from poor housing, low incomes, excessive crowding of transportation systems and other public facilities, lack of satisfying recreation, disruption of family life and community membership; (2) patterns of prejudice of complex origin established prior to the immediate situation; (3) a rapid change in relative numbers of the two contending groups; (4) a lack of intergroup familiarity because of segregation and other factors; (5) a rapid differential change in incomes of the two groups; (6) the presence of "hoodlum" elements emerging from prior social disorganization; (7) the presence of opportunistic leaders who can advance their own private interests through encouraging conflict; (8) absence of adequate, well trained, well organized, and relatively impartial law-enforcement forces. In the total situation each of these factors may be a necessary condition but no one of them may be sufficient to account for the occurrence of a riot in just the way it actually happened.[28]

Fortunately, the problem can be somewhat simplified if it is recognized that Williams is using the term "tension"

[27] Robin M. Williams, Jr., *The Reduction of Intergroup Tensions* (New York: Social Science Research Council, 1947), p. 60.

[28] *Ibid.*, 43–44.

broadly, to refer to psychological strains which arise from a variety of frustrations and which may be channeled into a variety of other reactions, as well as into intergroup hostility. The interracial tension being measured here, on the other hand, should not be regarded as a cause of interracial conflict at all; rather it is a result, reflecting the presence of some of the causal elements just enumerated. Thus, if "opportunistic leaders"—or neighborhood property owners' associations— are "encouraging conflict," the success of their efforts should appear as an increase in intergroup hostility in the community, that is to say, as interracial tension. Similarly if changes in intergroup relations cause conflict, this, too, is signalized by increased tension. So, the interracial tension scale serves as an index of several of the causal elements in interracial violence.

Nevertheless, prediction of violence from the tension scale can only be contingent. It can only be said that, *everything else being equal,* an outbreak of violence is more likely to occur in a community with a high level of interracial tension than in one with a low level. Before there could be an outbreak in a community with a low level of tensions, it could be presumed that there must be a sharp rise in the tension level. To put it another way, the prediction must be that, *if the other factors also conduce to it,* a high level of interracial tension will eventuate in interracial violence, if the situation does not alter; that is, *if no other factors intervene.* For example, given the situation Dr. Williams has described, and assuming a high level of interracial tension, the prediction would probably be that an outbreak of violence will occur unless something in the situation alters, but a change in one element—say, a reorganization of the police force—would be sufficient to lead to a reconsideration of the prediction.

In the case of the two communities under study, violence was more likely to be predicted in Greater Grand Crossing than in Auburn-Gresham, not because there was any substantial difference in tension levels between the two communities, but because, though tension levels in both communities were high, more of the other factors contributing to violent outbreaks were present in the Grand Crossing situation than in the Auburn-Gresham situation. To put it in its simplest terms, as long as there were no Negroes in Auburn-Gresham, no amount of interracial tension, however high, could eventuate in interracial violence within the community.

The tension potential for violence was there, nevertheless.[29] An exact prediction for Auburn-Gresham would be about as follows: (1) Given the level of interracial tension in the community, (2) if no effective group efforts are made to reduce tension, and (3) if group activities fostering tension continue, then (4) if movement of Negroes into the area were to begin, and (5) if police efforts were not more effective than they have been in other sections of the city, violence would occur.[30] Since condition (4) was

[29] The situation is comparable with that in another section of Chicago where violence occurred in November, 1949. The sight of a Negro entering a house (which was occupied by a white family who had moved in only a few weeks earlier) touched off the tension which had been accumulating around rumors that Negroes had moved or were about to move into the community. The facts of the situation were that a Negro had recently purchased property in the community, though he had not attempted to occupy it. This was a community in which violence would not have been expected, simply because no Negroes were in the community. For a full account see City of Chicago, Commission on Human Relations, "Interracial Disturbance at 7407–7409 S. Parkway and 5643 S. Peoria Street," Documentary Memorandum, Chicago, November 8, 1949 (mimeographed). Some of the Commission's conclusions were reported in the *Chicago Sun-Times,* January 8, 1950.

[30] The condition that "hoodlum elements" be present can safely be ignored, for these are present in every city, and easily drift to any scene of potential disturbance. In the interracial

not expected, it may be said, in a kind of shorthand, that violence in Auburn-Gresham was not expected. Judged by tension level alone, however, Auburn-Gresham had to be considered a community in which violence *could* occur.

In developing the tension scale to the point that it could be successfully used in the prediction of interracial violence, procedures cannot be based on the assumption that if violence fails to occur in a community in which the tension scale indicated a high level of tension, the scale's validity is disproved. The only necessary condition is that a community in which violence occurs should have had a recent high tension reading on the scale before the actual violence. The tension scale would thus place the community in the class of communities in which violence could occur, while objective or subjective estimates of other factors in the situation would still remain to be made before any outright prediction that violence will (or will not) occur is possible.

Needed Methodological Research

Before the tension scale can be used, in this qualified sense, for the prediction of violence, however, a number of questions remain to be answered. Two major technological problems need to be investigated before there can be precise knowledge of how to interpret tension scores.

The problem of norms.—In one sense, this is simply the problem of collecting further data bearing on the validity of the tension scale and the establishment of a reliable cutting-point to be used with it that has been mentioned earlier.

violence which occurred at Fernwood Project in Chicago, August, 1947, for example, a large number of the participants had come in from other sections of the city. See Homer Jack, "Chicago Has One More Chance," reprinted with added map from *The Nation*, September 13, 1947, by the Chicago Council against Racial and Religious Discrimination.

In operational terms, the tension score distributions of a large number of communities, varying with respect to their interracial tension levels (as judged by expert observers) and in other characteristics—size, region, economic status, rate of growth, etc.—must be examined in order to establish fully the amount of discrimination obtained with the scale and the points on the scale which are to be considered indicative of low, moderate, high, and extremely high tension.[31]

Beyond this, however, more complex questions pertaining to norms arise. There is as yet no evidence at all on the question of whether such norms as we have discussed can be established as one uniform standard for urban areas in the country as a whole or whether a set of more limited norms will have to be developed, with each norm pertaining only to a subclass of urban areas. For example, regional differences might require regionally limited norms, or norms might have to vary with city size or type. Carefully planned, the study previously outlined could answer these questions.

Once these norms are established, the tension scale may be used substantively, with no further technological research on the scale itself[32] in community research whose objective is the static description of the status of intergroup relations, for the tension scale would then

[31] If sufficient instances of this kind are collected, they can not only be compared in terms of their tension levels as rated by experts, but instances in which violence occurred shortly after the study can be singled out to see whether the tension scale would in fact have suggested the possibility of this violence. That is to say, this study could also be adapted to seeing whether the condition necessary to the use of the tension scale in prediction actually obtains. Other research problems relating to the use of the tension scale in prediction are discussed below.

[32] This, of course, assumes that the research done to establish norms will confirm the tentative conclusion that the tension scale has validity. Should the validity of the scale be seriously challenged by such research, it would naturally not be used further.

offer an objective measure of one aspect of intergroup relations, viz., the intergroup tension level. Before the tension scale could be used in the analysis of social change, however, the second set of methodological problems must be solved.

The problem of variability in tension scores.—At least three aspects of this problem need investigation:

The reliability of tension scores.—No research tool can be regarded as useful, unless it can be shown to obtain the same results under the same conditions; that is, to have a high degree of *reliability.* A test of this point is simple, requiring merely two applications of the tension scale to the same population or set of populations, after the lapse of sufficient time to avoid false consistency through respondents' remembering their first set of answers, but before the lapse of enough time to give reason to expect some real alteration in tension levels. The extent to which the tension scale classifies individuals and/or communities consistently with respect to their tension levels could then be determined.[33]

The interpretation of changes in tension scores.—Even with a reliable tension scale, there will still be changes in tension scores as community intergroup relations change and tension levels alter. The question then is what meaning a change in tension levels of any given size has. Suppose, for example, that the tension level of some community has twice been examined by means of the tension scale, and a statistically significant difference has been found between the two observations. It can then be said that an increase or decrease, depending on the direction of the change, in tension levels has occurred.

The serious question of *interpretation*

[33] Although the test of reliability is yet to be made, it is assumed in both the preceding discussion and the discussion that follows that the scale will prove to have acceptable reliability. It is likely that the scale will prove to have high reliability, but if it should not, these research suggestions would no longer be relevant.

arises, however, if the primary concern is with making a contingent prediction about violence. Suppose again, in the illustration, that the increase in tension levels, while statistically significant and a warning-signal in this sense, still does not place the community in the range of tension levels found in communities where violence shortly afterward took place. Because there is as yet no conclusion about norms, it cannot definitely be said that in such a community situation, no prediction of violence could be made. In theory, at least, research might indicate that community variations in tension levels cannot be interpreted in terms of absolute norms, whether these are "universal" or limited in application. It might be that changes in tension level can only be evaluated in relative terms, as deviations from the usual tension level of the community. In such an event the size of the deviation, rather than the absolute level would be the important consideration, and research would have to be directed toward establishing "usual" tension levels for communities and the meaning of various-sized deviations from these levels.

The earlier research suggestions must be carried out before it can be seen how real this problem is. It is suggested at this point only to indicate how complex the research problems which might arise in connection with the tension scale are.

The rapidity of change in tension scores. —If the tension scale is to be used in the prediction of violence, outbreaks of violence must be shown to be preceded by high tension levels. If such predictions are to have more than an academic interest, however, a further condition must be added: High tension levels must precede outbreaks of violence by sufficient time to permit the determination of the tension level and the prediction of violence prior to the occurrence. From the practical standpoint it might well be added that the time interval should also be long enough to permit preventive action between the time of prediction and the actual violence. It is at least theoretically possible that a sudden change in community relations could lead to an abrupt rise in tension and community outbursts in a matter of hours, in which case there would be no opportunity to measure tension soon enough beforehand to make a prediction.

The research needed here is a study of trends in tension levels in a number of communities in which sudden changes in race relations may be anticipated. These communities should, at the beginning of the study, have relatively low tension levels, like the city in upstate New York which was used in the present study. Periodic determination of the tension level of the communities could then be made at relatively short intervals. At periods of community intergroup crisis, the samples could be so designed that each day's interviewing offered a separate representative sample and daily fluctuations could be examined. Only at the conclusion of such a study, would there be sure knowledge of how tension levels alter under the impact of crisis events.

The answers to this set of research problems will determine the extent to which the tension scale can be adapted to studies of trends in intergroup tensions and to the prediction of intergroup violence.

Possible Substantive Studies

In the foregoing discussion of the technological research problems still to be undertaken, little attention has been given to the possible usefulness of the tension scale in substantive studies centering around theoretical interest in the concept of tension itself, as, for example, studies of the causes of interracial tension, its relationship to other kinds of societal tensions and conflicts and to individual emotional stresses and tensions, or its mitigation and control. If the concept of intergroup tension deserves investigation in its own right, apart from its possible practicality as a predictor of

outbreaks of violence, the tension scale could be used in such research without waiting for answers to the more technical scale problems just raised, requiring simply that its validity and reliability be firmly established.

Although the research here reported was not primarily designed for investigation of these problems, it contained enough data to permit a few tentative and preliminary conclusions about some of the factors associated with greater or lesser individual tension over interracial problems in the same community situation. Associated with greater tension are:

1. Parents' concern for their children, acting upon previously established prejudices.
2. Insecurity, viewed in terms of relative deprivation, or what people have to lose, rather than in terms of currently inferior position.

On the other hand, two sorts of interracial contacts appeared to decrease the possibilities for individual interracial tension:

1. Equalitarian interracial work experiences, possibly reinforced by similar contacts in labor unions.
2. Non-anxiety-provoking (unthreatening) interracial experience in community living.

This sketchy beginning may serve to illustrate the kinds of hypotheses that may be investigated by means of the tension scale.

Tension and the Minority Group

This approach to the measurement of tension has been strictly in terms of the attitudes of the majority group, even though interracial tension has been explicitly restricted to situations in which groups conflict. Certainly, there are two sides to a conflict, and many aspects of the interracial situations of communities currently involved in struggles over desegregation suggest an at best uneasy truce in which the tension of anticipating and waiting for the seemingly inevitable overt conflict builds up on both sides. Moreover, there have been occasional episodes of violence, like the 1943 Harlem riot,[34] where the mounting of tension and immediate precipitation of violence came more from the minority group than from the majority. Since both racial groups appear to experience tension and not always concurrently, why should not the tension of the minority group be explored?

On the face of it, there would seem to be little doubt that tension over intergroup relations can be measured equally well for the minority group, not by the present scale employed with whites, but by one which paralleled it in theoretical premises and in technical design. The situations giving rise to tension are much the same in both groups in that they are situations in which the minority group is attempting to better their social position or, as in recent South African history, to prevent deterioration in the face of majority group opposition to their aspirations. The emotions experienced are quite the same, the subjective signs of tension would be quite similar. So, such signs as mounting predictions of impending interracial trouble and violence, mounting conviction that minority group aspirations will not be peaceably granted, increasing feelings that nothing but force will achieve their goals, together with an increasing belief that whites are prejudiced, hostile to the aspirations of Negroes, determined to stop at nothing to thwart them, could rather easily be adapted to a set of questions quite analogous to those used with whites and equally likely to yield an analogous minority tension scale.

If such a scale were to be created, it would still face exactly the same methodological problems as were just reviewed for the present one; in addition, there would remain the question of whether its use would add sufficiently

new or different information to justify the extra effort. While the latter question is itself open to empirical determination, general knowledge of intergroup relations suggests that the situations out of which riots or other violence have emerged are generally situations of high tension to both whites and Negroes, while stable interracial situations are those in which there is relatively low tension in either group. Interracial situations in which one group is tense but the other is not appear to be relatively impermanent, transitional states dependent on partial barriers to communication. In the instance of the Harlem riots, for example, the relatively high tension of the Negro population had apparently not communicated itself effectively to the white population, especially not as active demands or moves for changes in interracial patterns; if it had, we would expect either falling Negro tension as whites granted the justice of Negro grievances or rising white tension as they prepared to resist Negro aspirations, but it is difficult to see how disparate tension levels could long persist.

If the foregoing analysis is at all correct, it suggests that measurement of Negro tension is not likely to add very much to the measurement of white tension, so far as its potential administrative use in the anticipation or control of violence is concerned.[35] Insofar as inter-

---

[34] Kenneth B. Clark, "Group Violence: A Preliminary Study of the Attitudinal Pattern of Its Acceptance and Rejection: A Study of the 1943 Harlem Riot," *Journal of Social Psychology*, XIX (1944), 319–37.

[35] We give preference to white over Negro tension in this event simply because the affected white population is easier to define and to reach. In the case of residential invasion, for example, the white group whose reactions are most relevant are the residents of the affected community, but the comparable Negro group are those who are or are likely to be moving into the community, a much harder group to delimit. Much the same may be said of the more recent, now chronic tension situation of communities undergoing school desegregation: it is relatively easy to pick out the whites whose schools will be affected, but it is not so easy to sample the Negroes who will attempt to send their children to desegregated schools, and it is not so clear that the entire Negro population is the universe to be considered.

est is addressed to increasing more basic understanding of intergroup relations, however, the "high-low" or "low-high" tension situations are likely to be particularly illuminating, suggesting as they do situations in which whites and Negroes fail to understand each other, with false security (high Negro tension only) or false alarm (high white tension only) the result, and the availability of double tension measures would assist greatly both in singling out such instances and in further analyzing them.

A RETROSPECTIVE NOTE

This study accomplished what it set out to do, which was simply to demonstrate that interracial tension *could* be measured, at least in the relative ranking terms that Guttman scales make possible. It produced an interracial tension scale which seemed to translate into quantitative terms the essential flavor of the concept as it was qualitatively employed and which was comparatively simple, inexpensive, and rapid to use in practical situations, but which still required a good deal of developmental research before it could be fully established as a standard device. This was the point at which research halted ten years ago; it is still the point at which it stands today.

A backward look at this research now suggests that the concept of tension was at the time endowed with undue luster and that pursuing the leads this study offered in the direction of attempting either to develop an administratively useful predictive device or to employ tension as a central concept in more theoretically oriented research would have proved disappointing. As conceptual refinement has proceeded and as the Supreme Court has provided us with more and more instances of intergroup conflict over fundamental changes in race relations in the United States both in the school desegregation cases and in other rulings, high interracial tension has more and more come to appear an inevitable accompaniment to all attempts at social change in the face of widespread social opposition and a phenomenon whose very inevitability makes it less interesting and less important.

Since tension is a component of conflict situations, the tension scale developed here may be a convenient way to represent the degree or depth of conflict and, as such, a reasonable predictor of violence on the negative side, for, where tension is low, conflict is low and there is no reason to expect violence. Once there is conflict, however—and experience has indicated that every attempt to wipe out discriminatory treatment of Negroes in community facilities, be it in housing, desegregated schools, buses, swimming pools, or what not, is productive of intense conflict—the invariably high level of tension is not very useful for differential diagnosis, and it is to much more variable factors that we must turn to predict or to understand the outcome. In the South, today, if a community's schools are successfully integrated or desegregated without violence, it is not mainly because this community was less tense about the issue than another in which events proceeded less smoothly. To the extent that race relations research is primarily interested in studying high conflict situations, a measure of tension will have little use except perhaps to demonstrate that the situation being studied is, in fact, an instance of high conflict. It cannot contribute to predicting the course and outcome of the conflict; and, as a reaction wholly derivative from the interaction of underlying prejudices, the symbolic importance of the particular interracial practice under challenge, the apparent strength of the forces arrayed to maintain and to change the practice, etc., there appears to be little about interracial tension, itself, that requires independent investigation and explanation.

Ten years later the question now appears to be whether interracial tension *should* be measured.

12. *Social Change and Prejudice*

MORRIS JANOWITZ

In the fifteen years since data were collected for *The Dynamics of Prejudice* there has been a fundamental transformation of attitude patterns toward Jews and Negroes in the United States.[1] Research evidence accumulated since the close of World War II documents that the level and intensity of ethnic prejudice toward Jews and Negroes has declined during this period. The decline in prejudice has been marked for both groups, but the Negro still remains much more the object of hostility than the Jew. This is not to overlook important short-term countertrends, new manifestations of latent hostility, or the persistence of a "hard core" of extremist attitudes.

Such a trend is all the more significant since the period was one in which public attention focused chronically on minority problems, with incidents of tension and violence given wide attention. Thus, ethnic prejudice declined at a time when there was great divergence of public opinion on policy questions and when ethnic relations stood at the center of local and national political events.

Our purpose here is to reassess some of the sociological findings of *The Dynamics of Prejudice* in the light of social change during the last fifteen years. We will examine trends in prejudice toward Jews and Negroes during this period and see how relevant were basic sociological variables in accounting for these trends.[2]

In the original study, 150 male veterans of World War II who were residents of Chicago were studied. They were interviewed intensively in order to probe underlying attitudes and sentiments toward minority groups. The extensive interview records were subjected to systematic content analysis in order to classify the men into four attitude patterns; tolerant, stereotyped, outspoken anti-Semitic, and intensely anti-Semitic. (The same procedure was used with respect to hostility toward Negroes.) From these procedures, the five most frequent anti-Jewish stereotypes were identified: (1) they are clannish; they help one another; (2) they have the money; (3) they control everything; (4) they use underhanded business methods; and (5) they don't work; they don't do manual labor. By contrast, for the Negro, the five most frequent stereotypes were: (1) they are sloppy, dirty, filthy; (2) they depreciate property; (3) they are taking over; they are forcing out the whites; (4) they are lazy; they are slackers in work; and (5) they are immoral. The objective of the study was not to

[1] Bruno Bettelheim and Morris Janowitz, *The Dynamics of Prejudice* (New York: Harper & Bros., 1950).

[2] In the revised edition of *The Dynamics of Prejudice* we further explore the link between social mobility, especially downward social mobility, and prejudice, on the basis of the replication studies that have been completed on this topic. We will also evaluate research that has continued the study of psychological mechanisms found related to ethnic hostility. Finally, we will seek to make more explicit the relations between the process of social control and the personal and psychoanalytic mechanisms which we found at work in tolerant and prejudiced attitudes. For this purpose, it becomes necessary to extend an analysis beyond social change in the United States and to encompass changes in the world community, even though such a task must be essentially speculative.

explain the historical genesis of prejudice, but to account for differences in levels of prejudice in this relatively homogeneous sample.

Four hypotheses supply a basis for summarizing some of the empirical findings. First, ethnic intolerance was related to a person's mobility within the social structure, and in particular intolerance was related to downward social mobility. While the study investigated the sociological correlates of prejudice, it was assumed and found that no single sociological variable or simple combination of variables could account for differences in ethnic intolerance. Second, hostility toward out-groups was a function of the hostile person's feelings that he has suffered deprivations in the past. Thus, the objective extent of the veterans' deprivation during the war was unrelated to prejudice while their subjective feeling of deprivation was positively related. Third, hostility toward out-groups was a function of the hostile person's anxiety in anticipation of future tasks, as inferred from his expectations of deprivation. Concern about economic employment and economic security was particularly important. Fourth, the question of the person's orientation toward the controlling institutions of society and his attitude toward authority was also investigated. This is a complex problem both sociologically and psychologically. From a psychological point of view there was reason to believe that the prejudiced person would be a person who lacked ego strength and have inadequate controls which favor irrational discharge and evasion rather than rational action. Such a person blames the out-group for his personal failures and limitations. From a sociological point of view, such a person blames existing authorities and social institutions for his personal limitations. In the particular sample we investigated it was expected that the highly prejudiced person would be generally hostile and negative to the controlling institutions, whether it be the economic system or the political party organizations. Considerable evidence was collected supporting this hypothesis, even though it is abundantly clear that our understanding of social control in the dynamics of prejudice remains most limited.

Social research is hard pressed when it is called upon to describe and analyze how historical and social change fashions and refashions human attitudes. In these fifteen years the United States has moved some stages further as an advanced industrial society. Superficially, the trends of advanced industrialization imply social change in the direction of less prejudice because of three sets of variables: higher levels of education, growth of middle income occupations and professions, and increased urbanization. Nor is it easy to separate internal social change from developments in the world arena.

We assumed in the original study that the "idea of progress" in industrial development does not carry with it automatically the "idea of progress" toward tolerance. By contrast, we saw the problem as one of tracing the consequences of those social trends that work to decrease ethnic hostility, and at the same time of probing their actual and potential countereffects. Thus, our basic orientation is that *in an advanced industrial society, especially one that emphasizes individualistic values, those sociological variables that account for much of the weakening of ethnic hostility have potential limits.*[3]

For example, even during a period of high prosperity and relative economic growth, some persons experience downward social mobility. Downward social mobility—the comparison of fathers and their sons—seems to affect as much as

[3] A similar position on "race relations" is argued by Everett C. Hughes and Helen M. Hughes, *Where Peoples Meet* (Glencoe: Free Press, 1952).

20 per cent of the male population.[4] And downward mobility is but one characteristic of an advanced industrialized society which we assumed to be a source of ethnic intolerance, as against those basic sociological trends toward greater tolerance.

TRENDS IN PREJUDICE

What, then, have been the long-term national shifts in attitudes toward Jews and Negroes? Despite the proliferation of national attitude surveys, no comprehensive and systematic body of trend

vey research professionals have not assumed the responsibility for writing current social history by means of systematic trend reporting. Nevertheless, there is convincing data to support the trend hypothesis that since 1945, for the nation as a whole, there has been a decline in the "average" or over-all level of anti-Jewish and anti-Negro attitudes. But there is little reason to believe the decline of percentage of persons with "hard core" extremist attitudes against these minorities has been as marked. The available data from national sam-

TABLE 1

"HAVE YOU HEARD ANY CRITICISM OR TALK AGAINST THE JEWS IN THE LAST SIX MONTHS?"*

National Samples: 1940–59†

(Percentage)

	1940	1942	1944	1946	1950	1953	1955	1956	1957	1959
Yes..............	46	52	60	64	24	20	13	11	16	12
No................	52	44	37	34	75	80	87	89	84	88
No opinion.........	2	4	3	2	1	......	......	......	......	......
Total.........	100	100	100	100	100	100	100	100	100	100
Number......	(3,101)	(2,637)	(2,296)	(1,337)	(1,203)	(1,291)	(1,270)	(1,286)	(1,279)	(1,470)

* Based on total white Christian population plus Negroes. Data supplied by Dr. Marshall Sklare, Division of Scientific Research, American Jewish Committee, New York City.

† Studies for the 1940 to 1946 period were conducted by Opinion Research Corporation, Princeton, New Jersey; for the 1950 to 1957 period by National Opinion Research Center, University of Chicago; the 1959 study was by Gallup Organization, Inc.

data has been collected over the last fifteen years. Investigations have been episodic and specialized. With the notable exception of survey findings by the Division of Scientific Research of the American Jewish Committee, and the more limited efforts of the National Opinion Research Center, there has been too little emphasis on the repeated use of standardized questions over time to chart contemporary social history.[5] Sur-

ples are by far more adequate for charting shifts in the moral "normal" levels of mild intolerance of Jews than for measuring the concentration of intense anti-Semitic attitudes. While the fifteen-year period has seen a long-term decline in prejudice toward Jews, much of the change occurred as a sharp shift after World War II, namely, during 1948–50.

Evidence of this shift appears in Table 1, which shows responses collected for

[4] Despite sociological interest in the question of social mobility in the United States, satisfactory data do not exist. The best estimates are derived from a study by the National Opinion Research Center, "Jobs and Occupations: A Popular Evaluation," *Opinion News* (September, 1947) and Richard Centers, "Occupational Mobility of Urban Occupational Strata," *American Sociological Review,* XIII (April, 1948), 198.

[5] It must be recognized that standardized questions are only a partial approach to charting trends in ethnic prejudice. The meaning of standardized questions change and new dimensions of prejudice emerge. On the basis of available evidence from a wide variety of studies, there is no reason to believe that these two limitations contributed in any significant degree to the over-all trend.

the Division of Scientific Research, American Jewish Committee, from comparable national samples from 1940 to 1959 to the question: "Have you heard any criticism or talk against the Jews in the last six months?" Although it has defects as a probe of anti-Semitic attitudes, the question is useful because it has been repeated in standardized fashion since 1940. It was apparently designed as a projective question, but it may reflect objective shift in public and private discussion about Jews rather than personal feelings of hostility, although the two are manifestly linked. Nonetheless, and despite limitations of the measure, the secular shift from roughly 50 per cent to 12 per cent "yes" is pronounced.

If it is argued that this downward trend is related to basic changes in the social structure of an advanced industrial nation state, it is still necessary to observe and explain the short-term shifts. The body of data underlines that anti-Semitic attitudes have a volatility that is apt to emerge with political and economic events. First, the period 1940 to 1946 revealed a definite increase in anti-Semitic attitudes that might be ascribed to the tensions of the war and the dislocations of postwar transition. Despite the fact that a war was being waged against a nation which persecuted the Jews, there is reason to believe that anti-Semitic attitudes were strengthened among those elements who believe that the Jews were a major cause of World War II. Second, the most dramatic short-term shift came during the years 1946 to 1950. The marked decline in "yes" responses during those years cannot be explained by changes in technical research methods, although these were at work because a different field agency collected the data. The same sharp drop in tolerance toward Jews around 1950 is documented by national sample responses to the question: "In your opinion are there any religious, nationality or racial groups in this country that are a threat to America?" (Table 2.) The frequency of the response "yes, the Jews," was 19 per cent in 1945, 18 per cent in 1946, and 5 per cent in 1950.

This short-term shift may well have been influenced by the exposure of Nazi genocide practices. Another possible explanation was the consequences of the "cold war" and the rise of the Soviet Union as an object of hostility. On the domestic front the Jews passed from a public prominence associated with World War II. This was also the period of the establishment of Israel, and the symbolism of the fighting Israeli Army may well have weakened anti-Semitic attitudes in the United States. Third, the downward trend continues after 1950, with a short-term rise in 1957 which might be linked to the economic recession.

Long-term data on the decline in prejudice toward Jews are also found in three samplings of college students over a period of 30 years by Emory S. Bogardus. Using his social distance scale, he found no difference in attitudes between 1926 and 1946. But in 1956, similar to the above data after World War II, there was a decline in feelings of social distance from the Jews.[6]

Data on the shifts in the percentage of "hard core" anti-Semites during this period are not fully adequate. In *The Dynamics of Prejudice*, four attitude patterns were identified for anti-Jewish and anti-Negro attitudes: tolerant, stereotyped, outspoken, and intensely prejudiced. As of 1945, the conclusion drawn from twenty national and specialized polls was that not more than 10 per cent

[6] Emory S. Bogardus, "Racial Distance Changes in the United States during the Past 30 Years," *Sociology and Social Research*, XLIII (November, 1958), 127–34. Similar findings on the relative stability of anti-Semitic attitudes until after World War II are contained in H. H. Remmers and W. F. Wood, "Changes in Attitudes toward Germans, Japanese, Jews, and Negroes," *School and Society*, LXV (June, 1947), 484–87.

of the adult population could be classified as intensely anti-Semitic. By intensely anti-Semitic was meant that persons held an elaborate range of negative stereotypes and sponstaneously recommended strong restrictive action against Jews. More specifically, the well-known *Fortune Survey* of 1946 revealed that 9 per cent of the nation's population had strongly anti-Semitic attitudes. The conclusion was based on the percentage who named the Jews either as "a group harmful to the country unless curbed," or who designated Jews as "people trying to get ahead at the expense of people like yourself." (There was no mention of the Jews in the questions by the interviewer.)

In Table 2, the responses are presented for 1945, 1946, and 1950 to the question designed to tap more extreme hostility, namely what groups are a "threat to America?" In this specific question the downward trend in anti-Semitic attitudes parallels the findings on other questions for the period up to 1950.

Unfortunately this type of question has not been used in national polls in recent years. However, in the 1950's the spontaneous expressed belief that Communists are most likely to be Jews became a useful measure of intense anti-Semitism, though the measure has an element of ambiguity. One cannot overlook the fact that among a very small group of sophisticated persons, the high incidence of Jews among the Communist party would be taken for granted as a political and social fact. But this group is probably too small to influence national opinion poll results. Therefore, the general question on which groups are likely to be Communists appears to tap intense prejudice among the population at large. In 1950, a national sample was asked the direct question: "In this country do you think any of the people listed here are more likely to be Communist than others?" Eleven per

cent named "the Jews" from the designated list.[7] In 1954, when the question was put in indirect form without specific reference to the Jews, "What kind of people in America are most likely to be Communists?" only 5 per cent of a national cross-section said that Jews were most likely to be Communists.[8] The difference between the two sets of responses could in large measure be attributed to the different form of the question and thus make it impossible to infer any actual decline in extremist anti-Semitic attitudes.

Have there been any significant changes in stereotypes about the Jews,

TABLE 2

JEWS AS A "THREAT TO AMERICA"*
National Samples: 1945–50†

(Percentage)

	1945	1946	1950
Yes.........	19	18	5
Number......	(2,500)	(1,300)	(1,250)

* In your opinion are there any religious, nationality, or racial groups in this country that are a threat to America?"

† 1945 and 1946 data collected by Opinion Research Corporation, 1950 data by National Opinion Research Center.

as well as in the level of hostility? Among the veterans' sample, the four most frequent groups of stereotypes were: (*a*) they are clannish, they help one another; (*b*) they have the money; (*c*) they control everything; they are trying to get power; (*d*) they use underhanded business methods. More contemporary patterns of stereotypes were revealed in the 1957 and 1959 national surveys by those who volunteered that they heard criticism of the Jews within the last six months. The striking change was that the "clannish" stereotype had

[7] Data collected by National Opinion Research Center from a sample of 1,250 white Christians.

[8] Data collected by American Institute of Public Opinion and National Opinion Research Center from a sample of 4,933 persons.

become very infrequent, while the other three stereotypes persisted with the same order of frequency. Comparison of stereotypes among Princeton undergraduates of 1932 and 1949 reveals that there has been a "fading of highly negative group stereotypes."[9]

TABLE 3

STEREOTYPES ABOUT JEWS:
HOUSING AND BUSINESS
National Samples: 1957–59*
(Percentage)

	NATION	
	1957	1959
"Jews Spoil Neighbor-hoods"[1]		
Strongly agree........	7	2
Agree..............	12	9
Uncertain..........	25	26
Disagree............	44	46
Strongly disagree.....	12	17
Total.............	100	100
Number..........	(1,058)	(1,294)
"Jewish Businessmen Are Shrewd and Tricky"[2]		
Strongly agree........	12	6
Agree..............	25	24
Uncertain..........	15	22
Disagree............	38	38
Strongly disagree.....	10	10
Total.............	100	100
Number..........	(1,058)	(1,294)

* Sample of Christian white persons. Data collected by Gallup Organization, Inc.

[1] "The trouble with letting Jews into a nice neighborhood is that sooner or later they spoil it for other people."

[2] "The trouble with Jewish businessmen is that they are so shrewd and 'tricky' that other people do not have a fair chance in competition."

Additional evidence of changing stereotypes comes from direct questions in the 1957 and 1959 national samplings. No significant shifts were expected in a two-year period, yet these data do show that stereotypes fluctuate. The direct questions probed the stereotypes that Jews spoil neighborhoods and that Jew-

[9] G. M. Gilbert, "Stereotype Persistence and Change among College Students," *Journal of Abnormal and Social Psychology*, XLVI (April, 1951), 245–54.

ish businessmen are so shrewd and "tricky" that other people do not have a fair chance in competition (Table 3). There was much more acceptance of the slogan that Jewish businessmen are shrewd and "tricky" than that Jews spoil neighborhoods (30 per cent strongly agreed, or agreed about business, as contrasted with 11 per cent about neighborhoods). However, both stereotypes weakened in the short two-year period, but the pattern of change differed. In the case of the Jews spoiling neighborhoods, the shift was in the more tolerant direction among all attitude groups. There was an increase among those who disagreed with the stereotype and a decrease among those who agreed with the stereotype. In the case of the stereotypes about Jewish businessmen, there was a decline in the percentage of those who agreed but no corresponding increase in the percentage of those who disagreed. The shift away from acceptance of the stereotype produced more uncertain responses. In other words, the decline in the stereotype about neighborhoods was more pronounced than the one about Jewish businessmen.

Stereotypes about the behavior of the Jews—namely, in spoiling neighborhoods—seem much more likely to weaken under the impact of direct contact than do those involving group characteristics that are illusive and hard to disprove—namely, that Jewish businessmen are shrewd and "tricky." Another plausible explanation of these shifts (if in fact the shifts are significant) is that Jews have come to be more integrated into community organization, residential location, and voluntary associations. During this period the Negro was becoming more of a "threat" to prejudiced persons as they pressed for residential movement into white areas. This pressure may well have reduced concern with Jews as neighbors. Since stereotypes are to some degree based on social reality, there has been a corroding of the stereotyped symbol of the "clannish Jews," living in a private world of high social solidarity—enforced though it may be by the non-Jewish world. Such an explanation flows from the assumption that those stereotypes which are in fact most easily checked against direct experience are also most likely to change as the intensity of prejudice declines. Thus, remote stereotypes such as "they control everything" and "they are trying to get power" would be expected to, and do in fact, persist most strongly.

The pattern of social change in "typical" attitudes toward the American Negro can be inferred from the data collected by the National Opinion Research Center of the University of Chicago by means of periodic national samplings since 1942. At four time periods, comparable national samples, excluding Negroes, were asked, "In general, do you think Negroes are as intelligent as white people—that is, can they learn things just as well if they are given the same education and training?" The results summarize a basic transformation in attitudes toward the Negro (Table 4).[10] For the total white population in the United States, attitudes have changed from 41 per cent who answered "yes" in 1942 to 78 per cent in 1956. A change of attitude among Southern whites on this question is equally marked during the same period, shifting from 21 per cent to 59 per cent answering "yes."

Residential and school integration became focal points for measuring changing attitudes about discrimination. In 1942, two-thirds of the population, as measured by national sampling, objected to the idea of living in the same block with a Negro; but by 1956 a majority declared they would not object.[11] In 1942 fewer than one-third of the respondents in the nation favored school integration;

by 1956 almost half endorsed the idea. This shift took place both in the North and in the South. In the North support for school integration had risen among white people from 41 per cent in 1942 to 61 per cent in 1956. In the South in 1942, only one white person in fifty favored school integration; by 1956 the figure increased to one in seven.

After 1956, as "massive" resistance to school desegregation temporarily developed, the national trend toward tolerant responses on this item continued but

TABLE 4

CHANGING ATTITUDES TOWARD NEGROES
National Samples: 1942–56

(Percentage)

Yes, Negroes Are as Intelligent as Whites[1]			
	Northern White Northern Population	Southern White Southern Population	Total U.S. White Population
1942..........	48	21	41
1944..........	47	29	42
1946..........	60	30	48
1956..........	82	59	76

[1] "In general, do you think Negroes are as intelligent as white people—that is, can they learn things just as well if they are given the same education and training?" Data collected by the National Opinion Research Center.

perhaps at a slower pace. By 1959 the over-all national level expressing support for integration stood at 56 per cent as compared with not quite 50 in 1956.[12] This slight upward trend was at work both in the North and in the South. What changes took place in the South were in the "Border States" as compared with the "Deep South." Breakdowns within the South reveal the percentage in the Deep South approving school integration as four, in the Border South as twenty-three.

Trends in response to "social distance"

[10] Herbert Hyman and Paul B. Sheatsley, "Attitudes toward Desegregation," *Scientific American,* December, 1956, 35–39.

[11] *Ibid.,* p. 38.

[12] American Jewish Committee Research Report, *The Nationwide Poll of 1959,* p. 5. Data collected by Gallup Organization, Inc., from 1,297 white Christians.

questions from national samples highlight the intensity and persistence of prejudice toward the Negro even during this period of social change. From 1948 to 1958, whatever changes took place in attitudes toward racial intermarriage hardly produced extensive tolerance. In answer to the blunt question, "Do you approve or disapprove of marriage between white and colored people," 4 per cent approved as of 1958 and most of the approval was among college graduates. In 1942, as noted earlier, two-thirds of the population objected to the idea

TABLE 5

CHANGING ATTITUDES TOWARD NEGROES

National Samples: 1944–56*

(Percentage)

Think Most U.S. Negroes Are Treated Fairly[1]

	Northern White Population	Southern White Population	Total U.S. White Population
1944.........	62	77	66
1946.........	62	76	66
1956.........	65	79	69

* Data collected by National Opinion Research Corporation.
[1] "Do you think most Negroes in the U.S. are being treated fairly or unfairly?"

of living in the same block with a Negro. By 1956 a majority did not object and in 1958, 56 per cent answered "no" to the question, "If colored people came to live next door would you move?"[13] In his study of college students, Bogardus found that between 1946 and 1956 "social distance" between these students and Negroes declined somewhat as measured by his paper and pencil tests.[14]

Finally, public perspectives on "America's dilemma" illuminate what has changed and what remains stable in American attitudes toward the Negro

[13] Data collected by American Institute of Public Opinion, from 1,650 whites.

[14] Emory S. Bogardus, *op. cit.*, p. 131.

during the last fifteen years. Gunnar Myrdal authored the phrase "America's dilemma" to emphasize the white man's involvement in race relations. In his comprehensive study of the position of the Negro in the United States before World War II, he stated that the majority's sense of conscience—its commitment to the creed of equality and dignity—created a powerful dilemma which was a constant source of pressure for social change. "The American dilemma" operates with greater force among community and political leaders he believed, but it was also a moral norm for society at large.

How strong is the awareness of this feeling of an "American dilemma"? What changes have reshaped these attitudes since World War II? The greater the sense of a "dilemma" the more likely the person seems to say that the Negro is being treated unfairly. The question, "Do you think most Negroes in the United States are being treated fairly or unfairly," supplies a crude but revealing index. It is crude because it mobilizes defensive sentiments; it is revealing because on this score, U.S. attitudes have changed over the years (Table 5). As of May, 1944, 66 per cent of a national sample thought that the Negro was being treated fairly; or "America's dilemma" was being felt by much less than a majority.[15] As was to be expected, the per cent who answered "fairly" was greater in the South than in the North (77 per cent in the South; 62 per cent in the North).

Moreover, the great transformation in attitudes toward the Negroes and the actual change in practices of the last fifteen years have brought no measurable changes in this response pattern. In May, 1946, the national percentage remained at 66 per cent and by April, 1956, it had risen only to 69 per cent. The stronger tendency of Southerners to

[15] Hyman and Sheatsley, *op. cit.*, p. 39.

give the answer "fairly" persisted. In short, there has been no increase in the popular sensitivity to an "American dilemma" during the period of greater agitation for equality within the United States and of a greater salience of race in international affairs. One plausible explanation is that the social, economic, and political progress of the Negro population during this period has served to prevent an increase in a sense of moral dilemma.

AGE, EDUCATION, AND SOCIO-
ECONOMIC STATUS

Having described recent trends in prejudice, we will take the next step of exploring the reasons for the shift toward greater tolerance in terms of basic changes in social structure during the last fifteen years. For this purpose, the social changes of advanced industrialism can be crudely highlighted by the key variables of age, education, and socioeconomic status. If the data were adequate, we could assess how important these variables were, singly and in combination, in accounting for the trend toward less prejudice. While the available data hardly approximate the research requirements, they offer some revealing findings.

In the original study we assumed, and the data supported the conclusion, that particular sociological variables, such as age, education, and socioeconomic status, would not be very powerful in accounting for patterns of ethnic hostility; a more interactive analysis was required. Melvin Tumin, in his review study of empirical work on American anti-Semitism, comes to the same conclusion.[16] "We are led first to the realization that no single sociological characteristic will suffice to give adequate understanding or prediction of where we will encounter the greatest amount and intensity of anti-

Semitism. Not age, nor income, nor education, nor religion, nor any other [sociological factor] by itself, is adequate. Nor can valid statements be made about the impact of various combinations of these characteristics, unless we specify the situational context. . . ."

Nevertheless, for each of the key sociological variables, a general trend hypothesis about its effect on prejudice is abundantly clear, although the impact of the variables is likely to be complex and interactive. First, younger persons are likely to be less prejudiced than older persons; second, better educated persons are likely to be less prejudiced than poorer educated persons; and third, higher socioeconomic status is likely to be associated with less prejudice than is lower status.

To what extent does later research evidence support or throw doubt on these general hypotheses? Moreover, to what extent have changes in the age, education, and socioeconomic structure of American society contributed to shifts in prejudice patterns during the last fifteen years? We have already seen that an important amount of the shift in attitude toward Jews took place in a short time span after the close of the war, and must therefore be linked to specific events—both domestic and international. On the other hand, the struggle for desegregation in the South after 1956 seems to have slowed but not stopped the trend toward greater tolerance toward Negroes. Despite these short-term shifts, we still need to explore the underlying shifts in social structure that might account for the longer term trends.

Age

A fundamental rationale for the hypothesis that younger persons are less prejudiced than older persons lies in the conflicts between the generations.[17] The

16 Melvin Tumin, *Inventory and Appraisal of Research on American Anti-Semitism* (New York: Freedom Books, 1961), p. 28.

17 The sample used in *The Dynamics of Prejudice* was not meant to be representative but

older generation is the carrier of basic values and norms in society, while the younger generations must be socialized into accepting these values. Invariably there is tension and struggle between the generations in an advanced industrialized society as the tempo of social change renders obsolete the standards of the older generation. Attitudes toward minority groups become one aspect of this tension, just as do style of clothes, and standards of morality. In the search for identity, the younger age groups tend to assert their independence from the older groups, and greater tolerance toward ethnic groups is a frequent expression of it. Thus, where the general trend in society is toward tolerance, the younger age groups are apt to be even more tolerant. In this sense, age is an index to the broader processes of social change. That is, the hypothesis that younger persons are less prejudiced than older persons is more than just a symptom of the conflict of generations. All of the changes of a more advanced industrialized society that might result in a decline in prejudice are likely to affect younger persons most.

This pattern of tolerance extends beyond minority groupings to political attitudes as well. Thus, Samuel Stouffer in his extensive national sample study of tolerance for political nonconformity found that young people were clearly more tolerant than older people. The concentration of "more tolerant" responses in the age group 21–29 were 47 per cent, and it dropped systematically with age. Those persons 60 years and over revealed only 18 per cent in the tolerant category.[18] Numerous studies of specialized samples have found the same

relation of age to attitudes toward minority groups.

In contrast to the findings on age grading, there is no adequate body of empirical data dealing with the life cycle of the individual and his attitudes toward minority groups. Is there any basis for speculating that as a person grows older his attitudes toward minority groups become less tolerant? It seems very plausible that this process does take place. Impressionistic accounts of the political behavior of older people emphasize a rigidity of outlook and more extremistic demands. However, the political attitudes of older people center on concrete economic issues, and there is less concern with minority groups and the social order in general.

Given a link between age grading and prejudice, the basic question remains: to what extent can the decline in ethnic hostility during the last fifteen years be explained by shifts in age composition among the population at large? Examination of the changes in gross age composition during this period, marked though they were compared with other periods in history, show them to be unimportant factors in the trends in prejudice. The age structure is still relatively stable, decade by decade, and those changes that have occurred would not explain the trend toward greater tolerance.[19]

The analysis of age structure and prejudice requires a more refined approach involving cohort analysis. Are the new

---

rather to concentrate on the young age group. Nevertheless, it was possible to divide the sample into younger and older veterans; the general hypothesis held that the young were more tolerant.

[18] Samuel A. Stouffer, *Communism, Conformity and Civil Liberties* (Garden City, N.Y.: Doubleday & Co., 1955), p. 92.

[19] During the 1950–60 decade the median age of the population declined for the first time since 1900; it dropped from 30.2 years in 1950 to 29.3 years in 1959. But the median is a poor measure of the changes in age composition. The important changes that have occurred are those in the age groupings under 17 years and those over 65 years. While the total increase in population during the decade was 17.2 per cent, those under 17 years and over 65 years grew at a much faster rate (14 to 17 years, 30.7 per cent; 65 years and over, 26.1 per cent). Middle age cohorts remained relatively stable or grew at a rate lower than the national rate.

cohorts of young people entering the adult population less prejudiced than the cohorts who are one and two decades older? Likewise, are the old cohorts above 60 years of age and who are dying off more prejudiced than the middle and younger cohorts? We have no direct data available to us on this subject, but we presume that a cohort analysis would highlight the greater incidence of tolerant attitudes among the young cohorts. Although such a cohort analysis is important, it does not answer questions concerning the process of attitude formation. In particular it remains to investigate whether growing older, even during a period of increased tolerance, produces a tendency toward rigidity of attitude toward minority groups.

The relationship between age and tolerance is complicated by the results of education. Young persons are more likely to be better educated and to have an education compatible with tolerant attitudes toward minority groups. In fact, one could argue that the general hypothesis of younger persons being more tolerant rests to a considerable degree on the fact that the younger are better educated. Therefore education, the second basic variable, is of crucial importance in assessing trends toward greater tolerance.

Education

Education correlates with a wide variety of social behaviors, from consumer behavior to political attitudes. But in analyzing the consequences of education and an ever rising level of attainment, we must distinguish between education in its "intellectual" and moral value content, and education as it is linked to and required for occupational mobility. However, the rationale for the hypothesis that better educated persons are likely to be less prejudiced does not rest solely on the argument that education is an index to socioeconomic position. Education

should be positively correlated with tolerance because of the impact of social experiences during the educational process and because of the selective processes influencing what kinds of persons will receive advanced schooling. It can be assumed that education will have different consequences for different social groups; for example, the higher the socioeconomic position the less effect education would have on intolerant attitudes. But education, per se, is designed in a political democracy to increase the power of one's personal controls and to broaden one's understanding of social reality (in Karl Mannheim's term, "substantive rationality"). These social processes are assumed to weaken ethnic prejudice.

The very fact that a significant portion of college graduates still hold stereotypes and support discriminatory practices reflects the limits of the educational system in modifying attitudes. On the basis of an examination of some twenty-five national sample surveys since 1945, the positive trend effect seems to involve the social experience of education and not merely the sociological characteristics of the population from which the educated are recruited.

However, the trend impact of education is not a simple process. The available data underscore areas in which education operates to reduce prejudice. However, the same body of data highlight the persistence of prejudice among the educated, and even some evidence of instability of attitudes. These data are relevant in accounting for the persistence of a "hard core" of very prejudiced persons.

Charles H. Stember in his careful review of the effects of schooling on prejudice concludes that the better educated are: (*a*) less likely to hold traditional stereotypes about Jews and Negroes, (*b*) less likely to favor discriminatory policies, and (*c*) less likely to reject casual contacts with minority group members.[20] Education seems to reduce traditional provincialism and to weaken primitive misconceptions. On the other hand the more educated, according to Stember, are more likely to: (*a*) hold highly charged and derogatory stereotypes, (*b*) favor informal discrimination in some areas of behavior, and (*c*) reject intimate contacts with minority groups.

Thus, for example, the better educated are more prone to accept the stereotypes that Jews are (*a*) loud, arrogant, and have bad manners, (*b*) are shady and unscrupulous, and (*c*) have too much business power. Moreover, the previously mentioned question administered in 1952 which asked: "In this country do you think any of the people listed here are more likely to be Communists than others?" revealed that there was a higher concentration of those answering "Jews" among the college graduates than among those with only grammar school education (17 per cent for college education, 10 per cent for grammar school). Evidence that this is not merely a sophisticated response comes from the findings that the better-educated are more likely to perceive Jews as a "threat to the country," and as unwilling to serve in the armed forces.

The limits of social acceptance are often sharply drawn by better-educated people. Covert discrimination continues to be acceptable and the desire to keep minorities at some social distance remains. These findings, as far as prejudice toward Jews are concerned, need to be interpreted in the light of the available data which reveals that college-educated persons (and thereby persons of higher socioeconomic status) have more actual contact with Jews than less-educated persons. Moreover, the better-educated show no greater concern with the prob-

lem of discrimination than others, on the basis of national sample studies. In particular, better-educated persons show marked concern about sending their children to school with Negroes, presumably because of assumed lower educational standards in such schools. There is an important regional difference in this finding. In the South, Melvin Tumin found that among his sample in Guilford County, North Carolina, the best-educated were the most prone to accept desegregation of the public school system.[21]

The data on education and stereotypes confirm the theory and findings of *The Dynamics of Prejudice.* Since stereotypes are rooted in social and psychological needs, schooling does not consistently bring a rejection of stereotypes. The better-educated are more likely to reject certain kinds of stereotypes, but old images persist and new ones emerge. The attitudes of the educated seem more liable to change under the impact of particular events. Apparently the less-educated are more stable in their attitudes. Clearly, these data indicate the resistance of prejudice despite the rising U.S. educational levels.

In recent years there has been, of course, swift progress in raising the educational level of the United States. During the period 1940 to 1957 the proportion of the population classified as functional illiterates (less than five years of elementary school) was decreased by one-third. Only a few years before 1940 the average citizen was a graduate of elementary school. By about 1965 the average citizen will be a high school graduate. These dramatic changes are important ingredients in the decline in prejudice although there is a different attitude pattern toward Jews and toward Negroes. Each increase in education seems to be linked to less prejudice, but in the case of anti-Negro attitudes there

[20] Charles H. Stember, *Education and Attitude Change: The Effects of Schooling on Prejudice against Minority Groups* (New York: Institute of Human Relations Press, 1961), pp. 168 ff.

[21] Melvin Tumin, *Desegregation: Resistance and Readiness* (Princeton: Princeton University Press, 1958), p. 193.

seems to be a threshold effect; college level is necessary before attitudes toward Negroes change significantly.

The findings on education must be assessed in the light of a crucial observation based on repeated surveys: that education as a separate factor has less consequences at the upper levels of the social structure. Within the upper socioeconomic groups, educational differences make less of a difference in prejudice (both toward Negroes and Jews) than at the lower levels. Again education seems to have built-in limitations as an agent of social change for reducing prejudice; those who get the most education have been and are the least likely to be influenced by it per se. If the trend toward a "middle class" society continues, it may well be that the future effects of expanding education will diminish. Or, to put it differently, the content of education as opposed to amount of it will grow in importance. We have spoken here of the consequences of education. However, access to education and the effects of education depend on a person's socioeconomic status and the changing pattern of stratification in society at large.

Socioeconomic Status

A number of sociological arguments would lead one to anticipate that persons of upper socieconomic status would be less prejudiced than those of lower status. It can be argued that higher social position, like education, serves to broaden personal perspectives and reduce intolerance. In the same vein upper status groups have a greater stake in the existing social arrangements and are therefore less likely to hold extremist attitudes, including those toward minority groups. This assumption implies that upper status groups would be less likely to hold extreme intolerant attitudes. It also means that they would not necessarily hold their tolerant beliefs with greater conviction or intensity. Portions of the

middle class, especially those in the new bureaucratic occupations, are also more immune to the pressures of economic conflict and are therefore less likely to express intolerance toward actual or potential competitors.

But such reasoning is of limited value for, in fact, there are important differences within the lower and middle classes as well as between them. To explain the trends of the last fifteen years these differences make it necessary to reject a simple economic conflict model of prejudice, although economic pressures are clearly important. Likewise, specific ethnic and religious group difference within the lower and middle class elements of the so-called majority group strongly modify the class patterns of ethnic intolerance. Finally, it was originally assumed in *The Dynamics of Prejudice* that to locate a person in the society-wide stratification system—as measured by his income or occupation—was only a first step. We then had to investigate the dynamics of mobility by which a person acquired his socioeconomic position.

Thus, it is possible to examine national surveys and observe that, for the population as a whole, for very broad socioeconomic groupings a limited association with very general forms of ethnic prejudice does emerge. The upper social groups are at least more inhibited in their expression of ethnic intolerance. But much more relevant is to select a particular metropolitan community rather than a national sample. Within the metropolitan community the interplay of social stratification and ethnic prejudice can be seen more precisely. Important regional differences are ruled out—the South versus the other regions of the country. The differences between urban and rural areas are also controlled, for there is a gradual decrease in the level of ethnic intolerance as one goes from rural areas to small towns to cities under a million to those over a million. The use of metropolitan community samples focuses more sharply on the realities of social stratification in what we now call the mass society.

In the metropolitan community, when occupation is the measure of socioeconomic status, the sharp differences in levels of prejudice within the middle and the working class emerge. Data collected by the Detroit Area Study in 1957, for a representative sample of the adult population, makes possible a breakdown of anti-Negro attitudes by heads of households (Table 6). The top of the social structure—the professional and managerial group—displayed the lowest amount

of both the middle and working class are less prejudiced than the lower strata of the same classes runs parallel to the distribution of the authoritarian syndrome in representative national samples.[23]

In the metropolitan community interpersonal contacts between majority groups and minority groups are stratified. These contacts influence stereotypes and ethnic hostility. The Jewish minority is essentially a middle and upper class group, although a Jewish "proletariat" exists in the largest metropolitan centers. In contrast, the Negroes in the urban centers are predominantly a working and

TABLE 6

SOCIOECONOMIC STATUS AND NEGRO PREJUDICE

Detroit Metropolitan Area Sample: 1957

	Tolerant	Mildly Intolerant	Strongly Intolerant	Total Number	
Professional, managerial, and proprietors.	32.6%	53.3%	14.1%	100%	(92)
Clerical, sales, and kindred.	28.9	44.6	26.5	100	(83)
Craftsmen and foremen.	31.7	50.0	18.3	100	(82)
Operatives, service, etc.	30.0	33.8	36.2	100	(80)
Total.	(104)	(154)	(79)		(337)

of intolerance while the very bottom—the operatives and service, etc.—had the highest amount. There was, however, no straight line progression as one moved down the hierarchy. While the professional and managerial category roughly represented the upper-middle strata with lower intolerance, the lower-middle strata (clerical, sales, and kindred) revealed a markedly higher level. Crossing the white collar–blue collar line, the upper-lower stratum (craftsmen and foremen) was more tolerant than the lower-middle stratum and very like the top professional and managerial group. The lower-lower group, the most intolerant, was more prejudiced than even the lower-middle which is often impressionistically described as particularly prone to extremist attitudes.[22] This pattern of ethnic prejudice in which the upper strata

lower-middle class group. These patterns of contact help explain the higher incidence of certain stereotypes about the Jews among gentiles in the better-educated and upper socioeconomic status groups. Earlier, we pointed out a decline in frequency of the stereotype that the Jews are "clannish" and stick together. This decline may well be linked to the

[22] Stratification in the metropolitan community involves not only the occupational category but differential risks of unemployment. The incidence of unemployment falls heaviest on the lower socioeconomic strata. The Detroit Metropolitan area during the 1950's was representative of the urban center where unemployment has persisted. The higher level of ethnic hostility expected among the unemployed, as compared with the employed labor force, was found present.

[23] Morris Janowitz and Dwaine Marvick, "Authoritarianism and Political Behavior," *Public Opinion Quarterly*, XVII (September, 1953), 185–201.

greater social integration of the Jews into the metropolitan community, mainly through membership in voluntary associations. Nevertheless, the "clannish" Jew is one of those select stereotypes more likely to be mentioned by upper status persons as compared with working class persons.[24] Middle and upper-middle class persons have most contact with Jews. It is plausible that they are more observant of the ambiguities that result from the interplay of Jewish demands for social equality and the practice of social withdrawal into Jewish communal life. Therefore, this stereotype increases rather than decreases as one moves up the social structure.

A very similar reaction was found in the case of the "inferior intelligence" of Negroes. This again is one of the select stereotypes about Negroes that increases with higher socioeconomic status. Presumably middle class persons have more chance to observe and judge the consequences of lack of cultural preparation for higher education among Negroes. For defensive reasons they are then more prone than lower class persons to label the Negroes as inferior in intelligence.

To summarize, there has been a trend downward since World War II in the United States in prejudice toward minority groups, as measured by attitudes toward Negroes and Jews. This trend can be linked to changes in the social structure of an advanced industrial society, namely, changes in the age structure, higher levels of education, and a broadening of the middle strata. While the consequences of change in the age structure are equivocal, the higher levels of education and the broadening of the middle strata have operated to weaken ethnic prejudice. These variables, singly or in combination, cannot account for the modification of patterns of prejudice over the last fifteen years. These basic

[24] Based on data collected from 3,000 Christians by Ben Gaffin, *Catholic Digest Religious Study,* 1952.

sociological variables, as they change under advanced industrialism, do not automatically result in "progress," if by progress we mean the further reduction of ethnic prejudice. The consequences of these variables are complex and we have observed limits on their impact, particularly in the case of education. Changes in the structure of social controls, such as the law, political organization, and the mass media, must be brought into the analysis.

In the years since the publication of *The Dynamics of Prejudice,* it has been fashionable for some social scientists to de-emphasize the study of prejudice. They have come to claim that they are mainly concerned with the processes of discrimination and desegregation. From the point of view of social action, these social scientists have announced that they are unconcerned with attitudes— private or public. Only overt behavior interests them. Both from a sociological and social problems point of view this is a partial approach of the processes of social change. Sociologists have traditionally postulated a crucial interplay between attitude patterns and social institutions. To be concerned with one, at the expense of the other, is to limit our understanding of the dynamics of social change. The goal of a free society is not only to eliminate discrimination, but also to develop sentiments and attitudes which have inherent respect for human dignity. Any action program that does not rely on brute force must take into consideration and understand the attitudes and sentiments of the persons involved.

There is every reason to believe that sociological studies of prejudice will be pursued with vigor in the next decade. Some of the work will by necessity take the form of national surveys designed to measure more accurately trends in attitudes toward minority groups. Only by establishing a national barometer or trend index will it be possible to chart the processes of social change and prejudice.

But such studies need to be matched by individual scholarship concerned with extensive approaches to the study of prejudice. One area that requires intensive investigation is the attitude patterns that develop between different minorities. In particular, there is need to study the structure of attitudes in the Negro community toward Jews and vice versa. On the American scene, in recent years, there has been an increase in immigration of "Spanish-Americans"—both from Mexico and Puerto Rico. What patterns of stereotypes are applied to these groups? To what extent are our theories of prejudice broad enough to understand the dynamics of hostility to this particular minority? In a real sense, the Southern white migrant in the Northern industrial centers, is a minority group. The structure of prejudice toward this minority has only been partially analyzed.

But in the decade ahead it is not very likely that sociologists will be content to re-do, elaborate, and expand the scope of past prejudice studies. It is most likely that they will take a more experimental approach. They will seek to study the new social action programs that are designed to modify attitudes and practices in the area of intergroup relations. The basic institutions of our society—the schools, the factory system, trade unions, governmental agencies, and religious organizations, in varying degrees—are explicitly developing new procedures and practices to eliminate discriminatory practices toward minority groups. Even in the area of residential housing, such as in the community of Hyde Park in the city of Chicago, the University of Chicago and local community associations are evolving procedures for creating an integrated racial community. The study of the impact of these social experiments on the dynamics of prejudice will be the research frontier of the next decade.

13. *The Negro Family in Chicago*[*]

E. FRANKLIN FRAZIER

The purpose of this chapter is twofold. The first is to give a summary review of *The Negro Family in Chicago,* indicating the sociological problem with which it is concerned, the general frame of reference of the study and the specific hypothesis which it tests, the sources and nature of the materials which are utilized, and the conclusions reached. The second is to assess the contribution of this study to urban sociology, especially in regard to the family and in view of the recent interest in sociological studies of cities in underdeveloped or preindustrial areas of the world.

THE PROBLEM

The problem with which this study was concerned was, broadly speaking, the demoralization of Negro family life but more specifically with the more acute manifestations of family disorganization in the cities to which Negroes had been migrating since emancipation. The explanations offered for the continued disorganization of Negro family life over the years ranged from such biological explanations as the compelling sexual appetite and the childlike mentality of the Negro to such anthropological and sociological explanations as the influence of the African cultural heritage and the lack of moral restraints in Negro life. All of these explanations seemed inadequate, especially since a knowledge of the social history of Negroes in the United States was necessary for an understanding of family disorganization among

[*] Based on the author's Ph.D. dissertation of the same title, Sociology, 1931, and recent research.

them. The social history of the Negro reveals the fundamental distinction between the loose family organization, based upon habit and affection, which was characteristic of the family among the slaves and among the rural folk Negro and the well-organized institutional families which developed among the Negroes who were free before the Civil War and their descendants. The widespread and continued family disorganization among Negroes in cities which had attracted the attention of students and social workers and officials is one of the results of the impact of the urban environment upon the simple and loose family organization of the Negro folk.

The mistake, then, of the various explanations of the disorganization of Negro family life was to treat the Negro population as a homogeneous group. The differences in the culture and social development of various elements in the Negro population were obscured, for example, in the statistics on the marital status of the Negro population as well as on the trend in the rate of illegitimacy in the United States as a whole. Even statistics on Negro family life for cities obscure important social differences in the Negro population. The inadequacy of the statistical treatment of the Negro population as a homogeneous group may be seen in the case of the statistics on Negro illegitimacy in the District of Columbia, where the rate had shown little change over a period of more than half a century. This was often cited as the classic illustration of the failure of the Negro to achieve the standards of American civilization in familial and sexual behavior. An alternate but obvious sociological explanation was never advanced, namely, that the District of Columbia was one of the focal points of the migration of the Negro folk from the rural South and that the process of family disorganization was only repeating itself with each new wave of migrants. Moreover, in the District of Columbia as in other cities of the country the disorganization of Negro family life was not characteristic of all sections of the Negro population and the impact of urban life on the Negro population was affected by differences in the social and cultural heritage of Negro families.

Hypothesis To Be Tested

The general hypothesis that gradually emerged from this view of the problem of family disorganization was that the disorganization and reorganization of Negro family life are part of the processes of selection and segregation of those elements in the Negro population which have become emancipated from the traditional status of the masses. A combination of circumstances made the Negro community in Chicago an ideal place in which to test the validity of this hypothesis. First, the Negro population of Chicago, which had increased rapidly along with the growth of the city, represented a cross-section of the Negro population of the United States. It included the descendants of both the slave and the free population and families accustomed to residence in northern and southern cities as well as those who had migrated recently from the plantations of the South. Still more important for the successful prosecution of this study were the research facilities and the resources provided by the local Community Research Laboratory at the University of Chicago. This laboratory provided statistical data on the Negro population for census tracts, thus making it possible to relate indexes of family life to the selection and segregation of

socially and culturally significant elements in the Negro population. Moreover, studies that had been carried on in connection with the laboratory served as models and showed the fruitful results of the point of view and methods represented in this study.[1]

However, from the standpoint of testing the hypothesis, the most important factor was Burgess' theory concerning urban expansion which he demonstrated could be measured by rates of change in poverty, home ownership, and other variable conditions for unit areas along the main thoroughfares radiating from the center of the city.[2] In the city of Chicago the Negro community which had expanded southward from the center of the city along one of the main thoroughfares, State Street, had cut across several of the concentric zones marking the expansion of Chicago. Therefore, it was logical to assume that if the processes of selection and segregation operated according to Burgess' theory of urban expansion, the processes of selection and segregation should be reflected in the Negro community. Therefore, the first step in this study was to determine if this was true.

The Seven Zones of the Negro Community

The Negro community which extended from Twelfth Street southward to Sixty-

[1] Outstanding among these studies were Harvey W. Zorbaugh, *The Gold Coast and the Slum* (Chicago: University of Chicago Press, 1929); Ruth S. Cavan, *Suicide* (Chicago: University of Chicago Press, 1928); and papers edited by Robert E. Park and E. W. Burgess in *The City* (Chicago: University of Chicago Press, 1925) and *The Urban Community* (Chicago: University of Chicago Press, 1926), edited by Ernest W. Burgess.

[2] See Ernest W. Burgess, "The Growth of the City" in *The City*, ed. by Robert E. Park and Ernest W. Burgess (Chicago: University of Chicago Press, 1925), and "The Determination of Gradients in the Growth of the City," *Publications of the American Sociological Society*, XXVI (1927), 178–84.

third Street and was bounded on the west by Wentworth Avenue and on the east by Cottage Grove Avenue could be divided on the basis of census tracts into seven zones which marked the expansion of the Negro community. That these zones provided a means of measuring the process of selection and segregation of elements in the Negro population

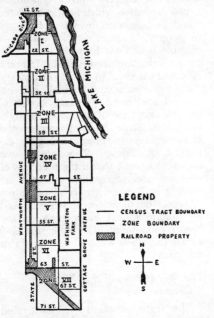

FIG. 1.—South Side Negro community of Chicago (*Negro Family in the United States*).

which were differentiated demographically and socially is indicated first by the character of the population in the seven zones (see Table 1). Although nearly four-fifths of the Negroes in Chicago in 1920 were adults, only the third zone or the bright light area and business center of the community showed a comparable preponderance of adults. The proportion of adults in the population was smaller in the first zone near the Loop in Chicago, where the poorer southern migrants settled, as well as in the areas of

more stable community life, Zones VI and VII, where the higher occupational classes resided. A process of selection and segregation was likewise revealed in regard to the proportion of males in the seven zones. Although Chicago, because of the opportunities for industrial employment, had attracted more men than women, the preponderance of males appeared only in certain areas—the deteriorated areas near the center of the city. The proportion of males in the Negro population declined in the succeeding zones, and in the better areas in the southern section of the community women actually outnumbered men.

One of the most striking features of the process of selection and segregation was the variation in the percentage of mulattoes in the population of the different zones. In the two zones near the center of the city or the Loop about one Negro man out of five and one Negro woman out of four was a mulatto or mixed blood. In Zone III the proportion of mulatto men mounted suddenly to one out of three and the proportion of mulatto women rose to two out of five. In the next two zones the proportion of mulatto men and women in the population of these zones was about the same as in the first two zones. But in Zone VI the proportion of mulatto men and women increased to about a third, while in Zone VII practically a half of the Negro men and women were mulattoes.

We shall see how the concentration of mulattoes in Zone VII was related to the concentration of the higher occupational classes in this zone. However, a word needs to be said concerning the concentration of mulattoes in Zone III. This zone was a bright light area of the Negro community.

Through the heart of this zone ran Thirty-fifth Street, the brightlight area of the Negro community. Here were found the "black and tan" cabarets, pleasure gardens, gambling places, night clubs, hotels, and houses of prostitution. It was the headquarters of the famous "policy king;" the rendezvous of the "pretty" brownskinned boys, many of whom were former bellhops, who "worked" white and colored girls in hotels and on the streets; here the mulatto queen of the underworld ran the biggest poker game on the South Side; here the "gambler de luxe" ruled until he was killed by a brow-beaten waiter. In this world the mulatto girl from the South who, ever since she heard that she was "pretty enough to be an actress," had visions of the stage, realized her dream in one of the cheap theaters. To this same congenial environment the mulatto boy from Oklahoma, who danced in the role of the son of an Indian woman, had found his way. To this area were attracted the Bohemian, the disorganized, and the vicious elements in the Negro world.[3]

When we turn from the demographic to the social aspects of the Negro population of the seven zones, we find the same process of selection and segrega-

[3] *The Negro Family in Chicago* (Chicago: University of Chicago Press, 1932), p. 103. This quotation from the study will indicate how documentary materials gathered through uncontrolled observations during "field studies" in modern communities will illuminate or, perhaps better, will make it possible for statistics to have meaning in terms of social processes.

tion. We note first that Zone I or the area in which the poorer migrants first get a foothold has the highest proportion of heads of families who were born in the South. The proportion declines steadily from nearly four-fifths in Zone I to slightly less than two-thirds in Zone VII. This decline in the proportion of heads of families who were born in the South is correlated with the decline in the proportion of illiterate Negroes in the seven zones. In Zone I the illiteracy rate among Negroes was about the same as it was in Houston and Dallas, Texas, and more than four times the rate for the Negro population as a whole in Chicago. The illiteracy rate declined rapidly after Zone I and in the three outermost zones it was less than 3 per cent.

The occupational status of the Negroes in the seven zones is of special interest because it reflects not only the social and cultural differences in the Negro population but provides an index to the class structure of the Negro community. It will be seen in Table 1 that the proportion of railroad porters or Pullman porters among employed males increases in the seven zones marking the expansion

TABLE 1

SOME INDEXES TO THE DIFFERENCES IN THE DEMOGRAPHIC AND SOCIAL CHARACTER
OF THE POPULATION IN THE SEVEN ZONES OF THE
NEGRO COMMUNITY IN CHICAGO

CHARACTERISTIC (per cent)	ZONES						
	I	II	III	IV	V	VI	VII
Persons 21 years and over..........	71.6	76.3	77.6	75.4	72.7	69.0	70.5
Males.........................	55.6	54.7	52.0	50.2	48.5	49.8	47.1
Mulattoes: 15 years and over							
Male........................	19.2	19.0	33.5	19.2	22.8	31.3	49.7
Female......................	27.2	23.8	40.2	24.0	24.7	32.8	48.5
Heads of families							
Southern born.................	77.7	77.0	74.7	73.8	72.6	69.0	65.2
Persons illiterate							
10 years and over..............	13.4	4.6	3.2	2.3	3.3	2.9	2.7
Occupational classes: Males							
Professional and white collar.......	5.8	5.5	10.7	11.2	12.5	13.4	34.2
Skilled........................	6.2	10.8	12.3	13.6	11.1	14.4	13.0
Railroad porters*................	1.4	3.4	6.7	6.5	7.5	7.7	10.7

* Presumably Pullman porters.

of the Negro community and that in Zone VII they constitute more than a tenth of the employed males. This is interesting because at one time Pullman porters were, on the whole, a group with comparatively good incomes and maintained a stable family life, and constituted an important element in the Negro upper class. But by the time this study was made in the late twenties they had been superseded by the professional and business classes in the Negro community. However, like the Pullman porters, the proportion of Negro men and women in professional and white-collar occupations, although the figures for women are not given in Table 1, increased regularly in the zones, marking the expansion of the Negro population from the area of first settlement near the center of the city. For example, in Zone I one out of every sixteen employed Negro males is employed in professional, business, and white-collar occupations as compared with one out of three in Zone VII. The tendency for the Negro women in this occupational group to be concentrated in areas of the outermost expansion of the Negro community is even more marked. Likewise, both Negro men and women in skilled occupations are concentrated in the same zones as the professional and business classes. And contrariwise, although the figures are not given in Table 1, Negro men and women in semiskilled occupations, domestic service, and employed as laborers are concentrated in the zones where the poorer newcomers to the cities are concentrated.

The census data which provided information on the demographic and social characteristics of the Negroes in the seven zones were supplemented by case materials including uncontrolled observations on the behavior of peoples in the seven zones, on the physical character and on the nature of the institutions in the seven zones. Some of this information could be treated statistically as, for example, in enumerating the number of the various denominational churches and "storefront churches," houses of prostitution, saloons, billiard halls, gambling places, and cabarets.[4] Moreover, materials were collected on the social organization of the community though, as we shall see, this material was inadequate for a thoroughgoing analysis of the social changes in the urban environment.

Indexes to Character of the Family

On the basis of the federal census data for the census tracts it was possible to secure some indexes to the character and organization of Negro family life in the seven zones (see Table 2). First, it will be noted that there were important differences in the marital status of men in the zones. In Zone I, nearly 40 per cent of the men were single and only slightly more than a half of them were married.

The proportion of single men declined for the successive zones to the point that in Zone VII only a fourth of them were single and more than two-thirds of them were married. The proportion of Negro men widowed did not show the same variation. However, there were variations in the proportion of divorced men which may have had some significance. In Zone VII, where the higher occupational classes were concentrated, there was a decidedly higher proportion of divorced males. The significance of this will be commented upon in relation to the marital status of Negro females.

It will be noted that the marital status of Negro females does not vary in the different zones as that of Negro males. An explanation of this difference can only be obtained from what is known of the social behavior of Negroes in case materials on the social and cultural life of Negroes. The census returns on the marital status of Negro women in the zones toward the outermost expansion of the Negro community are probably

[4] See *The Negro Family in Chicago*, Appendix B., p. 276.

TABLE 2

SOME INDEXES TO THE CHARACTER OF FAMILY LIFE IN THE SEVEN
ZONES OF THE NEGRO COMMUNITY IN CHICAGO

CHARACTERISTIC (per cent)	ZONES						
	I	II	III	IV	V	VI	VII
Marital status of males:							
Single....................	38.6	38.1	35.9	32.0	30.7	27.3	24.7
Married....................	52.1	54.4	55.8	61.1	62.5	65.6	68.5
Widowed....................	6.3	6.3	7.2	4.9	5.5	6.1	5.5
Divorced....................	0.9	0.9	0.7	1.4	1.5	1.8	1.2
Families with female heads..........	22.0	23.1	20.8	20.4	20.5	15.2	11.9
Married females 15–19 years........	2.8	2.5	2.1	2.1	1.8	2.1	0.7
House ownership..................	0	1.2	6.2	7.2	8.3	11.4	29.8

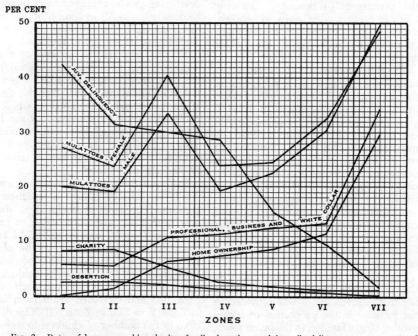

FIG. 2.—Rates of homeownership, charity, family desertion, and juvenile delinquency; percentage of mulattoes in the population; and percentage of males in professional, business, and white-collar occupations in the seven zones of the Negro community of Chicago.

accurate or nearly accurate. But generally speaking, from what is known concerning the marital status of Negroes, one cannot accept what the women say when they say that they are widowed. Many of the so-called "widowed" Negro females are unmarried mothers or women whose husbands or men with whom they have been living have deserted them. It is interesting to note, however, that in the zones on the periphery of the community the proportion of Negro women who are divorced is significantly higher than in the zones inhabited by the newcomers to the city. This only tends to confirm what was said concerning the validity of statistics on the marital status of the women in the various zones.

The difference in the character of the family was revealed in the difference in the proportion of families with female heads in the seven zones. In Zone I, where we have seen the poorer southern migrants first gain a foothold, in more than a fifth of the families the woman is head of the family. The proportion of families with female heads declined to less than an eighth in Zone VII, where the higher occupational classes and mulattoes are concentrated. In this connection another fact of interest is that in Zone VII only a fourth as many Negro females between the age of fifteen and nineteen were married as in Zone I.

Perhaps the most important index to the progressive stabilization of family life in the seven zones was provided in the increase in the proportion of home-owning Negro families in the seven zones. In Zone I, there was no home ownership among Negroes and only slightly more than 1 per cent in Zone II. But in Zone III, it was a little more than 6 per cent, and in Zones IV and V it continued to increase. In Zone VI more than an eighth of the families owned their homes and in Zone VII three out of every ten Negro families were home-owners. In the study, the progressive increase in home-

ownership was related to the changes in the physical and social character of the neighborhoods of the different zones. Moreover, it should be noted that the changes in rates of homeownership were related to the gradual decline in the average number of families and persons per dwelling unit in the seven zones.

Another index to the variation in the character of family life in the seven zones was provided by the census data on the average size of the household and on the number of children under 15, under 5, and under one to Negro women of childbearing age.[5] The average size of household, which was 3.8 in Zone I, increased to 4.2, 4.4, 4.3 in the next three zones and declined to 4.0 and 3.7 in Zones VI and VII.[6] The increase in the size of the household was related to the increase in the number of households with lodgers. But it is important to note that the size of the household in Zone VII was practically the same as the size in Zone I. The significance of this will become clear when considered in relation to the number of children to women of childbearing age in the zones.

In Zone I there were 70.7 children under 15 to each 100 women of childbearing age. The number declined in the next four zones and only began to increase in Zone VI and reached 74.1 in Zone VII. The same trend can be observed in regard to the number of children under five (not shown in Table 2) where the number of children declined from 19.8 and increased again from 20 in Zone V to 27.6 in Zone VII. The decline in the number of children to women of childbearing age in Zones II, III, and IV was undoubtedly the result of the decline of the importance of the family in these zones. However, when we consider the number of children under one (not shown in Table 2), one may

[5] See *ibid.*, Table XIII, p. 127.

[6] The average size of household and number of children under five and under one are not given in Table 2.

note that there is a slight increase in the number of children in Zone II but not in Zone III and that the significant increases were in the next four zones though the number is less in Zone VII than in Zone VI. The only explanation for the small number under one in Zone I is that since it is in this zone that the southern migrants first secured a foothold in the city, this was the area which would reflect the immediate effects of city life on the decline in the number of Negro births. Then it appears that among the more stable and more economically secure families in Zone VII, there are actually more children per family than in

was only about 1 per cent in the Zones VI and VII. A similar trend may be observed in regard to warrants for nonsupport and family desertion on the part of the men. In Zones VI and VII the rates for both of these forms of family disorganization declined to one-half of 1 per cent and even less. As one would expect, the decline in the rates of illegitimacy, based upon the number of unmarried mothers per 100 married women, 14 to 44 years of age, followed the same pattern of decline for the seven zones.

The decline in rate of adult delinquency but more especially juvenile delinquency in the seven zones is even more

TABLE 3

SOME INDEXES OF SOCIAL DISORGANIZATION IN THE SEVEN
ZONES OF THE NEGRO COMMUNITY IN CHICAGO

SUBJECT	ZONES						
	I	II	III	IV	V	VI	VII
Charity cases.................	8.0	8.2	5.3	2.8	1.9	1.0	1.1
Warrants for non-support..........	2.5	2.0	2.3	2.3	1.5	0.5	0.4
Family desertion................	2.5	2.6	2.1	1.5	1.1	0.4	0.2
Illegitimacy....................	2.3	1.1	1.2	0.9	0.6	0.4	0.2
Juvenile delinquency.............	42.8	31.4	30.0	28.8	15.7	9.6	1.4
Adult delinquency...............	9.4	6.7	3.8	2.5	2.9	3.2	1.2

the poor and disorganized families in the other areas of the community.

Indexes to Family Disorganization

In order to secure indexes as measures of family disorganization in the seven zones, it was necessary to utilize the records of the United Charities, the Juvenile Court, the Court of Domestic Relations, the Cook County Hospital, and the Institute of Juvenile Research. The rates of various forms of family disorganization and dependency are given in Table 3. First, it will be noted that about 8 per cent of the families in Zones I and II came to the charities for aid. The rate of dependency as measured by the number of families applying for aid declined sharply in the successive zones until it

striking. In Zone I where the poorer migrants from the South are concentrated, the number of inmates in the county jail represented nearly a tenth of the adult Negro male population. The proportion declined rapidly for the successive zones until it amounted to scarcely more than one out of a hundred men in Zone VII. In the case of juvenile delinquency, more than two boys out of five had been arrested for delinquency in Zone I. In the next three zones the rates kept close to 30 per cent but in the next three zones there was a sharp decline until it was only slightly more than 1 per cent in Zone VII.

The statistical materials were analyzed and interpreted on the basis of case materials, including family history documents, the results of interviews, and printed documents in order to throw light on the processes of social disorganization and reorganization in the seven zones. In the last section of the study an attempt was made to show how traditions have been built up in Negro families and how these traditions have been the means whereby the Negro has achieved social stability in a changing world and have taken over the patterns of family life similar to the American pattern.

Extension of Study to Other Areas

Before attempting an assessment of the study as a contribution to urban sociology, we shall indicate how the hypothesis in this study has been utilized in other studies carried on within the general frame of reference of this study. Since the publication of *The Negro Family in Chicago* nearly thirty years ago, I have engaged in the study of the Negro family on a larger scale including field studies in Brazil and in the West Indies.[7] However, the most immediately relevant study I undertook was the study of the Negro community in Harlem, New York City.[8] Although this study was undertaken to determine the economic and social causes of a race riot in 1935, during the course of the study I collected important materials on the ecological organization of the Negro community which permitted me to test my findings concerning the Negro community in Chicago, especially in regard to some aspects of family life.[9] The ecological organization of the Negro community in

[7] See "The Negro Family in Bahia," *American Sociological Review*, VII (August, 1942), 465–78.

[8] See "The Negro in Harlem, A Report on Social and Economic Conditions Responsible for the Outbreak on March 19, 1935," for the *Mayor's Commission on Conditions in Harlem*, New York, 1936. Unpublished.

[9] "Negro Harlem: An Ecological Study," *American Journal of Sociology*, XLIII (July, 1937), 72–88.

Harlem was found to differ in an important respect from the ecological organization of the Negro community in Chicago. As we have seen, the Negro community in Chicago had expanded along one of the main thoroughfares radiating from the center of the city and had cut across the concentric zones marking the expansion of the city as a whole. This was reflected in indexes to community life and in family organization and disorganization. In Harlem the Negro population had expanded from the center of the Negro community—Seventh Avenue and 135th Street—in all directions with the result that the ecological organization of the Negro community was similar to that of a self-contained city. It was possible to mark off on the basis of census tracts five concentric zones indicating the radial expansion of the Negro community in Harlem from its center. First, it was noted (see Table 4) that Negroes had taken over almost entirely Zone I or the center of the community and that the extent to which they had taken over the other four zones diminished as one went from the center to the periphery of the Negro community. Then, it may be observed also that the extent to which Negroes had taken over the successive zones corresponded with the decline in the percentage of non-residential structures in the five zones. The ecological organization of the Harlem Negro community showed in this respect the same relationship of the population to the physical habitat as the Chicago Negro community.

The differences in the social character of the Negro population in the Harlem community was shown in the marital status of the population in the five zones. There was a gradual but marked decline in the proportion of single men and women in the successive zones. Associated with the decline in the proportion of single men was a corresponding increase in the proportion of men and women who were returned in the fed-

eral census as married. Likewise, para-
doxical as it might seem, the increase in
the proportion divorced from Zone I to
Zone V was indicative of more conventional marital relations. In the case of
both the "widowed" and "divorced" it
was most likely that these terms represented more truly the marital status of
men and women in the peripheral zones
than in Zones I and II. These differences

of ten Negro families were receiving relief and the rate declined in the four
succeeding zones until it was less than
three out of ten families in Zone V. The
rates of juvenile delinquency tended to
fluctuate rather than decline though it
was less in the outermost zone than in
any of the other zones.

The statistics on births and on the
number of children to women of child-

TABLE 4

SOME INDEXES TO THE HOUSING AND THE SOCIAL AND DEMOGRAPHIC CHARACTER OF
THE POPULATION OF THE FIVE ZONES OF THE HARLEM
NEGRO COMMUNITY IN NEW YORK CITY

CHARACTERISTIC	ZONES				
	I	II	III	IV	V
Percentage of population Negro in 1930....	99.8	87.8	41.4	22.7	6.2
Percentage of non-residential structures in 1934..........	83.8	78.2	59.8	42.5	28.0
Marital status:					
Single {M........	42.6	38.5	35.3	34.0	31.1
{F........	30.9	27.6	26.3	25.6	23.5
Married {M........	49.8	56.0	60.3	62.3	64.2
{F........	50.5	54.8	57.6	59.8	60.1
Widowed {M........	7.3	4.7	3.6	2.9	3.8
{F........	17.6	16.4	15.0	13.0	14.4
Divorced {M........	0.2	0.5	0.4	0.6	0.5
{F........	0.6	0.8	0.7	1.1	1.6
Ratio of children under 5 to 1000 women 20–44 years of age: 1930............	115	176	225	315	462
Births per 1000 married women 15–44 years of age: 1930..............	66.1	81.5	91.9	141.6	168.4
Desertion rate per 1000 families.........	9.0	5.2	4.8	3.5	4.0
Families on relief per 1000 families.......	709	585	395	311	284
Boys arrested per 100 boys 10–16 years of age	5.5	4.5	5.7	4.8	4.3

in the marital status of the population
conformed to the problem of changes in
the desertion rates and family dependence as measured by relief cases obtained from the social agencies. The desertion rate declined from 9 per 1000
families in Zone I to 4 per 1000 families
in Zone V. This study was carried out
during the depression years in the thir-
ties, when large numbers of Negro families were dependent upon relief. But the
incidence of relief declined considerably in the five zones. In Zone I seven out

bearing age were both related to the
marital status of the population and to
the character of family life. In Zone I,
which was the center of the Harlem
community, where there were relatively
large numbers of single men and wom-
en, there was great dependence upon relief. In this same zone there were only
115 children under five years of age to
1000 women of childbearing age. This
indicated that not only did the family
tend to disappear but the population did
not reproduce itself. There was a pro-

gressive increase in the ratio of children and in the number of children born to women of childbearing age in the successive zones. In fact, in Zone V the ratio of 462 children to 1000 women of childbearing age and the birth rate of 16.8 equaled that of the rural Negro population.

Although there has been no systematic attempt to study the ecological organization of Washington, D.C., I was able to define on the basis of census tract materials five concentric zones which indicated the expansion of the city from the business center. It was found that the slum, concerning which there has been so much complaint that it was within the shadow of the nation's Capitol, fitted perfectly into the ecological organization of the city. However, more important for our interest here was the fact the rate of home ownership for Negroes increased regularly from the central zone or Zone I to Zone V and that it was practically the same as the rate of home ownership for white families in each of the five zones.[10]

It was pointed out at the beginning of this chapter that the important social and cultural differences in the Negro population provided the general frame of reference within which study of the Negro family in Chicago was carried out. The specific hypothesis which was being tested was that these important social and cultural differences were reflected in the traditions and patterns of Negro family life. On the basis of materials which were collected during a larger study of the Negro family in the United States, it was possible to define more precisely the differences in the social heritage and problems of family life.[11] It was possible to define four distinct types of traditional patterns of family life. An attempt has been made to describe and analyze the accommodations which these four types of families made to the urban environment.[12] Not only did these four types of families make different accommodations to the urban environment but the urban environment exercised a selective influence on these various family types. And it was out of this process that there emerged a new social and cultural organization of Negro life and in fact a new Negro personality. It was largely through the methods developed in these various studies that it was possible to organize and present in the general frame of reference the development of the Negro family as an institution.[13]

ASSESSMENT OF THE STUDY AS A CONTRIBUTION TO URBAN SOCIOLOGY

In order to make a proper assessment of *The Negro Family in Chicago* as a contribution to urban sociology, it will be necessary to give some attention to recent discussions of the definition of the city or urbanism. These discussions are the result of urbanization in underdeveloped or non-industrial areas in the world. In fact, some of the studies of urbanization in these areas are concerned with the problems with which the study in Chicago deals. It is felt that a redefinition of the city is necessary because the definition of the city as a large and dense population aggregate in which the family loses its importance and that as the result of mobility the contacts of people are impersonal and there is much anomie is descriptive of a special type of city which has grown up in the Western world. Therefore, an attempt has been made to differentiate the pre-industrial city which has been characteristic of Asia

[10] Unpublished materials in the Department of Sociology and Anthropology, Howard University.

[11] "Traditions and Patterns of Negro Family Life" in *Race and Culture Contacts*, ed. by Edward B. Reuter (New York: McGraw-Hill Co., Inc., 1934).

[12] "The Impact of Urban Civilization upon Negro Family Life," *American Sociological Review*, II (October, 1937), 609-18.

[13] *The Negro Family in the United States* (Chicago: University of Chicago Press, 1939).

and Africa from the Western industrial city.[14]

The problem of the definition of the city really concerns those features of social organization which are supposed to make urbanism a peculiar way of life.[15] In his article on "Urbanization among the Yoruba," Bascom contends that, while the distinction between pre-industrial and industrial cities is important, urbanization does not necessarily involve the decline in the importance of the family in the social organization and that primary forms of social control may still be effective in an urban environment.[16] The significance of Bascom's contention in this assessment of *The Negro Family in Chicago* becomes apparent when one views even casually the studies of social changes in the urban areas of Africa.[17]

The important factor, it seems to me, in differentiating the pre-industrial and industrial city concerns the difference in social organization. In the pre-industrial cities of Africa, kinship and lineages and primary forms of social control played the chief role in the social organization. But as these cities acquire the character of industrial cities, it is apparent in all the studies that these traditional forms of social organization are being dissolved. Then, too, as the Africans migrate to the new industrialized cities, despite their effort to maintain the traditional forms of social organization or create new forms of associations based upon the traditional culture, they are unable to do so. What is happening to

the urbanized African is very similar to what happened and continues to happen to the southern Negro who with his background of folk culture migrates to the industrial cities of the United States. Of course, the African's culture may be more resistant to change because the folk culture of the American Negro is essentially a subculture, since even the folk Negro lives in the twilight of American civilization. But the disintegration of the American Negro's traditional folk culture and the reorganization of his social life in the urban environment is very similar to what is occurring in the urban areas of Africa.

In view of the nature of the problem with which *The Negro Family in Chicago* is concerned, namely, social change as it is effected in the urban environment, one must recognize the limitations of the ecological approach to the problem. Human ecology, at least as Park conceived it, "was not a branch of sociology but rather a perspective, a method, and a body of knowledge essential for the scientific study of social life, and hence, like social psychology, a general discipline basic to all the social sciences."[18] Ecological studies were focused originally upon the community which was differentiated theoretically and for purposes of analysis from society, behavior in the former being characterized by the impersonal powers of competition and in the latter by norms and values which govern human behavior. As human ecology has developed as a scientific discipline, it has revealed through empirical studies the relevance of the physical basis of social life to the understanding of social and cultural phenomena. Moreover, the ecological approach to social studies has helped social scientists to define social problems and to discover in-

[14] Gideon Sjoberg, "The Preindustrial City," *American Journal of Sociology*, IX (March, 1955), 438–45.

[15] Louis Wirth, "Urbanism as a Way of Life," *American Journal of Sociology*, XLIV (July, 1938), 1–8.

[16] William R. Bascom, "Urbanization among the Yoruba," *American Journal of Sociology*, L (March, 1955), 446–53.

[17] See, for example, J. Clyde Mitchell, *Africans in Industrial Towns in Northern Rhodesia* (H.R.H. The Duke of Edinburgh's Study Conference, 1956).

[18] Louis Wirth, "Human Ecology," *American Journal of Sociology*, L (March, 1955), 484. This article is devoted to a systematic and critical analysis of the ecological approach to studies of social behavior.

terrelationships among social phenomena. But the relations which are revealed between phenomena in ecological studies are not explanations of social phenomena but indicate the selection and segregation of certain elements in the population. Thus, ecological studies are not a substitute for sociological studies but supplement studies of human social life. For a complete understanding of social phenomena it is necessary to investigate the social organization and culture of a community and the attitudes of the people who constitute the community.

The hypothesis which *The Negro Family in Chicago* undertakes to test is narrowly defined; family disorganization among Negroes was an aspect of the selective and segregative process of the urban community. The ecological approach to this study provided an adequate test of this hypothesis. However, the general frame of reference of the study was much broader. The study was really concerned with the fundamental social and cultural differences in the Negro population which determined the extent and nature of family disorganization and how these important social and cultural differences influenced the reorganization of life among Negroes on a different basis in the urban environment. Here we are brought face to face with the problem of the adequacy of the ecological approach to sociological problems involved in social changes resulting from urbanization. Quite aside from the question whether the new cities of Africa and Asia have the census materials for cities which would enable one to make an ecological study similar to the study which we are assessing, there is the more fundamental question of the adequacy of the ecological approach to this problem.[19] The sociological problem is essentially the problem of social organization.

The remainder of this chapter will be devoted to an assessment of the study as a contribution to the analysis and understanding of the processes of social organization or social reorganization which are involved in the social changes resulting from urbanization. It might be noted, first, that the study contains a description of the social organization of the Negro community which, it was stated, was shaped by the division of labor or occupational organization of the community.[20] This provided a sketchy description of the various types of associations and institutions in the Negro community. But there was no attempt to describe or analyze the social stratification of the Negro community which would have provided the most important frame of reference for studying social reorganization in the urban community.[21] Of course, in the social analysis which was designed to explain the process of selection and segregation, an attempt was made to analyze on the basis of case materials why, for example, there is more family stability and less family disorganization in the areas in which the higher occupational classes are concentrated. But this analysis is not specifically related to the new social stratification in the urban community nor is the analysis in terms of social processes. Such an analysis would be necessary, however, for an understanding of the processes of reorganization in the urban community. The ecological selection which the study revealed represented in fact changes

[19] In this connection reference should be made to the excellent ecological study by Leo Kuper, *Durban: A Study in Racial Ecology* (London: Jonathan Cape, 1958), which indicates what may be done in a South African city where statistics are available for census tracts. The study is restricted, however, to the relations of the races with reference to spatial distribution.

[20] *The Negro Family in Chicago*, pp. 112–15.

[21] In *The Negro Family in the United States*, I have devoted much attention to the analysis of the social processes by which new classes have come into existence among Negroes in the United States and the role of fundamental social and cultural differences in the formation of the new class structure as well as the new social distinctions.

which had occurred during two or more generations. Because of educational opportunities children acquired new skills and new ambitions and were able to rise in the new social stratification. It was because of the opportunity for this type of social mobility that they were able to escape from the condition of masses, that is, enter new occupations, become homeowners, maintain a conventional family life, and move to areas which were congenial to their way of life. It is only in the final chapter which deals with the manner in which traditions in the Negro family are built up that the social analysis deals with these processes of social change.

The study of social organization is especially important in the sociological studies which are being made among the urbanized Africans. The traditional forms of social stratification are being undermined or completely dissolved in the urban environment and a new and more complex type of social stratification is replacing them.[22] In this process the old social distinctions and prestige values are being supplanted by those which have meaning for the African in the new world of the city. This leads us to another aspect of the social reorganization of life in the city to which this study scarcely gives any attention but is especially important in areas like Africa. One of the most important phases of the reorganization of life among urbanized Africans is the development of new forms of associations. As the traditional African society dissolves or disintegrates the fabric of a new social life is coming into existence in the urban environment. These new forms of social life have a functional relationship to the needs of the new environment. Very often these new associations incorporate the attitudes and patterns of behavior of the traditional culture. But more often they

represent adjustments to new situations for which the traditional culture does not provide solutions. There are, for example, new types of economic associations which approximate in form and purpose the labor unions of the Europeans and perhaps even more important the new political organizations with nationalistic aims. Then as the traditional religions disintegrate, there are all sorts of cults formed to meet the new conditions of city living. Although the situation of the American Negro in the city is not exactly the same, there are many parallels. The study fails to deal with this aspect of adjustment to the urban environment.

Although the study is concerned with the problem of the family in the city, it does not deal with its crucial role in the social organization or the social reorganization of life in the city. This is of primary importance not only in studying the American Negro but in studying the African in the city. In the case of the American Negro the family in the plantation areas lacked an institutional basis and owed its cohesion and continuity to habitual association in the same household and the emotions and sentiments that grew out of this association. On the other hand, the African who comes to the city has been part of a family and lineage group with an institutional basis and social sanctions deeply rooted in their culture. However, in both cases the family had a functional relationship to the conditions of life and played an indispensable role in the social organization. In destroying both types of family groups the impact of the urban environment has resulted in social disorganization and created a cultural crisis. In dealing with this crisis, whether the family is organized on a different pattern or new types of associations are formed, it is in the family that the new norms of behavior and new conceptions of life and new values will provide the basis

[22] See, for example, A. L. Epstein, *Politics in an Urban African Community* (Manchester: Manchester University Press, 1958).

of the new social organization. These important aspects of the role of the family in social organization are only touched upon or implicit in this ecological study of the Negro family in the city.

In concluding this chapter, we shall attempt to sum up our assessment of *The Negro Family in Chicago* after a period of nearly thirty years since its publication. From the standpoint of its significance for human ecology, the study demonstrates in an unmistakable manner the validity of the theory of human ecology in the approach to the study of the urban environment and contains a broader and more developed conception of human ecology than the more restricted spatial aspects of human ecology. Moreover, it makes a distinct contribution to the theory of the ecological organization of the city especially in the application of its methods to the Negro community in New York. There it shows that gradients are not only found in the

growth of the city as a whole but that in cultural or racial communities within the city there are gradients similar to those in the city as a whole. Nevertheless, the study reveals the limitations of the ecological approach to the study of the important problem of social organization and social reorganization in the city. It fails to show the social stratification of the community which would provide the most important frame of reference for studying the social changes in the life of the Negro or any other urbanized group. Nor is there an analysis of the important role of the family in the social organization, although it is suggested in this study and carried out in the larger study of the Negro family. In brief this study in human ecology indicates and tends to define some of the sociological problems which need to be studied in the field of social disorganization and reorganization of life in the city.

14. Occupational Mobility of Negro Professional Workers*

G. FRANKLIN EDWARDS

INTRODUCTION

Approximately a decade ago an investigation was conducted on the occupational mobility patterns of Negro males in the District of Columbia who were working in the four professional occupations of medicine, dentistry, law, and college teaching.[1] The major objective of the research was to discover the occupational origins of Negroes who entered these professional fields and to assess those factors which were found to be associated with the mobility process. As there was reason to believe that the mobility pattern of Negroes varied from that found for other groups in the population, an attempt was made to relate the findings to existing theories of social mobility and stratification.

An interest in conducting the study stemmed largely from a desire to develop more knowledge than then existed of the mobility patterns of Negroes who entered high-status occupations. Early studies of occupational mobility in this country had concentrated on white males or on specific occupational groups.[2] Some stud-ies, though not focused on problems of mobility and stratification, had given passing attention to these phenomena among minority groups.[3]

These early studies had developed a fund of information which contributed to our understanding of the mobility process and provided important commentaries on the nature of American society. Among other things, they demonstrated that one did not move very far from the occupational level of his father; the propensity to enter an occupation on the same level as that of one's father was greater than that for entering any other occupational level. For those offspring who were occupationally mobile, the probability was high that most of them would enter occupations which were considered to be on levels adjacent to those on which their fathers were found. American society was not so replete with opportunity, nor yet so democratic, that everyone had an equal chance for entering a high-status profession. Those who succeeded in entering important government positions, the professions, and im-

---

* Adapted from the author's Ph.D. dissertation, "Occupational Mobility of a Selected Group of Negro Male Professionals," Sociology, 1952.

[1] A monograph, based upon the dissertation, appeared under the title *The Negro Professional Class* (Glencoe: Free Press, Inc., 1959).

[2] Dewey Anderson and Percy E. Davidson, *Occupational Mobility in an American Community* (Palo Alto: Stanford University Press, 1937), and F. Taussig and C. S. Joslyn, *American Business Leaders* (New York: MacMillan Co., 1932), are examples of these early studies.

[3] Among studies of this type the following may be mentioned: Edward K. Strong, Jr., *The Second-Generation Japanese Problem* (Palo Alto: Stanford University Press, 1934); S. Joseph Fauman, "The Factors in Occupation Selection among Male Detroit Jews," (unpublished doctoral dissertation, University of Michigan, 1948); Beulah Ong Kwoh, "The Occupational Status of American-Born Chinese Male College Graduates," *American Journal of Sociology*, VIII (November, 1947), 192–200; and Stuart Adams, "Regional Differences in a High-Status Occupation," *American Sociological Review*, XV (April, 1950), 228–35.

portant positions in the business world were likely to have had their social origins in families in which the economic and educational levels of their parents were above those of the average family. It was clearly indicated that sponsorship by the family played a significant part in determining the occupations followed by its offspring, and that such sponsorship took account of more than financial support. It entailed goal selection and/or direction and the constant nurture of aspirations in the form of motivations and incentives until the goal was reached. Family members and the social circle in which the family moved quite often provided occupational models of profound influence, however unwittingly these influences were experienced.

It was believed that an investigation of the mobility patterns of Negroes entering high-status occupations would enrich our understanding of this phenomenon, owing to circumstances peculiar to Negro life. At the time the investigation was planned, Negroes had been freed from slavery for only approximately three generations. During the slave period only a few Negro persons, limited to members of the free Negro population, were permitted to qualify for high-status occupations. Thus, the development of a professional structure, to administer to the service needs of the Negro community as it enlarged, occurred within the relatively short period elapsing since emancipation. This condition provided an excellent situation for assessing the amount of mobility and related factors which occur in a relatively fluid social system.

At approximately the time the study was planned, several students raised questions regarding the nature of social stratification, and hence mobility, in the mass society which gave the proposed study added theoretical interest. These students postulated that in the mass society there existed a dominant over-all pattern which was fairly uniform for the total society; but local communities, regions and groups, while living in conformity with the over-all stratification values, might show a considerable variation from them.[4] The investigation of mobility patterns among Negroes provided an excellent test case of the extent to which a group lived in conformity with and varied from the dominant pattern for the total society, with respect to the factors studied.

RESEARCH DESIGN AND METHODS

The professions were selected to represent a high-status occupational category among Negroes. While the professions are accorded high prestige by all elements of the society, among Negroes they rank especially high, owing mainly to the virtual absence of Negroes from executive positions in the business world. Studies of vocational choices of Negro youth show that predominantly they aspire to professional statuses; only infrequently are high-level positions in business and government mentioned as career choices. A further support for the selection was that, owing to the segregated pattern of community life, the Negro community supported a larger corps of professional functionaries than it did workers in any other occupational category which carries high prestige.

Several factors imposed limiting conditions on the research design. Since the plan was to compare the observed occupational mobility of Negroes with what was known of the phenomenon among whites, only males were selected as subjects. Previous studies had given attention only to the male population. In this

---

[4] This basic point was raised in each of the following articles: Paul K. Hatt, "Stratification in the Mass Society," *American Sociological Review*, XV (April, 1950), 216–22; Florence Kluckhohn, "Dominant and Substitute Profiles of Cultural Orientations: Their Significance for the Analysis of Social Stratification," *Social Forces*, XXVIII (May, 1950), 376–93; and Otis Dudley Duncan and Jay Artis, Jr., "Some Problems of Stratification Research," *Rural Sociology*, XVI (March, 1951), 17–29.

connection, the social work group, predominantly female in composition, was eliminated from consideration.

The limitation of the study to the District of Columbia required the selection of only those professions in which there was a sufficiently large Negro male population to permit cross-classification of the data without cell collapse. Several categories having small numbers of Negroes, including actors, musicians, architects, and engineers, were eliminated. The clergy qualified for inclusion from the viewpoint of numbers in the profession but this category was eliminated because the requirements for performance in this field are not as uniformly high as they are for the other professions selected. While many clergymen hold both undergraduate and professional degrees, others have had little formal training. College teachers were selected to represent the teacher group.

The Sample

The sample was drawn from lists of persons assembled for each of the professional groups. As the physicians, dentists, and lawyers each have a professional association, the rosters of these associations were secured. To these rosters were added the names of functionaries who were not members of their respective professional associations. The lists were alphabetized and numbered. Selection was done by random numbers, with one-half of the physicians, dentists, and lawyers appearing on the lists selected. All male college teachers in the arts and sciences at Howard University and at Miner Teachers College, a four-year institution engaged primarily in the preparation of teachers for the District of Columbia public school system, were included. As finally drawn, the sample totaled 300 persons, distributed among the several groups as follows: 90 physicians, 46 dentists, 72 lawyers, and 92 college teachers.

An inspection of certain demographic variables showed that the sample possessed the characteristics of professional populations in general. This held true for educational level (average of 19 years), marital status (90 per cent married), age at first marriage (27.5 years), and number of children (1.1 for the entire sample and 1.2 for those ever married).

Since comparisons of the income, occupational, and educational levels of the respondents' fathers with their contemporaries are made in other sections of this chapter, attention is here directed to one characteristic of the respondents' background which sharply distinguished them from the rest of the Negro population. The respondents of this study were a more urban group, as measured by their place of birth. Approximately 76 per cent of the respondents were born in places classed as urban at a time when 73 per cent of the total Negro population lived in rural communities. Of even greater significance is the fact that 40 per cent of the respondents were born in metropolitan communities in contrast to the 10 per cent of the total Negro population which lived in such places.

The Community

The District of Columbia, the community in which the study was conducted, offered a number of advantages for a study of this type. It had, in 1950, a total Negro population of 280,000 persons; it ranked fifth among the metropolitan areas of the country in the number of Negroes in the total population. This large Negro community provided economic support for a substantial corps of Negroes in the independent professions. There existed among Negroes of the district a strong professional tradition. The first Negro medical and dental societies in the United States, the precursors of the national organizations among these groups, were organized in the district and are still in operation. Negro lawyers have a professional association which is now forty years old. The area has the largest percentage of college graduates among Negroes 25 years of age and over of all communities in the country. The percentage of Negroes of this age category who are college graduates is two and a half times larger than the comparable percentage for the total Negro population and twice as large as the comparable figure for Negroes living in urban places.

Howard University, founded in 1867, is located in the district. It is the only institution of higher education among Negroes which offers training for most professional fields. The university has been a major influence in accounting for the large number of Negro college and professional school graduates in the community. Most Negro physicians, dentists, and lawyers who practice in the community were trained in the professional schools at Howard. The undergraduate college and the graduate school of arts and sciences have attracted to their faculties a large number of Negroes interested in teaching.

Freedmen's Hospital, a federally-supported facility of approximately 500 beds, serves as the training hospital for the Howard University School of Medicine. For a long period, it was the single most important training facility in the United States for Negro physicians who sought certification by specialty boards. The area has a larger number of Negro medical specialists than any other community in the country, and more Negro dentists than are to be found in any single state.

Finally, it should be pointed out that the occupational structure of Negroes in the District of Columbia is not greatly different from that of Negroes in other large urban areas of the country. It is somewhat more highly differentiated than the occupational structure of Negroes in metropolitan areas of the South, with the district having larger percentages of Negroes in professional and clerical occupations. The occupational structure of Negroes in the district, however, is not as differentiated as that of Negroes in large urban areas of the North.

Methods and Techniques

The data on which the study is based were gathered by means of a schedule and by interview. The schedule included items commonly found in mobility studies: identifying data on the respondent, questions on the educational, occupational, and economic status of his parents and other family data, methods of financing the respondent's education, and a series on the occupational aspirations of the respondent and the influences which shaped these aspirations. Appropriate tests of significance were used in a number of comparisons and values qualifying at the .05 probability level were accepted as significant. The method of expected cases was employed to compare the occupational status of the respondents' fathers with that of their Negro male contemporaries in the labor force.

MAJOR FINDINGS AND CONCLUSIONS

The major findings of this research are reported in this section: (1) occupational origins; (2) factors associated with occupational mobility; (3) occupational aspirations and motivations; and (4) the career profile of the respondent.

Occupational Origins

The respondents had their occupational origins in families in which the majority of the fathers were white-collar workers. Almost three-fifths of them (59.2 per cent) had fathers whose occupations were on this level. The largest single group of fathers in this category were professional workers (31.8 per cent), followed in order by clerical workers (15.4 per cent) and by proprietors (12.0 per cent). There was little variation among the professional respondents studied with respect to their origins within the white collar group, except for the dentists, who had fewer fathers at the professional level. The occupational origins of the several professional groups are shown in Table 1.

The occupational status of the respondents' fathers was superior to that of their Negro contemporaries in the labor force. This is indicated by the fact that fathers were represented in approximately their expected proportion, but there were fewer fathers than expected in farming.[5] The underrepresentation of fathers in farming is explained in large part by the predomniantly urban origin of the respondents. The expectancy val-

TABLE 1

OCCUPATIONAL LEVEL OF THE REGULAR OCCUPATIONS OF RESPONDENTS'
FATHERS BY OCCUPATION OF RESPONDENTS

OCCUPATIONAL LEVEL OF FATHER	No OF CASES	OCCUPATION OF RESPONDENTS (PERCENTAGE DISTRIBUTION)				
		Total	Physicians	Dentists	Lawyers	Teachers
White collar........	175	59.2	60.1	50.0	63.2	59.2
Blue collar.........	121	40.8	39.9	50.0	36.8	40.8
Total..........	296*	100.0	100.0	100.0	100.0	100.0

* In four cases the respondents did not know their fathers' occupation.

TABLE 2

COMPARISON OF THE OCCUPATIONAL CLASS OF RESPONDENTS' FATHERS
WITH THAT OF MARRIED NEGRO MALE WORKERS
IN THE LABOR FORCE (1910)

OCCUPATIONAL CLASS	ESTIMATED NUMBER OF NEGRO MALE WORKERS (1910)	PROPORTION OF LABOR FORCE (1910)	FATHERS		RATIO ACTUAL TO EXPECTED
			Actual Distribution	Expected Distribution	
White-collar......	66,802	.033	175	9.8	17.85
Blue-collar........	809,956	.398	99	117.8	.85
Farmers..........	1,157,517	.569	22	168.4	.13
Total........	2,034,275	1.000	296	296.0	....

the respondents had fathers in white-collar occupations 18 times more often than would be expected if no difference existed between the fathers' occupational distribution and that of other Negro males in the labor force. Fathers in professional occupations were represented 28 times as often as would be expected under the condition mentioned above, proprietor fathers ten times as often, and those in clerical occupations fifteen times as often. The manual workers among the

ues for broad occupational classes are shown in Table 2.

The presence in the sample of a considerable number of respondents born

[5] The values reported are derived from the expected cases method in which the occupations of the respondents' fathers are redistributed according to the proportion of Negro males in each occupational category in the labor force in 1910. The resulting value is a ratio of the actual number of fathers in the occupational category to the number derived from the redistribution.

and reared in the District of Columbia, and of others who migrated there during their youth, permitted a comparison along the line mentioned above with urbanization held constant. The result of this comparison shows a reduction in the overrepresentation of fathers in the white-collar group. In the district comparison the number of fathers in white-collar occupations was only five times larger than the expected number as compared with the previous comparison in which the number was 18 times the expectancy value. It is significant to observe, however, that even with the correction for rural-urban differences between the respondents' fathers and their Negro male contemporaries, the former group is superior in terms of occupational level.

By comparing the occupational origins of the respondents of the study reported here with the origins of professional workers reported in other studies,[6] some interesting facts are revealed. The respondents of this study are similar to those of other studies in having fathers whose occupations were predominantly in the white-collar group. Unlike the respondents of other studies, however, a larger proportion of the present study respondents came from families in which the fathers were blue-collar workers, particularly in service and semiskilled occupations. The data suggest that somewhat greater occupational mobility was experienced by Negro professional workers than by other professionals. This finding was reinforced by an analysis of the occupations entered by the adult male siblings of the respondents. The propensity to enter professional occupations was as

[6] These other studies are: Percy Davidson and H. Dewey Anderson, *Occupational Mobility in an American Community* (Palo Alto: Stanford University Press, 1937); Richard Centers, "Occupational Mobility of Urban Occupational Strata," *American Sociological Review*, XIII (April, 1948), 197–203; and C. C. North and Paul K. Hatt, "Jobs and Occupations: A Popular Evaluation," *Opinion News*, September 1, 1947.

strong for sons of semiskilled workers as for the sons of professional and clerical workers (approximately 50 per cent each), and about as strong for the sons of farm owners and service workers as for the sons of proprietors (approximately a third in each case).

There was, however, one striking difference which was noted in the points of origin within the white-collar group for the respondents of this study as compared with those reported in the other studies mentioned. Whereas the largest single group of sons in the present study had fathers who were professional workers, the largest contribution to professional workers among the sons in each of the other studies mentioned was made by fathers who were proprietors. In both the tendency to move further from their fathers' occupational level than white males and in a heavier concentration on the professions, Negro professional workers demonstrate a pattern which resembles that reported in studies of second-generation immigrants.

An examination of the occupations of the paternal grandfathers was carried out to gain a picture of intergenerational mobility. As may be expected, the occupations of a large number of the grandfathers were not known. This was true for approximately two-fifths of the grandfathers. For those for whom occupations were reported, there were more blue-collar than white-collar workers. One-quarter of the grandfathers were farmers, and this percentage is larger than the combined percentages for the professional, proprietor, and clerical categories. It is important to point out, however, that the grandfathers were superior in occupational terms to their Negro contemporaries in the labor force. Though most of them were manual workers, they were likely to be at the top of the occupational level in which they were found: there were more skilled than unskilled workers, and a larger number were farm owners than farm laborers and tenants.

It is clear from these data that the respondents of the present study came from families in which both their fathers and grandfathers were superior to their respective contemporaries in occupational terms. The intergenerational changes indicate that the development of a professional structure on a significant scale occurred in the fathers' generation, which coincided with the migration of Negroes to urban areas in large numbers. The formation of these large aggregations provided the economic base to support a substantial corps of professional workers. Only 13 per cent of the grandfathers

Negro males as late as 1950. (The respondents' mothers were high school graduates.) The median income of the respondents' families was $2,280, a figure far above that of Negro family income at the time the respondent was ready for college, about 1922, and approximately equal to non-white family income in 1952 ($2,338).

The higher educational and financial status of the parents were important factors in influencing the social mobility experienced by the respondents. Interview data provide the basis for asserting that the respondents' parents encouraged

TABLE 3

MEDIAN SCHOOL YEARS COMPLETED BY SONS AND PERCENTAGES
ENTERING PROFESSIONAL AND WHITE COLLAR OCCUPATIONS
ACCORDING TO INCOME LEVEL OF FATHER*

CATEGORY (SONS)	INCOME LEVEL OF FATHER				
	Total	Under $1,499	$1,500–$2,999	$3,000–$4,999	$5,000 and Over
Educational level........	14.5	13.1	13.9	14.4	16.4
Professional.............	38.7	31.3	38.9	46.5	50.0
White Collar............	64.7	56.7	65.3	73.3	75.0

* Only the adult male siblings of the respondents are used, as the respondent represents a special case.

were professional workers as compared with 32 per cent of the fathers. Almost two-thirds of the respondents and their adult male siblings had entered professional work, and it is suggested that the sons of the respondents will be represented in the professions in an even larger proportion.

Factors Associated with Mobility

The higher social origin of the respondents was indicated not only by their fathers' and grandfathers' occupational levels, but in other ways as well. The fathers were superior to their contemporaries in both income and educational status. The fathers had eleven years of schooling, a median which placed them far above the average for males of their time and above that of the median for

their children to aspire to high-status occupations and provided support for their children's education, particularly at the college level.

Of crucial importance is the finding that the chance of a son for upward mobility improved with an increase in father's economic level. With each increase in father's income, there was a commensurate increase in the percentage of sons entering white-collar occupations and in their educational attainment, as shown in Table 3.

The financial status of the respondents' families permitted a substantial contribution by the parents to the costs of schooling, but it is clearly indicated that the respondents were obligated to meet much of the costs through their own efforts. While parents contributed approximately one-half of the costs of under-graduate education, they supplied only one-fourth of the financial needs of the respondents at the graduate or profes-sional level. Some variations existed in the patterns of the several professional groups, with the families of physicians supplying a larger portion of the educa-tional costs at both levels. (The families of physicians had the highest incomes.)

Respondents from the South had less financial support from parents than those from other regions, owing to the lower incomes of families in the South; but there is abundant evidence that Southern families made innumerable sacrifices to get for their children the necessary train-ing to qualify for professional careers. The subjects from the District of Colum-bia enjoyed most financial support as a result of their ability to live at home while attending school.

An analysis of the differences in status origins by age groups uncovered some variations in the relationship between the occupation of father and that of his son. Our youngest respondents—those under 35 years of age—showed character-istics which distinguished them from the eldest group, aged 50 and over. The youngest group came from families in which the father had a significantly high-er occupational status than was the case of the fathers of the oldest group. More-over, the fathers of the youngest subjects averaged eleven years of formal school-ing as compared with an average of nine years for the fathers of those aged 50 years and above. As may be expected, the youngest respondents enjoyed great-er financial support from parents in meet-ing the costs of their education. In all of the comparisons, the age group 35–49 oc-cupied an intermediate position between the oldest and youngest subjects. It would appear that the oldest respond-ents represented a group of self-made professional men who were highly mo-bile. Over time, there has been less mo-bility and the respondents remain nearer

to their fathers' occupational and educa-tional levels.

One final factor which was considered in the analysis of mobility was that of skin color. It has been generally con-ceded that most of the first generation of Negroes in high-status positions were of light complexion or mulattoes. Some stu-dents have contended that the position of the mulatto resulted from his superior mental endowment; others viewed the situation as resulting from the advan-tages which light-skinned persons en-joyed during the period of slavery when many of them were house servants or free persons. The opportunity for con-tacts with whites gave them a head start on other Negroes, particularly those of dark complexion. The literature refers to this situation as the mulatto hypothesis.

Recently, some students have con-tended that with the urbanization of the Negro population the early advantages enjoyed by the mulattoes in terms of oc-cupational status and education have dis-appeared, and that dark-skinned persons now occupy a larger proportion of the high-status positions in Negro life as color prejudices are reduced and oppor-tunities for education have increased. Our data permit an evaluation of the contention that the high-status positions were disproportionately occupied by light-skinned persons, and that over time more dark-skinned persons have entered these positions.

Most of the respondents were brown skinned, either light brown or dark brown in color. When the light brown persons were assigned to the category of those classed as light and the dark brown persons assigned to the dark group, the total population was significantly lighter (than darker) in color.

By dividing the respondents into age categories (under 35; 35–49; 50 and over) and studying the color composi-tion of these categories, it was found that significant color changes have occurred. The most marked change was the reduction in the number of persons who were either very light or very dark in complexion. Whereas the oldest group—50 years of age and over—had larger proportions of very light and very dark persons, the other age categories had larger numbers of persons of intermediate colors—light but not very light, brown but not very dark or black. The percentage of persons classed as light brown remained rather constant for the three age groups, with approximately one-third of the subjects falling in this color group. A picture of these changes, using the division of those 50 and over and those under that age, is given in Table 4.

Occupational Aspirations and Motivations

The concentration of the subjects upon the professions has been referred to in an earlier section. Approximately one-half of the subjects had given serious thought to careers in fields other than those in which they are presently at work. But, significantly, these other fields of work are nearly all on the professional level. There were some fields which some respondents had wished to enter, but which they felt did not offer Negroes good prospects for making a decent livelihood. Included among these fields were architecture, engineering, journalism, the

TABLE 4

PERCENTAGE DISTRIBUTION OF RESPONDENTS ACCORDING TO COLOR AND AGE GROUPS

| AGE OF RESPONDENTS | COLOR | | | | | | |
	Total	Very Light	Light	Light Brown	Brown	Dark Brown	Very Dark
50 and over..........	100.1	11.9	11.9	33.7	22.8	17.8	2.0
Under 50............	100.1	7.0	16.1	32.7	32.7	10.1	1.5
Difference.......	....	− 4.9	+ 42	− 1.0	+ 9.9	− 7.7	− 0.5

It would appear from these data that the professions are not selective of any particular color group. The significance of the observed changes are obviously related to color changes which are occurring in the Negro population, owing to the intermarriage of persons of different complexions. The dominant skin color in the Negro group is becoming brown as the percentages of those of extreme colors, either very light or very dark, are reduced.[7]

[7] The analysis would be more significant if good statistics on the color composition of the Negro group existed. It would then be possible to determine if the professional occupations had a disproportionate number of persons of any given color. Unfortunately, no such color statistics exist on the present population. The statistics on color collected by the Bureau of the Census from 1850 to 1920 have been subject to criticism.

arts, and research in the biological and physical sciences. There were other fields which some subjects wished to enter but from which they were dissuaded by family members or other persons in the field, or for which they did not have the financial resources with which to get the necessary qualifying training.

The choices of the subjects show the rather restricted definitions which this minority has of occupational careers which offer the prospect of prestige and security. A career as medical doctor is regarded as the most prestigeful occupation open to Negroes.

There is a clear indication that a number of influences operated to shape the career aspirations of the subjects. The interest of the subject in the nature of the work and the influences of family members and other persons in the field are listed as the most significant determinants. Financial return from work in the field is not mentioned often as a motivating influence, but there is abundant evidence that this is an important consideration in having the respondents aspire to careers in certain fields and to give little attention to work in other fields.

The motivational patterns vary somewhat for the different professions studied. Teachers, for example, are more highly motivated by an interest in the subject matter of a particular discipline—mathematics, philosophy, literature, etc. Lawyers have been more concerned with opportunities for service. A larger percentage of the lawyers, as compared with the other professional groups, are from the South and have witnessed untoward situations in race relations. The welfare interests of the lawyers are clearly established. Physicians and dentists have been encouraged in larger numbers than other professional subjects by members of their families. The complex of factors which influenced physicians and dentists was so similar in nature that an attempt was made to discover variables which differentiated these two groups.

Many parents wished to have their children enter the medical sciences, and medicine was preferred to dentistry. The primary goal in the medical sciences, then, was to have the subjects become physicians. One-third of the dentists report that they wanted to become medical doctors rather than dentists. The analysis uncovered a number of factors which distinguished between those who became physicians and those who entered dentistry.

There was a significant difference in the income of the parents of physicians and dentists, with the former having a higher mean income. While no difference existed in the financial support received by physicians and dentists at the college level, physicians received greater financial support at the professional level. The family structures of the two groups varied to some degree. In 77 per cent of the cases, both parents were present in the families of physicians up until the time respondent was ready for college as compared with a figure of 63 per cent for this factor among the dentists. Though the difference here is not statistically significant, it is suggested that the physician subjects may have received greater emotional support as well as heavier financial backing for their career aspirations.

The differences in support doubtless played a part in allowing the physician subjects to make their career choices rather earlier in life and to move toward the medical goal in an unfaltering manner. The same was not true of the dentists. Sixty-seven per cent of the physicians made their career choice before entering high school. In contrast, 61 per cent of the dentists made the decision to study dentistry sometime after high school—in college or after graduation from college. Statistically, the difference was highly significant. It was observed, further, that a larger number of dentists experienced interruptions in their educational programs, both between high school and college and between college and the entering of professional school.

There may be other, non-situational factors which serve to distinguish between the two groups. It is suggested that differential intelligence may, indeed, be one factor. In the present study, for example, physicians were found to have superior intelligence as measured by high school grades, which is accepted as a measure of this factor.

One cannot stress too strongly the roles of the family in influencing careers. The parents of some Southern respondents, for example, left the South and migrated to Border or Northern cities to have their children receive better educational opportunities than those provided in their local communities. In some cases, the same result was accomplished by having the children live with relatives in large Border or Northern cities. The parents of the Southern respondents showed a strong desire to have their children prepare for the independent professions and to work as self-employed professionals, rather than work in institutional positions. They did much to discourage their children from careers in law. In contrast to this intimate identification with their offspring, the families of Northern respondents showed an entirely different pattern.

The Career Profile

The career profile describes the high points in the familial, educational, and occupational background of the respondents. Some attention already has been given to certain family and occupational characteristics. We are here concerned with detailing other characteristics relating to educational and job experiences.

The average subject was graduated from a public high school and went almost immediately to college. Four out of five subjects followed this pattern. Of those experiencing some interruption at this point, one-half of them remained out of school for only one year. The undergraduate degree was completed at 23 years of age, and the professional degree was received by the time the subject was 28 years old. Only slightly more than one-half of the respondents entered professional school immediately following the completion of the college degree or pre-professional work. The mean number of years out of school for the entire group at this point was 2.2 years. The subject began work in his chosen profession at 30 years of age and was likely to remain at work in the field once he had entered it.

As for most of the factors studied, some variation was discovered for the several groups. Teachers, for example, showed a different pattern once college work had been completed. They began their professional work earlier than other subjects and were likely to continue their training at periodic intervals. Most teachers had a master's degree, which was taken at approximately 27 years of age. Those who took the doctorate were 33 years old when the degree was received.

The subjects of this study had an average of three jobs since the time they were sixteen years of age, all of which were held for a period of eight months or more. The last regular job has been held for an average period of twelve years. The subjects married at 27.5 years of age, just prior to the completion of their professional training. Their wives were college graduates. As indicated elsewhere, they have one child.

SUGGESTIONS FOR FURTHER RESEARCH

As the present study considers only four professional fields, certain fields not covered should be investigated if one is to develop a more complete picture of the professional structure of the Negro community. The clergy constitutes a notable omission and should become the subject of objective investigation. It was the single most important professional group in Negro life in the generation following the emancipation and maintained high prestige for a long period thereafter. With the urbanization of the Negro population and the opening up of opportunities in other professional fields on a larger scale, the clergy lost some of its prestige. There is evidence today, however, that the clergy is recouping some of its lost prestige and is beginning to attract larger numbers of recruits of high level talent. The group is sufficiently important to become the subject of a major study.

Since the close of World War II, Negroes have entered certain professional fields in large numbers. This is true of social work in which a considerable number worked prior to the war, but in which their numbers have increased markedly. In certain other fields, where formerly there was limited representation, the number of Negroes has increased on a significant scale. This is true of architecture, engineering, and the biological and natural sciences. The increases in social work are the result in large part of the expansion of social services by governments, federal and local, and to the further professionalization of social work as a field, so that it has become more attractive as an area of employment in terms of salary and other conditions of work. The technological areas—architecture and engineering—and the biological and physical sciences have expanded markedly since World War II as a result of the boom in the construction industry and urban redevelopment, the emphasis on national defense connected with the cold war, and a greater support of scientific research. The demand for trained personnel in these areas has exceeded the available supply. Much of the work conducted in these fields has been supported in part by government funds and is covered by fair employment or non-discrimination contracts. Under these conditions, Negroes are finding careers in these areas open to them.

As many of the changes mentioned in the preceding paragraph have occurred since the end of World War II, they are to be understood in the context of the changing pattern of race relations. The group which has entered the professions in recent years doubtless has different occupational perspectives from most of the respondents in the study reported in this chapter. The inclusion of careers in the foreign service among possible careers today indicates the extent to which these perspectives have changed. A study of this most recent group of Negroes to enter professional fields against the background of what is known of earlier groups of Negroes in the professions should indicate the extent to which changes observed in the study reported have occurred on an even broader scale. A comparative study with whites entering the professions should reveal the extent to which convergence is occurring in occupational selection and training patterns as a result of the broader occupational opportunities for Negroes and the availability of substantially more fellowships and other forms of financial assistance.

It is interesting to observe in this connection that large numbers of Negroes in medicine remain in training after the medical degree is received and become specialists at the earliest possible time, a pattern which is typical among whites. Whereas there were only 92 Negro members of medical specialty boards in 1947, by 1959 the number had increased to 377, most of whom, 358, were living and represent graduates since 1947. The new opportunities open to them for residency training as well as the prospect of finding a field of service for their specialty training are contributing factors to this development. In 1959, the 74 medical graduates of the Howard University School of Medicine took their internships in 33 different hospitals; only 13 graduates were doing their internships in Negro hospitals. The 67 graduates of Meharry Medical College took their internships in 29 different hospitals; only 18 of these graduates were serving internships in Negro hospitals.[8]

Methodological Considerations

The restricted focus of this study of one community imposes a limitation on the interpretations which may be drawn from the findings. Communities differ in their objective characteristics and historical processes which, taken together, give to each a certain uniqueness. It is quite obvious that some replication of the present study is indicated, particularly in the large metropolitan centers. An understanding of the evolution of a professional structure among Negroes, and of the

8 These figures are taken from the *Journal of the Negro Medical Association*, LI, No. 4 (July, 1959), 314–17.

vertical mobility experienced by Negro persons entering the professions, should include professional persons located in communities of smaller sizes as well.

Many of the larger objectives of a study of this kind could be achieved by investigation of a cross-section of the Negro profesional population of the entire country. The selection of a sample for such a study would include all of the major professional occupations in which Negroes are found and would cover a range of communities of different sizes. Ideally, a projected national study should be developed on a comparative basis, so that comparable information would be collected on samples of the native white population and on other minorities— Jews, Italians, etc.—for the occupations studied. The logic of such a design is clear. It would eliminate the type of comparison, made by necessity in the present study, in which the subjects were compared with professional respondents in studies reported by others. As previously pointed out, these other studies were conducted in different communities and were reported for slightly different periods, generally about a decade before the present study.

Some students have pointed out that the extent and direction of vertical mobility is a function not only of personal and social factors, such as one's ambition or the occupation of one's father, but also of changes in the demand of the economy for workers of given types. Irrespective of personal qualities or the level of one's origin, the probability of movement, either upward or downward, is related to changes in the occupational structure. A recognition of changes in the demand factor is indispensable in comparing the mobility rates of different groups within the same society, two or more societies, or the same society at two different periods. In future studies, by employing schedule data which include questions on the occupations of the respondent's father and grandfather as well

as that of the respondent, the occupational changes represented in national censuses may be used to gain a measure of changes in the economic structure and thus to evaluate the demand factor.

While the observed pattern of mobility in the study reported in this chapter provides a picture of intergenerational occupational changes, our knowledge would be enriched if there were some method by which we could assess whether the observed changes were greater or less than should be expected on the basis of changes in the occupational structure of Negroes and of the country as a whole.

Mobility and Social Behavior

One major interest in the study of social mobility is the relationship of mobility to behaviorial correlates. While the study reported here did not have as one of its major objectives the analysis of the roles played by members of a highly mobile group, it is recognized that an analysis of the attitudes and values of persons belonging to the group would be of significance. Particular attention should be given to the behavior of those who are highly mobile vis-à-vis those who show less mobility.

Frazier[9] has furnished a lucid account of the changes in values and roles of members of the Negro middle class which came with the rapid urbanization of the Negro population and the related opportunities for mass education. The break with a past which was characterized by stable values resulted in the substitution of more superficial values as larger numbers achieved middle-class status. The excellent profile of the class provided by Frazier's account should be studied further with a view to accounting for variations within the class in terms of those who maintain much of the earlier traditional values of stable middle-class life as over against those whose value system incorporates more super-

[9] E. Franklin Frazier, *Black Bourgeoisie* (Glencoe: Free Press, 1957).

ficial attitudes and beliefs, and on a range of attitudes toward family life, economic values, religion, political behavior, and race relations.

The study of differential behavior between Negroes and other groups and of differences in attitudes and values within the Negro group inevitably would involve an investigation of the part played by the family as a mediator of larger community values and in the socialization of the young. The role of the family in conditioning the offspring for achievement levels and for the standards of personal and occupational conduct should be investigated for the light it would throw upon the variations observed among Negroes as well as on the observed differences between Negroes and other groups.[10]

Studies of New Elites

In one sense, the study reported in this chapter may be viewed as the process by which an occupational elite has been developed. To some extent, the same process is occurring elsewhere in other parts of the world, particularly in the so-called undeveloped and underdeveloped countries, where industrialization is expanding on a broad scale and, in some instances, where political independence recently has been won or is in process of being achieved. These political and industrial developments demand a larger corps of well-educated nationals. Recent statistics on foreign students in this country indicate a substantial increase in the number who are studying here. As recently as 1955, when systematic statistics were assembled for the first time, there

were 34,232 foreign students studying in American colleges and universities.[11] The number increased to 47,245 in 1958–59. Similar large increases are noted in the number of foreign faculty members and physicians at educational and medical institutions in this country.

It is clear that many, if not a majority, of these students do not come from advantaged classes in their home communities and thus are experiencing a considerable degree of mobility.[12] Support for this assertion is gained from the statistics on the pattern of financial support for meeting the costs of education. The largest single group among these students, 42 per cent, is self-supporting. Five per cent received their major support from their home governments, and another 5 per cent were supported mainly by the United States government. Only 28 per cent were privately supported; the remaining percentage received assistance from a combination of sources.

African students, the number of which increased from 351 in 1949[13] to 1,735 in 1958–59, are in great need of financial assistance in order to secure an education in this country. In 1958–59, for example, 27 per cent of them were receiving private grants, 26 per cent were the beneficiaries of foreign government awards, and 20 per cent were self-supporting. Owing in large part to the great surge of nationalistic sentiment in many areas of Africa, the governments of Africa were supporting a larger percentage of their students in this country through government awards than was true of gov-

---

[10] An undertaking of this type should be conducted on a comparative basis whenever possible. An interesting beginning on studies of this type already has been made. See, for example, Fred L. Strodtbeck, "Family Interaction, Values and Achievement," in Marshall Sklare (ed.), *The Jews* (Glencoe: Free Press, 1958), pp. 147–65; and Bernard C. Rosen, "Race, Ethnicity and Achievement," *American Sociological Review,* XXIV (February 1959), 47–60.

[11] The statistics reported in this section are taken from *Open Doors* (New York: Institute of International Education, May, 1959).

[12] The writer has had occasion to talk with large numbers of students from the British West Indies and Africa and has found that a preponderant majority of these students have lower middle-class origins.

[13] Ivor G. Cummings and Ruth Sloan, *A Survey of African Students Studying in the United States* (New York: Phelps-Stokes Fund, 1949).

ernments in any of the other major areas —the Far East, Latin America, etc.

Upon return to his home country, the foreign student is certain to have a high status as a result of his acquired skills and the prestige of study abroad. He will become a member of an occupational elite. His lower status origin vis-à-vis his status upon return poses many interesting questions regarding his personal and occupational conduct, his adjustment, and career development.[14]

Other Related Research

There are many other studies, related to the present investigation in diverse ways, which, if undertaken, would enhance our understanding of the process by which Negroes have developed a middle class. One greatly neglected area is the study of women in the professions.

Though Negro females have served as professional workers for many decades, they have been concentrated mainly in teaching. At the present time, larger numbers of Negro females are entering other fields of professional work: medicine, dentistry, law, science research, and some few are preparing for careers as architects and engineers. A study of their occupational perspectives, family backgrounds, patterns of educational support and career lives should reveal some interesting contrasts with males. The disappearance of many of the former restrictions upon female participation in many professional fields has not completely eliminated the role stresses which women experience in the world of work. In one sense, the investigation of the roles of women in the professions may be conceived of as a study of a new elite.

[14] The Social Science Research Council has sponsored a number of studies of the experiences of foreign students in this country and the adjustment of such students upon return to their home countries. It would appear from the available published reports that these studies have not given rigorous attention to the mobility factor.

Each of the major professions included in this study deserves more detailed investigation than the present study provides. Studies of a broader group of lawyers, for example, would confirm or invalidate the findings reported in this chapter, and would enlarge upon our understanding of current forces affecting Negroes in the legal profession. Whereas a generation ago Southern families discouraged their children from preparing for work in law, and few Negro lawyers practiced in Southern cities, the situation appears to have changed greatly in recent years. Many Negro lawyers are now locating in Southern cities.[15] Professions other than law are deserving of similar intensive study.[16]

One aspect of the formation of a Negro middle class which should be studied more intensively is the changing composition of the class in a number of cities. It has been observed in the present study that service and semiskilled occupations were the points of origin of many respondents who entered professional fields. At one period, persons in Negro life who worked in these occupations constituted a part of the "upper" or middle class and possessed the stable values to which Frazier has referred. With the broader opportunities for work in other areas, the composition of the class has changed, to some extent at least, and the professions have assumed much more importance as positions of prestige. Of great significance would be an evaluation of statuses by community members themselves and of the changes in the voluntary associations identified with class

[15] The graduates of the Howard University School of Law increasingly have located in Southern cities since World War II. I am informed that they are located in cities in every Southern state at the present time.

[16] Some professions have been studied in recent years. As an example of this work, see Daniel C. Thompson, "Teachers in Negro Colleges" (unpublished doctoral dissertation, Department of Sociology, Columbia University, 1956).

membership.[17] A study along this line would be of value in contributing knowledge of the impact made by urbanization upon the class structure of Negroes.

Finally, we need to know more of the personalities of those who enter given fields of work, and, as related more particularly to the present study, of the effects of mobility upon those who enter

[17] For a study in this vein, see, August Meier and David Lewis, "History of the Negro Upper Class in Atlanta, Georgia, 1890–1958," *Journal of Negro History*, XXVIII, No. 2 (Spring, 1959), 128–39.

the professions. One suggestion of our data which could not be followed in any detail was that those with the lowest-status origins often had more formal training than most of those whose families represented higher-status positions. Interviews with members of the former group suggested that marked uncertainties regarding their achieved status may be experienced. The interesting clinical work in the area of occupation selection may be applied to the study of minority group persons with profitable results.

PART 4

Urban Social Problems

The urban sociologist has found some of his most rewarding opportunities for empirical investigation through undertaking to do objective scientific research on social problems which either were unique to the city or were more prevalent or more severe in the city than in rural areas. In fact, the study of urban social problems has been a major driving force in the development of general sociology. Durkheim's study of suicide, as a reflection of urban social climate, or Thomas and Znaniecki's studies of personal disorganization of rural Polish peasant immigrants in the American urban community are familiar examples. Such basic sociological concepts as "attitude," "value," "anomie," "social distance," "marginal man," and "social solidarity" received their original formulation through the study of social problems of the city. Because urban social problems have often been so dramatic, so visible, and so acute, they have provided insights into social organization (through its breakdown, absence, or unusual pattern) which otherwise would not have been possible. We believe that a similar opportunity exists today, and that recent sociological research has not capitalized upon it as much as would have been desirable—both for the progress of the science and as a national service. Research on social problems can be basic fundamental scientific investigation; the researcher need not become a "do-gooder"; in fact, if he does, his research tends to suffer.

In this section we present samples of research contributions made in this tradition of using social crises to enlarge basic sociological knowledge, and to help build theory.

Writers undertaking to work out a systematic theoretical foundation for the study of social problems have tended to follow one of seven paths:

1. The social biology and individual organic pathology approach
2. The "social pathology" approach
3. The conflict of values approach
4. The deviant subculture approach
5. The social psychiatry approach
6. The social definition approach
7. The social interaction process approach

Limitations of space do not permit an exhaustive comparative treatment here of these approaches. The following notes are intended only to supply a context for the specific studies to be presented.

The social biology and individual organic pathology ("sick society" and "pathological person") approach.—By this view, social problems are presumed to be analogous to diseases. An organismic view of society underlies this approach,

255

which was popular in the nineteenth and first two decades of the twentieth century. Also allied to this view was the tendency to regard "problem" individuals (criminals, unwed mothers, etc.) as coming from biologically inferior stock or having a pathological body condition. Social problems were viewed as pathological conditions which afflicted the social body or the individual persons until appropriate treatment was administered. It was presumed that these disorders could be readily identified and catalogued and that few disagreements could arise concerning whether a given situation was pathological (a social problem) or normal (not a problem). Also, this view tended to assume that a specific "cure" could be found for each social ailment. Although this viewpoint is now no longer held as a basic theory, certain useful vestiges of its point of view remain. It declared that social problems were topics for scientific and objective study. It launched the "social survey" movement that emphasized objective fact-gathering about problems. It established the principle that scientific sociological research could produce knowledge which could be put to practical use by welfare workers to arrive at, improve, or remedy the conditions regarded as pathological. More than one sociologist still tends to use figures of speech and to draw analogies which reflect this outlook, even though as a complete explanation it is rejected.

The "social pathology" (social disorganization) approach.—The formulation of this approach, and its gradual elaboration into the status of a comprehensive theory of social change and social problems is one of the major accomplishments of the University of Chicago during the 1920's and early 1930's. It begins with the presumption that a social problem is a malady of society, but that *it is social rather than organismic processes that are deranged and in a pathological state.* It rejects the organismic analogy and declares that there are characteristic processes and interactions whereby individuals are socialized and social control and community organization is maintained. Whenever these processes and interactions are deflected and where morals and customs are violated, social problems arise. On the one hand individuals are incompletely or differentially socialized and on the other hand social solidarity and social control are weakened, so that both personal and social disorganization results. This theory was found to be highly useful in explaining many urban social problems. Burgeoning American cities were filled with migrants who had been released from old and established customs and definitions in their home communities, and who were relocated in a context where a new social organization and forms of social control had not yet been firmly established. The city was regarded as a type of human community where social organization was literally inadequate and incomplete, and hence where disorganization was common. Social problems could be regarded as a side effect of social change, and something that would tend to disappear as social reorganization (accommodation and assimilation) progressed.

A most important aspect of this theory, sadly neglected in much of the current writing, is an appreciation of the role which economic hardship and poverty (both absolute and comparative deprivation) play in social situations in creating intergroup strife, conflict, and disorganization.

This approach differed from the social biology approach in several fundamental ways. It identified the forces that tend to create social problems, and likened renewed social solidarity and re-establishment of social control as the sociological analogy of healing. It recognized that to each social problem a variety of solutions were possible—so long as they were collectively accepted. It recognized the fundamental role which tradition, customs, and mores play in community organization and in community problems. It warned that quick and easy "cures" would not be found, but that community-wide adoption of a new "definition of the situation" was the only long-range remedy for a condition of social pathology. It emphasized the internal conflict within the individual person caught in problem situations, and pointed out that much mass behavior is only an interaction between the persons involved and the larger society. The result is to create a feeling of profound uneasiness and awareness that the group is not in good "social health."

All of the remaining viewpoints draw to some extent upon this formulation. Most of them tend to select some particular aspect of it and give it greater emphasis, while not denying the general validity of the social disorganization approach.

The principal deficiency of this theory, in the light of a quarter-century of research and experience with it, is that although it is valid it is not exhaustive, and does not cover fully all social problems. Also, it is too broad and long-range to be used as a foundation for detailed research on specific propositions. Moreover, it implies that disorganization or lack of clear cultural directives is always pathological. It offers few suggestions for experiments concerning what types of deliberate intervention could be effective in reducing the severity of social problems— or where in the social organization such intervention would yield the greatest returns.

The conflict of values (anomie) approach.—This view emphasizes the cultural element in social organization and explains how social pathology and social disorganization come about. It holds that in the urban setting many cultures are brought into contact with each other, with the result that old and established customs and definitions cease to command adherence and exercise social control. Persons become familiar with two or more value systems, and feel loyalty or moral obligation to no one system. The result is comparative normlessness, and ego-centered and highly diverse behavior. Social problems arise because individuals are able to pursue their private goals with little concern for social rules or the welfare of a community with which they feel identified.

The cultural change approach is not inconsistent with the social disorganization approach, instead, it amplifies one aspect of it—the great importance for social order of possessing a set of culturally transmitted elements, which comprise an integrated and internally consistent set. It is not a complete theory, however, because it pays comparatively little attention to the nature of the forces that induce cultural elements into contact (and hence conflict) with each other.

The deviant subculture approach.—This approach is also cultural. It emphasizes that much of deviant behavior is nevertheless social behavior, performed by groups of persons acting in conformity with values that are at variance with those of the larger society. Delinquency, for example, is interpreted not as socially disorganized behavior, but as the activity of highly organized social groups acting in conformity with a set of values and norms of youth subculture having delinquency norms. Although this viewpoint is implicit in the social disorganzation theory, and is a logical extension of it, this insight is a powerful way of viewing social problems in their full-blown state. It recognized that the social problem itself has a set of social processes whereby it is perpetuated and transmitted, and that tradition, social control, and social organization characterize the deviant group as well as the "normal" groups. Certain passages from the works of Shaw and Burgess adumbrate this viewpoint, but it was not until such works as *Delinquent Boys: The Culture of the Gang* (1955) by Albert K. Cohen, that it became elevated to the level of systematic and integrated theory.

The social psychiatry approach.—This view has perhaps best been stated by Jessie Bernard in *Social Problems at Midcentury: Role, Status, and Stress in a Context of Abundance* (1957). "The central thesis of our study is that the pervasive motif of social problems has changed from concern with mere survival, poverty and dependency—to concern with the malfunctions of role and status. The principal form that suffering takes in a context of abundance is not physical pain, but anxiety." By this view, social problems are situations and conditions that cause anxiety and tensions within individuals. The remedy is tension reduction by mass social psychiatry, and by inducing social changes that remove the causes of tension.

This viewpoint also is a most valuable, even if incomplete, one. It calls attention more powerfully to the individual personality, the impact of social problems upon individuals, and the internal conflicts within persons which are generated by them. It does emphasize the fact that suffering from social problems is mental as well as physical. It is inadequate as a comprehensive theory, because the focus upon individuals fails to emphasize the role which social change, cultural reorganization, and social processes play in the reduction of anxiety-producing and tension-producing situations. Mass social psychiatry probably will not be the long-range solution to many problems situations. Instead of learning to adjust to a particular social situation as "given," by collective action people often change the situation itself.

The social definition ("definition-by-society") approach.—This viewpoint is purely pragmatic; a condition, a situation, or an activity is not a social problem until it is defined as a social problem by the group, and there is collective unrest and dissatisfaction concerning it. "Until an impelling aspiration for freedom has been kindled among slaves, slavery is not an active social problem," say Earl Raab and Gertrude Selznick in *Major Social Problems* (1959). This view performs the very important service of calling attention to the collective behavior aspect of social problems, and in the solution of social problems being arrived at through groups generating a new set of social definitions and social controls to gain compliance to the definitions.

The social interaction process approach.—This approach to social problems flows directly from the "interaction" theory of society, which the Chicago school of sociology has sponsored. It is sufficiently inclusive to encompass, as special cases, all of the sociological viewpoints described above, and yet adds additional insights and avenues for research of its own. This view is based on the recognition that personality and society both are products of social interaction, and that they exist and maintain their integrity only because of continued interaction. As quickly as these processes are suspended or interrupted, social disorganization sets in and personality begins to deteriorate. Since this interaction is always and everywhere adaptive, the social processes are continuously in a state of change—varying from minor shifts to major alterations. Adaptations of a major type tend to be formalized into mores, institutions, and culture and transmitted as right. Yet changing environmental conditions and the forces imposed by contact with other groups necessitate continually renewing social change and readjustment. In such a situation, it is natural and inevitable that social problems will emerge. It is natural and inevitable that in the collective efforts of unadjusted groups to arrive at new adjustments that subcultures should arise, and that some of these subcultures will be inimical to the major culture. It is also inevitable that during such periods there will be great anxieties and tensions—whether the society is affluent or poverty stricken. It is also inevitable that the larger society will sense its problems and will define the situation of maladjustment as being of communal concern.

This theory is unspecific concerning the origin of maladjustments, because these origins may vary. They may be environmental, as with the exhaustion of a basic resource. They may be technological, as with the invention of a new mode of production. They may arise from new contact and interaction with another culture. They could result from a new intellectual orientation, as with the rising level of education or the adoption of a rational instead of mystical view of the world. Whatever the source, it may be expected that there will be maladjustment, unrest, incompatible "definitions of the situation" and deviant behavior until the problem is resolved by a process of interaction. This interaction may involve conflict as well as accommodative behavior.

15. *Catholic Family Disorganization**

JOHN L. THOMAS

The study of family disorganization among members of a religious minority necessarily proceeds on the assumption that religious convictions will affect the family values, standards, and practices of its adherents in some measure. To be specific, since the Catholic system teaches that the family is founded on a sacramental contract characterized by perpetuity, indissolubility, and mutual fidelity, while marriage furnishes the only institutional framework within which the sexes may fully develop their mutual complementarity, we may validly assume that the beliefs and practices of Catholics related to sex and marriage will be vitally influenced by their religion.

Viewed against the backdrop of contemporary religious pluralism, many aspects of Catholic family disorganization will appear unique and specific, consequently justifying separate study and analysis. For example, belief in the indissolubility of the sacramental bond should be reflected in serious intent to preserve marital unity. Catholic teaching on the nature and purposes of sex can be expected to influence courtship patterns, as well as attitudes toward infidelity and family planning. Interfaith marriages will probably reveal some incompatibility in family goals and standards, with consequent loss of unity. Moreover, the diversity and varied degrees of ethnic solidarity so characteristic of the Catholic minority in this country may provide added sources of stress and strain in intergroup marriages and even

*Based upon the author's Ph.D. dissertation of the same title, Sociology, 1949.

between partners of the same national origin, since the process of acculturation does not proceed uniformly among all members of an ethnic group.

American Catholics may encounter special problems from other sources. Their families are predominantly urban and consequently experience the full impact of the extensive social changes characterizing contemporary society. Further, as members of a religious minority embracing a distinctive set of beliefs related to marriage and family life, they must work out their adjustments within a framework of values many elements of which are based on theological and philosophical premises not generally accepted in the dominant culture. Moreover, since family values have functional exigencies, that is, their continued realization in a given social milieu requires the support of related institutions and practices, Catholic families are subjected to additional strain, for a loosely integrated, pluralistic society is likely to furnish little of this requisite support.

THE PROBLEM

The present research was designed to obtain a general overview of disorganized Catholic marriages and the major factors related to their disruption. Hence the study has a broadly exploratory purpose, aimed both at furnishing useful information to marriage counselors and family life leaders, and at delimiting the field of broken Catholic marriages for future researchers. In line with this general consideration, we formulated several hypotheses. First, we assumed that since the Church teaches the indissolubility of

261

marriage, Catholic couples would seek a separation only for serious reasons and after making considerable effort to adjust. Second, we wished to test the contention that mixed marriages are less stable than others. Third, because a preliminary study of the data indicated that about 20 per cent of the couples had entered marriage under obviously unpropitious circumstances, we advanced the hypothesis that such cases must be considered separately if study of the relevant factors in marital breakdown among average couples was to prove useful. Fourth, pertinent characteristics of the couples studied were compared with the findings of other researchers, in an attempt to evaluate the relevance of some commonly held assumptions.

In presenting the major findings of our study, we shall proceed as follows. After discussing the source and nature of our data, we shall sketch a general view of the marriages in terms of ethnic background, type of marriage, length of acquaintance and engagement, age at marriage, number of children, duration, and source of petition for separation. This description will be followed by an analysis of the factors related to the breakdown, considering first the major group (roughly 80 per cent) constituted by couples apparently representative of the general average; and second, the several categories of non-typical cases requiring separate treatment according to our hypothesis. In the final section, we shall reconsider our initial assumptions and conclude with a brief evaluation of pertinent findings.

DISORGANIZED FAMILIES

According to Catholic teaching, spouses are obliged to make every possible effort to succeed in their marriages; consequently, if they petition Church authorities for permission to separate, we may conclude that their maladjustments are serious and their marriages have proved unsuccessful. Hence, in selecting such cases for study, we know we are dealing with truly disorganized families. To be sure, this approach does not uncover all cases of family disorganization among Catholics. Some couples may ignore religious norms and have direct recourse to civil divorce courts. More important, the failure to seek separation is not necessarily indicative of happiness and success in marriage. Despite the widespread social acceptance of separation and divorce, various religious and cultural values are still effective in keeping many couples from such action. As one cynic has remarked, there are many types of marriage: trial, conditional, and fight-to-the-finish!

Source of the Data

The couples we studied were members of the Chicago Archdiocese, which included at that time roughly the entire Chicago Metropolitan Area. The Chancery Office of the Archdiocese maintains a marriage separation court, staffed by twenty delegate judges with training in both canon law and marriage counseling.[1] Catholic couples seeking marital separation must appeal to this court, and since failure to do so involves severe religious sanctions, we may assume that all but nominal Catholics will comply with the Church's regulations in this regard. During the years 1942 to 1948, approximately seven thousand couples petitioned the court for separations. Out of this total we selected a representative sample of two thousand cases for intensive study.

The separation court maintains relatively complete case histories of all the couples interviewed by its judges. From

---

[1] The Church may deal with petitions for marital separation in one of two ways: either the bishop makes the decision through an administrative decree; or the petitions are submitted to a regular judicial procedure in which both parties are cited and their case is heard by a judge or several judges.

these records we obtained the following information: name, address, religion, parish, occupation of breadwinner, date, place and officiant at marriage, length of acquaintance and engagement, age at marriage, duration of marriage, number of children, source of petition for separation, and finally, the factors judged relevant to the breakdown of the marriage.

Reliability of Data

The separation court is not comparable to a civil divorce court. The judges seek to effect a reconciliation whenever possible, and the couples are aware that the court is not competent to deal with the marriage bond, so there is no question of obtaining freedom to remarry. Furthermore, in appearing before the court the partners are seeking a spiritual good that depends on their honesty in giving testimony. If they did not value their religion, they would simply bypass the court, as some couples apparently do. Hence, there appear no valid reasons for doubting either their good intentions or honesty in most cases.

On the other hand, one may well question the ability of spouses to give adequate and pertinent testimony concerning a situation that normally involves their emotions so deeply. However, granted that most couples contemplating separation may lack sufficient insight to analyze their difficulties competently, the judges who conduct the interviews are skilled in handling such problems and usually succeed in uncovering the principal factors contributing to the breakdown. It should be noted, however, that in a certain number of cases, the records throw little light on the basic sources of the maladjustment, and the labels "incompatibility" or "clash of temperaments" serve to cover a multitude of problems. Nevertheless, taken as a whole, these records furnish valuable information concerning major trouble spots among Catholic families.

Are They Representative?

Because we have only limited information concerning the Catholic minority in this country, it is difficult to determine the extent to which the population from which our cases were drawn is representative of the total group. There are sound reasons for believing that it resembles the major portion. Catholics in the Chicago Archdiocese are primarily urban; they are a minority—though a relatively large one (40 per cent); they are fairly typical of American industrial centers in ethnic composition as judged by the percentage of foreign-born; and they are characterized by a mixed-marriage rate (20 per cent) somewhat below the national average (25–30 per cent), but apparently similar to other industrial areas that include relatively large concentrations of ethnics.[2]

COUPLES IN TROUBLE

The following sections will describe briefly the major pertinent characteristics of Catholic couples who applied to the separation court. Since previous studies have uncovered a number of conditions and traits that proved significant for adjustment, a comparison of our findings with these studies may throw some light on why these couples failed.

Length of Acquaintance before Marriage

From the data presented in Table 1 we learn that over 17 per cent of our couples were acquainted for less than six months and nearly 45 per cent for one year or less. However 36 per cent were acquainted for over three years. To test the significance of these findings, we studied the association between duration of marriage and length of acquaintance. Well over one out of five of the

[2] For further information on ethnic solidarity and mixed marriages, see John L. Thomas, S.J., *The American Catholic Family* (Englewood Cliffs, N.J.: Prentice-Hall, Inc., 1956), pp. 107–26.

couples acquainted for six months or less before they married broke up within the first year of marriage. Since this was almost double the percentage of those who were acquainted for longer periods, and the latter represented a relatively uniform pattern, we may conclude that an acquaintance of less than six months is predictive of marital discord.

TABLE 1

DISTRIBUTION OF CASES ACCORD-
ING TO LENGTH OF
ACQUAINTANCE

Length of Acquaintance	Percentage
Less than 3 months....	6.6
3 to 6 months.........	11.0
7 to 12 months........	27.0
1 to 3 years...........	19.2
Over 3 years..........	36.2

Length of Engagement

For purposes of our study we take engagement to mean a formal agreement to marry plus some external symbol in the form of a ring or announcement. Table 2 shows that over one-third of the

TABLE 2

DISTRIBUTION OF CASES ACCORD-
ING TO LENGTH OF
ENGAGEMENT

Length of Engagement	Percentage
No engagement........	35.6
Less than 3 months....	14.3
3 to 6 months.........	20.2
7 to 12 months........	22.1
Over one year.........	7.7

couples had not been formally engaged, and an additional one-third for six months or less. Although these apparently unfavorable engagement characteristics may be significant, we lack comparable information on the total Catholic population from which our cases were drawn. A comparison between the couples who reported no engagement and others uncovered few differences, with the exception of "forced" marriages, 70 per cent of which revealed no engagement.

Age of Spouses at Marriage

Research on the relationship between marital adjustment and age at marriage suggests that early marriages, that is, under 19 or 20 for the bride and under 22 years for the groom, are closely associated with subsequent unhappiness. In analyzing this relationship, one may regard early marriage as a symptom of emotional instability or as a causal factor directly affecting the marital situation. Moreover, since many "forced" marriages involve relatively young couples, the possibility of this additional disrupting factor must be carefully weighed in any realistic discussion of early marriages.

TABLE 3

DISTRIBUTION OF CASES ACCORDING
TO AGE AT MARRIAGE

Age at Marriage	Husband	Wife
Under 18 years.......	.6	7.0
Under 19 years.......	2.8	17.7
Under 20 years.......	6.7	28.7
Under 21 years.......	13.0	39.6
Under 23 years.......	32.7	59.5
Under 25 years.......	51.9	73.2
Under 27 years.......	68.0	83.0
Under 30 years.......	80.6	90.5
Under 35 years.......	91.7	95.8

A study of the relationships between age at marriage and marital duration lent some support to the hypothesis that couples who marry relatively late find adjustment in the first years of marriage most difficult. Over 50 per cent of the cases in which the husband married after thirty broke up within the first five years, while only a little over one-third of the cases involving husbands who married between the ages of 20 and 25 failed in the first five years, and roughly 40 per cent endured for more than ten years. When the bride was past thirty at marriage, slightly more than 57 per cent of the cases did not survive the first five years, whereas among the cases in which the bride was between 20 and 25, all but 38.5 per cent weathered this initial period. On the other hand, a study of the relationship between age at marriage and the factors involved in the breakdown gave some support to the belief that early marriages face special problems. The rate of infidelity among wives decreased from 8.5 per cent for brides at 18 or younger to 0.7 per cent for those marrying after thirty. Among the grooms, the percentages ran from 25.5 per cent for those married at 20 years or younger to 11 per cent for those marrying after thirty. Also, marked irresponsibility was most likely to appear as a disruptive factor when the groom was under 23 or the bride under 21.

Husband's Occupation

The relationship between occupational status and marital stability is generally assumed in the literature, though so many other variables are involved that the precise nature of the relationship is far from clear. We used a seven-way breakdown of occupations for our data: (1) Dependents—no acceptable, regular employment; (2) Day laborers—jobs requiring no special training; (3) Semiskilled—jobs requiring some training; (4) Skilled—jobs requiring skill and experience; (5) Lower white-collar—jobs not primarily manual but requiring moderate education and skill; (6) Upper white-collar—jobs requiring considerable education, experience, and mental capacity; (7) Professional—jobs requiring professional training.

According to Table 4, the heaviest concentration of breadwinners is found in the "day laborers" category, while approximately 75 per cent are classified as "blue-collar" workers. Judged on the basis of occupation alone, it appears that only about 10 per cent of the couples would rank as upper class. Although we have only rough estimates of the socioeconomic status of the total Catholic

population, considering that we are dealing exclusively with urban Catholics, it appears that our findings do not differ significantly from national estimates.[3] Further, since our cases involve separation rather than divorce, we may expect a somewhat heavier representation among the semiskilled and day-labor categories than is usually found in studies of divorce, for the rate of separation has been found to be relatively high among the lower blue-collar classes.

TABLE 4

DISTRIBUTION OF HUSBANDS ACCORDING TO OCCUPATIONAL CLASS

Occupational Class	Percentage
Dependent	1.0
Day labor	26.8
Semiskilled	24.0
Skilled	22.9
Lower white-collar	15.3
Upper white-collar	8.6
Professional	1.2

Number of Children

During the period under consideration, the current baby boom was just getting under way, so that the various factors producing it probably had little influence on the size of the disorganized families we studied. Estimates gathered from the inadequate divorce statistics available in 1948 indicate that roughly 60 per cent of divorced couples had no minor children, while frequency of divorce varied inversely with the number of children under age 18 in the family; thus, for childless couples the divorce rate was 15.3 per 1,000 married couples, and 11.6, 7.6, 6.5, and 4.6 for one, two, three, and four or more children in the family, respectively.

The findings in Table 5 are not quite comparable to studies based on divorce court records because our data included children of all ages. Even when allowance is made for this possible source of

[3] For a summary of current estimates, see *The American Catholic Family*, pp. 134–38.

difference, it appears that the cases studied reflect the general tendency of Catholic couples to have a somewhat higher birth rate than others. At any rate, Table 5 indicates that a large number of children are involved in broken Catholic marriages, inasmuch as well over one-third of the couples had two or more children, and roughly one out of ten had four or more.

TABLE 5

DISTRIBUTION OF COUPLES AC-
CORDING TO NUMBER OF
CHILDREN

Number of Children	Percentage
No children	35.3
1 child	27.3
2 children	18.5
3 children	9.0
4 children	4.8
5 or more children	5.1

Duration of Marriage

Divorce statistics for the country as a whole indicate that about two-thirds of all divorces take place within the first ten years of marriage, while approximately two-fifths are granted to couples married for less than five years.

TABLE 6

DISTRIBUTION OF CASES ACCORD-
ING TO DURATION OF
MARRIAGE

Duration	Percentage
Less than 6 months	6.6
7 to 12 months	7.1
1 to 5 years	29.2
6 to 10 years	22.4
11 to 15 years	15.2
16 to 20 years	9.7
21 years and over	9.8

Table 6 indicates that our cases tend to follow the national pattern in this regard. Over 13 per cent separated before the end of the first year, roughly 43 per cent within the first five years, 65 per cent within the first ten, and only about one out of ten after 20 years. As we shall point out, the incidence of specific disintegrating factors varies considerably at each stage of the marriage.

Source of Petition

Over four-fifths of the petitions for separation were initiated by the wife. In civil divorce courts she appears as the plaintiff in about three out of four cases. Whatever may be the explanation of this distribution in civil divorce courts, our data suggest that among Catholic couples seeking permission to separate, it is the wife who feels the greatest need to have her changed marital status approved by the Church. Studies of mixed marriages indicate similar religious concern among Catholic women, inasmuch as they constantly outnumber men in seeking appropriate permission for such unions.

FACTORS RELATED TO MARRIAGE
BREAKDOWN

Marriage involves men and women in a set of uniquely intimate relationships calling for mutual adjustments and adaptations throughout the entire family cycle. Family disorganization obviously results from the failure of one or both partners to meet the demands of the situation. Although analysis of the functional exigencies of a given family system can reveal the general conditions normally conducive to marital success, it should be noted that some couples achieve happiness under circumstances that lead to disruption in others, so that it is not what happens but to whom it happens that seems most decisive. Evidently, if we had adequate criteria for measuring the potential of adaptability in couples, we could predict their success or failure in given situations. Lacking such criteria, we must be content to describe the conditions usually associated with family disorganization in a given cultural setting.

Particularly when analyzing the factors associated with marital failure, we must distinguish the conditions husbands and wives define as intolerable from those they regard as acceptable, though perhaps not wholly satisfactory. General knowledge of how a given culture defines the nature and purposes of marriage may prove helpful; but only an analysis of the factors affecting the decision to separate tells us how various groups really define the situation in this regard.

Finally, some students lightly dismiss factors like drink or infidelity as mere symptoms, apparently on the grounds that they do not constitute real "causes" of marital failure. This superficial view ignores the important fact that adjustment in marriage is a process, based on the intimate, continued interaction of partners within a more or less clearly defined framework of mutual expectations and goals. Partners may become involved in an "affair" or start drinking for any one of a number of reasons, but once this happens, the whole intricate web of marital and parental interaction is radically modified. The resulting tension and stress tend to further promote the deviant action of the offender and the disintegrating reaction of the spouse. Hence the symptomatic character of factors such as drinking and adultery is only one aspect to be considered. More important for the analysis of marital failure is how they affect adjustment by modifying the process of interaction within the family circle.

We have divided our cases into two broad groupings. The first, representing roughly 80 per cent of the cases, includes all the couples who entered marriage under apparently normal conditions. The second group contains marriages contracted under conditions or circumstances seemingly unpropitious to success. "War marriages," marriages in which the bride was pregnant, marriages in which children were absolutely excluded by one or both partners, and marriages of widows and/or widowers are placed in this group for separate treat-

ment. As later analysis reveals, marriages placed in the second group carry within themselves predisposing elements of instability, a point that the couples frequently noted during the interviews.

The following analysis is based on information gained from cases included in the first group. These represent what we consider typical maladjusted Catholic marriages. What factors started the chain of events that led to the disintegration of their unions, presumably founded on love between two people who apparently believed they were compatible and ready for marriage? Table 7 answers this ques-

TABLE 7

DISTRIBUTION OF CASES ACCORD-
ING TO DISINTEGRATING
FACTORS

Factors	Percentage
Drink	29.8
Adultery	24.8
Irresponsibility	12.4
Temperaments	12.1
In-laws	7.2
Sex	5.4
Mental illness	3.0
Religion	2.9
Money	0.8
Unclassified	1.7

tion on the basis of what we could learn from the interviews.

Drink and adultery, accounting for almost 55 per cent of the cases, appear as the most significant factors. Irresponsibility and clash of temperaments account for roughly one-fourth, while the remaining factors appear relatively less significant. We shall give a brief description of each factor and its major characteristics as they appeared in the interviews. Although one may not wholly agree with our system of classification, we believe that the factors described here reveal the chief marital problems the Catholic marriage counselor must deal with in practice.

Drink

In approximately 30 per cent of the cases excessive drinking appeared as the major disintegrating factor. When drinking occurs in the marital situation, it is generally associated either with nonsupport, abuse and cruelty, lack of companionship, or the suspicion of infidelity. Hence, in addition to excessive drinking, 37 per cent of the cases revealed lack of adequate support; an additional one-third, cruelty and abuse; and nearly one out of every five, the reasonable presumption of infidelity. Wives were guilty of excessive drinking in relatively few cases.

The majority of drinkers among our cases appeared to be periodic drinkers or "weekenders" rather than "alcoholics" as this term is usually defined. Most held fairly steady jobs but indulged heavily when not working. Husbands of Irish and Polish extraction were overrepresented, as were members of the blue-collar occupations. Drinking tended to be accompanied with infidelity among white-collar workers, but was generally associated with non-support and abuse among the lower occupational groups. These separations involved more children than any other category. Only 19 per cent were childless, while the remainder constituted roughly 36 per cent of the two- and three-child families, 54 per cent of the couples with four children, and 42 per cent of those with five or more children.

Adultery

In approximately one-fourth of the cases, family dissolution was precipitated by adultery. The husband was the transgressor in four out of every five cases. Because infidelity strikes at the very essence of marital solidarity as it has come to be defined in our culture, it is frequently very difficult to uncover the chain of circumstances leading up to the transgression. However, an analysis of the interviews suggests that it is superficial to regard all instances of adultery merely as symptoms of marital frustration. Some members of society evidently find monogamy both trying and monotonous; and, if the opportunity arises, they readily become involved in extramarital affairs.

The incidence of adultery among our cases was found to be relatively low among Polish husbands, Italians of both sexes, and Irish wives. Since we are studying only couples seeking separation, this finding may be indicative either of a low total rate of incidence or a high rate of tolerance. The white-collar classes were overrepresented, and though the number of children involved was not as great as in cases involving drink, the birth rate tended to be high. Age at marriage appeared to be significant. When the husband was the offender, the highest incidence occurred among those who were under 25 years old at marriage, while infidelity among wives decreased in direct relation to their age at marriage. However, when interpreting these findings, we should recall that opportunities for infidelity tend to decrease somewhat with age in our society.

Irresponsibility

Approximately one out of every eight cases was classified as irresponsible or immature. This category includes all marriages in which one or both partners displayed marked inability or unwillingness to accept the responsibilities of marriage as defined by the Church and society. The manifestations of this trait ranged from desertion to complete unawareness of the most obvious implications of the marriage contract. Some of the partners dated others within a few weeks after marriage, some spent little time in the company of their spouses, and many appeared both intellectually and morally shallow. A high percentage were found in the unskilled occupational class, suggesting that they were little inclined to acquire training or accept responsibility.

Most married at a relatively early age, and though there were many one-child families, there were few large ones.

The study of their interviews raises more questions than it answers. The reasons for the breakdown are usually apparent enough: the husband doesn't come home until late at night, he gambles his earnings away, he spends all his time with the "boys," he leaves home for days at a time; or, the wife is a hopeless housekeeper, she spends her time in the local tavern, she wants a good time without responsibilities, and so forth. Are we dealing with basic personality defects? Are these the products of poor family training? Or are they the refuse, the victim-products of our complex civilization? Neither the case records nor the available literature on the subject explains how people "get that way."

Temperaments

Incompatibility is the term usually employed to cover the approximately 12 per cent of our cases included in this category. We felt that a clash of temperaments was really involved, and since the term incompatibility is currently used to designate nearly all forms of maladjustment, we preferred to avoid it. A careful study of these marriages disclosed many traits predictive of success. The couples were responsible, relatively successful in their work, and apparently quite capable of meeting the economic and social demands of marriage. Yet they found it impossible to get along together. During the interviews there were frequent accusations of jealousy, "mental" cruelty, queerness, lack of considerateness, selfishness, "meanness," and so on, but further questioning revealed that these were highly relative terms, and it was usually admitted that in themselves they were not sufficient to explain the frequent quarrels and clashes. Many of the partners displayed a peculiar discontent either with life in general or with almost everything in their marriage. Among the older couples, trouble tended to develop after the children were raised and life in the "empty nest" revealed how widely the partners had grown apart during the early years.

A marked disparity of age may have played some part in the maladjustment noted among these couples, since approximately 30 per cent of the husbands were more than six years older than their wives. The skilled and lower-class white-collar groups were overrepresented here, and considering that social mobility tends to be relatively high among these classes, failure of the partners to share equal social aspirations may account for some of the conflicts. Most of the marriages endured for some time, suggesting that temperamental differences became sources of conflict only after initial marital relationships had been modified. In other words, at some stage in the marriage, either one or both partners became unwilling or incapable of the adjustments routinely required by cohabitation.

In-Laws

Problems related to in-laws probably account for more jokes than any other aspect of marriage. The mother-in-law theme, in particular, provides an inexhaustible source of questionable humor. Our findings indicate that the majority of in-laws are not out-laws, since in only a little over 7 per cent of our cases did in-law problems emerge as the chief source of conflict. Further analysis of the data also reveals that the charge of in-law interference sometimes appears as a *post factum* rationalization or is founded on a distorted view of normal extended family relationships.

The wife's in-laws figure in 47.7 per cent of our cases; the husband's, in 38.33 per cent; and in-laws of both, in 14 per cent. The mother-in-law was mentioned as the sole interfering relative by approximately 39 per cent of the couples. Partners of Polish or Italian descent were overrepresented and at about the same rate for in-group and out-group marriages. This suggests that the traditional extended family system characteristic of these two national minorities creates special problems of adjustment in our society. Members of the white-collar classes reported in-law conflicts somewhat more frequently than others. Although there was a housing shortage during the war years, "living-in" with relatives appeared as the source of difficulties in only 9.5 per cent of the cases.

In-law problems assume disruptive proportions primarily in the early years of marriage. Almost one-fourth broke up within the first year, two-thirds within the first five years, and only 16 per cent lasted longer than ten years. In line with this duration pattern, 42 per cent of the couples were childless, 37.4 per cent had one child, while only 8.5 had three or more children. We conclude that serious in-law problems appear early in marriage, and if not quickly resolved, readily lead to failure.

Sexual Incompatibility

Although failure to achieve mutually satisfactory sexual adjustment may lead to considerable frustration in married life, this factor was not regarded as a major source of conflict by most of the couples. Owing to the intimate nature of the marital act, we would expect that difficulties arising from other factors may ultimately be reflected in this relationship, though this does not always happen, as any experienced marriage counselor will testify. At any rate, among the couples studied, the factor of sex appeared as a seriously disruptive factor only in the nearly complete absence of marital relations.

When the wife was the defendant, failure to have marital relations was explained either by her alleged frigidity or by her downright refusal to run the risk of pregnancy. Perversion and sex crimes were the charges most often leveled against the husband, and in many cases these accusations were backed up by proof of arrest for violation of morals. Only a few couples reported physical incapacity. Most of these marriages broke up rather quickly, and roughly 75 per cent were childless.

Religious Differences

Although 17 per cent of our cases involved mixed marriages, conflicts centering directly on religion were surprisingly few, and only 80 per cent of these occurred in the context of a mixed marriage. About 15 per cent involved a convert at marriage, and in the remaining 5 per cent of the cases, both partners entered marriage as Catholics. The major areas of conflict were the education of children and the refusal of freedom to practice religion. Extensive research on mixed marriages throughout the country indicates that they present a serious threat to the faith in both these areas, yet on the basis of our present findings, we must conclude that many Catholic partners make concessions in this regard without disruptive conflict.[4] Among the cases studied here, quarrels over the religious education of the children arose when the non-Catholic partner denied the validity of the promises made at marriage and absolutely refused to allow the children to be baptized and/or educated in the parochial school. When refusal of freedom to practice religion appeared as a serious source of conflict, the defendent usually displayed a quasi-fanaticism in regard to any manifestation of the partner's religion.

The prevalence of hasty marriages among these cases is indicated by the 30 per cent who were married after an acquaintance of six months or less. There were few early marriages and age differences were normal. The lower whitecollar class was overrepresented. Few

---

[4] For a summary of research on mixed marriages, see *The American Catholic Family*, pp. 153–69.

children were involved, for one-third of the couples were childless, 50 per cent had one child, and there were no large families. The unions were of relatively short duration, 18 per cent separated within the first year, 47 per cent in the first five years, and an additional one-third in the next five years.

Mental Illness

This category includes only cases in which one of the partners had been either institutionalized or judged mentally ill by a competent psychiatrist. Unfortunately, the specific character of the mental illness is not indicated in the records. The petition for separation was motivated by fear of violence or the desire for security. The general characteristics of the group indicated stability. A good percentage of the couples married relatively late, although over 30 per cent had three or more children. Illness occurred in one-third of the marriages during the first five years, but only after 10 or more years in 50 per cent. The lower white-collar class furnished double the expected percentage of cases in this category.

Money

The term *money* is here used to cover only cases in which conflict arose over the use of money, that is, concerning either its investment or the way it was to be spent by the partners. Defined in this way, money was found to assume demoralizing proportions in few Catholic marriages. In general, writers who cite money as a major cause of marital breakdown use the term loosely to cover nonsupport. It seems scarcely necessary to point out that when the husband's drinking, infidelity, or irresponsibility deprives the family of adequate support, there will be quarrels over "money," but it seems meaningless to regard such quarrels as the real source of the conflict. Although too few of our cases fell in this category to merit detailed analysis, we hope that the present study has made some contribution to the clarification of terms.

SPECIAL TYPES OF BROKEN MARRIAGE

We have reserved for special treatment several types of marriages characterized by unusual features. War marriages, forced marriages, marriages in which children were positively excluded by one or both partners, and marriages of the widowed were judged atypical in this sense. They constitute approximately 20 per cent of all the cases studied; war marriages accounted for a little over one-third of this group, forced marriages for almost one-fifth, marriages excluding offspring, about one-third, and marriage involving the widowed, for roughly 7 per cent.

War Marriages

Under this term we include all marriages contracted during or just prior to World War II, and in which separation occasioned by military service prevented the establishment of normal married life. Since there is no information on the total number of such marriages among Catholics in the area, our findings apply only to the group that failed. These unions were short-lived. One out of six broke up within the first six months, and in 90 per cent of the cases, the partners had gone their separate ways within five years. Nearly 70 per cent did not attempt to resume marital life after the separation occasioned by the war. Infidelity or desertion and assumed adultery occurred in all these latter cases, though contrary to the usual pattern, wives were the transgressors in the ratio of three to two. Among the 30 per cent who had resumed family life after the war, the husband's instability and lack of family responsibility, together with the couple's marked incompatibility of backgrounds and temperament, appeared as the major factors in the breakdown.

The mixed marriage rate among these

couples was almost double the prevailing rate for the area. There were indications of hasty marriage, inasmuch as over 50 per cent of the couples separating because of infidelity and desertion had been acquainted for less than one year. The partners were younger than average at marriage. One out of five of the brides was 18 or under, and over 50 per cent were under 21; one out of five of the grooms was 20 or younger and nearly 50 per cent were under 23. Relatively few children were involved in these separations. For example, among cases in which the wife was unfaithful, 70 per cent were childless; when the husband was the offender, 63 per cent were childless; and even among the couples who had resumed family life after the war, over 50 per cent were childless.

Forced Marriages

We include under this term all marriages that would not have been contracted, at least when they were, if the bride had not become pregnant. We have little information concerning the prevalence of such unions among Catholics in the area, and consequently do not know what percentage eventually fails. Considering current dating patterns, however, we assume that a good number must succeed. Among the cases in our study, failure was related to adultery (41.9 per cent), irresponsibility (22 per cent), clash of temperaments (19 per cent), and in-law problems (18 per cent). About one out of six couples separated within the first year and over 56 per cent within the first five years. In 51.5 per cent of the cases the couple had only the one child alleged to have been the cause of the marriage, while another 9.5 per cent reported no living children.

Our cases were drawn primarily from the lower occupational classes: a little over 57 per cent were unskilled or semi-skilled, nearly 30 per cent were skilled, while only about 13 per cent were from the white-collar classes. Mixed marriages were overrepresented, accounting for approximately one out of four cases. Nearly two-thirds of the couples were acquainted for less than a year, and roughly 70 per cent had not been engaged. Age at marriage appeared highly significant since well over half the grooms were 21 or younger, while two-thirds of the brides were under 21, and well over half under 20.

Offspring Excluded

It is generally agreed that most couples in our society desire to have some children. The cases studied here represent marriages in which the explicit intention of excluding children was recognized as a disintegrating factor. Hence, not the absence of children but the disposition reflected by the intent to exclude them is significant, suggesting that one of the partners entered the marriage with mental reservations. Disintegration among these cases was associated with adultery (45 per cent), constant quarreling and bickering (40 per cent), and in-law problems (15 per cent). Mixed and convert marriages were overrepresented, particularly among cases involving adultery. Two-thirds of the marriages broke up within the first five years. Despite their intent, one out of seven couples had one child; however, it was not wanted by one or both parents, and in many cases its arrival was the occasion for the separation.

Marriages of the Widowed

Although we have no grounds for believing that marriages involving the widowed are particularly unstable, we have placed them in a separate category because they obviously have distinctive traits. In approximately 94 per cent of the cases, the grooms were past 30 and the brides over 27. Over 40 per cent of the husbands were six years or more older than their wives. Roughly three-fourths of the unions were childless. One-third broke up within the first year and two-thirds within the first five years. The maladjustment leading to separation in over 80 per cent of the cases was occasioned by the presence of children from a previous marriage. Among the remaining cases, drink and problems of sexual adjustment were prominent.

CONCLUSIONS

In some respects, this study raises as many questions as it answers. Although it enabled us to determine the principal factors usually associated with marital separation, we have gained only limited insight into their etiology. The high incidence of drink and adultery leaves us no room for doubting that they are seriously disruptive by nature, yet we may question whether modern Catholic husbands drink more heavily or are less faithful than their forefathers, among whom the rate of separation was minimal. A comparison with the findings of other studies related to such characteristics as length of acquaintance, engagement, age at marriage, and age differences, revealed a relatively high percentage of items usually judged predictive of maladjustment. Nevertheless, such comparisons may not be entirely valid. Our study was unique in that three-fourths of the husbands were blue-collar workers, and available evidence suggests that the various socioeconomic classes tend to differ considerably precisely in regard to the characteristics we have mentioned.

Despite the questions that remain to be studied, we have uncovered a few answers. When Catholic families became disorganized, the decision to separate was not taken lightly in the majority of cases. At least one partner regarded marriage as the source of serious obligations and duties binding in conscience. Failure was admitted only when the union had deteriorated to a mere external form or became a vehicle of physical and moral harm to the partner and children. This finding confirms our hypothesis that

religious beliefs will be reflected in the efforts made by Catholics to maintain their marriages.

On the other hand, secular attitudes were also in evidence. Many of the couples classified under "irresponsibility" and "clash of temperaments" manifested little understanding or appreciation of the sacred aspects of their marital vocation, while a good number among the non-typical cases displayed slight regard for the sacramental bond, either in contracting it or ignoring its practical significance. This finding presents a serious challenge to modern religious leaders. Evidently most Catholics acknowledge that a valid marriage is indissoluble, but a substantial number fail to recognize the implications of this belief for marriage preparation, the selection of a partner, or the will to succeed in marriage. If the functional exigencies of a religious belief are not recognized or fail to be realistically implemented, the belief itself runs the risk of becoming little more than an impossible ideal.

The assumption that valid mixed marriages tend to be relatively unstable is not confirmed by our findings. Disorganized mixed unions are probably underreported in the court records, yet the fact that disagreements over the religious education of children or the practice of the faith appeared in relatively few cases suggests that, other things remaining equal, many Catholic spouses will make broad concessions in religious matters rather than break up the marriage. Hence it appears that valid mixed marriages are more likely to endanger the practice of faith than the stability of the union.

Analysis of the non-typical cases bears out our contention that they should be treated separately. In most of the characteristics studied, they deviated significantly from the average, while their lack of stability as measured by duration indicated that they were apparently contracted under circumstances and conditions rendering them particularly vulnerable to disintegration.

Perhaps one of the most suggestive insights to emerge from this study is that disorganization had resulted in separation primarily because traditionally conservative, Catholic working-class wives were beginning to redefine their roles in the family. The present trend toward greater equality and independence for women, implying as it does a weakening of the foundations upon which the prerogatives of male dominance in marriage were based, has led many wives to be less tolerant and long-suffering than they have been. Contrary to the past, many prefer to support themselves and even their children rather than to put up with abusive, drunken, or unfaithful husbands. Under present conditions, many wives may feel that the best interests of the family can be served by seeking a separation. The crux of the problem in such cases is that husbands are loath to redefine their roles. Many Catholic men,

in particular, proceed on the assumption that their wives will not leave them, and since they may be conducting themselves only as their fathers did before them, they feel they are justified.

One final observation seems pertinent. Among Catholic couples at least, many factors leading to unhappiness and dissatisfaction have little relationship to the complete breakdown of the marriage. This is to say, many areas of conflict and tension are never thought of in terms of separation or divorce. Although, as we have indicated above, the margin of tolerance may shift, the average couple apparently accepts a considerable amount of frustration as a necessary concomitant of the marriage state. Disintegration occurs not primarily because temperamental differences, incompatibilities, and disagreements plague the union, but because marriage partners lose the will to resolve these differences under conditions that they have come to define as intolerable.

16. *Organized Crime in Chicago**

JOHN LANDESCO

The late John Landesco began his research on organized crime in Chicago as a research assistant in sociology under the auspices of the Local Community Social Science Research Committee.

His study was continued and expanded when it was incorporated into the research program of the Illinois Association of Criminal Justice.

Landesco was an ideal investigator for a study of the underworld of Chicago. He had a varied background of experience. He was born in Rumania and was brought to this country by his parents. He grew up in an immigrant neighborhood, and attended the University of Wisconsin, the University of Cincinnati, and the University of Chicago. He served as a welfare worker in Milwaukee, at that time the best governed large city in this country. This later gave him the opportunity of contrasting law and order in that city with the lawlessness and disorder of Chicago in the twenties.

In the conduct of his research Landesco made personal contact with a number of gangsters, several of whom later made newspaper headlines as prominent victims of gang warfare. He frankly told his friends of the underworld the purpose of his research and asked for and received their co-operation. He became known and was addressed as "Professor" by his underworld friends.

Some of the most outrageous manifestations of organized crime have been reduced in the past three decades and the

* Abstracted by the editors from Part III of *The Illinois Crime Survey,* sponsored by the Illinois Association for Criminal Justice, 1929.

effectiveness of law enforcement has been increased. But many problems of law enforcement still remain, according to the Chicago Crime Commission. Examples are the prevalence of illegal gambling, prostitution, gang warfare, intimidation of witnesses, serious defects in judicial administration, election frauds, and police and political corruption in Chicago and its suburbs. For example, a recent police scandal involved a series of burglaries carried on by men in uniform acting as partners of experienced criminals.

After thirty years a new study of organized crime is called for. There are many questions which should be answered. What changes have taken place in organized crime, now that the repeal of prohibition has cut off a main source of its revenue? What is the meaning of gang killings that still continue? To what extent has organized crime been repressed in certain of its activities or has shifted its operations to new areas? What is the evidence that the profits of organized crime are being invested in more or less legitimate businesses and enterprises? What has been the effect of the introduction of voting machines and the registration of voters upon election frauds? What is the validity of the evidence that crime is now nationally organized?

In the four months from January to April, 1926, there were 29 gangland killings in Chicago, ascribed by the police and newspapers to gangland wars over the monopoly of the beer racket. A climax in the murder activities of gangland was reached on April 27, 1926, when Wil-

275

liam H. McSwiggin, a young assistant state's attorney of Cook County, was one of three men killed by machine gun bullets in front of a Cicero saloon. His slain companions were known gangsters. It was never definitely established what the public official was doing in the company of notorious gangsters, but many supposed he was murdered with underworld friends for their part in a recent primary election in which rival gangs had each been politically active for candidates friendly to them. The murder was never solved, despite the fact that there was a coroner's inquest and six grand jury investigations (one of them federal). But the event aroused public indignation to a point demanding investigation and reform. The Chicago newspapers, especially the *Tribune*, were a driving force behind this reform, and helped keep the problem in the forefront of public discussion. One of the outcomes was the Illinois Crime Survey, in which the Department of Sociology of the University of Chicago was a major participant. This era of exposé brought to light some of the major facts of the relation between criminal gangs and political organization, and how the world of organized crime was able to control public officials, elections, and even the courts in Chicago.

The very failure of six grand jury investigations in the McSwiggin incident raised many puzzling and disturbing questions about the reasons for the breakdown of constituted government in Chicago and Cook County and its seeming helplessness when pitted against the forces of organized crime.

The present study was undertaken to arrive at a sociological accounting for the origin and growth of organized crime in Chicago and to trace the processes by which underworld organization can gain control of the municipal governmental machinery of the second largest metropolis in the nation.

Newspaper accounts of crime proved to be one of the very best sources of materials. In addition, the writer held many interviews with gangland members, both in and out of prison. He had access to the private files of leading Chicago daily newspapers and the police records. The day-by-day report of crime and vice for the 25 years preceding the study were systematically collected, compared, and classified. When this material was finally organized, it presented a consistent and coherent picture of the origin, growth, and ramifications of organized crime under the conditions of life in a modern metropolitan community. The newspaper and other accounts of testimony by public officials and other witnesses before various grand juries revealed conditions as they were in Chicago. The gravity of the problem of rule by organized crime was brought home to the public in the following two quotes from newspaper stories: Al Capone, chief suspect and briefly detained on a formal charge, is reported to have cleared himself with an interviewer by declaring he had no motive, saying, "I paid McSwiggin and I paid him plenty. I got what I was paying for." Charles A. McDonald, special prosecutor, after conducting five grand juries, said: "It is necessary to keep the names of these witnesses secret. The moment any of the witnesses learn that they are wanted, they disappear, or are even killed."

This study was conducted by following out a series of criminal developments, tracing the rise of specific gangs and specific leaders, using whatever materials could be assembled from all sources. The report presented these investigations in a series of chapters. Each chapter is summarized briefly here.

THE EXPLOITATION OF PROSTITUTION

This chapter poses three basic questions:

1. How has organized crime reached its present position of power?

2. How has organized crime persisted

in spite of successive drives against it by all law enforcement bodies?

3. What is the basis of the influence of gangs that enables them to resist, defy, evade, or control constituted authority? These questions are then answered by a historical survey of the origins and growth of organized crime in Chicago.

Organized crime existed in Chicago before 1900 and seems to have grown up to systematize the exploitation of prostitution. Al Capone, the overlord of Chicago gangs, got his start as a gunman-bodyguard to James Colosimo, first king of vice in Chicago. In 1912 it was reliably reported that the segregated vice district south of the Loop along the river at Eighteenth to Twenty-first streets contained at least 200 houses of prostitution under the management of Colosimo's vice trust. The trust collected from each of the houses and paid for arrangements with the police and for political contributions. It regulated competition. It required the houses to patronize certain grocery stores, to take out all their insurance in a company represented by a powerful politician. Particular physicians were especially endorsed. Cab drivers received a percentage of money spent by customers they brought to the house. The system was immune to police interference because it was protected by the aldermen of the district and the chief of police in the ward. The trust operated a string of saloons in the proximity or connected by passages with its houses of prostitution and clandestine flats.

Pressure from reform leaders in the community, from reform mayors, and from clergymen led to raids and "clean-up campaigns" which showed only that chiefs of police and other high political officials were regularly getting graft money from hotels and brothels. The vice syndicates prospered under mayors such as William Hale Thompson, who favored a "wide open" policy.

The historical review of vice in Chicago leads to the following conclusions:

1. Organized vice as a form of law-breaking is more deeply rooted in the social and political order in Chicago than is generally recognized. It began before 1900 and has perpetuated itself as an institutionalized part of the community since then.

2. The crusades against vice, even when they succeeded in achieving their objectives, do not seem to have extirpated the social evil; they have, however, driven it deeper into community life, where it tends to find concealed forms of expression.

3. Indeed, the effects of reforms designed to bring about change may place new opportunities for political corruption in the hands of vice and other law-breaking elements.

4. Politicians often capitalize on public sentiment against an evil and divert it to the purposes of factional politics. Reform becomes a means of winning elections rather than an instrument for correcting abuses. Under present conditions, vice lords, gamblers, and law breakers play as active a part in elections as any other element in the community. As they become a part of the political organization that can be relied upon, they invariably exercise an undue influence on the people who represent them in politics. Law enforcement under these circumstances tends to become a sham. Resorts protected by political influence are allowed to run, while other places are repeatedly raided.

5. Under these conditions the police, whose natural impulse is to enforce the law, become cynical and corrupt.

6. Every new administration, whether liberal or reform, is likely to disturb the previously existing arrangements between officials and law-breakers. Changes of administration, therefore, tend to be to the advantage of the abler and more experienced law-breakers. For Chicago, evidence is presented showing remarkable continuity and persistence of both major and minor personalities in organ-

ized vice over a period of twenty-five years. Indeed, there has been something like a royal succession of vice kings from Colosimo to Capone.

7. Finally, with the coming of prohibition, the personnel of organized vice took the lead in the systematic organization of this new and profitable field of exploitation. All the experience gained by years of struggle against reformers and concealed agreements with politicians was brought into service in organizing the production and distribution of beer and whiskey.

THE RULE OF THE UNDERWORLD: SYNDICATED GAMBLING

Syndicated gambling, as a phase of organized crime in Chicago, was developed under the initiative of one Mont Tennes. As proprietor of the General News Bureau, he controlled the wires for the gathering and dispensing of race-track news in Chicago and principal parts of the United States. He developed a string of handbooks and gambling houses in Chicago and other urban centers. The records and accounts of the day show that he gained control over politicians and officials for the purposes of protecting himself, his associates and subsidiaries, or of controlling the police to gain immunity or even to use police raids for the destruction of competitors and enemies. Since gambling is illegal, it cannot exist except by defeating the law, which is accomplished partly by influencing elections through contributions to campaign funds or by the bribery of officials. As it is an illegitimate business, gamblers cannot come into court in order to settle disputes with regard to their property rights; therefore they have settled disputes by bombing, killing, and arson. Gambling factions retain and support bombers and gunmen, whom they mobilize for action in times of gang war.

Shortly after 1900 there were three gambling syndicates in Chicago, one controlled by Tennes on the North Side, one in the Loop, controlled by the two aldermen involved in the vice trust, and one on the South Side. There was comparatively little sincere police activity to suppress gambling except during a brief time under Chief of Police Schuettler in 1904–6. With a wide-open town and profits of millions of dollars in sight, the gambling magnates of Chicago began waging war for supremacy. The richness of the prizes overturned the habitual caution and furtiveness of the trust gamblers who were reaching for them. Open bookmaking under the supervision of the rings could be found in every section of the city. The instigation of raids by gambling syndicates and the making of raids by a friendly and corrupt police organization upon gambling houses and places maintained without the permission of the syndicate were a successful means of crushing the competitors of the syndicate. The boss gamblers began quarreling over territories and the division of spoils. A series of bombings occurred in 1907, all seemingly aimed at Mont Tennes, who had already gained control of the wires carrying news from the race tracks.

Despite periodic attempts by private civic groups, such as the Chicago Law and Order League, to make inquiries into gambling and demonstrate connivance between the public officials and the gamblers, the syndicates grew and flourished and continued to war with each other. Raids by the police usually found no bookies, but newspaper reporters had no trouble finding them. In August, 1916, the Chicago *Daily News* published an exposé of handbooks operated without police interference and asked two questions, "Does Tennes control the police department?" and "Who is being paid how much?" It named the names of the protected establishments and quoted a "high police official" as saying: "It is just as necessary for a handbook or a gambling house to pay for protection as it is for a saloon or restaurant to pay for a city license. Any joint which is not paying for protection is promptly raided and closed. If a place is running, everybody is satisfied it is paying." The payment of protection, it was stated, was made either in political service or in cash. In October, 1916, Federal Judge Kenesaw Landis of the U.S. District Court managed to explore rather fully the gambling operations of the Chicago syndicates. Witnesses testified before him that the Tennes syndicate owned more than a dozen major handbooks in various parts of Chicago; that they and dozens of others that paid for the service were supplied with information from a secret central bureau in a hotel on Wabash Avenue; that their receipts were collected daily and turned in to the syndicate office; that this operation paid a $20,000 to $25,000 a month profit on the news racing wires leases alone. Along with race betting the syndicate and other establishments had other forms of gambling. Since the interstate transmission of racing news was not at that time prohibited, the federal inquiry came to naught.

During World War I gambling patronage declined. After the war a series of drastic raids, claimed by the newspapers to have been made in order to secure a larger interest in the proceeds for the politicians, weakened the old syndicate. The Al Capone gang moved in and began to add gambling to its list of income sources. With such weapons as bombs, sawed-off shotguns, machine guns, and the threat of "being taken for a ride," they threatened every gambling-house keeper, handbook owner, or other gambler into contributing a percentage of his income. The protection and immunity enjoyed by the syndicate members was almost conclusive indication that certain public officials and politicians were receiving their share of the booty from the syndicate.

THE RULE OF THE UNDERWORLD: BREWING AND BEER RUNNING

As quickly as the Eighteenth Amendment and the Volstead Act came into effect, the prostitution trust turned its attention to the organization of the business of manufacturing and distributing beer. Colosimo, the old vice king, had died and his leadership role had been taken over by John Torrio, a protégé acceptable both to politicians and gangsters. One of his first moves was to take possession of vice and gambling in Cicero, a western suburb, and to make it a base for the operations of beer distribution and gambling. He quickly rose to be Chicago's beer king. He purchased several breweries and was able to deliver beer almost anywhere in the metropolitan area with protection paid. Moreover, his gang was able to meet the competition of other would-be beer runners with police raids, murder, and hijacking. Federal agents trying to raid brewing and distribution points usually found the gangsters had been "tipped off."

Al Capone was Torrio's chief lieutenant, and served a valuable apprenticeship in this branch of racketeering. A change in city administration (Mayor Dever) led to greater police action against the syndicate, and the prestige and domination of the Torrio syndicate declined in 1924, when Torrio was sentenced to jail after being taken in a beer raid.

The author credits Torrio with developing the general plan of conducting criminal business on a large scale, which has been modified by successors, but followed in its main outlines.

1. Criminal business enterprises, like vice, gambling, and bootlegging, were carried on under adequate political protection. Torrio's power rested, in large part, on his ability to insure protection to his fellow gangsters. Immunity from punishment appears to be an almost

indispensable element in maintaining the prestige and control of a gangster chief, as indicated by Torrio's retirement after serving his prison sentence.

2. The gang leader must secure agreement among gangsters by the method of assignment of territory for operations. When he has enemies, he must resort to ruthless warfare and influence police into activity against his rivals, while maintaining immunity for his organization.

3. The gang leader must take advantage of the fact that the metropolitan region falls under many different municipal governments. He must control these suburban villages and their crime activities as a part of his empire, or they will become sources of competition.

4. The gang chieftain must assemble a group of men specialized in a variety of criminal occupations: assassins, thieves, bombers, and a variety of "safe" persons in respectable occupations: doctors, lawyers, merchants, and political chiefs.

THE BEER WARS

The administration of Mayor Dever undertook to enforce the laws against the production and sale of alcoholic beverage and made a genuine attack upon bootlegging. This disrupted the status quo of gangs in Chicago, led to the decline of Torrio, and hastened the outburst of a series of "wars" between gangs. In the four years 1923-26 inclusive, no less than 215 gangsters were murdered by other gangsters. The police, during these same four years, killed 160 beer gangsters in running battle. It was during this period that Al Capone, as leader of the old Torrio interests, was rising to power. In October, 1926, the feuding gangs made a truce, divided the territory, and brought out a more peaceable situation. This period of comparative quiet did not come from police or legal action but from a new set of peace terms among the gangster leaders.

The organized crime revealed in the beer wars cannot be regarded as an isolated phenomenon in the enforcement of an unpopular national prohibition law. This defiance of law and order by gunmen and their immunity from punishment had existed before the prohibition law, and existed simultaneously within other fields of extortion and crime.

TERRORIZATION BY BOMBS

Organized crime in Chicago has made systematic use of bombing since its early days. This chapter is based upon a study of over three hundred cases of bombings in the quarter-century 1904-29. It classified these bombings according to motive and the organization accused of using them.

Bombing in the Gambling Wars

As was shown in an earlier section, there was extensive use of bombing in the disputes of the various gambling factions. Bombs were used in disputes over territory, to intimidate witnesses, to expose to the press and the public the existence of gambling establishments in order to embarrass the police, to force a percentage of profits, and to expose the participation of public officials in gambling graft. In the quarter-century covered by this survey there was never a conviction of a gambler for bombing. The indications are that during the gambling war in 1907 and at other times specialized gangs of bombers were hired and that the police knew who the bombers were.

"Black Hand" Bombing

"Black Hand" is extortion by letters containing threats. The letters are sent anonymously, signed "Black Hand" or "La Mano Nera," indicating a sum of money to be paid for safety and the time and place for the delivery of the money. Shortly after the turn of the century this form of extortion became rife in the Italian community, and those who did not comply were usually bombed, or sometimes shot. Sicilians, who composed the overwhelming majority of the Italian population in Chicago, had been victimized by the "Black Hand" in Sicily, and men who were experienced in perpetrating this form of crime were undoubtedly among the immigrants. In Chicago this practice thrived because of the favorable conditions for crime; in Milwaukee and many other cities that received Sicilian immigrants it made only a weak beginning and soon died out. Most of Chicago's extortion by Black Hand was not done by the larger groups of organized criminals, but by small groups. The sums demanded were usually $1,000 to $5,000, and usually were paid. Italian leaders estimated that a half million dollars annually was paid to extortionists. In April and May of 1915 there were 8 bombings which resulted from disregarding demands made in threatening letters.

The Black Hand terror died out when the federal government began to investigate and prosecute for use of the mails. Extortion continued, but communication was by telephone, and murder rather than bombing was the reprisal for failure to pay.

At the height of the Black Hand extortion, the victims usually, in fear of death, refused to talk or aid the police in prosecution. The law-abiding Italian community was convinced, through experience, that it was futile as well as dangerous to give the police information, for there was never apprehension or prosecution save that by the federal government. The extortionists were often able to fix juries and officials through political connections. It is the purest banality to excuse the nefarious, bloody practices of Black Hand extortion and the widespread tribute paid by the victims by the historical explanation that blackmail and the conspiracy of silence are old-world traits transplanted. These practices originated in Sicily under conditions which were very similar to the

conditions which the Italians found in Chicago—politicians who would go to any length to paralyze the law and secure the release of any criminal for money or political following.

Political Bombing

In the early 1900's the political power of Chicago was concentrated in the hands of the native-born elements. As the Irish, German, and then the Italian and Polish communities grew, they gradually pushed their way into politics and endeavored to get representation in the City Council. In the first quarter of the century the Italian community was struggling hard to get political representation, but it was resisted by illegal as well as legal means. Bombing of political meetings was resorted to by both sides, and there were murders of political leaders, and finally the Italian aldermanic candidate himself was killed.

A similar series of bombing incidents and violence took place as quickly as the Negro population began to move toward political representation. In the Twentieth Ward, a Negro attorney, the first to run for nomination, was shot down on April 10, 1928, the night of the election, after the polls closed. A series of conditions had exacerbated Negro-white relations for many years: unionizing of colored labor, unemployment after World War I, congestion of population, poor transportation, lack of school facilities, and bad housing and living conditions. In those days the white population suffered severe economic losses when a Negro invasion of their block began, for the white tenants scattered and the property values depreciated, only to recover as Negroes moved in, to the profit of realtors. Race riots in 1919 were only a culmination of many bombings directed against Negroes, and these continued steadily throughout the 1920's as Negroes advanced into new neighborhoods.

There were many political bombings that did not directly involve an ethnic or racial group's expansion, but only partisan ideological differences—and a fight to retain or gain control of the flow of funds coming from organized crime. Just as the gangsters used bombs to eliminate their competition, so corrupt politicians not infrequently resorted to similar tactics in order to gain similar ends.

Labor Union Bombing

Certain trades became notorious in Chicago for demanding and obtaining graft. The building trades were at the forefront of this practice. Both employers and the building trades unions actively engaged in grafting. The contractors were asked for graft money to get the contract or to get production from the workers, and were forced to accept uneconomic rules and work arrangements. Efforts to escape these unwritten obligations were punished by bombing. All concerned came to consider it a normal part of operating in Chicago; public officials and the unions came to accept it as a normal part of building to be paid graft money. An effort to put an end to the building trade grafts, by Judge Kenesaw Mountain Landis in 1922, resulted in a series of bombings. Contractors who tried to abide by the rulings made by the Judge had their buildings bombed. A reign of terror in the building trades was brought to a climax by the shooting of policemen and the arrest of the leaders. The cases against all but one, a minor gangster, were dismissed under conditions that suggested there had been tampering with justice. Some of the largest manufacturers of building materials assisted in the defense expenses of the union leaders charged with the violence.

Bombing as a Business

As early as 1921 it became evident that certain gangs were in bombing as a business. They would accept any job of bombing for pay. Any union out on strike could add punch to its demands by having a commercial bombing job done in its behalf. Barber shop owners who did not work in agreement with barbers' rules were coerced by commercial bombers retained for this purpose. Gangsters began to make use of bombers to punish businessmen who refused to join so-called business organizations which were only extortion rackets. Thus, the professional bomber aided in the perfection of racketeering techniques.

RACKETEERING

"Racketeering" is the exploitation for personal profits by means of violence of a business association or employees' organization. A racketeer may be the boss of a supposedly legitimate business association; he may be a labor union organizer; he may pretend to be one or the other or both; or he may be just a journeyman thug. Whether he is a gunman who has imposed himself upon some union as its leader or whether he is a business association organizer, his methods are the same; by throwing bricks into a few windows, an incidental and perhaps accidental murder, he succeeds in organizing a group of small businessmen into what he calls a protective association. He then proceeds to collect what fees and dues he likes, to impose what fines suit him, regulates prices and hours of work, and in various ways undertakes to boss the outfit to his own profit. Any merchant who doesn't come in or who comes in and doesn't stay in and continue to pay tribute is bombed, slugged, or otherwise intimidated.

In 1927, a businessman's group reported that there were 23 separate lines of business in which racketeers were said to be in control or attempting to control: window cleaning, machinery moving, paper stock, cleaning and dyeing, laundries, candy jobbers, dental laboratories, ash and rubbish hauling, grocery and delicatessen stores, garage owners, physicians, drug stores, milk dealers, glazers, photographers, florists, bootblacks, restaurants, shoe repairers, fish and poultry, butchers, bakers, and window shade men.

At the time of the Illinois Crime Survey in 1929 the list of essential economic activities under the control of racketeers had risen to over ninety. Al Capone, overlord of organized crime, was now a stockholder in thousands of business enterprises, ensuring them "the best protection in the world." Racketeering has flourished in Chicago more than in most cities because of its tradition of lawlessness and violence.

THE GANGSTER AND THE POLITICIAN

The relation of the gangster and the politician becomes most obvious to the public on election day. Post-election contests and recounts expose the election frauds committed by the gangsters in behalf of the politicians. The manipulation of elections by machine politicians with underworld assistance is an old practice in the river wards of Chicago and has been gradually spreading to other districts. But election frauds do not disclose the entire picture of the reciprocal relations of politician and gangster.

Residents of the so-called bluestocking wards frequently receive the erroneous impression that if the ballots in the river wards were freely cast and honestly counted they would show a majority against the ward boss, his henchmen, and his gangster allies. Nothing could be further from the truth. Even if all the election frauds of most elections were disclosed, the extent of the fraudulent vote would not greatly exceed twenty thousand votes (1929). What needs to be appreciated is the element of the genuine popularity of the gangster, home-grown in the neighborhood gang, idealized in the morality of the neighborhood.

Political history in Chicago has been written at least partially by the activities of hoodlum and youth gangs who have done "strong arm" work in the elections.

One such gang helped the Irish to retain political control in the Back-of-the-Yards district long after the arrival of fresh waves of Polish, Czech, and other eastern Europeans. These gangs were centered around athletic or other clubs and often were highly regarded in their local neighborhoods. The emergence of the totally mercenary gang, not of a neighborhood, which controls elections for the profits of illegitimate or contraband commerce, became a strong trend after 1920.

In April, 1924, when the Torrio interests took over Cicero, they did it "legally" by backing the Republican ticket with a slate of picked candidates. On the Monday night preceding the election gunmen invaded the office of the Democratic candidate for clerk, beat him, and shot up the place. Automobiles filled with gunmen paraded the streets, slugging and kidnaping election workers. Polling places were raided by armed thugs, and ballots were taken at the point of the gun from the hands of voters waiting to drop them into the box. Voters and workers were kidnaped, brought to Chicago, and held prisoners until the polls closed.

The Capone gang was an organization of professional gangsters. It differed from the neighborhood gang in that it was not an outgrowth of a social or play group. The Capone gang was formed for the business administration of establishments of vice, gambling, and liquor.

During primaries and elections, the evidence of the alliance of gangster and politician has again and again become a public scandal. The mutuality of their services is not difficult to discover. The gangster depends upon political protection for his criminal and illicit activities. He therefore has a vital interest in the success of certain candidates whom he believes will be favorably disposed toward him. The politicians, even the most upright, have a lively sense of the part played in politics and elections by underworld characters. The gangsters and their allies always vote and bring out the vote for their friends, but the church people and the other "good" citizens stay away from the polls, except for presidential elections and those occasional local elections when the issue of good citizenship versus organized crime is dramatically staged.

Election frauds are one of the ways in which gangsters and gunmen have repaid politicians for favors received. Fraudulent voting has been a perennial problem of municipal study by academicians in Chicago, and repeated investigations have been made.

An examination of vote fraud investigations since 1900 discloses the following facts:

(1) The geographic area within which vote frauds occur is limited and can be traced on the map of the city.

(2) The authorities over the election machinery, the county judge, the election commission, and the state's attorney's office, repeatedly carry on the same conflicts around the same legal points, arising out of duplication of function and overlapping and division of authority.

(3) The partisanship of the County Board of Commissioners determines its action in appropriating funds for special investigations.

(4) The encumbent state's attorney always opposes and impedes the appointment of a special prosecutor and a special grand jury to investigate election frauds if possible: (a) by efforts to stop the County Board's appropriations, and (b) by efforts to gain priority in the appointment of a favorable special prosecutor and a favorable grand jury. Repeatedly there have been two or more special grand juries investigating vote frauds at the same time.

(5) The encumbent state's attorney tries to capture the services of the attorney general, who is in a position to take charge of as many grand juries as are in the field at any given time.

(6) When the dominant party is in the process of splitting into factions and factional bipartisan alliances occur, there is great activity in vote fraud investigation, with all the jockeying and maneuvering to capture the control of election machinery and prosecution and to secure advantageous publicity. This activity has seemed more often, in the past, to have as its aim factional advantage in political battle rather than the impartial suppression of vote frauds.

(7) The actual frauds that can be legally proved are committed by underlings. They refuse to testify to the identity of their superiors in the conspiracy, and it is, therefore, always impossible to convict the "higher-ups." The underlings under the gag of silence are usually sentenced for contempt of court by the county judge. Where prosecution is undertaken in a criminal court, it fails in a large number of cases because of lack of evidence. The political bosses furnish the money and attorneys to fight the cases, but they are seldom or never implicated by the testimony.

(8) The earlier centers of vote frauds were the areas in which dives, saloons, "flops," and rooming houses abounded, and the homeless or transient man was available in large numbers as purchaseable votes. This area was increased by the new immigration into territories dominated by political manipulators of the previous generations. Later, foreign leaders were developed under the tutelage of the earlier crooked politicians. In all of the foreign districts there have always been great numbers of immigrants who would stand aloof from politics because of what they regard as "low-down" local leaders and their crooked methods. The registration and the voting in these wards has always been small compared to the total population, and largely limited to the controlled vote. When racial or national group consciousness can be awakened through conflict situations, the politician can turn out a large number of legitimate votes.

(9) The young of the immigrant

groups, beginning with the child at play in the street, were assimilated uncritically to all of the traditions of the neighborhoods in which they lived. Street gangs were their heritage, conflict between races and nationalities often made them necessary—conflict and assimilation went on together. The politician paid close attention to them, nurturing them with favors and using them for his own purposes. Gang history always emphasizes this political nurture. Gangs often become political clubs.

(10) Through every investigation the most constant element is the connivance of the police, witnessing and tolerating the vote frauds and resisting investigation by refusing to give testimony. Through it all is the evidence that the police defer to the politician because of his power over their jobs.

(11) Slugging and intimidation of voters is a chronic complaint through this entire period. With the advent of

bootlegging arose the new phenomenon of the armed wealthy gun chief becoming the political boss of an area.

(12) While every type of fraud ever committed has been practiced within the last eight years, it can also be said that within the last few years there has been the most effective, impartial fight upon vote frauds through prosecution. For this, civic agencies, supported by private funds, and an honest county judge, impartially driving toward the objective of clean elections should be credited; the more emphatically because of the disadvantages of the chaotic governmental machinery which the prosecution has to employ and the odds against them in fighting the most powerful political organization in the history of Chicago.

The technique of vote frauds during the entire period can be analyzed and listed under three heads: (a) irregular practices of election officials, (b) irregular activities of party workers, and (c) proceedings subsequent to the announcement of the election returns.[1]

---

1 Mr. Landesco then lists the following practices:

A. Irregular Practices of Election Officials.
  1. Padding Registration Books.
      (a) The insertion of fictitious names in the register to enable fraudulent voters to vote those names on election day.
  2. Abuse of the Suspect Notice Provision.
      (a) Deliberate failure to send notices to irregularly registered persons, fictitious names and other names suggested by independent canvassers.
      (b) Mailing notices to legal voters hostile to the machine on the expectation that they will neglect to answer the notice and consequently be barred.
  3. Substitution of Election Officials.
      (a) A scheme by which the duly appointed election official is either kidnapped from the polls or intimidated into remaining away, so that a "machine" worker conveniently at hand is given the appointee's place in the polling place. The selection of the new official is made by the judges at the polling place.
  4. Failure To Initial Ballots.
      (a) The intentional omission of the election officials' initials from the ballots handed to voters known to be hostile

to the "machine," thus invalidating the ballot.
  5. Short-penciling, Double Marking.
      (a) A trick whereby the election officials counting the ballots furtively fill in crosses opposite names left blank by the voter, or by double marking invalidate the vote cast by the voter. Double marking is a trick by means of which a vote cast is invalidated by marking a cross opposite the name of the opposing candidate for the same office. Since this can occur even with the bona fide voter, there is little chance of detection.
  6. Transposition of Totals on the Tally Sheet.
      (a) The apparently innocent and entirely plausible error of transposing the totals of votes with the benefit of the error going to favored candidates.
  7. Alteration of Totals on the Tally Sheet.
      (a) The doctoring of totals while watchers are supposedly present during the count at the polling place.
  8. Wholesale Changes on the Tally Sheet.
      (a) In the more notorious wards totals are inserted without regard to the

A WHO'S WHO OF ORGANIZED
CRIME IN CHICAGO

One part of this study was to make a
card catalogue of criminals in Chicago
and select from these a certain number
of the more active, successful, and prominent for a "Who's Who of Organized
Crime in Chicago." The following available sources of information were con-
sulted:

1. Every name appearing in the crimi-

number or distribution of votes cast.
This requires the connivance of the
entire staff and party watchers.
9. Substitution of Tally Sheets.
  (a) The substitution of the original sheet
      marked under the observation of the
      watchers for a false one marked by
      "machine" workers in accordance
      with instructions from party bosses.
10. Substitution of Ballots.
  (a) The opening of sealed envelopes con-
      taining the ballots after they have
      left the polling place and the substi-
      tution of false ballots marked in
      accordance with the instructions of
      party bosses.
B. The Irregular Activities of the Party Workers.
  1. Registration.
    (a) Non-resident vagrants registering un-
        der fictitious names and addresses.
    (b) Making false statement as to length
        of residence at correct address.
    (c) Bona fide voters of one precinct reg-
        istering in another as a favor to some
        political boss in exchange for favors.
    (d) The actual housing of colonized
        vagrants for at least thirty days in
        order to conform with the lodging
        house law. This enables the ward
        bosses legitimately to control a large
        number of actually fraudulent votes.
  2. Pledge Cards.
    (a) The use of pledge cards, obtained
        before election day, to determine the
        desirability of unregistered voters
        to party interests, and if found favor-
        able, the precinct boss somehow man-
        ages to have the names inserted after
        the registration books have been
        closed.
  3. Ballot Box Stuffing.
    (a) Inserting a bundle of ballots already
        marked into the ballot box before the
        opening of the polling place.
    (b) Raids on polling places by armed

nal news of Chicago newspapers for a
period of one year was listed, the stories
clipped, classified and filed, and the
names catalogued.

2. The names of criminals entered in
the daily police bulletins were also classified and catalogued.

thugs and the stealing of ballot boxes
before the count begins.
  (c) The intimidation of election officials
      during the counting of the ballots
      while fraudulent ballots are being
      added.
  (d) The wholesale stealing of a large
      block of ballots before the opening
      of the polling place. These ballots
      are marked and later mixed with the
      valid ballots at counting time.
4. Irregular Voting.
  (a) Chain system—stringing. The first of
      a string of voters is given a marked
      ballot to take into the polling place
      and place in the ballot box. He brings
      out with him the blank ballot given
      him by the clerk, which is again
      marked by a party worker on the
      outside and given to the next "string-
      er" voter, ad infinitum.
  (b) Voting for former residents who have
      left the precinct since registration.
  (c) Voting for registered voters who fail
      to vote.
  (d) Voting for registered voters who do
      not appear at the polling place until
      shortly before closing time. These
      voters are then refused the right to
      vote on the ground that they have
      already voted.
  (e) Removing ballots from the polling
      place avowedly for the use of bed-
      ridden voters, but actually for pur-
      poses of fraudulent marking.
  (f) Armed sluggers intimidating legal
      voters into leaving the polls without
      voting.
  (g) Shooting up of polling places and
      driving voters from the polls.
  (h) The purchase of votes by faction
      leaders, both from those who control
      the repeaters and from those count-
      ing the ballots.
5. Kidnapping of Workers.
  (a) This is resorted to when the party
      worker becomes too loud in his pro-
      test against the "machine" in the ma-
      nipulation of ballots or he is known
      to be an important, uncompromising

3. From the current news the names of gang leaders were noted and their gangs traced through the newspaper archives for twenty-five years. This method yielded not only the names of those

affiliated with the leaders, but the names and activities of conflicting gangs or syndicates and leaders.

4. The life histories of the leaders in their gang settings were compiled, and geographical locations of the gangs, as well as the motives for conflict and co-operation, were traced.

5. For a period of three and a half

worker for the opposition; also so as to instill fear into the opposing party so that their workers will refuse to come out for their faction at future elections.

6. Open Conflict of Workers.
   (a) When both factions employ thugs to control the polling place, open warfare sometimes takes place when the thugs of one faction resist the fraudulent practices of the other faction.

7. Liberation of Arrested Workers.
   (a) When the police do make an arrest of a fraudulent voter, the latter is usually released, either by armed thugs at the point of a gun, or by deputized bailiffs of the municipal court placed at the polls to insure order, or by a judge who is actively engaged in politics who holds court at the polling place or on the sidewalk, and frees the fraudulent voter by judicial process.

8. Control of the Police.
   (a) Forcing the police to do the bidding of the ward boss under threat of demotion or on the promise of favorable mention to supervisors. Usually the policeman is called away from the polls on a ruse while the fraud is being committed. This leaves the police blameless.

9. Murder.
   (a) The deliberate assassination of party workers and political candidates of opposing factions where it is evident that such candidates are certain of election.

10. Support of Business Enterprises.
    (a) The owners of business profiting by the patronage of the gangs of hoodlums are required to furnish automobiles for the transportation of these fraudulent workers. Once the "hoodlum" is seated in the automobile, he can show little resistance to gangster persuasion.

C. Proceedings Subsequent to the Announcement of Election Returns.
   1. Recounts.
      (a) As a means of settling factional dis-

putes and to discredit the opposing faction.
      (b) As a means of keeping the ballots from those seeking to have a recount made by the election commissioners.
      (c) As a means of keeping the ballots from special grand juries investigating ballot frauds.
      (d) Refusal by the custodian of the ballots to surrender them to the opposing faction or to the grand jury until compelled to by court order.

   2. Opposition of the State's Attorney.
      (a) Opposition in the impaneling of a special grand jury.
      (b) Opposition in the appointment of a special state's attorney.

   3. Opposition by the County Board.
      (a) Refusal to appropriate funds for a special grand jury or special state's attorney.
      (b) Injunction in the name of a taxpayer to enjoin the use of already appropriated funds by the special state's attorney.
      (c) Refusal of the County Board to appropriate additional funds for the continuance of the vote fraud prosecution.

   4. Quashing Indictments.
      (a) After the indictments have been secured and the funds are exhausted, it is found that the indictments are faulty because of some technicality.

   5. Challenging the Jurisdiction of the County Court in the Handling of Vote Fraud Prosecutions.
      (a) Appealing convictions obtained by the County Court.
      (b) Obtaining writs for the release of convicted vote manipulators but applying to the Circuit or Superior Court with a consequent clash of judges over jurisdiction. The disappearance of the convicted persons pending an appeal to the Supreme Court.

years, firsthand contacts were established wherever possible with both leaders and followers in gangland. A collection of a limited number of life histories of gangsters who were also ex-convicts, fairly well distributed over the city, was also assembled.

6. From the Crime Commission of Chicago twenty-six hundred probation records furnished names, which were classified and added to our catalogue.

7. From the Illinois Association for Criminal Justice, one hundred names, selected for their use of the habeas corpus, were obtained and added to the list.

The catalogue thus compiled contains approximately seven thousand names. It is certainly not complete, but may be taken as fairly representative of recent criminal activity in Chicago.

Out of these seven thousand records, four hundred names were selected for the "Who's Who of Organized Crime." The first consideration was the persistence of the name appearing in current news through a considerable period of the twenty-five years covered by the historical studies. The second point was the position of the man in criminal news and criminal history, his importance, prestige, or notoriety. From the standpoint of organized crime, the affiliation of a person with a gang was also a main factor in his selection. Finally, this list of the four hundred men most persistent, most notorious, and most clearly affiliated with organized crime was cleared through the Bureau of Identification of the Police Department and the office of the secretary of police. This netted valuable additional information which was abstracted and entered for purposes of comparison upon analytical charts. A major discovery was that most of the really important gangsters had very skimpy records or no records at all in the police file. The criminals were followed through in groups, according to type. This analysis of specialized criminal occupations showed the risk of punishment in Chicago was much smaller than in other communities and other states. This shows the importance of local acquaintance and political influence in securing protection and immunity from the penalties of the law.

It was discovered that for certain forms of organized crime in Chicago only the underlings receive punishment and, almost without exception, petty punishment. The men higher up, the criminal overlords who reap enormous profits, go almost completely free. These forms of crime exploited by criminal profiteers are bootlegging, gambling, vice, and labor and merchant "racketeering." At present the risk incurred of prosecution and conviction in conducting these illegal operations is very small.

THE GANGSTER'S DEFENSE OF
HIS MODE OF LIFE

The gangster achieves status by being a gangster, with gangster attitudes, and enhances his reputation through criminal exploits. Usually the gangster is brought up in neighborhoods where the gang tradition is old. He grows up into it from early childhood in a world where pilfering, vandalism, sex delinquency, and brutality are an inseparable part of his play life. "Copper hating" is the normal attitude toward the law. Without the gang, life would be grim and barren for these children. The immigrant father usually is a laborer for an industrial establishment, and the mother cares for a large family and tries to gain extra money by such additional work as taking in washing. Toiling hard to make ends meet, they grudge spending pennies for pleasure.

The gang youth takes as his pattern the men in the neighborhood who have achieved success. His father, although virtuous in his grime and squalor and thrift, does not present as alluring an example to him as do some of the neighborhood gangsters. The men who frequent the neighborhood gambling houses

are good-natured, well-dressed, sophisticated, and above all, they are American,
in the eyes of the gang boy. The con-
spicuous expenditures and lavish display of the *nouveau riche* of the underworld confuse and pervert the traditional
standards and values of even the law-
abiding persons in the community.

The risks of an illicit or criminal career are calculated, and, in certain cases,
due precautions are taken. The experienced criminal or the boy brought up in
gang culture approaches his "trouble
with the law" as a matter which can be
met in a thousand ways—there are friends
and "fixers," perjury, bribery, and intimidation. There is a certain behavior which
befits a man of character in his society.
He must give no information about his
friends; he must not believe the police
when they say that his friends have
"squealed." From the stories he has heard
from childhood up, he knows that he
may have to stand a beating or the ex-
cruciating third degree, but in his mind
he knows it is an experience that will
bring him the plaudits of his group, just
as a young soldier does after his first
combat experience.

The world of the gangster is one in
which the burglar is convicted and the
"fence" retains the goods. Indeed, the
"fence" may be an important figure in
the neighborhood's political life. The
gangster grows to consider the world a
place in which everyone has a racket but
the "poor working sap," because as he
looks around he finds ample customers
for his loot, ample police protection for
money, and almost anything in his world
can be "fixed." The youthful gangster
makes invidious comparisons between
the opportunities for success in a criminal versus a legitimate career. He contrasts the "easy money" and the "good
time" of the gambler, beer runner, "stick-
up artist" and "con man" with the low
wages and long hours of the working-
man. He speaks in flowing admiration of
the power, the courage, the skill, the

display, and the generosity of the outstanding gang leaders. His glorification
of the life and the characters of the underworld is complete evidence of the
absence of any feeling of inferiority or
shame about his own criminal aspirations.

When the gangster becomes moralistic
in defense of himself, he presents an ar-
ray of facts to prove his claim that everybody has a "racket." He begins with the
police. The gangster is situated where
he observes the policeman as the bene-
ficiary of his earnings. At times these
exactions by the police become so heavy
that he finds himself in a situation where
he actually is working for the police.
The politician in the neighborhood
where the gangster lives grafts on the
criminals when they need "political pull"
and uses them for the purposes of fraud
and intimidation, as in elections. The
gangster does not exaggerate when he
says that he has never seen a straight
election. His own gang fellows, once
given even the minor jobs where they
have entree to big politicians and holders
of public office, become rich on the basis
of the graft they receive for information,
favors, and protection.

In prison he may be associated for the
first time with the defaulting banker or
the unscrupulous promoter of dubious
ventures. In making comparisons between himself as a criminal with grafting businessmen, police, and politicians,
the gangster feels his own superior virtue. This universal attitude of the underworld has been perhaps best expressed
by Al Capone in an interview:

There is one thing worse than a crook and
this is a crooked man in a big political job—
a man that pretends he is enforcing the law
and is really taking dough out of somebody
breaking it. Even a self-respecting "hood"
hasn't any use for that kind of a fellow. He
buys them like he would any other article
necessary in his trade, but he hates them in
his heart.

Many law-abiding citizens imagine the criminal to be constantly tortured with the pangs of remorse. It is difficult for them to believe that the gangster is seldom, if at all, conscience-stricken because of his crime. In four years' association with criminal gangsters, the writer encountered little or no remorse among Chicago gangsters. Certainly he feels remorse, not for his crimes but for being caught and convicted. Remorse arises when the effort to escape prosecution is blocked and one reaches an impasse. As long as there is practical hope, then in one's own mind there is a continual surging of possibilities of action. Within the friendly group interested in one's case, there is a stirring about, a great amount of discussion, rumor, argument, and counter-argument about means that can be used and about the resources that can be marshalled. When there is nothing to be done about one's trouble, the thoughts turn inward in a self-appraisal. A man mopes about his trouble and remorse follows. Thus, the remorse of the gangster is not based on his original guilt for the crime, but in a mistaken maneuver of a mistaken choice of friends or misplaced confidence.

Although the criminal gangster is untroubled about his crimes, he is stirred to the depths of his feeling and sentiment by any charge of personal treachery to his friends. Betraying a comrade is the only crime in the underworld for which its members are one and all likely to feel genuine remorse.

If the gangster does not feel remorse, what are the motives that lead to his reform? All students of criminology are aware that many criminals do forsake the life of crime and turn to law-abiding pursuits. There are many reasons but the main consideration seems to be the conclusion that "crime does not pay."

Often the criminal, upon his release from the state reformatory or the state penitentiary, attempts to follow a law-abiding life. He frequently succeeds, even against great odds. But many ex-convicts find the difficulties in the way of reformation almost insuperable. When he comes out, he has trouble finding a job. He may struggle along on skimpy pay and watch his friends' big financial success in underworld occupations that are protected from the encroachment of the law. Often the ex-convict is untrained, the school period having been wasted through truancy and delinquencies, working intermittently at blind alley jobs or never having worked at all. This makes getting a job doubly difficult. Another powerful factor in the return to a criminal career is the assistance and kindness of old associates in crime. Their aid is frequently given with more human sympathy than is the more formal help extended by welfare agencies. This contact with old acquaintances in the underworld not only places him under obligation to them, but prevents his carrying out his purpose of reformation.

Those members of the gang who have been punished by conviction and sentence never quite recover from the puzzling outrage of their fate. In their speculations of how it came about, there is always an increasing number of possibilities of who could have been the enemy or who could have been the "squealer," or what the ulterior motives might have been for him or the prosecution that they were actually sent up. The welfare, standards, and laws of organized society evoke no response in their hearts and minds. They seem to have no conception of justice, of laws, and of courts except as some external superimposed system of oppression which they must by hook or by crook obstruct and evade.

The picture of the gangster presented here differs widely from the current descriptions of him, whether those of soft-hearted sentimentalists or of hard-headed realists. When allowed to speak for himself, he is seen to be neither an innocent youth led astray by bad companions but ready to make good if given a chance, nor a hardened and vicious individual who has deliberately and vindictively chosen to wage war on society.

The story which he gives of his own life shows him to be a natural product of his environment—that is, of the slums of our large American cities. These slum areas have been formed in the growth of the city. They have been ports of first entry for each new wave of foreign immigration. These slum areas inhabited by national groups, as well as industrial areas like Back-of-the-Yards, are subject to the constant misfortune of losing their legitimately successful citizens. The constant ambition that grows with the rise of the people is to get out into the better districts of the city. As the successful families move away, they leave behind the unsuccessful, laboring foreigner, who is not accepted as a model for the children and youth in their process of Americanization. But there also remain the gangster and politician chief, who become practically the only model of success.

It follows that the gangster is a product of his surroundings in much the same way that the good citizen is a product of his. The good citizen has grown up in an atmosphere of obedience to law and of respect for it. The gangster has lived his life in a region of law-breaking, of graft, and of "fixing." That is the reason why the good citizen and the gangster have never been able to understand each other. They have been reared in two different worlds.

The stories which the gangsters tell of their own lives should enable the good citizens to deal more intelligently and therefore more effectively with the problem of organized crime. In the first place, it will enable the public to realize how deep-rooted and widespread are the practices and philosophy of the gangster in the life and growth of the city. In the second place, an understanding of this should make possible a constructive program that will not content itself with punishing individual gangsters and their allies, but will reach out into a frontal attack upon basic causes of crime in Chicago.

SUMMARY AND RECOMMENDATIONS*

The final and summary conclusion of our study is that the control of organized crime is always, in the last analysis, a *problem of public opinion.* Organized crime always seeks to commercialize and to exploit human nature. Society through legislation and other measures strives to protect its citizens against wayward impulses that are destructive of human happiness and social order. Public opinion in our largest American cities seems ever to fluctuate between endorsement of a wide-open town with little or no enforcement of the laws regulating personal conduct and reform supported by crusades.

Crusades arouse public sentiment against some existing abuse or disorder, but they are so sweeping in character that they are usually only temporarily successful and a reaction sets in against them. One reason for the failure of crusades against crime and vice is that they seek to endorse some general policy of law enforcement. They are seldom or never based on a study of the problem. What is needed is a program that will deal with the crime problem in detail and consecutively, that is, by analyzing the crime situation into its different elements, by taking up each crime situation separately, and one by one working out constructive solutions. This is only the application of business methods and scientific procedure to the study and solution of the crime situation. The order of the selection of individual crime situations for specialized treatment would depend upon many factors, such as existing conditions, the given state of pub-

* Written by E. W. Burgess in 1928 as a supplement to the report.

lic opinion, and the relative efficiency of available methods of control.

The wave of public sentiment that is aroused by the crusade needs direction; otherwise it is dissipated and lost. Public sentiment is a great force if properly directed. But direction requires fact-finding and research. Public opinion as expressed at the ballot box gives a public official a mandate to act, but it requires more wisdom than the public usually possesses to direct his activity.

A permanent policy and program of law enforcement cannot be based upon crusades but must rely upon creating public opinion that is informed upon the actual workings of organized crime and political machines. Newspapers render a valuable service in giving relatively accurate day-by-day reports of crime. But the vivid accounts of current events in the newspapers do not give their readers the balance and perspective necessary for formulating a permanent policy and program. The present study has indicated how, in the past, *crusades against crime have repeatedly failed* although public opinion had each time been inflamed to white heat.

While the original sources of the gangster's power lie in his own neighborhood, the overlords of vice, gambling, and bootlegging have taken full advantage of the complexity of county, city, town, and village government in the *greater Chicago region*. Crime control can no longer function with a system of administrative machinery which has been rendered obsolete by the growth of the city and the new means of rapid transportation like the automobile. Problems of health and recreation as well as organized crime demand the organization of a municipality of metropolitan Chicago. The consolidation of the City of Chicago and Cook County is a practical first step.

This study shows that *no one agency* can cope with the range of problems presented by organized crime in gam-

bling, commercialized vice, bootlegging, and gang activities. The diversity of the problems requires special handling by the Crime Commission, which stimulates the efforts of law enforcement agencies and the permanent interest of special groups.

But in addition to the efforts of the Crime Commission some way should be found of co-ordinating its efforts with the other organizations in order to avoid duplication and to insure co-operation. Co-ordination will perhaps best be secured, not by the amalgamation of these organizations as has been proposed, but by provision for an organization that will specialize in fact-finding, crime-reporting, and special study as occasion may require. This organization should not be tied up with any special policy or program but should be disinterested in order to insure public confidence in its findings and reports. It would seem that the Illinois Association for Criminal Justice is the best qualified of existing organizations to assume this function. The undertaking of this service would be a natural and logical sequence of the survey which it is now bringing to completion.

The importance of this service cannot be overestimated. No one today knows how much crime there is in Chicago or in any other large city in this country. No one knows the total cost of crime to the community. Yet these facts are essential to any adequate program of crime accounting. To develop intelligent public opinion in the field of crime control there is just the same need of getting exact and accurate information as in the fields of fire prevention and public health. And just as great improvement in crime prevention and control may be expected from systematic and continuous reports on crime conditions and law enforcement as have resulted from similar publicity measures in the field of public health.

17. The Delinquency Research of Clifford R. Shaw and Henry D. McKay and Associates*

ABSTRACT PREPARED BY THE EDITORS

The late Clifford R. Shaw was the father of modern scientific research in juvenile delinquency. As head of the Department of Research Sociology, Institute for Juvenile Research, he continued the study of delinquency which he began as a graduate student at the University of Chicago. With Henry D. McKay as his research associate, he developed a close collaboration with the urban studies program of the University of Chicago which lasted for almost three decades. Because of the daily contacts which his organization maintains with a wide variety of delinquents and with judges, probation officers, court social workers, and civic

* The materials for this chapter have been extracted by the editors from the following monographs and reports of which Clifford R. Shaw was principal author: *Delinquency Areas* (Chicago: University of Chicago Press, 1929), in collaboration with Frederick M. Zorbaugh, Henry D. McKay, and Leonard S. Cottrell; "The Juvenile Delinquent," Chapter XIV in *The Illinois Crime Survey* (Illinois Association for Criminal Justice, 1929), with Earl D. Meyers; *The Jack-Roller: A Delinquent Boy's Own Story* (Chicago: University of Chicago Press, 1930); *The Natural History of a Delinquent Career* (Chicago: University of Chicago Press, 1931); *Social Factors in Juvenile Delinquency*, for National Commission on Law Observance and Enforcement, Publication No. 132, Vol. II of *Report on the Causes of Crime* (Washington, D.C.: Government Printing Office, 1931), with Henry D. McKay; *Brothers in Crime* (Chicago: University of Chicago Press, 1938), with Henry D. McKay and James F. McDonald; and *Juvenile Delinquency and Urban Areas* (Chicago: University of Chicago Press, 1942) edited by Henry D. McKay, with chapters by Norman Hayner, Paul Cressey, Clarence Schroeder, Earl Sullenger, Earl Moses, and Calvin Schmidt.

leaders throughout the community, his research was able to bring a realism to criminology and especially the study of juvenile delinquency which had been conspicuously scarce in American sociology before 1920. In fact, empirical American sociology was perhaps popularized and transmitted to all corners of the world by the Shaw monographs more than by any other examples of this brand of social research. As a strong supporter of the personal document and life history approach to sociological research, he was a central figure in the stormy controversy over "qualitative versus quantitative" research methods, yet his organization calmly turned out more statistical research on sociological topics than most of his critics. In the writings of Shaw and McKay can be found rather full expositions of ideas that currently are regarded as the latest thinking in the field of delinquency research.

EARLY INTERPRETATION OF THE DELINQUENCY PROBLEM

In a report for *The Illinois Crime Survey* of 1929, Shaw, with the assistance of Henry D. McKay and other younger investigators, was called upon to make a rather comprehensive interpretation of the nature of the delinquency problem, its causes, and the shortcomings of the methods of treatment being used. This section is a brief summary of the contents of that report. Shaw's statements and interpretations, now more than three decades old, are a bench mark against which sociologists should measure their progress in developing greater insight and more profound theories of delinquency. In this report Shaw (a) developed statistical measures of delinquency and evaluated their shortcomings, (b) studied the spatial pattern of concentration of delinquency, and (c) noted the ties between delinquency, the family, and the neighborhood and school situation. Moreover, he declared delinquency to be a product of the social situation and proceeded to trace the roots of delinquency to the community characteristics, the family situation, and the role of companionship and gang membership in delinquency. As early as 1929 he had made it abundantly clear that a delinquency career was *developed* as an adjustment to life and was not an independent individual phenomenon resulting from inborn tendencies or accidental psychological abnormalities. From the very first he emphasized the presence of a delinquency "subculture" or "contraculture" in high delinquency areas.

Definitions of Juvenile Delinquency and Their Shortcomings

There are three ways of measuring the extent of delinquency: (a) number of police investigations of cases involving children, (b) number of children brought before the juvenile courts per year, and (c) number of delinquent children per year committed to correctional institutions by the courts. The monthly reports of the juvenile police probation officers assigned to the various police stations in Chicago were used to compile statistics of the number of cases investigated by the police. To get data on children in juvenile courts, records from the Juvenile Court on the number of cases filed were used. From the very first the weaknesses of these statistics were recognized. There are offenders, even some who persistently engage in delinquent practices, who are never known to the police. In some communities certain types of offenses are so prevalent that there is very little intervention on the part of the police. This is especially true in certain districts contiguous to railroad yards, where stealing from freight cars is more or less accepted by the community and police. It is also known that there are apprehended offenders whose names are omitted from the police records and a much larger number who are never brought to court because of the intervention of friends and relatives. Since an individual may be brought into police stations or to the court several times during a year, the number of police cases will always exceed the number of individuals.

In Chicago of the 1920's, only about 10 per cent of the children handled by the police were being brought into juvenile court. The cases brought to court were restricted primarily to more serious offenders over twelve years of age. The less serious cases were disposed of by the police—usually by calling in the child's parents. From a study of the records of the police probation officers it was found that a large number of children as young as eight and nine years of age had been involved in numerous instances of stealing, although many had never been in court. It is apparent that the number of cases of delinquent children brought to court in a given year represents only a fraction of the total number of cases of serious delinquents known to the police.

The third and most conservative index of the extent of delinquency is the number of cases of delinquent children committed to correctional institutions by the court.

There has been a rather constant ratio over several years between the three indexes, about 20 to 3 to 1. It is probable that the group of police cases most nearly approximates the actual numerical extent of delinquency. As an index to measure the comparative severity of delinquency in various areas, Shaw preferred the second index, the number of juvenile court cases.

Geographical Location of Delinquencies

As a first step in the general study of the social and cultural background of the delinquent child it is important to determine the geographic distribution of places of residence of delinquents in the community in question. By this means the problem is immediately localized, and the way is prepared for an intensive analysis of the particular social world to which the delinquent belongs. With this in mind, one of the first research projects at the University of Chicago was to prepare spot maps showing these distributions. This mapping revealed the following:

1. There are very definite "delinquency areas" in which large numbers of cases of delinquency are concentrated. The areas of concentration are adjacent to the "Loop" and contiguous to the large industrial districts near the Chicago River, the Union Stock Yards, Calumet Lake, and South Chicago.

2. A statistical measure termed the "rate of delinquents" was computed by expressing the number of male delinquents as a ratio to the total number of boys of the same age group. It was computed for each square mile in area of the city and showed wide variations between various parts of the city.

3. When the rate is represented along lines radiating from the "Loop" a very striking gradation from the "Loop" to the boundary is revealed. Along most radials there is a continuous decrease in the rate toward the boundary of the city. Along some radials the high rate continues much farther than it does along other radials.

4. A similar rate map was made for female delinquents, and aside from the fact that the rates were lower, the general pattern was the same.

5. It is extremely significant that the variations in the rate of delinquents show a rather consistent relationship to different types of community background.

Thus, the area in which the highest rate is found is the area of greatest physical deterioration, poverty, and social disorganization. Surrounding the area of deterioration there is a large area of disorganization populated chiefly by immigrant groups. In this area of confused cultural standards, where the traditions and customs of the immigrant group are undergoing radical changes under the pressure of a rapidly growing city and the fusion of divergent cultures, delinquency and other forms of personal disorganization are prevalent. In the outlying exclusive residential districts of single family dwellings and apartment buildings the rate of delinquents is invariably low.

Personality of Delinquent Offenders

The problem of delinquency is to a certain extent a community problem. Delinquent conduct is involved in the whole social life and organization of the community. The study of detailed life histories of delinquents reveals that the experience and behavior trends of offenders reflect the culture and spirit of the community in which they have lived.

In a 1927 study of 6,000 instances of stealing, it was found that in 90.4 per cent of the cases two or more boys were known to have been involved in the act. Thus, delinquency was shown to be primarily group behavior. In instances of petty stealing in the neighborhood there were usually five or six participants, most of whom were very young offenders. In instances of holdup, a more highly specialized type of offense, there were usually only two or three boys involved, most of whom were older and more experienced delinquents.

Delinquency frequently becomes an established social tradition in certain gangs and is transmitted from the older members to the younger. It is not infrequent to find gangs in which the requirement for membership is participation in the delinquent activities of the group.

To understand the delinquent behavior of a member of one of these gangs it is necessary to know the traditions and social values of the group.

Diffusion of Delinquent Patterns of Conduct

From a study of life histories of delinquents it appears that delinquent patterns, particularly those of stealing, are transmitted from one individual to another and from one group to another in much the same manner that any cultural form is disseminated through society. The boy who participates in the life of a delinquent gang naturally assimilates the prevailing patterns of behavior in his group, thus becoming a delinquent. For example, the idea of stealing is not only transmitted but the particular technique used in committing the act may be transmitted as well.

The foregoing considerations lead quite naturally to the assumption that if the delinquent is to be adequately understood and adjusted it will be necessary to study his behavior in relation to the situation in which it occurs. Any effort to deal with the delinquent as a separate entity, apart from the social and cultural world in which his behavior trends have arisen, necessarily neglects important aspects of the situation.

THE WICKERSHAM REPORT

In 1931 Shaw and McKay prepared a report entitled, *Social Factors in Juvenile Delinquency: A Study of the Community, the Family, and the Gang in Relation to Deviant Behavior.* Preparation of this report (which is Volume II of *Report on the Causes of Crime*) was sponsored by the National Commission on Law Observance and Enforcement, of which the Honorable George W. Wickersham was chairman. In this report, the sociological ideas sketched out in the 1929 report for the Illinois Crime Survey are here developed more fully, given a more profound theoretical underpinning,

and illustrated with case materials and statistics drawn from several American cities. Not only the authors, but other renowned delinquency experts regard this report as the best and fullest statement of the Shaw-McKay theories; their later researches were directed toward probing further specific phases of it.

Shaw and McKay begin the report with a statement concerning the social genesis of deviant behavior which expresses simply yet elegantly the fundamental hypothesis which was to guide delinquency research for the next thirty years and is still guiding it today:

The attitudes and habits underlying the behavior of the child are built up in the course of his experiences, developing in the process of interaction between the child and the successive situations in which he lives. Among the more important social groups involved in the development of the attitude and behavior trends of the child are the family, the play groups, and the neighborhood. These groups are particularly significant, since they are the first groups to which the child belongs. Through participation in these groups the child is subjected to an increasing number and variety of personalities and social values to which he must make some sort of an adjustment. In this process of adjustment to the expectations and standards of these various groups, beginning with the family, the play group, and the neighborhood, the child's attitudes and behavior trends are gradually built up. Delinquency (should be) studied in its relation to the social and cultural situation in which it occurs.

Shaw and McKay illustrate with the case study of Nick, a delinquent boy, how the family, the play group, and the community are all involved in behaviors defined by society at large as delinquent. By reporting the father's story, the mother's story, and the boy's story, they illustrate just how different are the explanations placed upon the same set of "delinquent" acts by the child and his parents.

It is clear that the parents had very little appreciation of the nature of Nick's problem and the sort of social world in which he was living. Although his behavior was, for the most part, strictly in conformity with the socially approved standards of the play group and neighborhood, it was a violation of the family traditions and expectations. He was torn between the demands and expectations of two conflicting social groups. Their conflict is made more acute because the boy was conscious of the economic and social inferiority of the family and had accepted the contemptuous and superior attitudes of the (community at large) toward his family. It is in this conflict of values that the boy's open defiance of authority occurred. From this point of view it may be assumed that his behavior problems were incidental to the larger cultural conflict between the family and the prevailing social values of the neighborhood.

Part II of the Wickersham report deals with "The Community Background of Delinquency." It reviews the spatial patterning and distribution of delinquency rates, as measured by the various indexes. Shaw and McKay had compiled a time series from old records for each of several subareas of Chicago indicating the change over time in delinquency rates to show that there is great persistence in the areas having high delinquency. They then examine in greater detail the social and economic characteristics of the high delinquency areas, and find them to have the following outstanding traits:

1. Prevalence of physical deterioration;

2. Widespread poverty;

3. Residence mixed with industry and commerce;

4. Concentration of foreign-born population;

5. High residential mobility—families moving out of the neighborhood as quickly as possible;

6. Dearth of facilities for maintaining an adequate neighborhood organization in support of conventional community life;

7. High incidence of adult crime.

Apart from the social institutions which are supported and controlled by persons from more prosperous communities, there are few agencies in delinquency areas for dealing with the problem of delinquent behavior. The comparative lack of common community ideals and standards prevents cooperative social action either to prevent or to suppress delinquency. There is little spontaneous and concerted action on the part of the inhabitants of the areas of high rates of delinquency to deal with the delinquent. In this type area, the community fails to function effectively as an agency of social control.

They also point out that the high concentration of adult offenders in these areas makes it possible for criminalistic older boys and men to become "models" to be emulated by the younger boys.

One of the most significant findings in this part of their study was the fact that, while the relative rate of delinquency in these high rate areas remained more or less constant over a period of 20 years, the nationality composition of the population changed almost completely in this interval. As the older national groups moved out of these areas of first immigrant settlement, the percentage of juvenile delinquents in these groups showed a consistent decrease. Delinquency, therefore, seems to be attached to the situation rather than to the particular people who lived there.

A trail-blazing chapter in this part of the book, "The Spirit of Delinquency Areas," undertakes to spell out what the world of the delinquent is like.

Children who grow up in these deteriorated and disorganized neighborhoods of the city are not subject to the same constructive and restraining influences that surround those in the more homogeneous residential communities farther removed from the industrial and commercial centers. These disorganized neighborhoods fail to provide a consistent set of cultural standards and a wholesome social life for the development of a stable and socially acceptable form of behavior in the child. Very often the child's access to the traditions and standards of our conventional culture are restricted to his formal contacts with the police, the courts, the school, and the various social agencies. On the other hand his most vital and intimate social contacts are often limited to the spontaneous and undirected neighborhood play groups and gangs whose activities and standards of conduct may vary widely from those of his parents and the larger social order. These intimate and personal relationships, rather than the more formal and external contacts with the school, social agencies, and the authorities, become the chief sources from which he acquires his social values and conceptions of right and wrong.

In many cases, the child's relationship to his parents assumes the character of an emotional conflict which definitely complicates the problem of parental control, and greatly interferes with the child's incorporation into the social milieu of his parents. In this situation the family is rendered relatively ineffective as an agent of control and fails to serve as a medium for the transmission of cultural heritages.

Delinquency persists in these areas not only because of the absence of constructive neighborhood influences and the inefficiency of present methods of prevention and treatment, but because various forms of lawlessness have become more or less *traditional* aspects of the social life and are handed down year after year through the medium of social contacts. Delinquent and criminal patterns of behavior are prevalent in these areas and are readily accessible to a large proportion of the children.

This view of the delinquent and his world has been elaborated and exploited fully by scholars since Shaw and McKay. It provides the basis for the hypothesis of the delinquency "subculture" and "contraculture."

Oddly enough, in later years Shaw and McKay came to the opinion that in their strenuous efforts to combat the prejudice among judges and court workers that delinquency springs from inherently vicious "bad blood" or "inferior stock," they seem to have "oversold" the sociologists on the notion of a delinquency tradition and culture. Some, especially those who had comparatively little firsthand research contact with the delinquency world, came to view the delinquency subculture as a whole and complete social system in itself—a self-sustaining society at war with established society—a more or less autonomous social entity and reality. Shaw and McKay did not take this extreme a view, and regarded this as a somewhat mischievous overstatement of the delinquency reality that exists. In their view, the delinquency tradition exists in constant interaction with the larger culture of the community and neighborhood, and bears the unmistakable stamp of that culture. For example, the status of boys in the gang is found not to be independent of the status of their parents in the neighborhood, independently of the gang's own standards for prestige on the basis of achievement in gang activities.

In reviewing the present abstract, Mr. McKay requested the editors to remind our readers that they warned, "Many of the boys in these areas do not become delinquent," and "It should not be assumed that the parents of the delinquents in the areas under consideration are necessarily indifferent to the needs and welfare of their children. In many cases their efforts to control and direct the behavior of the children are rendered futile because of the more powerful demoralizing influences operating in the community."

The remainder of Part II is devoted to a review of the evidence concerning juvenile delinquency in other American cities, a topic which was to be explored even more fully later (see below, p. 403).

Next, in Part III, the authors turn their attention to "The Companionship Factor in Juvenile Delinquency." Thrasher had been studying gangs in Chicago and had published his famous book *The Gang* in 1927. Following the lead of Thrasher, Shaw and McKay do not tend to regard the gang as a *cause* of crime, but saw it as a contributing factor which facilitates the commission of crime and greatly extends its range. To Shaw and McKay the gang was a unique social invention, a new creation growing out of urban living. Of itself gang behavior is neither bad nor good. Under certain combinations of conditions gangs can become specialized in delinquency behavior.

The development of relationships with play groups outside of the home represents a significant enlargement of the child's social world. Through them he is subjected to the influence of an increasing number and variety of personalities, social activities, and moral norms. That these play group relationships are important factors in determining behavior traits is indicated in the study of the life histories of both delinquent and non-delinquent boys. They are particularly important as a medium through which new social values are acquired and new attitudes and interests defined.

The tendency of boys to organize themselves into some form of social group is more or less characteristic of the social life in the deteriorated and disorganized sections of the city as well as in the outlying residential neighborhoods. Such groupings are usually spontaneous in origin and constitute a form of primary group relationship. While these groups are more or less universal in all sections of the city and possess many common characteristics with respect to the mechanisms of control within the group, they differ widely in regard to cultural traditions, moral standards, and social activities. In certain areas of the city the practices and social values of many of these groups are chiefly of a delinquent character. Frequently these groups develop persistent delinquent patterns and traditional codes and standards which are very important in determining the behavior of the members. Some of these groups are highly organized and become so powerful in their hold on members that the delinquent traditions and patterns of behavior persist and tend to dominate the social life throughout the area.

In order to explore more deeply the relationship between gang behavior and delinquency, Shaw and McKay made an extensive study of boys' gangs in Chicago. One important phase of this study pertained to the relationship between gang activities and juvenile delinquency. In order to secure a more exact measure of the extent to which juvenile delinquency is group behavior, a study was made of the relative frequency of lone and group offenders among cases of delinquent boys appearing in the juvenile court of Cook County. This analysis was made at the end of 1928, and included all boys who appeared in this court during that year. It took into consideration the delinquency record of each boy from the date of his first appearance in the court as a delinquent. The findings of this study indicated quite conclusively that most juvenile offenses, at least those offenses charged against delinquents appearing in the juvenile court in Chicago, are committed by groups of boys; few by individuals. Approximately 90 per cent of the instances of delinquency behavior were performed with one or more companions, while only about 10 per cent were performed alone. Not all such group delinquencies are committed by well-organized gangs. While many of the delinquents may be members of such gangs, they usually commit their offenses in the company of only one or two other boys.

In a chapter entitled, "The Activities and Traditions of Delinquent Boys," they review the evidence of the existence of a delinquent "tradition" that is transmitted from one generation of gang boys to another. They report that within some gangs there exists a "delinquency code," a set of standards and ethical values to which the members must adhere if they are to preserve their membership in good standing. They state:

The ethical values of these groups often vary widely from those of the larger social order. In fact the standards of these groups may represent a complete reversal of the standards and norms of conventional society.

Types of conduct which result in personal degradation and dishonor in a conventional group, serve to enhance and elevate the personal prestige and status of a member of the delinquent group. Thus, an appearance in the juvenile court or a period of incarceration in a correctional institution may be a source of pride to the young delinquent, since it identifies him more closely with his group.

The delinquent group, like all social groups, tends to develop its own standards of conduct by which it seeks to regulate and control the behavior of its members. It inflicts punishment upon those who violate its rules and rewards those who are loyal and conform. In the older delinquent and criminal groups there tends to be a definite hierarchy of social grouping, which ranges all the way from the petty thief to the gangster.

Apparently the motives underlying the delinquent boy's participation in the delinquent activities of his group are essentially not unlike those observed among members of non-delinquent groups. Like the non-delinquent boys he is apparently motivated by those common and universal desires for recognition, approbation, and esteem of his fellows, for stimulation, thrill, and excitement, for intimate companionship, and for security and protection. In the delinquency areas of the city these fundamental human desires of the boy are often satisfied through participation in the activities of delinquent groups.

Undoubtedly, it is passages such as these that lead Albert Cohen, in his book *Delinquent Boys: The Culture of the Gang,* to state: "A classic statement of this cultural-transmission theory of juvenile delinquency is contained in Clifford R. Shaw and Henry D. McKay, *Social Factors in Juvenile Delinquency.*"

Part IV of the Wickersham Report is entitled "Family Situations and Juvenile Delinquency." This is a topic which in recent years has been somewhat neglected in favor of studying and working directly with boys through clubs and "corner workers." One of the major inquiries of this section concerns the relationship between delinquency and broken homes. Their findings on this subject are worthy of caution today in making generalizations on this subject. In slum areas there is a very high incidence of broken homes. Hence, it is possible to establish a very high correlation, by census tracts, between broken homes (separated, widowed, divorced) and delinquency. But when Shaw and McKay undertook, in 1930, to determine whether within the slum area the boys who came from broken homes had a significantly higher probability of becoming delinquent than boys who did not come from broken homes, they failed to discover evidence that would support a clear-cut assertion that this was the case. Although some of the subsequent research has tended to support the existence of such an association, at least in some situations, the relationship is far looser than had been claimed by court workers before the Shaw-McKay research. (This topic is badly in need of intensive investigation today, because of a renewed theory of delinquency based on a possibly similar fallacy. Because Negro slum areas have a high percentage of households without a father, unmarried mothers, families where the father has deserted, and divorced or widowed mothers, it is claimed that the adolescent boy has a problem of sex-identification because no father-figure is present to help him establish his adult role. While this may be a significant force, it is scientifically unsound to claim as evidence the correlations between area rates for delinquency and the prevalence of fatherless families. There is need for a careful further probing of the kind performed three decades ago by Shaw and McKay.)

In a chapter on "Family Relations and Juvenile Delinquency," they continue to develop the theme that family discord and lack of a stable family life probably *are* related to juvenile delinquency. They assert:

Although the formal break in the family may not in itself be an important determining factor it is probable that the conflicts, tensions, and attitudes which precipitate the disorganization may contribute materially to the development of the delinquency and the personality problems of the child. The actual divorce or separation of the parents may not be so important a factor in the life of the child as the emotional conflicts which have resulted in the break in family relationships. Our case histories suggest that the subtle emotional relationships between members of the family are often significantly involved in the boy's delinquent behavior.

Shaw and McKay believe that subtle interrelationships are far too complex to unravel with formal statistical data, and so they rely upon case histories and personal documents. (Their findings in this area are discussed in the next section.)

The last section of the book deals with the topic, "The Development of Delinquent Careers." The authors develop the thesis (now widely accepted) that a criminal is *developed*, over time, by a very definite process which has a typical "life history." Beginning with various forms of petty stealing in the neighborhood and truancy from school, the boy progresses to more serious deviant activities. He is influenced at first by his play group and other neighborhood contacts. In the early stage, his contacts with his parents may be congenial but not sufficiently effective to counteract the more powerful demoralizing influences in the area where he resides. By a succession of experiences involving arrest, court appearances, reform school, tougher gangs, and finally imprisonment as a young adult, the criminal career unfolds. (The details of this process also are amplified in the next section.)

THE LIFE HISTORY RECORD AS AN INSTRUMENT OF JUVENILE RESEARCH

Methodologically, the research of Shaw and his associates was characterized by a very great reliance upon the "life history" or personal document approach. Although this mode of research was widely used in psychological research before the 1920's, it was introduced into sociology in the urban studies of the Chicago Department of Sociology. Shaw made such extensive use of it that he became its leading exponent as a research method. Three of his monographs rely almost wholly upon this method: *The Jack-Roller, The Natural History of a Delinquent Career,* and *Brothers in Crime.* In the opinion of the editors, these materials are much more than "ancient history" of sociological methodology. We believe that for theory formulation and for discovering new social forces and factors, this type of approach is essential. Hence, in this section we begin by explaining the viewpoint and justification for it, extracted from writings of the time. This is followed by a short summary of two of the life history monographs of Shaw and his associates.

The Life History Method of Research

In his editor's preface to *The Natural History of a Delinquent Career,* E. W. Burgess gave the following statement concerning the life history method in sociological research:

The life-history record is a relatively new instrument for the study of human behavior. As such it should be used with full consciousness of its values, limitations, and possible shortcomings.

No one will question the value of the life-history as a human document when written freely and frankly. It admits the reader into the inner experience of other men, men apparently widely different from himself: criminals, hobos, and other adventurers. Through the life-history he becomes acquainted with those far removed from the sheltered routine of his own existence in much the same intimate way that he knows himself or a friend. As he lives, for the time being, their careers and participates in their memories and mistakes, aspirations and failures he comes to realize the basic likeness of all human beings, despite the differences, real as they are, of biological endowment and social experience.

Granted that the life-history possesses this unique human value, what if any is its function as an instrument of scientific inquiry? Is the writer of the document telling the truth? Is he not influenced, consciously or unconsciously, by his conception of his audience? Does any person know sufficiently well the causes of his own behavior for his statement, sincere though it may be, to be given full credence?

These and other questions must be squarely faced before any final decision may be made upon the merits of the life-history as an instrument of scientific research. No attempt will be made to give an answer here. But attention should be called to the care and discrimination used in the securing and checking of the documents in this volume and the other life-histories in preparation for this series. First of all the person is asked to write the history of his experience in his own way uninfluenced by a series of detailed guide questions. The events of the history are then checked by interviews with parents, brothers and sisters, friends, gang associates, school teachers and principals, probation officers, and social workers. Official records are secured and the accounts of delinquencies checked against written reports.

Finally, it is realized that it is hazardous to venture generalizations based upon the data in a few case studies. The comparison and analysis of a sufficiently large collection of these documents ought to throw light upon the validity of their use in the scientific inquiry into human behavior.

From E. W. Burgess' preface to *The Jack-Roller,* the following excerpt reveals by analogy the unique power envisaged for this technique.

In the biological sciences, the invention and use of the microscope has made possible many, if not most of the scientific discoveries in the study and treatment of disease. For the microscope enabled the research worker to penetrate beneath the external surface of reality and to bring into clear relief hitherto hidden processes within the organism.

In a very real sense, the life-history document performs an identical, or at least a similar, function for the student of personality. Like a microscope, it enables him to see in the large and in detail the total interplay of mental processes and social relationships.

The life history is the person's own account of his experiences, written as an autobiography, as a diary, or presented in the course of a series of interviews. The unique feature of such documents is that they are recorded in the first person, in the subject's own words. A hidden stenographer (or a tape recorder) often is employed. Clifford Shaw explains the nature of the procedure and the mode of interpretation in chapter 1 of *The Jack-Roller:*

It should be pointed out that validity and value of the personal document are not dependent upon its objectivity or veracity. It is not expected that the delinquent will necessarily describe his life situations objectively. On the contrary, it is desired that his story will reflect his own personal attitudes and interpretations, for it is just these personal factors which are so important in the study and treatment of the case. Thus, rationalizations, fabrications, prejudices, exaggerations are quite as valuable as objective descriptions, provided, of course, that these are properly identified and classified. As a safeguard against erroneous interpretations of such material, it is extremely desirable to develop the "own story" as an integral part of the total case history. Thus each case study should include, along with the life-history document, the usual family history, the medical, psychiatric, and psychological findings, the official record of arrest, offenses, and commitments, the description of the play group relationships, and any other verifiable material which may throw light upon the personality and actual experiences of the delinquent in question. In the light of such supplementary material, it is possible to evaluate and interpret more accurately the personal document. It it probable that in the absence of such additional case material any interpretation of the life history is somewhat questionable.

The child's "own story" is of particular importance in the diagnosis and treatment of cases of delinquency. The attitudes and intimate situations revealed in the life story not only throw light upon the fundamental nature of the behavior difficulty, but, along with the other case material, afford a basis for devising a plan of treatment adapted to the attitudes, interests, and personality of the child.

Life history data have a theory-building as well as therapeutic value. They not only serve as a means of making preliminary explorations and orientations in relation to specific problems in the field of research, but afford a basis for the formulation of hypotheses with reference to the causal factors involved in the development of delinquent behavior patterns. The validity of these hypotheses may in turn be tested by the comparative study of other detailed case histories and by formal methods of statistical analysis.

The "own story" reveals useful information concerning at least three important aspects of delinquent conduct:

The delinquent boy's point of view.— The boy's own story is of primary importance as a device for ascertaining the personal attitudes, feelings, and interests of the child; it shows how he conceives his role in relation to other persons and the interpretations which he makes of the situations in which he lives. It is in the personal document that the child reveals his feelings of inferiority and superiority, his fears and worries, his ideals and philosophy of life, his antagonisms and mental conflicts, his prejudices and rationalizations.

The delinquent's social world.—It is undoubtedly true that the delinquent behavior of the child cannot be understood and explained apart from the cultural context in which it occurs. By means of the personal document it is possible to study not only the traditions, customs, and moral standards of neighborhoods, institutions, families, gangs, and play groups, but the manner in which these cultural factors become incorporated into the behavior trends of the child. The life record discloses also the

more intimate, personal situations in which the child is living; that is, the attitudes, gestures, and activities of the persons with whom he has intimate contact.

Sequence of events in the life of the delinquent.—Very often the delinquent behavior may be traced back to experiences and influences that occurred very early in life. In many of these cases it is possible to describe the continuous process involved in the formation and fixation of the delinquent behavior trend. In the search for factors contributing to delinquency in a given case, it is desirable, therefore, to secure as complete a picture of the successive events in the life of the offenders as possible. Here again the "own story" has proved to be of great value.

The Jack-Roller

This was the first of the case studies of young male delinquents published in the University of Chicago Sociology Series. It is a case study of the career of a young male delinquent identified as Stanley. It is based on six years of contact with the boy, from age sixteen to twenty-two. This particular person specialized in jack-rolling (robbing drunken hobos on Skid Row). The principal objective of this monograph is to illustrate the value of the "own story" in the study and treatment of the delinquent child. Since Stanley was able to express his thoughts and feelings with great clarity, the document reveals the process of becoming delinquent and the great struggle involved in trying to reform—in terms of the feeling states of the child himself.

In introducing the study, Shaw states:

The reader is cautioned against drawing conclusions regarding causes of delinquency or the relative merits of different methods of treatment upon the basis of this single case record. Perhaps its chief value consists in the fact that it affords a basis for formulating tentative hypotheses which may be tested by the comparative study of other detailed cases or by formal statistical methods.

This boy was picked up first by the police as a runaway at the age of six years and six months. He was picked up seven more times as a runaway in the next six months. By the time he was nine years old he had been in the police station and Detention Home many times as a truant or runaway. He came from a broken home. His mother had died and his father was living with his third wife. The boy did not like the stepmother. Because of his repeated truancy and running away he was committed to institutions. In rapid succession he was sent to the Detention Home, the Chicago Parental School (for chronic truants), the County Boys Reformatory and the State Boys Reformatory, but the treatment at these correctional, reformatory, and penal institutions failed to check his delinquent career. In these places he mingled with other "bad boys" and learned much about delinquency, sex perversion, and criminal gangs. Between confinements he started to live away from home. He drifted to the neighborhood of West Madison Street. In his own words, "I worked and romped West Madison Street. I developed a hankering for these crowds of hobos and spent my evenings in them. . . . I quit my job and went down to Madison Street. . . . I slept in alleys and begged food and ofttimes ate from garbage cans." He was caught, sent to reformatory again, and upon his return he had matured into a young adolescent "tough." He returned to West Madison Street's skid row. After getting fired from his job he went on a spree with his wages. He describes how he became a jack-roller:

I was lord of all for a few days. We had our wild women, went to movies, and had plenty to eat. We also shot crap, and in a few days the dough was gone. This little spurt of fortune had turned my head. Now I wanted a good time. But I was in a predicament, for I had no money, and you can't enjoy life without dough. My buddy, being an old "jack-roller," suggested "jack-rolling"

as a way out of the dilemma. So we started out to "put the strong arm" on drunks. We sometimes stunned the drunks by "giving them the club" in a dark place near a lonely alley. It was bloody work, but necessity demanded it—we had to live.

Several oportunities were given to this boy to "go straight." He was once paroled to a farmer but quickly got lonesome for the bright lights of the city and ran away. A wealthy vice president of a company took him into his own home and tried to rear him as a son. On several other occasions social workers and citizens tried to help, but each time he drifted back into his pattern of stealing and hanging around skid row.

At the age of fifteen he was arrested for jack-rolling and sentenced to the Pontiac prison. Shortly after completing his term he was back on skid row jack-rolling the homeless men. Within a few months he was caught and at the age of seventeen was sentenced to one year in Bridewell, Chicago's house of correction. Stanley described the house of correction as follows:

The cell was made of old and crumbling brick. The dampness seeped through the bricks, and the cracks were filled with vermin and filth. The cell was barren except for the dirty bunk and the open toilet bucket in the corner. . . . I fell into a slumber, only to be awakened by vermin crawling all over my face and body. . . . The horrors of that House of "Corruption" cannot be described. I can only say that when there I lost all respect for myself, felt degenerated and unhuman. In my anguish I planned vengeance and hatred. Hanging, life imprisonment in Joliet—anything would be better than a year in that vermin-ridden, unsanitary, immoral, God-forsaken pit. It wasn't discipline that I hated and resented; I was used to that. But it was the utter low-downess, animal-like existence that it forced me down to.

Mr. Shaw and his associates became interested in the jack-roller during his stay in Bridewell. When he was released, they helped to plan a program of rehabilitation for him which proved to be successful. This program was worked out by Dr. Shaw on the basis of the boy's life story and a full inventory of his needs. He was transplanted to a completely new environment and helped to get work that fitted his egocentric nature. During the early phase of his treatment Stanley wrote and dictated his "own story," which was edited and published after he had "gone straight" for five years and was a successful salesman with a wife and family.

In his discussion of this case in the final section of the monograph, E. W. Burgess observes that the jack-roller's story is typical in many respects of a large proportion of other juvenile delinquents. Although the jack-roller was highly egocentered and had other personality traits that were extraordinary, sociologically he was typical of his environment. Dr. Burgess made a distinction between "social type" (attitudes, values, and philosophy of life derived from copies presented by the social environment) and "personality pattern" (the sum and integration of those traits which characterize the typical reactions of one person toward other persons). The jack-roller is typical as a social type, even though many elements of his personality pattern were extraordinary.

Brothers in Crime, 1938

This monograph is concerned with a study of the lives of five brothers, all of whom had long records of delinquency and crime. It extends over a period of fifteen years, and the materials which comprise the case history have been secured directly from the members of the family and from the records of the many social agencies, behavior clinics, and institutions which have attempted to provide for the economic, medical, and social needs of the family. Along with the study of the case continuous efforts were made to assist the brothers in making an

adjustment to conventional standards of behavior. Four of them, for a period of six to ten years, had been engaged in self-supporting activities of a legitimate character. At the time the report was published the fifth brother was still in prison.

The extent of the participation in delinquent and criminal activities of these brothers is clearly indicated by the fact that they served a total of approximately 55 years in correctional and penal institutions. They were picked up and arrested by the police at least 86 times, brought into court 70 times, confined in institutions for 42 separate periods, and placed under supervision of probation and parole officers approximately 45 times. The cost of their collective total of 55 years of institutional care was in excess of $25,000 (1920–29). The value of the jewelry, clothing, and money secured in more than three hundred burglaries in well-to-do homes amounted to many thousands of dollars. The value of the 45 or more automobiles which were stolen and the salaries of the various workers who were assigned at various times to supervise the brothers would comprise another substantial item in the total cost entailed in this case.

The problem of juvenile delinquency in this case was of such a character that it was not susceptible to the methods of treatment employed by the Juvenile Court, the behavior clinics, the correctional institutions, and social agencies. Despite the therapeutic efforts of all these organizations, the five brothers continued in delinquency throughout the period when they were wards of the Cook County Juvenile Court and four of them served sentences in penal institutions.

A careful review of the sequence of events in the start, development, and flowering of the delinquent and criminal career of each brother revealed several common elements. In the period of early childhood all of them engaged in begging, played truant from home and school, and were involved in various forms of petty stealing. From this early beginning there was in each case a progression to more serious and complicated types of delinquency and crime. Apparently the influences which were most immediately responsible for their earliest delinquencies were inherent in the home situation.

To understand fully the delinquent acts of these brothers as human experiences, it is necessary to indicate the circumstances in which they took place, the manner in which they occurred, and something of their meaning and significance as interpreted by the brothers. In short, it seems desirable to describe the offenses not simply as isolated acts abstracted from their social context, but as aspects of the whole system of interpersonal relationships and social practices which comprised the social world of the brothers. Viewed from this standpoint, the offenses may be regarded as a function of the efforts of the brothers to secure certain common human satisfactions in the particular situation in which they lived.

An analysis of the autobiographical documents revealed that in the early stage of their delinquency (before the age of nine) the brothers were only vaguely aware of their implications from the standpoint of conventional society. Apparently they engaged in stealing because it was one of the forms of activity which prevailed in the groups to which they belonged; from the standpoint of these groups stealing was an approved and accepted practice. The realization that there was a larger conventional society whose standards of conduct were in opposition to the standards of their immediate social world was not distinctly impressed upon the brothers until they were taken into court and committed to correctional institutions.

Between the ages of 9 and 15 years the brothers engaged in the burglary of residences in well-to-do neighborhoods. To do this they employed more refined techniques, exercised greater deliberation and premeditation in planning offenses, and made greater use of "fences" for the disposal of stolen goods. Their attitudes of suspicion and hostility with regard to the police, the courts, and the officers to whom they were assigned for supervision while on probation and parole were more crystallized. The transition from the initial experiences in petty stealing to the burglary of residences was a continuous process of education, habituation, and increasing sophistication in the art of stealing.

After the age of 15 the brothers began to specialize in different types of crime. It became necessary for them to change their pattern for a number of reasons. Because of their size their presence in well-to-do neighborhoods aroused suspicion and they could no longer elicit a sympathetic reaction from the persons to whom they appealed for aid. In the second place the brothers were separated from each other during long terms of confinement in different correctional schools and penal institutions. As each brother returned home under parole supervision he established contacts with other offenders in the neighborhood and with these companions engaged in new forms of delinquent and criminal conduct. The divergent forms of delinquent and criminal conduct into which each brother drifted conformed to the type of criminality which was current among the other offenders with whom each brother became associated on his return from correctional institutions.

A study of the community background from which the brothers came revealed it to be one of great physical deterioration and low economic status. The presence of a large number of old deteriorated buildings provided an appropriate situation for the practice of junking (stealing iron, lead pipes, and lumber from vacant buildings and disposing of them to junk dealers) which is one of the most common initial forms of delinquency. For the most part the residents were unskilled laborers who had been forced to work at those types of employment which are relatively low-paying and provide little security. In times of prosperity the standards of living were low, while in times of depression a large segment of the population was dependent upon charity for subsistence. This stood in sharp contrast to the standards of living maintained by a large proportion of the communities in the city. Children in this area were forced to accept whatever employment happened to be available regardless of how irregular, uninteresting, or unremunerative it may be or how little it may offer for the future. However, they are exposed to the luxury standards of life which are generally idealized in our culture but which are beyond their attainment. To many of them the fact that they cannot possess the things which they see others enjoy does not nullify their eagerness and determination to secure these things—even by illegitimate means when such means have the support and sanction of the groups to which they belong. Very often crime and the rackets offer the only means of employment. Only a small proportion of the men who return to the community on parole from penal institutions are able to secure any kind of legitimate renumerative work. However, the fact that some delinquency is found in neighborhoods with higher socioeconomic status should not be overlooked. The effect of economic conditions in any given case of delinquency is a relative matter; apparently its significance is dependent upon its relationship to many other things in the total situation.

Perhaps one of the most important characteristics of the brothers' home community was the confusion and wide diversification of its norms or standards of behavior. The local population comprised many national groups with widely divergent definitions of behavior, standards, and expectations. The moral values of these different social worlds range from those that are strictly conventional to those that are delinquent or criminal in character. Thus, acts of theft are sanctioned in certain groups and condemned in other groups. The children living in this community are exposed to a variety of interests, forms of behavior, and stimulations, rather than to a relatively consistent pattern of conventional standards and values. There is a disparity of interests, standards of philosophy of life between European-born parents and their American-born children. Where the children belong to street crowds, play groups, or organized gangs, the free, spontaneous, colorful and glamorous life in these groups is stimulating, exciting, and enticing. These groups afford satisfactions and exert an influence and control upon the lives of their members with which the family, the school, and the character-building agencies in the community can scarcely compete. The attitudes of many adults in the community toward delinquency are characterized by indifference, tolerance, or tacit approval. In a very real sense delinquency is an established and integral part of the pattern of life of the community; it is one of its social traditions. This tradition is assimilated by groups of young boys and transmitted by them to succeeding ones. Whether or not a child becomes a delinquent seems to depend, in many cases at least, upon which of the varied social worlds or systems of relationships he becomes associated with.

The five brothers grew up in a group where delinquency was a part of the culture. They became members of a boys gang that engaged in theft and early had contact with adult criminals. The gang exerts a strong influence in holding a youthful offender in a career of delinquency. This is illustrated in the instance of one of the brothers being given a good job in a Loop bank by a kind-hearted citizen. Although he had a genuine desire to succeed in his work, the ridicule he received from his fellow workers because of his language, manners, and ragged clothes and the constant solicitation on the part of his companions to return to delinquency made it impossible for him to hold his position. Gang experience also debilitates the youth in his contacts with conventional society. Because of his previous experiences he often assumes toward such persons the same attitude of distrust which characterizes his feeling toward the police, probation and parole officers, guards in institutions, and court workers.

The major value of this study is that it illustrates how much more important social factors can be than individual personality traits in influencing delinquency behavior. The entrance and progress of each of the five brothers in a delinquent career appears to be almost a direct outcome of the residence of a poverty-stricken immigrant family in a neighborhood of boys' gangs and criminal traditions. Counteracting factors were present, such as parental concern over the behavior of the boys, the efforts of the juvenile authorities in their behalf, and the kindness of citizens who gave them opportunities to "go straight." But the appeal to the boys of conventional patterns of behavior was weak in comparison with the thrill of adventure and the easy rewards of stealing.

Shaw did not intend this interpretation to be taken to mean that in all cases of crime social influences predominate. He pointed out that the spectacular crimes which make headlines in the newspapers are generally those in which some particular constitutional or psychological characteristic is present and appears to be an essential factor in the crime. There is good reason to believe, however, that the vast majority of cases of delinquency and crime in American cities is due to social influences. The cases of the brothers may be taken as typical of the formation of criminal careers. They are usual and not exceptional cases. They are to be looked upon as normal persons who had the misfortune of adjusting themselves to a weaker part of the community. Many of these, if they were brought up outside the criminal environment, would have matured to be well-adjusted persons.

It has been traditional to impute to the criminal certain distinctive and peculiar motivations and physical, mental, and social traits and characteristics. Historically, crime has been ascribed to innate depravity, instigation of the devil, constitutional abnormalities, mental deficiency, psychopathology, and many other conditions inherent in the individual. Criminals have been thus set off as a distinct class, qualitatively different from the rest of the population. The practice of diagnosing all or a large proportion of the inmates of prisons as pathological personalities probably has no more validity than the former extravagant claims that feeble-mindedness or constitutional abnormality was the chief cause of delinquency and crime.

The delinquent careers of the brothers had their origin in the practices of the play groups and gangs with which they became associated as children. The initial acts of theft were part of the undifferentiated play life of the street. From these simple beginnings the brothers progressed, by social means, to more complicated, more serious, and more specialized forms of theft. The situation in their home community not only failed to offer organized resistance to this development, but actually there were elements which encouraged it and made any other course of action difficult.

Lack of social controls that would combat delinquency behavior tendencies is thus shown to be a primary characteristic of high-delinquency neighborhoods. The controls traditionally exercised by such social groups as the family, the neighborhood, and the church have been weakened. The wide ramifications of this finding suggest the need for developing treatment and prevention programs of a community-wide character. Programs which seek to deal with single individuals or small segments of the community life are not likely to be any more effective in the future than they have been in the past. It appears that to bring about a substantial reduction in the volume of delinquency in these areas it will be necessary to develop an effective organization of conventional sentiments, attitudes, and interests as a substitute for the present situation in which socially divergent norms and practices prevail.

Effective procedures for bringing about such changes in the organization of the social life in these areas are not known at the present time. Efforts to impose from the outside programs of ready-made activities have not yielded satisfactory results. There is reason to believe that more satisfactory results might be achieved by programs in which primary emphasis would be placed upon the responsible participation of the local residents. In such an enterprise the objective would be to effect a greater unanimity of attitudes, sentiments, and social practices in the community by giving to the local residents every possible assistance in developing their own programs to promote the physical, moral, and social well-being of their own children.

JUVENILE DELINQUENCY AND URBAN AREAS

Shaw and McKay review the evidence of a lifetime of research and restate their theories in *Juvenile Delinquency and Urban Areas*. The report explores further the ecology of delinquency and crime by extending the analysis to twenty American cities. The findings establish conclusively the fact of far-reaching significance, namely, that the distribution of juvenile delinquents in space and time follows the pattern of the physical structure and of the social organization of the American city.

The method employed by the authors to test this hypothesis is ingenious but simple. If the main trend in city growth is expansion from the center to the periphery, then two consequences follow. Physical deterioration of residences will be highest around the central business district, lowest at the outskirts, and intermediate in between. Social disorganization will correspondingly be greatest in the central zone, least at the outer zone, and moderate in the middle zone. Accordingly, for the majority of the cities studied, concentric zones were set up by arbitrarily marking off uniform distances of from one to two miles. Delinquency rates were calculated by taking for each zone the ratio of official juvenile delinquents to the population of juvenile court age.

The findings were astonishingly uniform in every city. The higher rates were in the inner zones, and the lower rates were in the outer zones. Even more surprising was the discovery that, for all the cities but three for which zonal ratios were calculated, the rates declined regularly with progression from the innermost to the outermost zone. The main point established by these findings is that juvenile delinquency of the type serious enough to appear in juvenile courts is concentrated in the more deteriorated parts of the American city and that it thins out until it almost vanishes in the better residential districts.

In generalizing from these data, Shaw and McKay make it abundantly clear that they see nothing inherently significant in the zonal pattern, other than that this is the pattern of distribution of those combinations of social and economic characteristics that give rise to high delinquency. If the spatial pattern of the city were to change, they would expect a corresponding change in the pattern of delinquency rates.

In a supplementary analysis for selected cities, the authors correlate the rates of delinquency with various measures of social organization. Juvenile delinquency is shown to be highly correlated with a number of presumably separate factors, including population change, bad housing, poverty, foreign-born and Negroes, tuberculosis, adult crime, and mental disorders.

The correlation of juvenile delinquency is so high with each of these that if any one were considered separately from the others it might be deemed the chief factor in juvenile delinquency. Since, however, juvenile delinquency is highly correlated with each of them, then all of them must be more or less intercorrelated. Therefore, all these factors, including juvenile delinquency, may be considered manifestations of some general basic factor. The common element is social disorganization or the lack of organized community effort to deal with these conditions. Juvenile delinquency, as shown in this study, follows the pattern of the physical and social structure of the city, being concentrated in the areas of physical deterioration and neighborhood disorganization. Evidently, then, the basic solution of this and other problems of urban life lies in a program of the physical rehabilitation of slum areas and the development of community organization.

If juvenile delinquency is essentially a manifestation of neighborhood disorganization, then evidently only a program of neighborhood organization can cope with and control it. The Juvenile Court, the probation officer, the parole officer, and the boys' club can be no substitute for a group of leading citizens of a neighborhood who take the responsibility of a program for delinquency treatment and prevention. If we wish to reduce delinquency, we must radically change our thinking about it. We must think of its causes more in terms of the community and less in terms of the individual.

We must plan our programs with emphasis upon social rather than upon individual factors in delinquency. We must expect that prisons, reformatories, boys' and girls' schools, and even work camps will continue to fail in the treatment of delinquency. We must realize that the brightest hope in reformation is in changing the neighborhood and in control of the gang in which the boy moves, lives, and has his being, and to which he returns after his institutional treatment. We must reaffirm our faith in prevention, which is so much easier, cheaper, and more effective than cure, and which begins with the home, the play group, the local school, the church, and the neighborhood.

Ecological Aspects

The ecological approach to the study of crime and delinquency is more than a century old. As early as 1833 statistical tabulations had been prepared by André Guerry to show that crime rates in certain of the *départements* of France were much greater than in other *départements*. During the nineteenth century similar studies of interregional differences in crime were made in England and Wales, Italy, Germany, Austria, and other nations. Systematic studies of the relative incidence of delinquency in local districts within cities are of more recent development. Henry Mayhew noted the great concentration of juvenile thieves in London's "low neighborhoods" in his *London Labor and the London Poor* (1862). In the United States, in 1912, Sophonisba P. Breckinridge and Edith Abbott published a study, *The Delinquent Child and the Home,* in which the geographic distribution of juvenile delinquency in the city of Chicago was shown. This study showed only concentrations of numbers, and did not relate the number of delinquents to the juvenile population. In 1915 Ernest W. Burgess conducted a survey of social conditions in Lawrence, Kansas, in which rates of delinquency were shown for each of several districts into which the city was divided. Two years later R. D. McKenzie developed similar statistics for Columbus, Ohio. After the Institute for Juvenile Research and the University of Chicago jointly initiated their studies of ecological research in delinquency, matching studies were made for several cities in America as well as several other nations. In all of these studies the technique is to allocate delinquency cases to their place of residence, and to divide the number of delinquents by the number of boys of juvenile court age, in order to compute rates for small areas. These rates are then used to make shaded maps or compute correlations. Shaw and McKay emphasize,

While these maps and statistical data are useful in locating different types of areas, in differentiating the areas where the rates of delinquency are high from areas where the rates are low, and in predicting or forecasting expected rates, they do not furnish an explanation of delinquency conduct. This explanation, it is assumed, must be sought in the field of the more subtle human relationships and social values which comprise the social world of the child in the family and community.

The later ecological studies revealed that not only is there a higher rate of delinquency in the inner zones of the city, but within these zones one finds that (*a*) truancy is more closely linked to delinquency, (*b*) recidivism is much greater, and (*c*) a substantially higher percentage of delinquents is committed to institutions for treatment or punishment than is the case in the outer zones. Thus, the general finding from a series of data extending over thirty years is that the higher the rate of delinquency in an area the greater is the average number of court appearances per delinquent and also the greater the proportion of delinquent boys committed to

correctional institutions. Moreover, relatively more delinquents in the high-rate areas are arrested later as adult criminals.

Community Factors in Delinquency

What is it, in modern city life, that produces delinquency? Why do relatively large numbers of boys from inner urban areas appear in court with such striking regularity, year after year, regardless of changing population structure or the ups and downs of the business cycle? The study *Juvenile Delinquency and Urban Areas* examined the correlation of three sets of factors with delinquency rates in Chicago. It was demonstrated that there are significant and high correlations between delinquency and (1) population decline, (2) proportion of families on relief, (3) proportion of homes rented rather than owned, and (4) low rental—cheap housing.

Yet these measures are not explanations of delinquency. For example, the economic crash of 1929, bringing with it a great rise in unemployment, dependency, and economic hardship did *not* cause a sudden and dramatic rise in delinquency throughout the city as a whole. In fact, there was little or no change in the rate of delinquents for the city of Chicago as a whole from 1929 to 1934 when applications for assistance were mounting daily and the rates of families dependent on public and private relief increased more than tenfold. This would seem to indicate that the relief rate is not itself causally related to the rate of delinquency. The patterns of distribution for both phenomena during these years, however, continued to correspond. The distribution within Chicago of several other social problems was mapped, and rates were computed for subareas of the city. The rates for these social problems were then correlated with the rates for juvenile delinquency, with the following results:

Social Problem	Correlation with Rate of Delinquency (Juvenile Court Rates)
Rate of school truants	.89 ± 0.1 (140 areas)
Rate of young adult offenders	.90 ± 0.1 (140 areas)
Infant mortality....	.64 ± 0.4 (119 areas)
Rate of tuberculosis	.93 ± 0.01 (60 areas)
Per cent of families on relief..........	.89 ± 0.01 (140 areas)
Median rent........	.61 ± 0.04 (140 areas)

In addition, rates by successive outward zones for delinquents, truants, boys' court cases, and a variety of measures of social problems were computed for five successive zones outward from the center of the city. Table 1 presents these statistics. It will be noted that there is not a single instance in which the measures of delinquency and the measures of social problems do not vary together. Relief, rentals, and other measures of economic level fluctuate widely with the business cycle; but it is only as they serve to differentiate neighborhoods from one another that they seem related to the incidence of delinquency. It is when the rentals in an area are low, *relative to other areas in the city*, that this area selects the least-privileged population

groups. On the other hand, rates of delinquency, of adult criminals, of infant deaths, and of tuberculosis for any given area remain relatively stable from year to year, showing but minor fluctuations with the business cycle.

Many people have noted that the delinquency rates are much higher in areas where the foreign-born and Negroes live than in other areas. The meaning of this association is not easily determined. One might be led to assume that the relative-ly large number of boys brought into court is due to the presence of certain racial or national groups were it not for the fact that the composition of many of these neighborhoods has changed completely, without appreciable change in their rank of the rates of delinquency. Clearly, one must beware of attaching causal signficance to race or nativity. For in the present social and economic system, it is the Negroes and the foreign-born, or at least the newest immigrants, who have the least access to the necessities of life and who are therefore least prepared for the competitive struggle. It is they who are forced to live in the worst slum areas and who are least able to organize against the effects of such living. A closer look at the available data

TABLE 1

RATES FOR SELECTED COMMUNITY PROBLEMS BY ZONES
OUTWARD FROM THE CENTER OF CHICAGO

COMMUNITY PROBLEMS	ZONES				
	I	II	III	IV	V
Rates of delinquency, 1927–33..............	9.8	6.7	4.5	2.5	1.8
Rates of truancy, 1927–33..................	4.4	3.1	1.7	1.0	0.7
Boys' court rates, 1938......................	6.3	5.9	3.9	2.6	1.6
Rates of infant mortality, 1928–33...........	86.7	67.5	54.7	45.9	41.3
Rates of tuberculosis, 1931–37..............	33.5	25.0	18.4	12.5	9.2
Rates of mental disorder, 1922–43...........	32.0	18.8	13.2	10.1	8.4
Rates of delinquency, 1917–27..............	10.3	7.3	4.4	3.3	3.0
Rates of truancy, 1917–27..................	8.2	5.0	2.1	1.5	1.4
Boys' court rates, 1924–26..................	15.8	11.8	6.2	4.4	3.9
Rates of adult criminals, 1920..............	2.2	1.6	0.8	0.6	0.4

SOURCE: *Delinquency and Urban Areas*, p. 100.

reveals that *within* the foreign-born and Negro communities there is great variation, and that those among the foreign-born and the recent immigrants who lived in physically adequate residential areas of higher economic status displayed low rates of delinquency, while conversely, those among the native born and among the older immigrants who in that period occupied physically deteriorated areas of low economic status displayed high rates of delinquency. Negroes living in the most deteriorated and disorganized portions of the Negro community possessed the highest Negro rate of delinquency, just as whites living in comparable white areas showed the highest white rates. And equally important, those population groups with high rates of delinquency now dwell in preponderant numbers in those deteriorated and disorganized inner-city industrial areas where long-standing traditions of delinquent behavior have survived successive invasions of peoples of diverse origins.

In the face of these facts it is difficult to sustain the contention that, by themselves, the factors of race, nativity, and nationality are vitally related to the problem of juvenile delinquency. It may be that the correlation between rates of delinquency and foreign-born and Negro heads of families is incidental to relationships between rates of delinquency and apparently more basic social and economic characteristics of local communities. Evidence that this is the case is seen in two partial correlation coefficients computed. Selecting the relief rate as a fair measure of economic level, the problem is to determine the relative weight of this and other factors. The partial correlation coefficient between rate of delinquency and per cent of families on relief, holding constant the percentage of foreign-born and Negro heads of families in the 140 subareas of Chicago, is .76 ± 0.2. However, the coefficient for rates of delinquency and the percentage of foreign-born and Negro

heads of families, when percentage of families on relief is held constant, is only .26 ± .05. It is clear from these coefficients, therefore that the percentage of families on relief is related to rates of deliquency in a more significant way than is the percentage of foreign-born and Negro heads of families.

Differences in Social Values and Organization among Local Communities

In the areas of low rates of delinquency there is more or less uniformity, consistency, and universality of conventional values and attitudes with respect to child care, conformity to law, and related matters; whereas in the high-rate areas, systems of competing and conflicting moral values have developed. Even though in the latter situation conventional traditions and institutions are dominant, delinquency has developed as a powerful competing way of life.

In the areas of high economic status there is a unanimity of opinion on the desirability of education and constructive leisure-time activities and of the need for a general health program. There is a subtle, yet easily recognizable, pressure exerted upon children to keep them engaged in conventional activities, and in the resistance offered by the community to behavior which threatens the conventional values. Children living in the low-rate communities are, on the whole, insulated from direct contact with deviant forms of adult behavior.

In contrast, children living in areas of low economic status are exposed to a variety of contradictory standards and forms of behavior rather than to a relatively consistent and conventional pattern. More than one type of moral institution and education are available to them. A boy may be familiar with, or exposed to, either the system of conventional activities or the system of criminal activities, or both. Similarly, he may participate in the activities of groups which engage mainly in delinquent activities, those concerned with conventional pursuits, or those which alternate between the two worlds. His attitudes and habits will be formed largely in accordance with the extent to which he participates in and becomes identified with one or the other of these several types of groups. Conflicts of values necessarily arise when children are brought in contact with so many forms of conduct not reconcilable with conventional morality as expressed in church and school. A boy may be found guilty of delinquency in the court, which represents the larger values of society, for an act which has had at least tacit approval in the community in which he lives. It is perhaps common knowledge in the neighborhood that public funds are embezzled and that favors and special consideration can be received from some public officials through the payment of stipulated sums. The boys assume that all officials can be influenced in this way. They are familiar with the location of illegal institutions in the community and with the procedures through which such institutions are opened and kept in operation; they know where stolen goods can be sold and the kinds of merchandise for which there is a ready market; they know what the rackets are; and they see in fine clothes, expensive cars, and other lavish expenditures the evidences of wealth among those who openly engage in illegal activities. All boys in the city have some knowledge of these activities; but in the inner-city areas they are known intimately, in terms of personal relationships, while in other sections they enter the child's experience through more impersonal forms of communication, such as motion pictures, the newspaper, and the radio. The presence of a large number of adult criminals in certain areas means that children who live there are brought into contact with crime as a career and with the criminal way of life, symbolized by organized crime. This means that delinquent boys in these areas have contact not only with other delinquents who are their contemporaries but also with older offenders, who in turn had contact with delinquents preceding them, and so on back to the earliest history of the neighborhood. This contact means that the traditions of delinquency can be and are transmitted down through successive generations of boys, in much the same way that language and other social forms are transmitted.

The cumulative effect of this transmission of tradition is seen in two kinds of data. The first is a study of offenses, which reveals that sometimes certain types of delinquency have tended to characterize certain city areas, or to be specialized in by particular gangs. The execution of each type involves techniques which must be learned from others who have participated in the same activity. Each involves specialization of function, and each has its own terminology and standards of behavior. Jack-rolling, shoplifting, stealing from junkmen, and stealing automobiles are examples of offenses with well-developed techniques passed on by one generation to the next.

The second body of evidence on the effects of the continuity of tradition within delinquent groups comprises the results of a study of the contacts between delinquents, made through the use of official records. The names of boys who appeared together in court were taken in a special study of "Contacts between Successive Generations of Delinquent Boys in a Low-Income Area in Chicago," and the range of their association with other boys whose names appeared in the same records was then analyzed and charted. It was found that some members of each delinquent group had participated in offenses in the company of other older boys, and so on, backward in time in an unbroken continuity as far as the records were available.

Another characteristic of the areas

with high rates of delinquency is the presence of large numbers of non-indigenous philanthropic agencies and institutions—social settlements, boys' clubs, and similar agencies—established to deal with local problems. These are, of course, financed largely from outside the area. They are also controlled and staffed, in most cases, by persons other than local residents and should be distinguished from indigenous organizations and institutions growing out of the felt needs of the local citizens. The latter organizations, which include American institutions, Old World institutions, or a synthesis of the two, are rooted in each case in the sentiments and traditions of the people. The non-indigenous agencies, while they may furnish many services and are widely used, seldom become the people's institutions, because they are not outgrowths of the local collective life. The very fact that these non-indigenous private agencies long have been concentrated in delinquency areas without modifying appreciably the marked disproportion of delinquents concentrated there suggests a limited effectiveness in deterring boys from careers in delinquency and crime.

Tax-supported public institutions, such as parks, schools, and playgrounds are also found in high-rate as well as in low-rate areas. These, too, are usually controlled and administered from outside the local area; and, together with other institutions they represent to the neighborhood the standards of the larger community. However, they may actually be quite different institutions in different parts of the city, depending on their meaning and the attitudes of the people toward them. If the school or playground adapts its program in any way to local needs and interests, with the support of local sentiment, it becomes a functioning part of the community; but, instead, it is usually relatively isolated from the people of the area, if not in conflict with them. High rates of truants in the inner-

city areas may be regarded as an indication of this separation.

Negroes and Delinquency

The physical, economic, and social conditions associated with high rates of delinquency in local communities occupied by white population exist in exaggerated form in most of the Negro areas. Of all the population groups in the city, the Negro people occupy the most disadvantageous position in relation to the distribution of economic and social values. Their efforts to achieve a more satisfactory and advantageous position in the economic and social life of the city are seriously thwarted by many restrictions with respect to residence, employment, education, and social and cultural pursuits. These restrictions have contributed to the development of conditions within the local community conducive to an unusually large volume of delinquency. The problems of education, training, and control of Negro children and youth are further complicated by economic, social, and cultural dislocations that have taken place as a result of the transition from the relatively simple economy of the South to the complicated industrial organization of the large northern city. The effect of this transition upon social institutions, particularly the family, have been set forth in the penetrating studies of E. Franklin Frazier.

THE CHICAGO AREA PROJECTS

While Dr. Shaw and his associates were pursuing research, they also developed a program of action based upon their theories of delinquency. From their theories they inferred that agencies *external* to the neighborhood in which delinquent children live would have comparatively little influence in reaching the problem. Also from the theory they inferred that what is required is a fundamental change in the environment, and that this change should consist in the growth of indigenous elements of social control favoring conventional behavior. Social organization and institutional structure in the delinquency neighborhoods are not adequate to control deviant behavior by social means. This inadequacy results not only from the cultural confusion resulting from heavy immigration from Europe and the rural South, but also from the presence of indigenous delinquency-bearing and pro-criminal cultures that are in conflict with the prevailing norms of society. As a result, these neighborhoods are unable to resist or control delinquent gangs by public opinion and other social pressures and guide their behavior into better channels. By sociological theory, this "vacuum" eventually would be filled by a new type of organization that would enforce the larger society's values.

The Chicago Area Projects were efforts to hasten this process of new growth of constructive indigenous social organization. Shaw and his associates hypothesized that in each delinquency area there is local "right-minded" talent and leadership that can be mobilized to fight delinquency. They began a series of projects to help this talent to coalesce into an effective neighborhood organization—completely indigenous, completely independent, and fully self-determining. They fostered the idea of a neighborhood discussion group patterned after the idea of the New England town hall, with a panel of community leaders organized under its own program to improve their neighborhood. These organizations tended to be patterned along ethnic lines: Polish, Italian, etc. The basic stimulus for this organization and the guidance in how to proceed were furnished by Dr. Shaw's agency, but in every way these organizations were autonomous—they were even free to reject further assistance from Dr. Shaw. Several incorporated as non-profit organizations under the laws of Illinois and established neighborhood community centers.

This movement led to some heated attacks from professional social workers in public and private agencies throughout Chicago. These critics believed not only that professional persons could direct such programs more effectively, but also were convinced that the neighborhood organizations would be ineffective because many of these committees contained members who were ex-convicts and men with long police records. Dr. Shaw and his associates, especially Dr. McKay, spent many years working "behind the scenes" with these committees. Several of them were moderately successful in improving conditions in their neighborhood, and in redirecting the activities of delinquent groups. Unfortunately, because each was dominated by a particular ethnic composition, they have died as the old ethnic communities have been broken up by suburbanization and the invasion of Negro and Puerto Rican and Southern white immigrants.

The Chicago Area projects have demonstrated that the areas of high crime and delinquency do contain elements of indigenous leadership and desire for making the social environment more conventional, and that with proper stimulation and encouragement these can be mobilized into units for self-help in gaining the upper hand of delinquency through social and communal preventive means. There is urgent need to re-evaluate this type of program and to experiment further with it, incorporating the findings of recent research.

RECENT ACTIVITIES

During recent years, under the guidance of Henry D. McKay, the Institute for Juvenile Research has continued to experiment and develop new lines of inquiry. Solomon Kobrin has continued the study of gangs and street corner groups and has been especially focusing his attention upon cultural forces in the neighborhood which influence the nature of gang activities and the system of values and traditions the gang develops. In the early 1950's, the Institute conducted a drug addiction study among young persons in Chicago. Some of the highlights of this study are reported in "Cats, Kicks, and Color" an article in *Social Problems* for July, 1957. Currently the Institute is studying the relationship between delinquency and disturbed children. It is also measuring delinquency in the suburban areas of Chicago and in other parts of Illinois, and undertaking to reformulate basic theory to incorporate the apparently rising rate of delinquency in more well-to-do neighborhoods. Also, they are carefully reassessing the rates of delinquency within Negro areas, in an effort to measure the impact of rising levels of living and lessening discrimination in the fields of employment.

They are finding that the criteria for status within delinquent groups is *not* necessarily prowess at performing delinquent acts as many sociologists contend. Instead, they are reaffirming the thesis that the values of the local community are accepted in many cases and the criterion of status is similar to that for the neighborhood.

Another line of current research is a follow-up of delinquent boys into adulthood, to determine what proportion and which ones become criminals, or how many and which ones lead law-abiding lives. They are especially interested in the role which incarceration seems to play in furthering the development of a criminal career.

Index of Names

319

General Index